Lecture Notes in Artificial Intelligence 9904

Subseries of Lecture Notes in Computer Science

More information about this series at http://www.springer.com/series/1244

Gerhard Friedrich · Malte Helmert
Franz Wotawa (Eds.)

KI 2016: Advances in Artificial Intelligence

39th Annual German Conference on AI
Klagenfurt, Austria, September 26–30, 2016
Proceedings

 Springer

Editors
Gerhard Friedrich
Alpen-Adria Universität Klagenfurt
Klagenfurt
Austria

Franz Wotawa
Technische Universität Graz
Graz
Austria

Malte Helmert
University of Basel
Basel
Switzerland

ISSN 0302-9743   ISSN 1611-3349 (electronic)
Lecture Notes in Artificial Intelligence
ISBN 978-3-319-46072-7   ISBN 978-3-319-46073-4 (eBook)
DOI 10.1007/978-3-319-46073-4

Library of Congress Control Number: 2016950419

LNCS Sublibrary: SL7 – Artificial Intelligence

Printed on acid-free paper

This Springer imprint is published by Springer Nature
The registered company is Springer International Publishing AG
The registered company address is: Gewerbestrasse 11, 6330 Cham, Switzerland

Preface

This volume contains the conference proceedings of the 39th German Conference on Artificial Intelligence, KI 2016, which was held on September 26–30, 2016. Having started as German Workshop on AI (GWAI) in 1975, this annual event traditionally brings together academic and industrial researchers from all areas of AI, providing a highly regarded international forum for research on the foundations and applications of artificial intelligence systems and algorithms.

This year, the conference took place in Klagenfurt, Austria, in conjunction with the Austrian Society for Artificial Intelligence (ÖGAI). Five workshops on specialized topics within Artificial Intelligence as well as the workshop on Current AI Research in Austria (CAIRA) were held on the first two days of the conference, followed by three days featuring the main technical program of the conference.

The conference received 44 submissions from 18 countries, which were evaluated in a rigorous single-blind peer reviewing process by a Program Committee including 49 experts. Of the 44 submissions, 8 (18 %) were accepted for inclusion in these proceedings as full papers, and a further 12 (27 %) were accepted as technical communications. Technical communications are shorter papers that can report on research in progress, important implementation techniques or experimental results, novel interesting benchmark problems, or other issues of interest to the AI community.

We thank all Program Committee members and additional reviewers for their efforts in reviewing and discussing the submissions to the conference. The selectivity of the review process shows the dedication of the Program Committee to maintaining high quality standards and is a major reason for the ongoing success and vitality of the KI conference series.

In order to further promote the role of the KI conference as a venue for the exchange of ideas between AI researchers and practitioners in the German-speaking countries, in a new initiative, KI 2016 also invited researchers from Germany, Austria, Switzerland, and neighboring regions who have published papers at the flagship international AI conferences in 2016 to present this work at KI. This initiative was very well received, resulting in 18 additional conference presentations. In addition, the presenters were given the opportunity of providing a report on their research to the KI audience in the form of an extended abstract, an opportunity that 16 of the 18 presenters made use of. These extended abstracts are included in an appendix of these proceedings.

Last but certainly not least, the KI 2016 program included four keynote presentations by distinguished scientists. Our heartfelt thanks goes to Michael Wooldridge ("From Model Checking to Equilibrium Checking"), Thomas Eiter ("Artificial Intelligence at the Gates of Dawn?"), Michael May ("Towards Industrial Machine Intelligence"), and Ulrich Furbach ("Automated Reasoning and Cognitive Computing").

Concluding these remarks, we would like to thank everyone who helped make KI 2016 a success. This, of course, includes all authors, Program Committee members, reviewers, and keynote speakers, as well as the organizers, reviewers, and authors of the workshops.

In addition to the conference and program chairs, the organizing team included Konstantin Schekotihin, Gerald Steinbauer, and Stefan Wölfl, who dedicated much of their time and deserve many thanks for organizing the workshop program, liaising with the German and Austrian AI societies, advertising the conference, and providing general advice. Our final thanks goes to the the participants of KI 2016, the heart and soul without which the conference could not exist.

September 2016

Gerhard Friedrich
Malte Helmert
Franz Wotawa

Organization

General Chair

Gerhard Friedrich   University of Klagenfurt, Austria

Program Chairs

Malte Helmert   University of Basel, Switzerland
Franz Wotawa   TU Graz, Austria

Doctoral Consortium Chair

Stefan Wölfl   University of Freiburg, Germany

Workshop Chair

Konstantin Schekotihin   University of Klagenfurt, Austria

Publicity Chair

Gerald Steinbauer   TU Graz, Austria

Local Organization

Organizing Committee of INFORMATIK 2016

Program Committee

Sven Behnke   University of Bonn, Germany
Ralph Bergmann   University of Trier, Germany
Mehul Bhatt   University of Bremen, Germany
Philipp Cimiano   Bielefeld University, Germany
Cristobal Curio   Reutlingen University and Max Planck Institute
     for Biological Cybernetics, Germany
Stefan Edelkamp   University of Bremen, Germany
Thomas Eiter   TU Vienna, Austria
Gerhard Friedrich   University of Klagenfurt, Austria
Stefan Funke   University of Stuttgart, Germany
Johannes Fürnkranz   TU Darmstadt, Germany
Birte Glimm   University of Ulm, Germany

Christian Guttmann	Institute of Value Based Reimbursement System (IVBAR), Sweden
Malte Helmert	University of Basel, Switzerland
Joerg Hoffmann	Saarland University, Germany
Steffen Hölldobler	TU Dresden, Germany
Jean Christoph Jung	University of Bremen, Germany
Gabriele Kern-Isberner	TU Dortmund, Germany
Kristian Kersting	TU Dortmund, Germany
Thomas Kirste	Rostock University, Germany
Roman Kontchakov Birkbeck	University of London, UK
Ralf Krestel	Hasso Plattner Institute, Germany
Antonio Krüger	DFKI, Germany
Andreas Lattner	Otto Group, Germany
T. Marius Lindauer	University of Freiburg, Germany
Volker Lohweg	inIT - Institute Industrial IT, Germany
Robert Mattmüller	University of Freiburg, Germany
Till Mossakowski	University of Magdeburg, Germany
Giuseppe Pirrò	Institute for High Performance Computing and Networking (ICAR-CNR), Italy
Gabriele Röger	University of Basel, Switzerland
Jörg Rothe	University of Düsseldorf, Germany
Sebastian Rudolph	TU Dresden, Germany
Martin Sachenbacher	TU München, Germany
Torsten Schaub	University of Potsdam, Germany
Stephan Schiffel	Reykjavík University, Iceland
Malte Schilling	ICSI Berkeley, USA
Ute Schmid	University of Bamberg, Germany
Lutz Schröder	FAU Erlangen-Nürnberg, Germany
Daniel Sonntag	DFKI, Germany
Steffen Staab	University of Koblenz-Landau, Germany
Gerald Steinbauer	TU Graz, Germany
Hannes Strass	Leipzig University, Germany
Heiner Stuckenschmidt	University of Mannheim, Germany
Thomas Stützle	Université Libre de Bruxelles (ULB), Belgium
Matthias Thimm	University of Koblenz-Landau, Germany
Ingo J. Timm	University of Trier, Germany
Martin Wehrle	University of Basel, Switzerland
Stefan Wölfl	University of Freiburg, Germany
Stefan Woltran	TU Vienna, Austria
Franz Wotawa	TU Graz, Austria

Additional Reviewers

Gregor Behnke	University of Ulm, Germany
Eric Bouillet	IBM Research, Ireland
Martin Dyrba	Rostock University, Germany
Wilfried Elmenreich	University of Klagenfurt, Austria
Johannes Fichte	TU Vienna, Austria
Martin Gebser	University of Potsdam, Germany
Lisa Grumbach	University of Trier, Germany
Frank Gurski	University of Düsseldorf, Germany
Andreas Hertle	University of Freiburg, Germany
Roland Kaminski	University of Potsdam, Germany
Seongyong Koo	University of Bonn, Germany
Hagen Langer	University of Bremen, Germany
Matthias Liebeck	University of Düsseldorf, Germany
German Martin Garcia	University of Bonn, Germany
Nysret Musliu	TU Vienna, Austria
Clemens Mühlbacher	TU Graz, Austria
Fabian Neuhaus	University of Magdeburg, Germany
Matthias Nieuwenhuisen	University of Bonn, Germany
Tobias Philipp	TU Dresden, Germany
Florian Pommerening	University of Basel, Switzerland
Adrian Rebola Pardo	TU Vienna, Austria
Volker Roth	University of Basel, Switzerland
Zeynep Gözen Saribatur	TU Vienna, Austria
Marvin Schiller	University of Ulm, Germany
Max Schröder	Rostock University, Germany
Tim Schwartz	DFKI, Germany
Michael Siebers	University of Bamberg, Germany
Kristina Yordanova	Rostock University, Germany

Contents

Sister Conference Contributions/Extended Abstracts

Full Papers

Providing Built-In Counters in a Declarative Dynamic Programming Environment

Michael Abseher, Marius Moldovan$^{(\boxtimes)}$, and Stefan Woltran

Institute of Information Systems 184/2,
TU Wien, Vienna, Austria
{abseher,moldovan,woltran}@dbai.tuwien.ac.at

Abstract. D-FLAT is a framework for developing algorithms that solve computational problems by dynamic programming on a tree decomposition of the problem instance. The dynamic programming algorithm is specified by means of Answer-Set Programming (ASP), allowing for declarative and succinct specifications. D-FLAT traverses the tree decomposition and calls an ASP system with the provided specification at each tree decomposition node. It is thus crucial that the evaluation of the ASP program is done in an efficient way. As experiments have shown, problems that include weights or more involved arithmetics slow down this step significantly due to the grounding step in ASP, which yields large ground programs in these cases. To overcome this problem, we equip D-FLAT with built-in counters in order to shift certain computations from the ASP side to the internal part of D-FLAT. In this paper, we highlight this new feature and provide empirical benchmarks on weighted versions of the DOMINATING SET problem showing that our new version increases D-FLAT's robustness and efficiency.

1 Introduction

Many computationally hard problems become tractable if the graph structure underlying the problem instance at hand exhibits certain properties [17,23]. An important structural parameter of this kind is treewidth [9,25]. By using a seminal result due to Courcelle [13] several fixed-parameter tractability (FPT) results have been proven in the last decade for this parameter. Moreover, small treewidth often occurs in practice, for instance, in traffic networks[1].

To turn such tractability results into efficient computation, designing a suitable dynamic programming (DP) algorithm that works directly on tree decompositions of the instances is necessary (see, e.g., [14,23]). D-FLAT [1,2] is a system for rapid prototyping of such DP algorithms by making use of Answer-Set Programming (ASP) [12]. The key features of D-FLAT are that (i) ASP is used to specify the DP algorithm by declarative means; this allows for a convenient way to describe table transitions which are the typical operations in DP [23];

---

[1] In [4] it was shown that the treewidth of metro and urban train systems even of large cities like Singapore is relatively small and often not much higher than 5 or 6.

© Springer International Publishing AG 2016
G. Friedrich et al. (Eds.): KI 2016, LNAI 9904, pp. 3–16, 2016.
DOI: 10.1007/978-3-319-46073-4_1

(ii) the burden of computation and optimization is delegated to existing tools for finding tree decompositions and to ASP solvers; and (iii) D-FLAT relieves the user from tedious non-problem-specific tasks, but stays flexible enough to offer enough power to solve a large number of problems [8]. D-FLAT is free software written in C++ and internally uses the answer set solving systems *gringo* and *clasp* [20], as well as an improved version of the *htdecomp* library[2] for heuristically generating a tree decomposition of the input [16].

As experiments have shown, problems which include weights or more involved arithmetic operations slow down D-FLAT. This can be explained by the grounding step in ASP which yields large ground programs in such cases. To overcome this problem, we present in this paper a new version of D-FLAT which offers built-in counters in order to shift certain computations from the ASP side to the internal part of D-FLAT, but keeping the ASP interface of D-FLAT fully declarative. We shall describe the usage of this new feature via some examples and provide empirical benchmarks on weighted versions of the DOMINATING SET (DS) problem. However, the aim of this work is not to outperform existing ASP solvers (where the unsatisfiable-core option is often the most efficient) but to simplify the process of developing complex dynamic programming algorithms.

Several attempts to separate more involved computational operations from the actual ASP evaluation exist, resulting in systems which are termed as hybrid or ASP-modulo solvers, see e.g. [22,24]. However, in the case of D-FLAT, shifting certain operations from the ASP side to the D-FLAT functionality is even more natural, since D-FLAT already takes care of several tasks in-between the calls of the ASP system (for instance, to remove duplicate information in the subsolutions of the DP). The latest version of the D-FLAT system is available at www.dbai.tuwien.ac.at/proj/dflat/system/. This page also contains further examples of how to use the new built-in counters.

2 Background

Answer Set Programming. Answer Set Programming (ASP) is a declarative language where a *program* Π is a set of *rules*

$$a_1 \vee \ldots \vee a_k \leftarrow b_1, \ldots, b_m, \text{not } b_{m+1}, \ldots, \text{not } b_n.$$

The constituents of a rule $r \in \Pi$ are $h(r) = \{a_1, \ldots, a_k\}$, $b^+(r) = \{b_1, \ldots, b_m\}$ and $b^-(r) = \{b_{m+1}, \ldots, b_n\}$. We call r a *fact* if $b^+(r) = b^-(r) = \emptyset$, and we omit the $\leftarrow$ symbol in this case. A set of atoms I satisfies a rule r if $I \cap h(r) \neq \emptyset$ or $b^-(r) \cap I \neq \emptyset$ or $b^+(r) \setminus I \neq \emptyset$. I is a *model* of a set of rules if it satisfies each rule. I is an *answer set* of a program Π if it is a subset-minimal model of the program $\Pi^I = \{h(r) \leftarrow b^+(r) \mid r \in \Pi, b^-(r) \cap I = \emptyset\}$ [21].

In this paper, we use the language of the grounder *gringo* [18,19] (version 4) where programs may contain variables that are instantiated by ground terms

---

[2] Free software, available at github.com/mabseher/htd.

(elements of the Herbrand universe, i.e., constants and compound terms containing function symbols) before a solver computes answer sets according to the propositional semantics stated above.

Example 1. The following program solves the DOMINATING SET (DS) problem for graphs that are given as facts using the predicates `vertex/1` and `edge/2`, i.e. we have to determine sets S such that each $v \in V$ is either contained in S or adjacent to at least one vertex from S. In the latter case we call v dominated.

```
{ selected(X) : vertex(X) }.
dominated(Y) :- selected(X), edge(X,Y).
:- vertex(X), not selected(X), not dominated(X).
```

The first rule chooses which of the vertices are selected for the dominating set. The second rule derives `dominated/2` for each vertex which is adjacent to a selected vertex. Finally, the last rule ensures that each vertex is selected or dominated.

Dynamic Programming on Tree Decompositions. The ideas underlying the concept of dynamic programming on tree decompositions stem from the field of parameterized complexity. Many computationally hard problems become tractable in case a certain problem parameter is bound by a fixed constant. This property is referred to as *fixed-parameter tractability* [17], and the complexity class FPT consists of problems that are solvable in $f(k) \cdot n^{\mathcal{O}(1)}$, where f is a function that only depends on the parameter k, and n is the input size.

For problems whose input can be represented as a graph, an important parameter is *treewidth*, which measures "tree-likeness" of a graph. It is defined by means of tree decompositions (TDs) [25]. A *tree decomposition* of a graph $G = (V, E)$ is a pair $\mathcal{T} = (T, \chi)$ where $T = (N, F)$ is a (rooted) tree and $\chi : N \to 2^V$ assigns to each node a set of vertices (called the node's *bag*), such that the following conditions are met: (1) for every $v \in V$, there exists a node $n \in N$ such that $v \in \chi(n)$; (2) for every edge $e \in E$, there exists a node $n \in N$ such that $e \subseteq \chi(n)$; and (3) for every $v \in V$, the subtree of T induced by $\{n \in N \mid v \in \chi(n)\}$ is connected. The *width* of $\mathcal{T}$ is $\max_{n \in N} |\chi(n)| - 1$. The *treewidth* of a graph is the minimum width over all its tree decompositions. Although constructing a minimum-width TD is intractable in general [5], it is in FPT [10] w.r.t. parameter treewidth, and moreover, there are polynomial-time heuristics giving "good" TDs [11,15,16]. Variants of the DOMINATING SET problem are examples for problems in FPT when considering treewidth as parameter.

Example 2. Let us consider the enumeration variant of the MINIMUM DOMINATING SET (MDS) problem on a graph $G = (V, E)$. This means we want to determine all dominating sets S of minimal cardinality. An example graph G_{Ex} and a possible TD $\mathcal{T}_{Ex}$ are given in Fig. 1. The width of $\mathcal{T}_{Ex}$ is 2. Note that $\mathcal{T}$ contains unnecessarily many nodes: We could obtain another valid TD for G_{Ex} by arranging n_3, n_2 and n_1 in a path. However, we chose $\mathcal{T}_{Ex}$ to serve for our example because it is more suitable for illustrating DP algorithms (cf. Example 3).

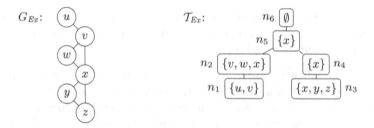

Fig. 1. Example graph G_{Ex} and a TD T_{Ex} for G_{Ex}.

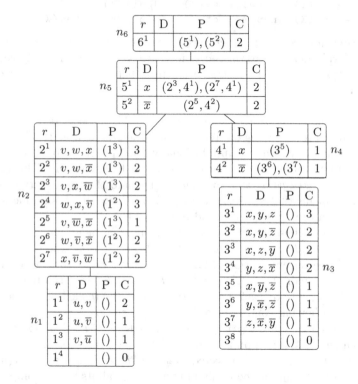

Fig. 2. DP computation for MDS

Algorithms for DP on TDs generally traverse the TD in post-order. At each node, partial solutions for the subgraph induced by the vertices encountered so far are computed and stored in a data structure associated with the node. The goal of DP algorithms on TDs is generally to compute every such data structure in polynomial time, assuming the treewidth of the instances is bounded. This results in an algorithm that decides the problem in polynomial time because the number of TD nodes is linear in the input size. So if the width is bounded by a constant, the search space for subproblems is constant as well, and the number of subproblems only grows linearly for larger instances.

Example 3. Figure 2 illustrates the DP computation for MDS. The tables are computed as follows. For a TD node n, each table row r consists of data $D(r)$, which stores partial solutions (subsets of dominating sets) over vertices in $\chi(n)$. Here, $D(r)$ contains vertices which are selected into a dominating set and dominated vertices. To distinguish the two groups in Fig. 2, dominated vertices are highlighted via a bar above the vertex name. All vertices in $\chi(n) \setminus D(r)$ have to be dominated during the further steps of the tree traversal. The set $P(r)$ contains so-called extension pointer tuples (EPTs) that denote the rows in the children which r was constructed from. The value in column C denotes the cost (number of selected vertices) of the cheapest solution which is consistent with the selection in $D(r)$. Partial solutions with higher costs are not propagated. First consider node n_1: Here, $\chi(n_1) = \{u, v\}$ allows for four solution candidates. In n_2, the child rows are extended, the partial assignments are updated (by removing vertices not contained in $\chi(n_2)$ and guessing which of the vertices in $\chi(n_2) \setminus \chi(n_1)$ are to be selected and which become dominated). In n_3 we proceed as described before. In n_4, data related to removed vertices y and z are projected away. (Observe that row 4^2 is constructed from two different child rows.) In n_5, additionally only partial solutions that select the same subset of common vertices are to be joined. We continue this procedure recursively until we reach the TD's root.

The overall procedure is in FPT time because the number of nodes in the TD is bounded by the size of the input graph and each node n is associated with a table of size at most $\mathcal{O}(2^{|\chi(n)|})$ (i.e., the number of possible selections). Solutions (minimum dominating sets of G_{Ex}) can be enumerated with linear delay by starting at the root and following the EPTs while combining the partial assignments associated with the rows. For instance, the minimum dominating set $\{v, x\}$ is constructed by starting at 6^1 and following EPTs (5^1), $(2^3, 4^1)$, (1^3) and (3^5), thereby combining $D(6^1) \cup D(5^1) \cup D(2^3) \cup D(4^1) \cup D(1^3) \cup D(3^5)$.

3 D-FLAT: A Quick Tutorial

D-FLAT [1,7] is a framework for developing algorithms that solve computational problems by dynamic programming on a tree decomposition of the problem instance. It proceeds in the following way:

1. D-FLAT parses a representation of the problem instance and automatically constructs a tree decomposition of it using heuristic methods.
2. It provides a data structure that is suitable for representing partial solutions for many problems. The programmer only needs to provide an ASP program of how to populate the data structure associated with a TD node.
3. D-FLAT traverses the tree decomposition in post-order and calls an ASP system at each tree decomposition node for computing the data structure corresponding to that node by means of the user-specified program.
4. The framework automatically combines the partial solutions and prints all complete solutions. Alternatively, it is also possible to solve decision, counting and optimization problems.

Table 1. Reserved predicates for specifying the DP via ASP in D-FLAT.

Input predicate	Meaning
`initial`	The current tree decomposition node is a leaf
`childNode`(N)	N is a child of the current decomposition node
`current`(V)	V is an element of the current bag
`introduced`(V)	V is a current vertex but was in no child node's bag
`removed`(V)	V was in a child node's bag but is not in the current one
`childRow`(R, N)	R is a table row belonging to decomposition node N
`childItem`(R, I)	The item set of table row R contains I
`childAuxItem`(R, I)	The auxiliary item set of table row R contains I
`childCost`(R, C)	C is the cost value corresponding to the table row R
Output predicate	Meaning
`item`(I)	The item set of the current table row shall contain the item I
`auxItem`(I)	The auxiliary item set (for the default-join) of the current table row shall contain the item I
`extend`(R)	The current table row shall extend the child table row R
`cost`(C)	The current table row shall have a cost value of C
`currentCost`(C)	The current table row shall have a current cost value of C

The system is free software and can be downloaded at www.dbai.tuwien.ac.at/research/project/dflat/system/. In our presentation of the initial D-FLAT prototype [7] we were able to successfully apply it to several problems, and we showed in [8] which modifications could further extend its applicability.

Before we move on to introducing new functionality we first want to draw the reader's attention to the most important input and output predicates used in D-FLAT. Here we restrict ourselves to those predicates in D-FLAT's table mode that are crucial for this paper. D-FLAT also offers an item tree mode for problems at higher levels of the polynomial hierarchy, which we will not handle here. The full set of input and output predicates supported by D-FLAT together with their detailed semantics can be found in [1].

Table 1 shows available input predicates which are provided to the ASP solver in each decomposition node and refer to the structure of the tree decomposition and to the information which was computed in the child nodes of the current decomposition node, respectively. To enable D-FLAT to store partial solution candidates and other relevant information which should be propagated to the parent nodes of the TD, certain output predicates are required. Also these predicates are shown in Table 1.

In Listing 1.1 we provide a simple example which shows how to solve the problem of MINIMUM WEIGHTED DOMINATING SET (MWDS) (i.e., given a

```
1    1 { extend(R) : childRow(R,N) } 1 :- childNode(N).
2    { item(in(X)) : introduced(X) }.
3    item(in(X)) :- extend(R), not removed(X), childItem(R,in(X)).
4    auxItem(dominated(X)) :- extend(R), not removed(X),
         childAuxItem(R,dominated(X)).
5    auxItem(dominated(Y)) :- item(in(X)), current(X),
         current(Y), edge(X,Y).
6    :- extend(R), removed(X), not childItem(R,in(X)),
         not childAuxItem(R,dominated(X)).
7    cost(0) :- initial.
8    cost(CC + IC) :- extend(R), childCost(R,CC), IC =
         #sum{ W,X : item(in(X)), introduced(X), weight(X,W) }.
9    currentCost(CC) :- CC =
         #sum{ W,X : item(in(X)), weight(X,W) }.
```

Listing 1.1. MWDS encoding for D-FLAT with default-join.

graph with weights associated to vertices, find all weight-minimal subsets S of vertices such that each vertex is either contained in S or directly adjacent to a vertex in S) using D-FLAT on semi-normalized[3] tree decompositions. In Line 1 we guess a child row which should be extended. In Line 2 we guess which of the introduced vertices X are actually in S. Via Lines 3 and 4 we retain information computed in the child nodes which is still relevant and in Line 5 we update which of the vertices is dominated by S. For each vertex which is removed from the bag we have to make sure that it is either selected or dominated; this is handled by the constraint in Line 6.

This solves the problem of DS. To retain only weight-minimal solutions we have to add the rules in Lines 7–9 in the previous versions of D-FLAT. For leaf nodes (they are empty by default in D-FLAT) we assign a cost of 0. In Line 8 we set the cost of the current node equal to the cost of the child node plus the sum of weights of newly added vertices to the dominating set and via Line 9 we keep track of the cost generated by vertices which are in the current node bag and in the dominating set by summing up their weights. In join nodes, D-FLAT uses the so-called default-join where candidates with equal item sets are merged and the costs are updated automatically using the inclusion-exclusion principle which ensures in our case that a single selected vertex is counted only once.

This approach works well only in cases when the grounding of the rules having cost/1 or currentCost/1 in the head can be done fast. The larger the bags and/or the more complex the required arithmetics become, the more possibilities there are for the outcome of the cost predicates so grounding a rule like those in Lines 8 or 9 will take more and more time.

4   Built-In Counters

In order to overcome the aforementioned problems, we extend the functionality offered for tracking the cost of each solution to any type of counter, such that D-FLAT now also stores the value for any defined counter, not only for the cost of

---

[3] Each node n has at most two child nodes; in case of two child nodes, the bags of n and its children contain the same vertices.

a solution, internally. To this end we introduce new output predicates: `counter/2` and `currentCounter/2`. `counter/2` takes an identifier and an integer value and sets the value of the counter denominated by the first argument, in the current table row. If the counter does not exist yet, it is created with its first occurrence as argument of the predicate `counter/2`. `currentCounter/2` also takes a string and an integer value, yet it sets the value of the counter denominated by the first argument only corresponding to the current node. The latter is necessary when using the option `--default-join`, which D-FLAT now uses to automatically merge counter values from different branches at join nodes by the inclusion-exclusion principle, just as it used to do for costs in previous versions. On the one hand, this feature makes the post-processing node with identical bag elements above each join node, when using the default-join, superfluous, on the other hand it offers the possibility to write encodings that are easier to understand and maintain.

Furthermore, D-FLAT now offers another feature that also boosts its performance. Instead of having to calculate the value for each counter every time, we can specify by how much a certain counter will be incremented. For this purpose, D-FLAT offers output predicates `counterInc/2+` and `currentCounterInc/2+`. These can be used alternatively to `counter/2` and `currentCounter/2` to increment the counter, or current counter, respectively, denominated by the first argument, by the value given in the second. The values of the counter and the current counter, respectively, to be incremented are taken by D-FLAT from the extended table row of the child node, or the extended item tree leaf of the child node, respectively. Further, we need to add as many arguments as needed to make each instantiation of the predicate unique. The uniqueness in turn is required to ensure that the different instantiations with the same cost do not overlap. Hence the predicates have arity of at least two. Again, if the counter does not exist yet, it is created with its first occurrence as argument of the predicate `counterInc/2+`. In the worst case, the performance does not improve significantly, on average however, it improves due to smaller program groundings. The latter can be achieved as the use of aggregate functions is not necessary anymore when incrementing, as opposed to calculating, counter values.

When these new predicates are used with "cost" as first parameter, they act as a cost declaration and D-FLAT optimizes the set of solutions specifically on the values stored in this counter. Further, if counters other than the "cost" counter have different values for identical item sets, the partial answer sets are not merged. For removing counters which will not be used anymore, D-FLAT provides the output predicate `counterRem/1`, which takes the name of the counter to be removed as its argument. Further, besides the predicate `childCost/2`, also `childCounter/3` is printed for each counter, at each node, and passed as input for the parent node of the tree decomposition. The first argument indicates the extended table row of the child node, or the extended item tree leaf of the child node, respectively, while the second denominates the counter and the third bears its value.

```
1  counterInc(cost,W,X) :- introduced(X), item(in(X)),
       weight(X,W).
2  currentCounterInc(cost,W,X) :- introduced(X), item(in(X)),
       weight(X,W).
3  currentCounterInc(cost,-W,X) :- extend(R), removed(X),
       childItem(R,in(X)), weight(X,W).
```

Listing 1.2. Cost calculation for MWDS using counters.

Table 2 shows the newly introduced predicates in D-FLAT's table mode. The same functionality is provided in item tree mode by analogous predicates.

Table 2. New reserved predicates for specifying counters in D-FLAT.

Input predicate	Meaning
childCounter(R, T, C)	C is the counter value corresponding to the table row R and the counter T

Output predicate	Meaning
counter(T, C)	The counter T of the current table row shall have a value of C
currentCounter(T, C)	The current counter T of the current table row shall have a value of C
counterInc(T, C)	The value of the counter T of the current table row shall be increased by a value of C
currentCounterInc(T, C)	The value of the current counter T of the current table row shall be increased by a value of C
counterRem(T)	The counter (and current counter) T shall be removed

Usage of the New Features. In order to illustrate the use of the newly introduced predicates in a simple manner, we present the cost calculation for the MWDS encoding for D-FLAT with default-join on semi-normalized tree decompositions using the counterInc/2+ and currentCounterInc/2+ predicates in Listing 1.2, replacing Lines 7–9 from Listing 1.1. Instead of summing up vertex weights in each inner node and having to use time-costly aggregate functions, we only increment the value of the cost by the weights of the newly introduced vertices that are part of the dominating set (Line 1). For the current cost, we increment this value by the weights of the newly introduced vertices that are part of the dominating set (Line 2), and decrement it by the weights of the newly removed vertices that are part of the dominating set (Line 3).

Further, if we wanted to implement a generalization of MINIMUM WEIGHTED PERFECT DOMINATING SET (MWPDS), where one can specify for each vertex by how many other vertices it is allowed to be dominated, we would need to use

```
1 auxItem(dominated(Y,N,CR)) :- extend(R), currentNode(CR),
       introduced(Y), not item(in(Y)),
       1 #count { CH: childAuxItem(R,n(CH)) } 1,
       N = #count { X : item(in(X)), edge(X,Y) }.
2 auxItem(dominated(Y,N1+N0,CR)) :- extend(R),
       currentNode(CR), current(Y),
       1 #count { CH: childAuxItem(R,n(CH)) } 1,
       childAuxItem(R,dominated(Y,N1,CH1)), N0 =
       #count { X : item(in(X)), edge(X,Y), introduced(X) }.
3 auxItem(dominated(Y,N1+N2-N12,CR)) :- extend(R),
       currentNode(CR),
       current(Y), childAuxItem(R,dominated(Y,N1,CH1)),
       childAuxItem(R,dominated(Y,N2,CH2)), CH1 != CH2,
       N12 = #count { X : item(in(X)), edge(X,Y) }.
4 auxItem(n(CR)) :- currentNode(CR).
5 :- extend(R), removed(X), not childItem(R,in(X)),
       childAuxItem(R,dominated(X,N,CH)), lowerBound(X,B),
       N<B.
6 :- extend(R), removed(X), not childItem(R,in(X)),
       childAuxItem(R,dominated(X,N,CH)), upperBound(X,B),
       N>B.
```

Listing 1.3. Generalized MWPDS encoding: auxiliary items and constraints.

some rather cumbersome constructs, namely the code in Listing 1.3, replacing Lines 4–6 from Listing 1.1. Instead of using an auxiliary item dominated/1, with one argument, now we would need one that takes three arguments: besides the name of the dominated vertex, the number of vertices it is dominated by and the name of the current node. The latter is necessary together with another option that inserts a so-called post-processing node with identical bag content right above each join node (option --post-join), where the dominated/3 predicate can be adjusted, as the default-join just passes auxiliary items through without merging them. In Line 1 we count for each vertex newly introduced into a bag of exchange nodes, by how many other vertices it is dominated, in Line 2 we instantiate the dominated/3 predicate for vertices which are not new to the tree decomposition by adding the number of dominating vertices in the child node to the number of newly introduced dominating vertices, while in Line 3 we merge the dominated/3 instantiations in a post-processing node, coming from different branches of the join node below, by the inclusion-exclusion principle. Line 4 defines the n/1 predicate which is used when checking that we are not dealing with a post-processing node. Finally, in Lines 5 and 6 we throw away all those partial solution candidates for which there is at least one newly removed vertex that does not comply with the number of vertices it must be dominated by in case it is not part of the dominating set.

Using the newly implemented built-in counters simplifies the encoding for two reasons: we do not need auxiliary items and post-processing nodes are not necessary anymore, as the counters replacing dominated/3 are now merged

```
1  counter(Y,N) :- introduced(Y), not item(in(Y)),
       N = #count { X : item(in(X)), edge(X,Y) }.
2  counter(Y,N0+N1) :- extend(R), current(Y),
       childCounter(R,Y,N1), N0 =
       #count { X : item(in(X)), edge(X,Y), introduced(X) }.
3  currentCounter(Y,N) :- current(Y), not item(in(Y)),
       N = #count { X: item(in(X)), edge(X,Y) }.
4  counterRem(Y) :- removed(Y).
5  :- extend(R), removed(X), not childItem(R,in(X)),
       childCounter(R,X,N), lowerBound(X,B), N<B.
6  :- extend(R), removed(X), not childItem(R,in(X)),
       childCounter(R,X,N), upperBound(X,B), N>B.
```

Listing 1.4. Use of built-in counters for generalized MWPDS.

automatically in join nodes when using the default-join. Thus, the counters need to store only their name, which coincides here with the name of the vertex they describe, and the number of vertices that dominate the former, as shown in Listing 1.4, which illustrates the use of counter/2 and currentCounter/2. The rule in Line 1 instantiates the counters for newly introduced vertices that are not part of the dominating set. The next rule defines the counters for vertices that are not newly introduced by adding the value of the counter of the vertex in the child node to the number of newly introduced vertices it is dominated by in the current node. In Line 3, we now define the current counter for each vertex that is not in the dominating set as being the number of vertices that dominate the former, for the default-join to be able to correctly merge the counters in join nodes by the inclusion-exclusion principle. Line 4 is needed for D-FLAT to stop carrying counters of vertices that are not in the current bag anymore and the last two lines again throw away those partial solution candidates for which the number of dominating vertices is out of the specified range. These improvements to the MWPDS encoding are rather small in terms of runtime, being attributed to the fact that a post-processing node is not needed anymore. However, the readability of the code is strongly improved.

5   Experimental Results

In order to check possible performance improvements of the new features, we compared the implementation for D-FLAT of the MWDS problem, that does not use the newly implemented features, as seen in Listing 1.1, and the one in which Lines 7–9 from Listing 1.1 are replaced by Listing 1.2, using the newly introduced built-in counters to calculate the costs of the solutions. Further, we used a standard ASP encoding for the MWDS problem, which we fed to *clingo* [20] using two different strategies, branch-and-bound and unsatisfiable-core, for having a general reference. The complete benchmark set-up is available online[4].

---

[4] See www.dbai.tuwien.ac.at/proj/dflat/system/files/counters.zip.

As benchmarks we used 50 graphs based on real world instances of rail transportation networks in and around cities, namely combinations of train, metro and tram networks. They all have a treewidth of at most three and less than 400 vertices. For each graph we generated random weights and compared how the total number of rules generated in the grounding steps and the runtime varied when the weights took values of at most 1, 10, 100 and 1000, respectively. The tests were performed using ten different seeds for each instance on D-FLAT implementations on a machine with an AMD Opteron 6308@3.5 GHz processor operated with Debian 8 (jessie, kernel 3.16.0-4-amd64), on which clingo 4.5.0 and D-FLAT 1.2.0 were executed.

Figure 3 shows the results on 32 of the preliminary experiments, the rest exceeding the time bound of 30 min for *clingo* with branch-and-bound. As we can see, without using the new features, the runtime of D-FLAT grows linearly with an increase of the weights of the vertices and there is a clear correlation between the total number of rules in the groundings used by D-FLAT and the total necessary computation time. This can be easily explained by the fact that aggregate functions were used, whose groundings also grow with the existence of higher weights. The wider the span of weights gets, the smaller the probability becomes that some rules coincide by the summed value of weights in the grounding, and the larger the number of rules to be processed gets, as can also be seen on the left figure. Compared to this exponential growth, the implementation with built-in counters makes aggregates unnecessary and shows a major improvement in runtime, backed again by the total number of rules in the groundings. Now the growth in runtime is only logarithmic, growth which can be explained by the mere fact that *clasp* has to operate with higher numbers. We further notice that D-FLAT performs better than *clingo* with branch-and-bound strategy when making use of the built-in counters. Nevertheless, when using the unsatisfiable-core strategy, *clingo* is highly efficient on this problem.

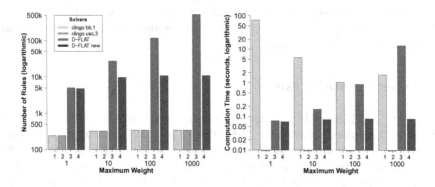

Fig. 3. Performance comparison between D-FLAT variants and ASP-system *clingo*.

6   Conclusion

In this paper we introduced a new feature to the D-FLAT system, namely built-in counters. These counters make encodings more convenient to write and much easier to maintain compared to encodings done for older versions of D-FLAT. Moreover, encodings using counters need considerably less computation time when minimizing the optimal solution based on weights. Future work will comprise experiments on further applications where dynamic programming algorithms require involved arithmetics, for instance, versions of the SECURE SETS PROBLEM [3].[5] Furthermore, we want to integrate counters also to a recently proposed lazy-evaluation variant of D-FLAT [6].

Acknowledgments. This work has been supported by the Austrian Science Fund (FWF): P25607-N23, Y698-N23. The authors thank the reviewers for their helpful comments which allowed to clarify the presentation of our work in the final version of this paper.

References

1. Abseher, M., Bliem, B., Charwat, G., Dusberger, F., Hecher, M., Woltran, S.: D-FLAT: progress report. Technical report DBAI-TR-2014-86, Vienna University of Technology (2014)
2. Abseher, M., Bliem, B., Charwat, G., Dusberger, F., Hecher, M., Woltran, S.: The D-FLAT system for dynamic programming on tree decompositions. In: Fermé, E., Leite, J. (eds.) JELIA 2014. LNCS, vol. 8761, pp. 558–572. Springer, Heidelberg (2014)
3. Abseher, M., Bliem, B., Charwat, G., Dusberger, F., Woltran, S.: Computing secure sets in graphs using answer set programming. J. Logic Comput. (2016). Accepted for publication
4. Abseher, M., Musliu, N., Woltran, S.: Improving the efficiency of dynamic programming on tree decompositions via machine learning. Technical report DBAI-TR-2016-94, TU Wien (2016). http://www.dbai.tuwien.ac.at/research/report/dbai-tr-2016-94.pdf
5. Arnborg, S., Corneil, D.G., Proskurowski, A.: Complexity of finding embeddings in a k-tree. SIAM J. Algebraic Discrete Methods **8**(2), 277–284 (1987)
6. Bliem, B., Kaufmann, B., Schaub, T., Woltran, S.: ASP for anytime dynamic programming on tree decompositions. In: Proceedings of the IJCAI (2016). Accepted for publication
7. Bliem, B., Morak, M., Woltran, S.: D-FLAT: declarative problem solving using tree decompositions and answer-set programming. TPLP **12**(4–5), 445–464 (2012)
8. Bliem, B., Pichler, R., Woltran, S.: Declarative dynamic programming as an alternative realization of Courcelle's theorem. In: Gutin, G., Szeider, S. (eds.) IPEC 2013. LNCS, vol. 8246, pp. 28–40. Springer, Heidelberg (2013)
9. Hans, L.: Bodlaender.: a tourist guide through treewidth. Acta Cybern. **11**(1–2), 1–22 (1993)

---

[5] See www.dbai.tuwien.ac.at/proj/dflat/system/files/counters.zip for such an encoding example.

10. Bodlaender, H.L.: A linear-time algorithm for finding tree-decompositions of small treewidth. SIAM J. Comput. **25**(6), 1305–1317 (1996)
11. Bodlaender, H.L., Koster, A.M.C.A.: Treewidth computations I. Upper bounds. Inf. Comput. **208**(3), 259–275 (2010)
12. Brewka, G., Eiter, T., Truszczyński, M.: Answer set programming at a glance. Commun. ACM **54**(12), 92–103 (2011)
13. Courcelle, B.: The monadic second-order logic of graphs. I. Recognizable sets of finite graphs. Inf. Comput. **85**(1), 12–75 (1990)
14. Cygan, M., Fomin, F.V., Kowalik, L., Lokshtanov, D., Marx, D., Pilipczuk, M., Pilipczuk, M., Saurabh, S.: Parameterized Algorithms. Springer, Heidelberg (2015)
15. Dechter, R.: Constraint Processing. Morgan Kaufmann, Burlington (2003)
16. Dermaku, A., Ganzow, T., Gottlob, G., McMahan, B., Musliu, N., Samer, M.: Heuristic methods for hypertree decomposition. In: Gelbukh, A., Morales, E.F. (eds.) MICAI 2008. LNCS (LNAI), vol. 5317, pp. 1–11. Springer, Heidelberg (2008)
17. Downey, R.G., Fellows, M.R.: Parameterized Complexity. Monographs in Computer Science. Springer, New York (1999)
18. Gebser, M., Kaminski, R., Kaufmann, B., Lindauer, M., Ostrowski, M., Romero, J., Schaub, T., Thiele, S.: Potassco User Guide 2.0. (2015). https://sourceforge.net/projects/potassco/files/guide/2.0/guide-2.0.pdf
19. Gebser, M., Kaminski, R., Kaufmann, B., Schaub, T.: Answer Set Solving in Practice. Synthesis Lectures on Artificial Intelligence and Machine Learning. Morgan & Claypool Publishers, San Rafael (2012)
20. Gebser, M., Kaufmann, B., Kaminski, R., Ostrowski, M., Schaub, T., Schneider, M.T.: Potassco: the potsdam answer set solving collection. AI Commun. **24**(2), 107–124 (2011)
21. Gelfond, M., Lifschitz, V.: Classical negation in logic programs and disjunctive databases. New Gener. Comput. **9**(3/4), 365–386 (1991)
22. Lierler, Y.: On the relation of constraint answer set programming languages and algorithms. In: Proceedings of the AAAI, pp. 521–527. AAAI Press (2012)
23. Niedermeier, R.: Invitation to Fixed-Parameter Algorithms. Oxford Lecture Series in Mathematics and its Applications. OUP, Oxford (2006)
24. Ostrowski, M., Schaub, T.: ASP modulo CSP: the Clingcon system. TPLP **12**(4–5), 485–503 (2012)
25. Robertson, N., Seymour, P.D.: Graph minors. III. Planar tree-width. J. Comb. Theory Ser. B **36**(1), 49–64 (1984)

Model Based Augmentation and Testing of an Annotated Hand Pose Dataset

Richárd Bellon[1], Younggeon Choi[2], Nikoletta Ekker[1], Vincent Lepetit[3],
L. Mike Olasz[1], Daniel Sonntag[4], Zoltán Tősér[1(✉)], Kyounghwan Yoo[2,5],
and András Lőrincz[1]

[1] Faculty of Informatics, Eötvös Loránd University, Budapest, Hungary
zoltan.toser@gmail.com
[2] Department of Applied Computer Engineering,
Dankook University, Yong-in, Korea
[3] Institute for Computer Vision and Graphics,
Graz University of Technology, Graz, Austria
[4] German Research Center for Artificial Intelligence, Saarbrücken, Germany
[5] Neofect Co., Ltd., Yong-in, Korea

Abstract. Recent advances of deep learning technology enable one to train complex input-output mappings, provided that a high quality training set is available. In this paper, we show how to extend an existing dataset of depth maps of hand annotated with the corresponding 3D hand poses by fitting a 3D hand model to smart glove-based annotations and generating new hand views. We make available our code and the generated data. Based on the present procedure and our previous results, we suggest a pipeline for creating high quality data.

1 Introduction

The big leap Deep Learning technology (DLT) is making today has its roots in the two different ways it can be used:

Component 1: DLT learns to map inputs to outputs
Component 2: It can be run in reverse, working as a generative model to create an input-like *imaginary* structure

The combination of these two components was already present in the autoencoding scheme developed many years ago [4, 11]. The breakthrough is due to the inclusion of Component 2 into deep learning architectures in diverse manners. Steps of the technology include the stacked autoencoder system, the the end-to-end learning schemes using rectified linear units, the very recent variational autoencoder [10] and the brute force inversion methods [6, 14], among many others. For thorough reviews, the interested reader is referred to the literature [1, 21].

The fast progress of DLT is constrained by an obstacle: present day deep learning methods need large training datasets with high quality annotations.

© Springer International Publishing AG 2016
G. Friedrich et al. (Eds.): KI 2016, LNAI 9904, pp. 17–29, 2016.
DOI: 10.1007/978-3-319-46073-4_2

Such high quality and numerous annotations, however, are hard to produce. For example, as pointed out in [13,25], there are many misplaced joints in the 3D hand pose dataset of [26]. Errors in the annotations make training and – more importantly – the evaluation unreliable. Different solutions have been put forth

1. for extending datasets and improving tracking capabilities, such as data generation from synthetic models [18,19], high tech complex camera setup [27] or data gloves [28] for data collection and
2. for improving tracking capabilities by means of error correction via regenerating the inputs as in [14], and exploiting spatial, temporal and appearance constraints for fine pose estimation [12]

among others. They all have certain drawbacks, such as the lack of proper noise in the synthetic data, the cost (multiple cameras) or the inaccuracies of the high tech tools of the annotation procedure, errors in data collection, imprecision coming from the sensor noise, or the differences between the noise of the training samples and the noise of the actual sensor. These issues are to be overcome by the combination of methods and by means of novel and efficient algorithms, including automated and robust outlier filtering in the training examples and the labels themselves [3,7,24].

Our contributions are as follows. We exploit (i) the synthetic open source LibHand software tool[1] [20], which provides a realistic articulated 3D hand model, (ii) the ICVL dataset of 3D hand poses [26], (iii) the DeepPrior architecture [13] that predicts a 3D hand pose given a depth map and which was rewritten in Caffe [25] and Lasagne, (iv) the Neofect data glove [23], and (v) a temporal series dataset collected for some examples of the American Sign Language by taking advantage of the capabilities of the data glove and fitting the data to the LibHand model. We shall make the new dataset and the related software tools available in order to accelerate their developments. We demonstrate the advantages of joining the methods; we increase the range of the orientation where tracking is feasible.

The paper is organized as follows. The next section (Sect. 2) describes the methods and the tools we used. Sections 3, 4, and 5 detail our results, discuss them, and conclude, respectively.

2   Tools, Datasets, and Methods

Below, we report about the tools we used, such as the NeoFect data glove, the LibHand software, ICVL hand posture dataset and our data collection method (Sect. 2.1). This subsection is followed by the description of the dataset extension pipeline (Sect. 2.2). Finally, we sketch the details of the ConvNet architecture called Deep Prior that we used for learning (Sect. 2.3) and list the open source software tools that are available already or will be made available soon (Sect. 2.4).

---

[1] http://www.libhand.org/.

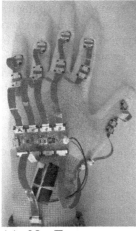

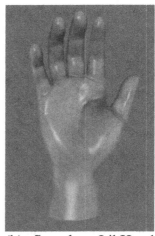

(a) NeoFect proto-
type data glove

(b) Sample LibHand
model

Fig. 1. The NeoFect prototype data glove and the LibHand graphics model.

2.1 Smart Glove, Model Software, Dataset

The NeoFect prototype data glove: We have used a prototype of the
RAPAEL Smart Glove^{TM} (Fig. 1(a)). The data glove has 14 pieces of 9 degree-
of-freedom inertia sensors and a software that outputs the relative angles
between them.

The LibHand software: We applied the open-source LibHand library [20] for
rendering hand poses (Fig. 1(b)). This tool was used to fit the ICVL dataset.

ICVL Dataset: The hand posture dataset of the Imperial College Vision and
Learning Lab has a large number of depth images, mostly taken from the
direction of the palm. This is the direction, where occlusions for different
hand poses are minimal. The dataset has 16 markered joints (Palm, Thumb
root, Thumb mid, Thumb tip, and root, mid tip for the Index, Middle, Ring,
and Pinky fingers.

Data Collection: The prototype NeoFect data glove has considerable uncertainties. In order to collect feasible hand poses that cover the most relevant
hand pose configurations, we turned to the signs of the American Sign Language (ASL). We configured the LibHand model to 22 ASL signs, set the
experimenter's hand to e achsign with the data glove on and recorded different motions starting from the signs and also from open hand configurations.
Different motions were recorded with the gloves both by starting from the
same pose and by using different starting poses.

Data, if played backwards end up in ASL positions and could be used for
temporal recognition of ASL signs, e.g., by means of recurrent neural networks
(for a review on 3D skeletal data of people and related methods, see [8] and the

references therein) or using temporal kernels [5,9]. Since ASL configurations that our time series start from have been carefully designed and are very different and since our time series end up in more prototypical hand poses, we expect that the data we collected cover a large portion of relevant hand poses. We fitted the data to LibHand and if the fit corresponded to some impossible configuration (due to the imprecision of the glove), then we deleted it from the dataset.

2.2 Database Generation for Extending the ICVL Dataset

We developed mappings between the data types and extended the available dataset in different ways.

Mapping: We connected three data types; the angles of the sensors of the data glove, the parameters of the LibHand model, and the markers of the ICVL dataset. The goal was to compare the data and to combine them such a way that synthetic data can be created. The pipeline for generating synthetic depth images is shown in Fig. 2 and is detailed below:

  (i) We get the angles from the glove,
  (ii) construct a rotation-invariant pose representation with joint angles that we
  (iii) fit to the LibHand model and then we
  (iv) generate the new depth image with different hand orientations.

ICVL integration: Due to the synthetic nature of our dataset, it is easy to derive new orientations. Beyond our collected dataset, we also fit the LibHand model to the ICVL dataset and rotated the dataset to novel orientations. This step was to produce additional depth and marker data with a large variety of real hand configurations. The original ICVL data was also kept since it contained data with real noise content. The procedure is as follows:

  (i) We get the 3D markers from the ICVL dataset
  (ii) construct a rotation-invariant pose representation with joint angles using the Deep Prior software
  (iii) fit to the LibHand model and that enables us to
  (iv) generate the new depth images with different hand orientations.

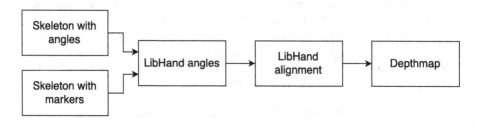

Fig. 2. Database generation pipeline

2.3   DeepPrior-Lasagne CNN

Training was performed with a ConvNet architecture shown in Fig. 3. The inputs are 128×128 normalized images processed first by a tandem made of a convolutional layer (8 pieces of 5×5) and pooling layer (with 4×4 pooling region). The architecture has two more similar, but somewhat smaller double layers followed by two dense layers having 1024 units each. The final layer is also a dense layer, which has 30 units. Units of the two large dense layers are rectified linear units, whereas units of the output layer are linear. Another important feature of the architecture concerns the processing of the marker data. They undergo principal component analysis and only the largest 30 dimensions are kept. This PCA filtered dataset forms the output of the training sessions.

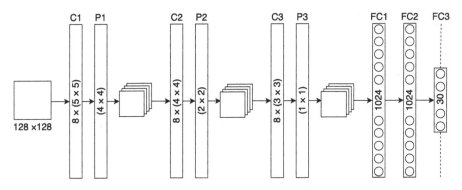

Fig. 3. 'DeepPrior' parameters for ConvNet: 3 convolutional and pooling layers, 2 dense layers and a linear output layer

2.4   Open Source Contributions

We open our dataset. We add crowdsourcing annotation options for further extensions and quality assurance [16]. Deep Prior is already available under GPLv3[2] [13] and there is a Caffe implementation[3] [25], too. We make our code available in Lasagne that includes the fitting tool to the LibHand library [20].

3   Results

3.1   Non-linear Mapping from ICVL 3D Markers to the LibHand Model

Skeleton angles are the basic control features of LibHand. ICVL, on the other hand, provides marker points on the hand. To our best knowledge, marker points on the fingers and on the hand are at middle points between corresponding surface points of the forehand and backhand poses. We assigned forehand and backhand surface vertex points of LibHand to the ICVL marker points.

---

[2] https://cvarlab.icg.tugraz.at/projects/hand_detection/.
[3] https://github.com/jsupancic/deep_hand_pose.

The other element of the generation took advantage of the NeoFect glove. The angles of the NeoFect sensors have considerable uncertainties from day-to-day and also for large orientation changes. On the other hand, precision of measuring small changes of the pose is sufficiently precise. With the glove on our hand, we imitated fixed hand poses that we constructed in the LibHand model. We had 22 of those, most of which correspond to basic positions of the American Sign Language. We modified all poses in relatively small ranges allowed by the precision of the gloves and measured the angle changes. In addition, we developed a simple mapping between the angles of the glove sensors and the angles of the LibHand model. This way, to each hand pose changes we had a corresponding LibHand model.

Taking together, we collected over 20,000 LibHand poses with LibHand angles, LibHand forehand and backhand vertex positions and estimated ICVL marker positions within the LibHand model. We paired the ICVL marker positions and LibHand angle vectors. We used these pairs for training a deep learning of architecture made of four dense layers and rectified linear units. 3D marker point positions of the fitted ICVL model served as the input and skeleton angles were the outputs during training. We tested the mapping on samples not used in the training sessions and found that in the front-hand and the backhand poses the errors in the angles were slightly above 4° and around 4.7°, respectively.

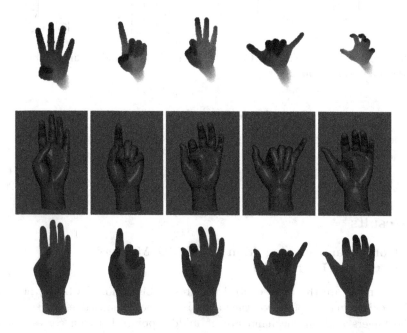

Fig. 4. Realistic set of pose models generated by means of the NeoFect gloves, LibHand model and the ICVL. **Top row:** original depth images. **Middle row:** conservative Lib-Hand fits. Such fits enable the generation of any orientations. **Bottom row:** LibHand generated depth images.

Performance of the trained network is shown in Fig. 4. In turn, we could unify the models generated by means of the NeoFect glove and the models generated by means of the ICVL dataset. In the following, we shall present our results concerning (a) the network trained on the *ICVL dataset*, (b) the network trained on the *Glove dataset*, i.e., the dataset contained no data from the ICVL dataset, (c) the network trained on the *augmented ICVL* (A-ICVL dataset), and (d) the network trained on *rotated and augmented ICVL dataset* (RA-ICVL dataset). We shall also use the shorthand expression *IGT* for the ICVL marker point ground truth as well as *GGT* for the glove marker point ground truth.

3.2 Tests on the New Datasets

We conducted a number of tests with artificial and real data.

First test: Comparison between the networks trained on the ICVL on the A-ICVL datasets. We found that networks trained on ICVL and A-ICVL perform equally well (Fig. 5).

Second test: Comparison between Glove and A-ICVL datasets. We found that the samples generated from the Glove dataset are not sufficient for generating good fits to the Glove depth data themselves. However, the combined dataset, i.e., the A-ICVL dataset fits the Glove dataset well (Fig. 6).

Third test: Testing in real scenarios. We trained networks for frontal and backward poses. The procedure was the following:

(a) We collected the data of a real frontal hand pose detected by a Senz3D depth camera.

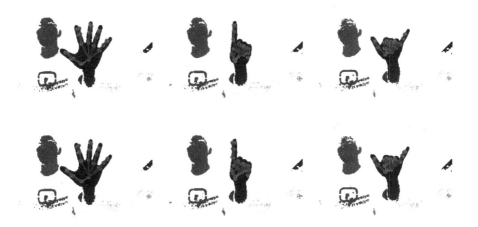

Fig. 5. Training results with the ICVL dataset and the augmented ICVL dataset. ICVL depth images: grey, ICVL ground truth (IGT) markers: green dots. **Upper row:** IGT pose + prediction with model trained on the ICVL frontal dataset. **Lower row:** IGT pose + prediction with model trained on the frontal augmented ICVL dataset. (Color figure online)

Fig. 6. Training results with the Glove dataset and the augmented ICVL dataset. Glove depth images: grey, Glove ground truth (GGT) markers (green dots). **Upper row:** GGT pose + prediction with model trained on the Glove dataset for frontal orientation. **Lower row:** GGT pose + prediction with model trained on the frontal augmented ICVL dataset. (Color figure online)

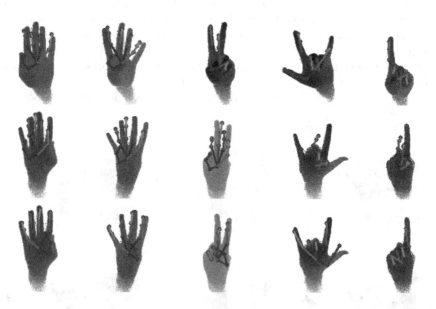

Fig. 7. Testing on real hand data taken with Senz3D depth camera. In four out of the five examples, occlusion is considerable. **Top row:** real data in frontal pose and fits generated by the model trained on the frontal ICVL data; **Middle row:** real data taken from the back and fits generated with the same model as above. **Bottom row:** Results are very similar for the fits generated by the model trained on the data collected with glove alone and when it is combined with the fitted and rotated ICVL data restricted to the direction of the back side of the hand. Here we show the latter. Mean errors for the former and the latter are 9 mm and 8.8 mm respectively with about 50 % higher values for the V-like pose in the middle.

(b) We estimated the hand pose with the DeepPrior architecture

(c) We rotated the hand in front of the camera while maintaining the hand pose

(d) We estimated the hand pose with models trained on different datasets (see, Fig. 7).

Fits are best on the rotated and augmented ICVL dataset

Fourth test: Results as a function of the rotation range. We used our datasets and trained networks for different central hand orientations having different orientation ranges. Central orientations were set to 0°, 45°, 90°, 135°, and 180°, respectively along the vertical axis. Training angle ranges were 0°, ±20°, ±40°, ±60°, and ±80°, respectively. Results are shown for overall mean and for overall max errors in Figs. 8 and 9, respectively.

Results are very similar for the different orientation angles: the low error range increases as the range of rotation angle grows. At the same time, precision barely decreases as it can be seen on the (g)–(i) subfigures of both figures.

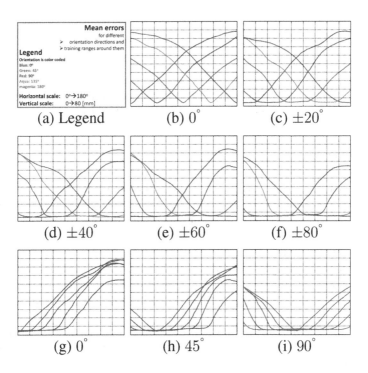

Fig. 8. Mean errors of all models trained on different central orientations and different orientation ranges. Central orientations: 0°: blue, 45°: green, 90°: red, 135° aqua, 180°: magenta. Training ranges around the central orientations: (b): 0°, (c): ±20°, (d): ±40°, (e): ±60°, (f): ±80°. Subfigures (g)–(i): curves reordered according to the training ranges. Symmetrical cases are not shown. (Color figure online)

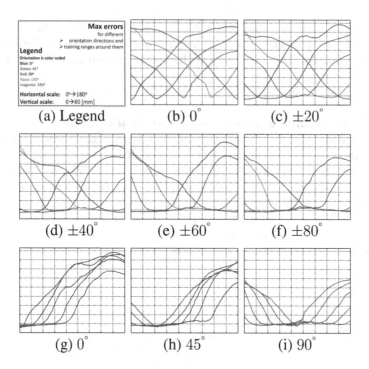

Fig. 9. Max errors of all models trained on different central orientations and different orientation ranges. Notations are the same as in Fig. 8. (Color figure online)

4 Discussion

Having a hand model, the task is to fit it to the detected data. There are different approaches for such optimizations, including particle filtering [2], particle swarm optimization [15] that can be combined with deep learning methods [22]. Our method exploits marker based and model based approaches, alike [29]. Such methods can also be extended by interpolation techniques to improve precisions [12]. These methods can learn specific artifacts arising from sensor noise and can improve tracking capabilities by the richness of model generated databases. We demonstrated that such enlarged databases can improve the performance of deep learning methods in both directions: collected data improves model based tracking (Fig. 6) and the model can be used to extend the variety of data, including, e.g., hand orientations (Figs. 8 and 9). We also note that the two component role of deep networks – as mentioned in the introduction – can be used for reducing problems arising from particular types of sensory noise [14]. These technology elements can greatly reduce the DLT needs for high quality human annotations.

Here we presented a set of methods for dataset extension for hand pose tracking. Some of the tools are already available on the Internet, and we are making the new tools and the new database open for further improvements.

We list the drawbacks that if overcome may improve performance considerably.

(i) The depth images need larger dynamic ranges: We used Unity3D and the distance of the near and far clipping planes (of the virtual camera) together with the 8 bit precision of the software is not sufficient should be increased. We lost a great amount of depth information and the mapping of the generated dataset to the ICVL is not sufficiently precise.

(ii) The generated dataset contains no noise. When we combined it with the ICVL database we experienced considerable improvements on real data taken with a Senz3D depth camera. Noise data for structured light sources may be necessary for fitting the data taken with such cameras if the method of brute force inversion [14] is not sufficient.

Furthermore, the advances in deep learning technology are very fast and more efficient architectures are being developed see, e.g., [6,10,14,17] and may give rise to considerable improvement in performances when combined.

5 Conclusions

Human-computer (human-robot) interactions require human models with fast tracking capabilities. 3D depth cameras offer novel solutions especially if they are combined with deep learning methods. The latter is constrained by the need of large datasets with high quality annotations that can be expensive. Here we put forth a combination of methods that can simplify the problem for real time hand tracking. In addition, we make our tools and the database available for further works.

Acknowledgments. This work was supported by the EIT Digital grant (Grant No. 16257).

References

1. Bengio, Y., Goodfellow, I.J., Courville, A.: Deep Learning. MIT Press, Cambridge (2015, in preparation). http://www.iro.umontreal.ca/~bengioy/dlbook
2. Bray, M., Koller-Meier, E., Van Gool, L.: Smart particle filtering for 3D hand tracking. In: Proceedings of the Sixth IEEE International Conference on Automatic Face and Gesture Recognition, pp. 675–680. IEEE (2004)
3. Cho, M., Sun, J., Duchenne, O., Ponce, J.: Finding matches in a haystack: a max-pooling strategy for graph matching in the presence of outliers. In: Proceedings of the IEEE Conference on Computer Vision and Pattern Recognition, pp. 2083–2090 (2014)
4. Cottrell, G.W., Munro, P., Zipser, D.: Learning internal representations from gray-scale images: an example of extensional programming. In: Ninth Annual Conference of the Cognitive Science Society, pp. 462–473 (1987)
5. Cuturi, M.: Fast global alignment kernels. In: Proceedings of the 28th International Conference on Machine Learning (ICML 2011), pp. 929–936 (2011)

6. Dosovitskiy, A., Tobias Springenberg, J., Brox, T.: Learning to generate chairs with convolutional neural networks. In: Proceedings of the IEEE Conference on Computer Vision and Pattern Recognition, pp. 1538–1546 (2015)

7. Fu, J., Wu, Y., Mei, T., Wang, J., Lu, H., Rui, Y.: Relaxing from vocabulary: robust weakly-supervised deep learning for vocabulary-free image tagging. In: Proceedings of the IEEE International Conference on Computer Vision, pp. 1985–1993 (2015)

8. Han, F., Reily, B., Hoff, W., Zhang, H.: Space-time representation of people based on 3D skeletal data: a review. arXiv preprint arXiv:1601.01006 (2016)

9. Jeni, L.A., Lőrincz, A., Szabó, Z., Cohn, J.F., Kanade, T.: Spatio-temporal event classification using time-series kernel based structured sparsity. In: Fleet, D., Pajdla, T., Schiele, B., Tuytelaars, T. (eds.) ECCV 2014, Part IV. LNCS, vol. 8692, pp. 135–150. Springer, Heidelberg (2014)

10. Kingma, D.P., Welling, M.: Auto-encoding variational bayes. arXiv preprint arXiv:1312.6114 (2013)

11. Kohonen, T., Lehtio, P., Oja, E., Kortekangas, A., Makisara, K.: Demonstration of pattern processing properties of the optimal associative mappings. In: Proceedings of the International Conference on Cybernetics and Society (1977)

12. Oberweger, M., Riegler, G., Wohlhart, P., Lepetit, V.: Efficiently creating 3D training data for fine hand pose estimation. In: Proceedings of the IEEE Conference on Computer Vision and Pattern Recognition (2016, accepted)

13. Oberweger, M., Wohlhart, P., Lepetit, V.: Hands deep in deep learning for hand pose estimation. In: Proceedings Computer Vision Winter Workshop (CVWW) (2015)

14. Oberweger, M., Wohlhart, P., Lepetit, V.: Training a feedback loop for hand pose estimation. In: Proceedings of the IEEE International Conference on Computer Vision, pp. 3316–3324 (2015)

15. Oikonomidis, I., Kyriazis, N., Argyros, A.A.: Tracking the articulated motion of two strongly interacting hands. In: 2012 IEEE Conference on Computer Vision and Pattern Recognition (CVPR), pp. 1862–1869. IEEE (2012)

16. Palotai, Z., Lang, M., Sarkany, A., Toser, Z., Sonntag, D., Toyama, T., Lorincz, A.: Labelmovie: semi-supervised machine annotation tool with quality assurance and crowd-sourcing options for videos. In: 2014 12th International Workshop on Content-Based Multimedia Indexing (CBMI), pp. 1–4. IEEE (2014)

17. Rasmus, A., Berglund, M., Honkala, M., Valpola, H., Raiko, T.: Semi-supervised learning with ladder networks. In: Advances in Neural Information Processing Systems. pp. 3532–3540 (2015)

18. Riegler, G., Ferstl, D., Rüther, M., Bischof, H.: A framework for articulated hand pose estimation and evaluation. In: Paulsen, R.R., Pedersen, K.S. (eds.) SCIA 2015. LNCS, vol. 9127, pp. 41–52. Springer, Heidelberg (2015)

19. Rogez, G., Supancic, J.S., Ramanan, D.: Understanding everyday hands in action from RGB-D images. In: Proceedings of the IEEE International Conference on Computer Vision, pp. 3889–3897 (2015)

20. Šaric, M.: Libhand: a library for hand articulation. Version 0.9 (2011)

21. Schmidhuber, J.: Deep learning in neural networks: an overview. Neural Netw. **61**, 85–117 (2015)

22. Sharp, T., Keskin, C., Robertson, D., Taylor, J., Shotton, J., Kim, D., Rhemann, C., Leichter, I., Vinnikov, A., Wei, Y., et al.: Accurate, robust, and flexible real-time hand tracking. In: Proceedings of the 33rd Annual ACM Conference on Human Factors in Computing Systems, pp. 3633–3642. ACM (2015)

23. Shin, J.H., Kim, M.Y., Lee, J.Y., Jeon, Y.J., Kim, S., Lee, S., Seo, B., Choi, Y.: Effects of virtual reality-based rehabilitation on distal upper extremity function and health-related quality of life: a single-blinded, randomized controlled trial. J. Neuroeng. Rehabil. **13**(1), 1 (2016)

24. Sukhbaatar, S., Bruna, J., Paluri, M., Bourdev, L., Fergus, R.: Training convolutional networks with noisy labels. arXiv preprint arXiv:1406.2080 (2014)

25. Supancic, J.S., Rogez, G., Yang, Y., Shotton, J., Ramanan, D.: Depth-based hand pose estimation: data, methods, and challenges. In: Proceedings of the IEEE International Conference on Computer Vision, pp. 1868–1876 (2015)

26. Tang, D., Chang, H., Tejani, A., Kim, T.K.: Latent regression forest: structured estimation of 3D articulated hand posture. In: Proceedings of the IEEE Conference on Computer Vision and Pattern Recognition, pp. 3786–3793 (2014)

27. Tompson, J., Stein, M., Lecun, Y., Perlin, K.: Real-time continuous pose recovery of human hands using convolutional networks. ACM Trans. Graph. (TOG) **33**(5), 169 (2014)

28. Xu, C., Cheng, L.: Efficient hand pose estimation from a single depth image. In: Proceedings of the IEEE International Conference on Computer Vision, pp. 3456–3462 (2013)

29. Zhu, X., Lei, Z., Yan, J., Yi, D., Li, S.Z.: High-fidelity pose and expression normalization for face recognition in the wild. In: Proceedings of the IEEE Conference on Computer Vision and Pattern Recognition, pp. 787–796 (2015)

Lifted Junction Tree Algorithm

Tanya Braun[(✉)] and Ralf Möller

Institute of Information Systems, Universität Zu Lübeck, Lübeck, Germany
{braun,moeller}@ifis.uni-luebeck.de

Abstract. We look at probabilistic first-order formalisms where the domain objects are known. In these formalisms, the standard approach for inference is lifted variable elimination. To benefit from the advantages of the junction tree algorithm for inference in the first-order setting, we transfer the idea of lifting to the junction tree algorithm.

Our lifted junction tree algorithm aims at reducing computations by introducing first-order junction trees that compactly represent symmetries. First experiments show that we speed up the computation time compared to the propositional version. When querying for multiple marginals, the lifted junction tree algorithm performs better than using lifted VE to infer each marginal individually.

Keywords: Probabilistic logical models · Lifted inference · Junction tree · Belief propagation

1 Introduction

New probabilistic logical representation formalisms support first-order logic, rather than just propositional logic, and one can reason about sets of individuals in a relational domain. To express patterns or symmetries in the relation between individuals, we combine random variables (randvars) with logical variables (logvars) to denote a whole set of randvars (parameterized randvars, PRVs). In an undirected formalism with known domain objects, the idea of lifting is to use these patterns and symmetries to infer knowledge faster.

A small example that serves as a running example for the upcoming sections is a knowledge base (KB) G_{ex} with PRVs $epidemic(D)$ and $sick(D, P)$. The PRV $epidemic(D)$, for example, could stand for two propositional randvars if logvar D had the two instantiations flu and $measles$.

In general, we study the inference task of computing marginal distributions. Many approaches and applications need optimizations to enhance efficiency. For propositional representation languages, variable elimination (VE) [19] speeds up computation. VE decomposes a KB into parts that we can solve faster. In the first-order context, lifted VE [12] aims at answering queries more efficiently by exploiting symmetries captured in PRVs. More specifically, with PRVs in a KB, we have parameterized factors (potential functions), called parfactors for short, that have PRVs as arguments. A parfactor represents a set of factors with an identical potential function, e.g., a probability distribution. Lifted

© Springer International Publishing AG 2016
G. Friedrich et al. (Eds.): KI 2016, LNAI 9904, pp. 30–42, 2016.
DOI: 10.1007/978-3-319-46073-4_3

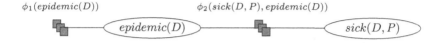

Fig. 1. Parfactor graph for G_{ex}

VE uses the symmetries in the potential functions to reduce the number of computations carried out. Figure 1 shows a graphical representation of G_{ex} with PRVs $epidemic(D)$ and $sick(D, P)$ and parfactors $\phi_1(epidemic(D))$ and $\phi_2(sick(D, P), epidemic(D))$. The graph consists of two variable nodes, one for each randvar in G_{ex}, and two factor nodes for the two parfactors. The factor nodes have edges to the nodes of the randvars involved. E.g., factor $\phi_1(epidemic(D))$ denotes that all randvars for which $epidemic(D)$ stands have the same potential function ϕ_1, e.g., a prior probability for some epidemic to occur.

When asking multiple queries in the propositional case, an optimization is the junction tree algorithm [7]. It allows to compute all marginal distributions efficiently instead of answering queries individually with VE. The junction tree algorithm is designed for query answering with respect to KBs specified with undirected formalisms. We can transfer directed formalisms into undirected ones by moralizing the underlying graphs or by building decomposition trees (dtrees) [7]. Dtrees are tree representations of the decomposition of a KB during VE. The junction tree algorithm supports exact reasoning through message passing where we basically apply VE in all directions at a time. In the context of junction trees, message passing distributes "knowledge" in a graph. It does not approximate in itself. With symmetries present, many unnecessary messages are sent. We transfer the idea of lifting to the junction tree algorithm to optimize the junction tree representation and message handling. We illustrate our findings in the evaluation with an extended example where we show that the advantages of a junction tree transfer from the propositional to the first-order setting.

This paper contributes the following: We propose a lifted junction tree algorithm for inference in probabilistic logical KBs. We lift the algorithm by building a lifted (first-order) junction tree (FO jtree). To this end, we introduce parameterised clusters (parclusters) that, similar to parfactors, support logvars to capture symmetries. We modify the message passing scheme to operate on FO jtrees. When calculating messages and results to queries, we integrate lifted VE.

The representation language and lifted VE operators we use heavily rely on Taghipour's work [17] (and the papers cited therein). Taghipour also introduces lifted (first-order) dtrees (FO dtrees) based on [6] and gives a simple algorithm to find one for a given KB. We use FO dtrees to build FO jtrees.

In terms of performance, the lifted junction tree algorithm imposes some static overhead due to the junction tree construction and message passing. But, with multiple queries or varying evidence where the tree is reusable, the overhead amortizes and becomes more and more negligible compared to the junction tree speed-up. According to our experiments, we significantly speed up run times in the presence of symmetries compared to the grounded version. Additionally, we speed up inference compared to lifted VE if asking multiple queries.

The remainder of this paper starts with related work on lifted inference and belief propagation followed by background information on the junction tree algorithm, parameterized KBs, and FO dtrees. Next, we introduce our lifted junction tree algorithm. Additionally, we present an evaluation of our algorithm with promising results. We conclude the paper by looking at future work.

2   Related Work

We present related work in the area of probabilistic (first-order) formalisms, focusing on the junction tree algorithm and lifted inference.

Basic junction tree algorithms, specifically, their message passing schemes, use one of two architectures. Shafer and Shenoy [13] propose the first architecture under the name probability propagation, often called Shafer-Shenoy. Jensen et al. [9] introduce the second architecture, nowadays referred to as Hugin. Both architectures have a *collect* and a *distribute* phase but vary with respect to what they store and how they compute messages. On the one hand, Shafer-Shenoy is more space-efficient than Hugin. On the other hand, Hugin usually is faster. Hugin saves time by doing fewer computations per message but requires more space to store larger intermediate results. We adapt the ideas of both architectures to pass and process messages in our lifted algorithm.

Darwiche [7] provides the foundation for the dtrees as we use them and the connection between dtrees and junction trees. His work on recursive conditioning [6] and local symmetry (the latter together with Chavira and Darwiche [5]) provides ideas on how to further utilize first-order structures in different ways.

Lifted inference has been the focus of research for some years now. The first formalizations of lifted inference go back to [12], named FOVE for first-order VE. The research presented in [3,10,17] extends the formalism to the standard form GC-FOVE of lifted VE with generalized counting. We use the lifting operators in GC-FOVE for internal lifted calculations in our algorithm.

Parallel to lifted VE, weighted first-order model counting emerges using the lifting idea applied to weighted model counting for inference [4]. Another branch, lifted belief propagation (BP), picks up the idea of probability propagation and combines it with lifting. Often, the work on belief propagation is accompanied with lifted representations. The work of Singla and his colleagues includes BP on a lifted network, using hypercube-based representations, and an approximate lifted BP, to approximate lifting in presence of noise [14–16]. Gogate uses hypercubes as well for a lifted representation [8]. Ahmadi et al. [1] provide a counting BP using a coloring algorithm including an extension to dynamic Bayesian networks. Though lifted BP uses belief propagation similar as we do, none of the approaches given uses a lifted version of junction trees.

The junction tree algorithm provides an efficient alternative to inference if confronted with the need to answer multiple queries or queries under varying evidence. Lifting provides an idea to further optimize inference by handling symmetries in an efficient way. We take the propositional version and adapt it to a first-order setting by modifying the underlying tree structure. Additionally, we revise the propositional algorithm to deal with first-order constructs efficiently. We alter the computing instructions for delivering results to queries as well as assembling messages to incorporate lifted VE instead of ground VE. Overall, we propose a lifted algorithm that compactly represents clusters in a KB and efficiently handles inference on them.

3 Background

This section presents the standard junction tree algorithm and introduces definitions for parameterized KBs and FO dtrees. The first subsection is based on [7], the second on [17]. Taghipour [17] calls the KB we work on a model. We use the term model for the remainder of this paper. We assume familiarity with common notions such as dtrees and its properties cutsets, contexts, and clusters (for an introduction, see also the appendix in [2]).

3.1 Junction Tree Algorithm

In inference, we query models, e.g., a factor graph, given some evidence. For one query, VE is the standard approach. With multiple queries, we look for a data structure that allows to pre-compute recurring calculations for faster query answering. Junction trees (jtrees) serves as such a data structure. Jtree nodes represent sets of variable nodes of the underlying model, called clusters. One algorithm run distributes knowledge in the underlying jtree. At the end, a node holds all information to compute marginal probabilities for its variables.

Intuitively, clusters consist of elements (i.e., randvars) that share close relations, through factors, otherwise not present in the model. Randvars that contribute to various clusters inform the structure of the jtree. All clusters that share a randvar build a subgraph to ensure that if local changes in one cluster influence a randvar, the effect is communicated to the other clusters. To construct a jtree, we build a dtree and compute its clusters. A dtree represents a decomposition of a model during VE. The dtree structure and its clusters associated with each node form a jtree.

A factor is associated with a cluster that includes the factor's arguments. Evidence influences arguments. If we enter evidence in the graph at one end, we propagate that information to other parts using messages. After propagating all information (factors are information as well), we answer queries by looking at clusters that contain the query variables. Starting from evidence, we compute aggregations of factors by propagating information from node to node. We reuse the jtree with new evidence.

Next, we formalize the dtree and jtree data structure and the junction tree algorithm. A dtree for a graph G is a tree whose leaf nodes correspond to the factors in G. An inner node represents a decomposition of its factors into partitions, one for each child, containing the factors in the child's subtree. The cluster of a dtree node N is the union of its cutset and context. The cutset of N is the set of randvars shared between any pair of its child nodes. In case of N not being the root, we subtract the randvars appearing in its ancestor cutsets. The context of N is the intersection of its randvars and those in its ancestor cutsets.

A jtree for a graph G is a pair $(\mathcal{J}, \mathbf{C})$ where $\mathcal{J}$ is a tree (the structure of the jtree) and $\mathbf{C}$ is a function that maps each node i in $\mathcal{J}$ to a label $\mathbf{C}_i$ called a cluster. The mapping function effectively makes the clusters and nodes of $\mathcal{J}$ interchangeable. A jtree must satisfy three properties: (i) A cluster $\mathbf{C}_i$ is a set of nodes from G. (ii) For every edge X—Y in G, variables X and Y appear in some cluster $\mathbf{C}_i$. (iii) If a node from G appears in clusters $\mathbf{C}_i$ and $\mathbf{C}_j$, it must appear in every cluster $\mathbf{C}_k$ on the path between nodes i and j in $\mathcal{J}$. $\mathbf{S}_{ij}$, called the separator of edge i—j, holds those randvars shared by clusters $\mathbf{C}_i$ and $\mathbf{C}_j$ and is given by $\mathbf{C}_i \cap \mathbf{C}_j$.

A jtree is minimal if by removing a variable from any cluster, the jtree stops being a jtree The clusters of a dtree fulfil the jtree properties. But, the resulting jtree is seldom minimal. We merge two neighboring clusters if the randvars in one of them is a subset of the randvars in the other.

The main workflow to answer queries is to construct the jtree, pass messages, and then answer queries. We modify the junction tree algorithm from [7] using potential functions instead of conditional probability tables (CPTs). The algorithm consists of a preparation phase and the actual algorithm. The preparations incorporate three steps: (i) Construct a jtree. (ii) Assign each potential function ϕ to a cluster that contains its randvars. (iii) Assign for each randvar X an evidence indicator λ_X to a cluster that contains X. We use evidence indicators to assign an observed value of a randvar. By multiplying an indicator with a potential function, we incorporate the evidence into the model. For each cluster, we multiply the assigned factors.

The algorithm itself is short: We enter evidence $\mathbf{e}$ through the indicators. Then, the algorithm sends messages to distribute knowledge. Message M_{ij} from node i to node j holds new information for j encoded in a readable way: M_{ij} is a product of the factor assigned to i and the messages received from other nodes but j projected onto $\mathbf{S}_{ij}$ by summing out $\mathbf{C}_i \backslash \mathbf{S}_{ij}$. Message computation is a form of VE, summing out variables unknown at the receiver node. We can interpret a message as a factor with the separator variables as arguments. After passing two messages per edge, we can compute, e.g., marginal $P(\mathbf{C}, \mathbf{e})$ for every cluster $\mathbf{C}$. To answer a query, we can now use any cluster that contains the query variables and sum out all other variables.

3.2   Parameterized Models and FO Dtrees

Parameterized models provide a compact way to specify KBs using first-order constructs allowing lifted VE. To enable a compact dtree representation, we need a first-order version, which we use for constructing FO jtrees.

First, we define a few useful shortcuts. Consider the PRV $epidemic(D)$ representing a set of randvars depending on the instantiations of D. We call the possible values of D its domain, denoted $\mathcal{D}(D)$. Assuming $epidemic(D)$ is binary, the range of each randvar represented by $epidemic(D)$ is $true$ and $false$: $range(epidemic(D)) = \{true, false\}$. The term $logvar(P)$ denotes the logvars in a set or sequence of randvars P (e.g., $logvar(epidemic(D)) = \{D\}$). Domains constrain the instantiations of a PRV to a given set by specifying the values of its logvars. As PRVs are arguments to parfactors, parfactors are subject to constraints as well. We introduce a constraint C to specify instantiations of logvars. Taghipour defines a constraint C as a tuple $(\mathbf{X}, C_{\mathbf{X}})$, with $C_{\mathbf{X}} \subseteq \times_{i=1}^n \mathcal{D}(X_i)$ where $\mathbf{X} = (X_1, \ldots, X_n)$ is a tuple of logvars.

To specify a parfactor g, we need the potential function with its arguments, i.e. PRVs, and a constraint on the logvars in g. Formally, g is given by

$$g := \forall \mathbf{L} \ : \ \phi(\mathcal{A}) \mid C$$

where $\mathbf{L}$ is a set of logvars that the factor generalizes over. $\mathcal{A} = (A_1, \ldots, A_n)$ is a sequence of randvars. If $\mathbf{L} = logvar(\mathcal{A})$, we omit $\forall \mathbf{L}$ in the parfactor. $\phi = \times_{i=1}^n range(A_i) \to \mathbb{R}^+$ is a potential function with values of $\mathcal{A}$ as input.

A model G is given by a set of parfactors $\{g_i\}_{i=1}^n$. Model G_{ex} becomes the parfactor model $G_{ex} = \{g_1, g_2\}$ with $g_1 = \phi_1(epidemic(D))|C_1$, $g_2 = \phi_2(sick(D, P),$ $epidemic(D))|C_2$. Let $\mathcal{D}(D) = \{flu, measles\}$ and $\mathcal{D}(P) = \{alice, eve, bob\}$. Then we could define C_2 by $((D, P), C_{(D,P)})$ and $C_{(D,P)} = \{(flu, eve), (flu, bob), (flu, alice), (measles, eve), (measles, bob), (measles, alice)\}$.

Lifting uses the fact that we can decompose a model into isomorphic subproblems and solve only one representative. For our algorithm, we use the lifting operators defined by Taghipour (for full definitions including pre- and postconditions, see [17]). For example, we use lifted absorption when entering evidence in the FO jtree or lifted summing-out when computing messages.

First-Order Dtrees. We now define a compact representation of the decomposition of a model. Logvars allow us to ground models partially by grounding a subset of the logvars and work with representatives of the grounded logvars. If a model is in a certain normal form, we can decompose it into partial groundings isomorphic up to permutations of inputs. For details on the normal form and decomposition into partial groundings (DPG), see also the appendix in [2].

Isomorphic decomposition (ID) nodes represent isomorphic partial groundings in the FO dtree. An ID node $T_{\mathbf{X}}$ is given by a triplet $(\mathbf{X}, \mathbf{x}, C)$ where $\mathbf{X} = \{X_1, \ldots X_k\}$ is a set of logvars all of the same domain $\mathcal{D}_{\mathbf{X}}$, $\mathbf{x} = \{x_1, \ldots x_k\}$ is a set of *symbolic constants* from $\mathcal{D}_{\mathbf{X}}$, and C is a constraint on $\mathbf{x}$, such that for $i, j : x_i \neq x_j \in C$. We denote $T_{\mathbf{X}}$ by $\forall \mathbf{x} : C$ in the FO dtree. $T_{\mathbf{X}}$ has one child named $T_{\mathbf{x}}$. The model under $T_{\mathbf{x}}$ is a representative instance of $T_{\mathbf{X}}$.

An FO dtree represents a decomposition of a parfactor model during lifted VE with parfactors in its leaves and ID nodes to model representative instances. Formally, an FO dtree is a tree that can have ID nodes and in which (i) each leaf contains a factor (possibly with symbolic constants), (ii) each leaf with symbolic constant x is the descendent of exactly one ID node $T_{\mathbf{X}}$ such that $x \in \mathbf{x}$, (iii) each leaf that is a descendent of ID node $T_{\mathbf{X}}$ has all symbolic constants $\mathbf{x}$ in its factor, and (iv) for each ID node $T_{\mathbf{X}}$, $\mathbf{X} = \{X_1, \ldots X_k\}$, $T_{\mathbf{x}}$ has $k!$ children $\{T_i\}_{i=1}^{k!}$, which are isomorphic up to a permutation of symbolic constants $\mathbf{x}$.

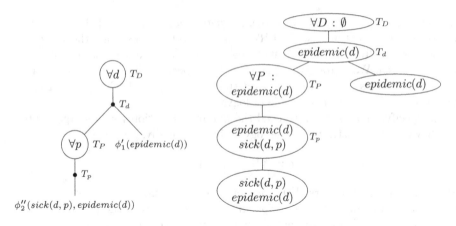

Fig. 2. FO dtree for G_{ex} **Fig. 3.** FO jtree for the FO dtree in Fig. 2

For an FO dtree, one can compute a cluster for each node analogously to computing clusters for propositional dtrees. The appendix in [2] shows how to build an FO dtree for a model and how to compute clusters for FO dtrees.

Figure 2 shows an FO dtree for G_{ex}. For readability purposes, we only write the element for singleton sets and omit $\top$ constraints. The root is an ID node $T_D = (D, d, \top)$ (logvar D allows a DPG). T_D has a child T_d with the model $G' = \{g_1' = \phi'(epidemic(d)), g_2' = \phi'(sick(d, P), epidemic(d))\}$. G' does not allow a DPG (g_1' has no logvar). Hence, G' is split based on the occurrence of P. Thus, T_d gets two children. The right child with the model $\{g_1' = \phi'(epidemic(d))\}$ is ground. It has only one factor in its model which results in a leaf node with factor $\phi'(epidemic(d))$. The left child with the model $\{g_2' = \phi'(sick(d, P), epidemic(d))\}$ has a logvar, P, that permits a DPG. Hence, the child is an ID node $T_P = (P, p, \top)$ with a child T_p with the model $\{g_2'' = \phi''(sick(d, p), epidemic(d))\}$. g_2'' is ground and only consists of one factor as well, so the child is a leaf node with factor $\phi''(sick(d, p), epidemic(d))$ contained in it.

4   Lifted Junction Tree Algorithm

This section presents our lifted version of the junction tree algorithm including FO jtrees and parclusters.

4.1   First-Order Junction Trees

FO jtrees follow the idea of ground jtrees. Clusters combine PRVs with close relations and message passing distributes knowledge to enable efficient query answering of many queries. A ground jtree in the presence of symmetries has many nodes with identical factors where messages propagate information that basically is already present. We allow parameterized randvars to capture symmetries and parameterize the notion of a cluster to represent a subgraph of grounded clusters with identical potential functions.

Algorithm 1. Constructing an FO Jtree for a Model G Using an FO Dtree

---

    function FO-JTREE(G)
        FO dtree T = FO-DTREE(G)
        Compute clusters for T
        Construct FO jtree J
        Minimize J
        return J

Parclusters. Intuitively, parclusters are the nodes of an FO jtree formed by FO dtree clusters. A parcluster describes the set of randvars in a cluster and can have factors assigned. It generalize over logvars if ID nodes are involved.

Formally, a parcluster $\mathbf{C} = \forall \mathbf{L} : \mathcal{A}|C$ is a set of randvars $\mathcal{A}$. The parameters of $\mathbf{C}$ are the set of logvars $\mathbf{L}$ and $logvar(\mathcal{A}) \subseteq \mathbf{L}$. The constraint C puts limitations onto logvars and symbolic constants. A factor $\phi(\mathcal{A}_\phi)|C_\phi$ assigned to $\mathbf{C}$ has to fulfil (i) $\mathcal{A}_\phi \subseteq \mathcal{A}$, (ii) $logvar(\mathcal{A}_\phi) \subseteq \mathbf{L}$, and (iii) $C_\phi \subseteq C$.

As jtrees built from dtrees often are non-minimal, we define a merge operation for parclusters. Parclusters $\mathbf{C}_i$ and $\mathbf{C}_j$ with possibly assigned factors ϕ_i and ϕ_j can merge if $\mathcal{A}_i \subseteq \mathcal{A}_j \vee \mathcal{A}_j \subseteq \mathcal{A}_i$ holds. The merged parcluster $\mathbf{C}_k$ and its assigned factor ϕ_k are determined by

- $\mathcal{A}_k = \mathcal{A}_i \cup \mathcal{A}_j$,
- $\mathbf{L}_k = \mathbf{L}_j \cup \mathbf{L}_i$,
- $C_k = C_i \cup C_j$, and

$$
- \phi_k = \begin{cases}
\phi_i & \text{if only } \phi_i \text{ exists} \\
\phi_j & \text{if only } \phi_j \text{ exists} \\
\phi_i \otimes \phi_j & \text{if both exist} \\
undefined & \text{otherwise.}
\end{cases}
$$

The new node k takes over all neighbours of i and j. To merge a parcluster with logvars and another with corresponding symbolic constants, we first perform an inverse substitution from symbolic constants to logvars and then merge.

FO Jtrees. An FO jtree for a model G is a graph with parclusters as nodes. It must also satisfy the three properties introduced for ground jtrees. Grounding an FO jtree leads to a jtree that could have been built by converting a ground dtree into a jtree. The set of factors in the grounded version of the FO jtree is identical to the set of factors in the ground jtree. Algorithm 1 shows pseudo code for constructing an FO jtree for a model G. First, it constructs an FO dtree and computes its clusters. Then, it builds an FO jtree using the clusters. Finally, the FO jtree is minimized by merging parclusters.

The clusters of the FO dtree in Fig. 2 lead to the FO jtree in Fig. 3. The labels next to the nodes indicate from which node a cluster came. The FO jtree shown is not minimal. Iteratively merging leaf parclusters with their neighbor leads to a single parcluster $\mathbf{C} = \forall D, P : \{epidemic(D), sick(P, D)\}$ with ϕ_1 and ϕ_2 assigned to it.

Algorithm 2. Lifted Junction Tree Alg. for Model G, Queries Q, Evidence E

---

    function FOJT(G, Q, E)
        FO jtree $J = $ FO-JTREE(G)
        J.ENTEREVIDENCE(E)
        J.PASSMESSAGES
        J.GETANSWERS(Q)

4.2 Algorithm Description

Our lifted junction tree algorithm has the following workflow: (i) Construct an FO jtree for a given model G. (ii) Enter evidence E into the tree. (iii) Pass messages. (iv) Compute answers. Algorithm 2 shows a corresponding pseudo code description, which uses Algorithm 1.

FO jtree construction uses the clusters of an FO dtree for model G. After the FO jtree construction, we enter evidence E, a set of evidence parfactors. We assign an evidence parfactor to a parcluster if the represented set of the parcluster randvars includes the randvars of the evidence parfactor.

Message passing on FO jtrees proceeds analogously to the one on grounded jtrees. A message from node i to node j is a factor over the randvars in separator $\mathbf{S}_{ij}$ where all other randvars in parcluster $\mathbf{C}_i$ are summed out. The messages and factors include PRVs which allow us to use lifted VE for computations. Message passing starts from the leaves and moves inward (*collect* phase). When all neighbors but one have sent messages to a node, the node itself sends a message to the remaining neighbor. Sending messages in such a way leads to one or two nodes in the center of the jtree to have received messages from all neighbors. Then, the *distribute* phase begins. The one or two nodes send messages to all its neighbors. If now a node receives a message (from the node to which it sent a message during the *collect* phase), it sends messages to all other neighbors. With new evidence, we repeat message passing.

To answer a query, we identify a cluster with the query terms in its domain and sum out all other terms in its parfactor and messages received. For answering queries (or handling evidence), we need the lifted VE operator splitting to rewrite the model to permit lifted summing out. (A parfactor is split into one parfactor for the query term (or the terms for which we have evidence) and one for the other instances of the logvar.)

Compared to the ground version, we do not change the algorithm structure much to lift it. We enter evidence and pass messages. The preparation phase and how we handle evidence, messages, and queries vary. In a dtree, the leaves hold the factors and every factor appears in exactly one leaf. Therefore, clusters have assigned factors and our merge operation maintains them. Additionally, we do not assign evidence indicators as we use evidence parfactors to handle evidence in a lifted manner. So, the preparation phase (construction, assign factors, assign indicators) melts down to construction. For message and query computation, we incorporate lifted VE operators to further optimize calculations.

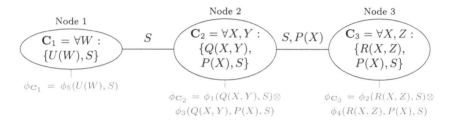

Fig. 4. FO jtree for G_{ex2}

5   Evaluation

We compare our lifted algorithm with GC-FOVE and a propositional version of the junction tree algorithm. We have implemented our lifted junction tree algorithm with Shafer-Shenoy message passing as a Java program that builds on GC-FOVE [18] which is an extension of C-FOVE [10] in BLOG [11].

First experiments exhibit promising results. Since lifting is relevant in the presence of symmetries, the experiments focus on models with symmetries. Additionally, inference benefits from our approach particularly if asking several queries. Although GC-FOVE has to eliminate all non-query randvars in the model, it is usually faster than our algorithm if asking only one query as it does not have to construct an FO jtree. With multiple queries, though FO jtree construction and message passing impose some static overhead, our algorithm needs considerably fewer computations to answer queries. If evidence changes, we can reuse the FO jtree and only add the overhead of a message passing run.

We illustrate our findings with an extended model $G_{ex2} = \{g_1, g_2, g_3, g_4, g_5\}$. The parfactors are defined as follows:

- $g_1 = \phi_1(Q(X,Y), S)$
- $g_2 = \phi_2(R(X,Z), S)$
- $g_3 = \phi_3(Q(X,Y), P(X), S)$
- $g_4 = \phi_4(R(X,Z), P(X), S)$
- $g_5 = \phi_5(U(W), S)$

The domains of the four logvars are of size four. The randvars are binary and the potential functions are CPTs with random entries. We have no evidence and the queries are $P(S)$, $P(U(w_1))$, $P(P(x_1))$, $P(Q(x_1, y_1))$, and $P(R(x_1, z_1))$. Figure 4 displays the minimized FO jtree for G_{ex2} consisting of three nodes with the associated parfactors as labels. The two parfactors of parclusters $\mathbf{C}_2$ and $\mathbf{C}_3$ are multiplied into one parfactor using lifted multiplication during merging.

Comparison with GC-FOVE. We feed our algorithm with the model and the five queries as input and receive as answers five probability distributions. We run GC-FOVE with the same model and each query individually. Asking multiple queries in GC-FOVE may lead to dependencies between query terms which causes GC-FOVE to abort.

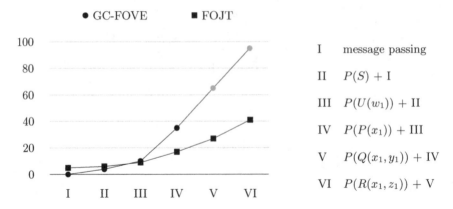

Fig. 5. Accumulated number of calls to lifted VE operators during query answering by GC-FOVE and FOJT (The lines between data points are only there for readability. The gray dots denote that the counts include queries that GC-FOVE aborted.)

For the queries $P(S)$, $P(U(w_1))$, and $P(P(x_1))$, we get three probability distributions identical to the ones from our algorithm. The query $P(Q(x_1,y_1))$ leads GC-FOVE to terminate and prompt the following error message: `Fatal error: Parfactor[qe(x1, y1), qe($318, y1)]` `:{constraint} still contains a non-query term.` When GC-FOVE aborts, it has already performed 30 split and sum-out operations to no avail. Query $P(R(x_1,z_1))$ causes the same problem.

Figure 5 shows the accumulated number of calls to lifted VE operators during answering the five queries for GC-FOVE and our algorithm called FOJT in the figure. We initialize the accumulated counts with the number of calls to lifted VE operators during message passing for FOJT. The order of the added counts is from the shortest to the longest query in terms of operator calls. GC-FOVE has to always eliminate all randvars in the model except for the query randvar. In contrast, after message passing, FOJT only has to eliminate all non-query randvars in a parcluster. E.g., for $P(U(w_1))$, we take the final parfactor at $\mathbf{C}_1$, $\phi_{\mathbf{C}_1}$, and sum out $U(W), W \neq w_1$ (with lifted VE) and S. GC-FOVE has to additionally sum out $P(X)$, $Q(X,Y)$, and $R(X,Z)$.

With the second query, FOJT needs fewer overall calls. Considering that we also need to construct the FO jtree, the test run supports our statement that with only very few queries to answer, the overhead of our lifted junction tree algorithm does not amortize. But with an increasing number of queries, our approach becomes more and more efficient.

Overall, GC-FOVE calls the splitting operator over three times more and the summing-out operator over one and a half times more than our algorithm as it has to eliminate all non-query terms for each query. We pay the savings in calls with time spent on constructing the FO jtree and passing messages. The message passing, which involves four messages being sent, takes another five calls to the summing-out operator.

A brief look at runtimes shows that FOJT appears to be competitive. GC-FOVE has an accumulated runtime of $\sim$55 ms for model G_{ex2} and the three queries it can answer. The runtime of the implementation of our algorithm is $\sim$40 ms which $\sim$15 ms faster and answers two more queries. With only the three queries GC-FOVE can answer, our algorithm needs $\sim$24 ms.

Comparison with Ground Version. The ground jtree for G_{ex2} has 36 clusters, 4 clusters of form $\{U(w_i), S\}$, 16 clusters of the form $\{Q(x_i, y_j), P(x_i), S\}$, and 16 clusters of the form $\{R(x_i, z_j), P(x_i), S\}$. If we merge the clusters of the dtree to have one virtual root, e.g., $\{Q(x_1, y_1), P(x_1), S\}$, with 35 neighbors, we send 70 messages instead of 4. In the *collect* phase, we perform 35 grounded sum-out operations. For each message in the *distribute* phase, we calculate a product with 35 multiplicands and sum out one or two ground randvars. At the end, each leaf node has to multiply the received message into its factor and the virtual root has to multiply all its messages and its factor. To answer queries, we have less work as we only need to sum out one or two ground randvars.

For the grounded-out version, the Hugin architecture is advantageous. We would not calculate 35 products with 35 multiplicands but multiply each incoming message into the stored factor once (leading to overall 35 multiplications) and divide the stored factor by the received message if sending the return message (35 divisions). Using Hugin in our lifted algorithm does not have a huge effect on the number of computations given the FO jtree for G_{ex2}.

6   Conclusion

Most applications need efficient inference algorithms. As first experiments with our lifted junction tree algorithm show, our proposal performs inference more efficiently when dealing with multiple queries in the presence of symmetries. The junction tree construction imposes overhead but only once per fixed knowledge base. If the evidence changes, message passing is repeated. For different queries for a model and given evidence, the algorithm only needs to run once.

Currently, we are fleshing out our algorithm and implementation to fully handle evidence. Additionally, we intend to optimize the basic implementation of the algorithm and extend it to include message passing based on the Hugin architecture. We plan to thoroughly evaluate different settings and analyze the behavior of our algorithm in terms of growing knowledge bases. In a broader scope, we investigate ideas to further use the data structures with respect to other theoretical constructs as well as practical applications that could benefit from our algorithm. Symmetries within a factor present an area of interest to potentially refine the data structures and increase efficiency. Dynamic structures to incorporate temporal constructs are another branch of work to look at.

References

1. Ahmadi, B., Kersting, K., Mladenov, M., Natarajan, S.: Exploiting symmetries for scaling loopy belief propagation and relational training. Mach. Learn. **92**, 91–132 (2013). Kluwer Academic Publishers, Hingham
2. Braun, T.: Lifted junction tree algorithm. Technical report, Universität zu Lübeck (2016)
3. de Salvo Braz, R.: Lifted first-order probabilistic inference. Ph.D. thesis, University of Illinois at Urbana-Champaign (2007)
4. Van den Broeck, G.: Lifted inference and learning in statistical relational models. Ph.D. thesis, KU Leuven (2013)
5. Chavira, M., Darwiche, A.: Compiling bayesian networks using variable elimination. In: Proceedings of the 20th International Joint Conference on Artificial Intelligence. Morgan Kaufman, San Francisco (2007)
6. Darwiche, A.: Recursive Conditioning. Artif. Intell. **2**, 4–41 (2001). Elsevier Science Publishers, Essex
7. Darwiche, A.: Modeling and Reasoning with Bayesian Networks. Cambridge University Press, Cambridge (2009)
8. Gogate, V., Domingos, P.: Exploiting logical structure in lifted probabilistic inference. In: Working Note of the Workshop on Statistical Relational Artificial Intelligence at the 24th Conference on Artificial Intelligence. The AAAI Press, Menlo Park (2010)
9. Jensen, F.V., Lauritzen, S.L., Oleson, K.G.: Bayesian updating in recursive graphical models by local computations. Comput. Stat. Q. **4**, 269–282 (1990). Physica-Verlag, Vienna
10. Milch, B., Zettlemoyer, L.S., Kersting, K., Haimes, M., Pack Kaelbling, L.: Lifted probabilistic inference with counting formulas. In: Proceedings of the 23rd Conference on Artificial Intelligence, pp. 1062–1068. The AAAI Press, Menlo Park (2008)
11. Milch, B., Li, L.: Bayesian Logic Programming Language. https://bayesianlogic.github.io
12. Poole, D.: First-order probabilistic inference. In: Proceedings of the 18th International Joint Conference on Artificial Intelligence, pp. 985–991. Morgan Kaufman Publishers Inc., San Francisco (2003)
13. Shafer, G.R., Shenoy, P.P.: Probability propagation. Ann. Math. Artif. Intell. **2**, 327–351 (1989). Springer, Heidelberg
14. Singla, P., Domingos, P.: Lifted first-order belief propagation. In: Proceedings of the 23rd Conference on Artificial Intelligence, pp. 1094–1099. The AAAI Press, Menlo Park (2008)
15. Singla, P., Nath, A., Domingos, P.: Approximate lifted belief propagation. In: Working Note of the Workshop on Statistical Relational Artificial Intelligence at the 24th Conference on Artificial Intelligence. The AAAI Press, Menlo Park (2010)
16. Singla, P., Nath, A., Domingos, P.: Approximate lifting techniques for belief propagation. In: Proceedings of the 28th Conference on Artificial Intelligence, pp. 2497–2504. The AAAI Press, Menlo Park (2014)
17. Taghipour, N.: Lifted probabilistic inference by variable elimination. Ph.D. thesis, KU Leuven (2013)
18. Taghipour, N.: GC-FOVE. https://dtai.cs.kuleuven.be/software/gcfove
19. Zhang, N.L., Poole, D.: A simple approach to bayesian network computations. In: Proceedings of the 10th Canadian Conference on Artificial Intelligence, pp. 171–178. Morgan Kaufman Publishers, San Francisco (1994)

Improved Diversity in Nested Rollout Policy Adaptation

Stefan Edelkamp[1]([✉]) and Tristan Cazenave[2]

[1] Fachbereich Mathematik und Informatik, Universität Bremen,
Am Fallturm 1, 28359 Bremen, Germany
edelkamp@tzi.de
[2] PSL – Université Paris-Dauphine, LAMSADE UMR CNRS 7243,
Place du Maréchal de Lattre de Tassigny, 75775 Paris Cedex 16, France

Abstract. For combinatorial search in single-player games *nested Monte-Carlo search* is an apparent alternative to algorithms like UCT that are applied in two-player and general games. To trade exploration with exploitation the randomized search procedure intensifies the search with increasing recursion depth. If a concise mapping from states to actions is available, the integration of policy learning yields *nested rollout with policy adaptation* (NRPA), while Beam-NRPA keeps a bounded number of solutions in each recursion level. In this paper we propose refinements for Beam-NRPA that improve the runtime and the solution diversity.

1 Introduction

Cazenave [4] has invented *nested Monte-Carlo search* (NMCS), a randomized search algorithm inspired by UCT [12] but specifically designed to solve single-player games. Instead of relying on a playout at each search tree leaf, the decision-making in level l of the algorithm relies on a level $(l-1)$ search for its successors.

With *nested rollout policy adaptation* (NRPA), Rosin [14] came up with the idea to learn a policy within the recursive procedure. NRPA has been very successful in solving a variety of optimization problems, including puzzles like *morpion solitaire*, but also hard optimization tasks in logistics like *constraint traveling salesman problems* [9] combined *pickup-and-delivery tasks* [8], *vehicle routing* [10], and *container packing* [7] problems.

Monte-Carlo tree search algorithms balance entering unseen areas of the search space (exploration) with working on already established good solutions (exploitation). Many Monte-Carlo search algorithms including NRPA, however, suffer from a solution process that has many inferior solutions in the beginning of the search. If policies are learnt too quickly, the number of different solutions reduces, and if not strong enough they will not help sufficiently well to enter parts of the search space with good solutions.

In other words, the diversity of the search remains limited. Beam-NMCS [5] is a combination of memorizing a set of best playouts instead of only one best playout at each level. This set is called a beam and all the positions in the set are

© Springer International Publishing AG 2016
G. Friedrich et al. (Eds.): KI 2016, LNAI 9904, pp. 43–55, 2016.
DOI: 10.1007/978-3-319-46073-4_4

developed. Beam search carries over to improve NRPA, enforcing an increased diversity in a set of solutions. In Beam-NRPA [6], for each level of the search, the algorithm keeps a bounded number of solutions together with their policies in the recursion tree. In selected applications, Beam-NRPA improves over NRPA.

In this paper, we reengineer the implementation of Beam-NRPA. We show that the solution quality can be improved by applying a selection of refinements. In particular, we study more closely how to increase the diversity.

2   NRPA and Beam-NRPA

NRPA is a randomized optimization scheme that belongs to the wider class of Monte-Carlo tree search (MCTS) algorithms [3]. The main concept of MCTS is the random *playout* (or *rollout*) of a position, whose outcome, in turn, changes the likelihood of generating successors in subsequent trials. Prominent members in this class of reinforcement learning algorithms are *upper confidence bounds applied to trees* (UCT) [12], and *nested monte-carlo search* (NMCS) [4]. MCTS is state-of-the-art in playing many two-player games [11] or puzzles [2], and has been applied also to other problems than games like mixed-integer programming, contraint problems, mathematical expression, function approximation, physics simulation, cooperative pathfinding, as well as planning and scheduling.

What makes NRPA [14] different to UCT and NMCS is the concept of learning a policy through an explicit mapping of moves to selection probabilities. The pseudo-code of the recursive search procedure is shown in Fig. 1 (left). NRPA has two main parameters that trade exploitation with exploration: the number of levels l and the branching factor N of recursion calls. If r is not better than *best*, on the first glance it looks like the same call to NRPA is performed within the loop on i. However, rollouts change due to randomness, and policy adaptation in other level of the recursion.

Beam-NRPA is an extension of NRPA that maintains B instead of one best solution in each level of the recursion. The motivation behind Beam-NRPA is to warrant search progress by an increased diversity of existing solutions to prevent the algorithm from getting stuck in local optima. The basic implementation of Beam-NRPA algorithm [5] is shown in Fig. 1 (right). Each solution is stored together with its score and the policy that was used to generate it. Better solutions are inserted into a list that is sorted wrt. the objective to be optimized.

As the NRPA recursion otherwise remains the same, the number of playouts to a search with level L and (iteration) width N rises from N^L to $(N \cdot B)^L$. To control the size of the beam, we allow different beam widths B_l in each level l of the tree. At the end of the procedure, B_l best solutions together with their scores and policies are returned to the next higher recursion level. For each level l of the search, one may also allow the user to specify a varying iteration width N_l. This yields the algorithm Beam-NRPA to perform $\prod_{l=1}^{L} N_l B_l$ rollouts.

procedure NRPA(level l, policy p)
  if $l = 0$
    $Best \leftarrow$ Playout(p)
  else
    $p_l' \leftarrow p$
    $Best \leftarrow (\text{Init},\langle\rangle)$
    for $i = 1, \ldots, N$
      $r \leftarrow$ NRPA($l - 1, p_l'$)
      if r better than $Best$
        $Best \leftarrow r$
        Adapt($Best, p, p_l'$)
  return $Best$

procedure Beam-NRPA(level l, policy p)
  if $l = 0$
    $(score, rollout) \leftarrow$ Playout(p)
    return $(score, rollout, p)$
  $Beam_l \leftarrow (\text{Init},\langle\rangle,p)$
  for $i = 1, \ldots, N$
    $SL \leftarrow \emptyset$
    for $t \leftarrow (score, rollout, p) \in Beam_l$
      $SL \leftarrow SL \cup \{t\}$
      $T \leftarrow$ Beam-NRPA($l - 1, p$)
      for $t' \leftarrow (score', rollout', p') \in T$
        Adapt($rollout', p', p$)
        $SL \leftarrow SL \cup \{t'\}$
    $Beam_l \leftarrow B$ best in $Beam_l \cup SL$
  return $Beam_l$

Fig. 1. NRPA and Beam NRPA. To cover both minimization and maximization problems, score ordering is imposed by means of implementing *Init*, *better*, and *best*. SL is implemented as a sorted list.

3 Refinements

We propose several refinements to Beam-NRPA.

Dropping Policy Information. First, we have observed that copying the policy in each rollout of Beam-NRPA is a rather expensive operation that can dominate the runtime of the entire algorithm.

    In fact, further code analysis showed that the policy update is always performed wrt. the currently best solution found in a level and the policy one level up, so that it is not required to store the policy attached each solution, as long as we keep B_l best policies alive for each level l of the recursive search procedure.

Employing Faster Adaptation. For a faster processing of policy adaptation, we avoid the regeneration of successors by providing all the information that is needed at the time we construct the solution in the rollout. Hence, we store the sequence of codes $Code_l$ and successor node codes $Succ_l$ for each best solution (relative to a level l) produced, where the *code* is a user-specified domain-specific address into the policy table calculated based on the current state and the current move executed in this state [14].

    The implementation in Fig. 2 shows that this strategy is already applicable to the original NRPA algorithm. It leads to minor extensions to the implementation of the generic *playout* function: each time a successor is checked for availability the corresponding code is stored. We see that the update in *Adapt* affects only the codes of the good solution to be adapted and its successor codes, to balance the positive effect put on choosing it as negative effect to all of its successors.

procedure NRPA-Adapt (rollout *best*, level l, policy p, policy p)
    $p' \leftarrow p$
    for $i \in best_l$
        $c_i \leftarrow$ code of move $best_{l,i}$
        $Succ_{l,i} \leftarrow$ successors codes of $best_{l,i}$
            $p'[c_i] \leftarrow p'[c_i] + \alpha$
        $z \leftarrow 0$
        for $c' \in Succ_{l,i}$
            $z \leftarrow z + exp(p[c'])$
        for $c' \in Succ_{l,i}$
            $p'[c'] \leftarrow p'[c'] - \alpha \cdot exp(p[c'])/z$

procedure NRPA-Adapt-Improved(level l, policy p, policy p')
    $p' \leftarrow p$
    for $c_i \in Code_l$
        $p'[c_i] \leftarrow p'[c_i] + \alpha$
    $z \leftarrow 0$
    for $c' \in Succ_{l,i}$
        $z \leftarrow z + exp(p[c'])$
    for $c' \in Succ_{l,i}$
        $p'[c'] \leftarrow p'[c'] - \alpha \cdot exp(p[c'])/z$

Fig. 2. Old and new policy adaptation procedure for NRPA reproducing rollout data and its successors (left) and recorded solution information (right); z is used for normalization, α is the learning rate, usually $\alpha = 1$.

Avoiding Memory Defragmentation. To avoid fragmented access to the memory and operating system calls to provide memory, high-speed algorithm implementations often avoid dynamic memory allocation or have their own memory maintenance and allocators. Beam-NRPA pre-allocates the information in the beam in static arrays and operates on the stored information directly. Besides faster insertion and deletion this allows to follow the progress of the search by showing the top $k \leq B_l$ elements.

4 Improving the Diversity

Beam-NRPA itself is inspired by the objective of higher diversity in the solution space of NRPA. In larger search spaces NRPA often got stuck with inferior solutions. It simply takes too long to backtrack to less determined policies in order to visit other parts in the search space. The beam is stored in a bounded number of *buckets*. The information contained in the buckets is visualized in Fig. 6. Instead of the moves executed in a rollout we store the *Code* of the chosen move and the code of its successors *Succ*. Additionally, the length of the rollout and its score is stored for each bucket in the beam.

Improving Diversity in the NRPA Driver. When looking at a beam, a natural aim is to keep solutions in the beam substantially different. This can be imposed by a matching the best obtained rollout with of the ones stored in the beam. Duplicate solutions wrt. this criterion are excluded from the beam. Figure 3 provides a pseudo-code implementation.

    The application of a filter to improve diversity is implemented in method *Similar*. We expect that $s_i = s_j$ implies $Similar(s_i, s_j)$ and $Similar(s_i, s_j) = Similar(s_j, s_i)$. The output is a truth value (interpreted as a number in $\{0, 1\}$). The beam is scanned for similar states, and if present, the new insertion request

procedure Diversity-NRPA(level l, policy p)
    for $b = 1, \ldots, B_l$
        $score_{l,b} \leftarrow$ Init
    if $l = 0$
        $Score_{0,1} \leftarrow$ Playout(p)
        return $Score_{0,1}$
    for $i = 1, \ldots, N_l$
        $score \leftarrow$ Diversity-NRPA$(l - 1, p)$
        if $score$ better than $Score_{l,B_l}$
            for $b' = 1, \ldots, B_{l-1}$
                if $\neg$ Similar$(Score_{l,b'}, Length_{l,b'}, l)$
                and $Score_{l-1,b'}$ better than $Score_{l,B_l}$
                    insert $(Score_{l-1,b'}, Length_{l-1,b'}, Code_{l-1,b'}, Succ_{l-1,b'})$ into $Beam_l$
        if $(i > \Theta_l)$
            Diversity-Adapt (l, p_l')
    return $Score_{l,1}$

Fig. 3. Beam-NRPA with high diversity; B_l is the size of the beam $Beam_l$ maintained in level l, $Score_{l,b}$ is the score of the rollout in bucket b_l in level l, $Length_{l,b}$ is the length of the rollout in b_l, $Code_{l,b}$ is an array with codes for the rollout in bucket b_l, $Succ_{l,b}$ is a matrix for the successor codes for the rollout in bucket b_l.

is rejected. Such similarity can be implemented on top of the score of the solution, the solution length, or other features of the rollout. The example implementation in Fig. 4 looks at the score and the length of the rollout.

The concept of similarity implies a formal characterization of *solution diversity*. Let $\mathcal{S}$ be a set of solutions of an optimization problem with and let $Similar$ be a pairwise similarity score (being large for high similarity and small for low similarity) between every two solution s_i and s_j in $\mathcal{S}$, then the diversity is defined as the sum of the pairwise similarities, i.e., $Diversity(\mathcal{S}) = \sum_{s_i, s_j \in \mathcal{S}} Similar(s_i, s_j)$. This means that if the solutions are pairwise similar the diversity is low. A similar concept is that of pre-sortedness in an input array by adding the pairwise number of inversions.

One important aspect is that adaptation is now applied in every iteration, while before it was applied only for improved solutions. This increases the number of calls significantly, but allows more information exchange between the members in the beam. If the parameters are chosen carefully, the efforts for the playouts and for executing policy adaption are roughly the same.

We also skip some Θ_l iterations before we start learning. The motivating objective is the *secretary problem*, in which the best secretary out of n rankable applicants should be hired for a position. Applicants are interviewed one after the other and the final decision has to be made immediately after the interview. The stopping rule rejects the first applicants after the interview and then stops at the first applicant, who is better than every applicant interviewed so far.

Diversity is an objective that has to be dealt with care. In some domains the solution length (like the *snake-in-the-box*) already is the score, so that only

procedure Similar(score s, length r, level l)
    for $b = 1, \ldots, B_l$
        if $Score_{l,b} = s \wedge Length_{l,b} = r$
            return true
    return false

Fig. 4. Example of applied similarity measure, returning true iff both the score and the length of a solution matches one in the beam $Beam_l$ of size B_l.

solutions of different lengths are kept in the beam. This may limit the number of good solutions in the beam (too) drastically. As a solution to this problem, we propose to include other state features into the fractional part of the solution.

A good compromise has to be found. Using the entire state vector for similarity detection requires comparing regenerated solutions, which can be slow, or storing the full state in the rollout to be retrieved in later calls of the policy adaptation, which would results in a significant overhead in space and time.

procedure Other(level l, index b, i, j)
    $LC \leftarrow \emptyset$
    for $c_j \in Succ_{l,b,i}$
        if $(c_j, c_i) \notin Beam_{l,1..b-1}$
            $LC \leftarrow LC \cup \{c_j\}$
    for $b' = b+1, \ldots, B_l$, $c_{i'} \in Code_{l,b'}$
        if $c_i = c_{i'}$
            for $c_{j'} \in Succ_{l,b',i'}$
                if $c_{j'} \notin LC \wedge (c_{j'}, c_i) \notin Beam_{l,1..b-1}$
                    $LC \leftarrow LC \cup \{j'\}$
    return LC

procedure Diversity-Adapt(level l, policy p, policy p')
    $p' \leftarrow p$
    for $b \in 1, \ldots, B$
        for $c_i \in Code_{l,b}$
            if $c_i \notin Beam_{l,1..b-1}$
                $p'[c_i] \leftarrow p[c_i] + \alpha$
                $CL \leftarrow$ Other(l, b, i, j)
    $z \leftarrow 0$
    for $c \in CL$
        $z \leftarrow z + exp(p[c])$
    for $c \in CL$
        $p'[c] \leftarrow p'[c] - \alpha \cdot exp(p[c])/z$

Fig. 5. Policy adaptation within Diversity-NRPA, with function *Other* checking for *fork* duplicates; CL and LC are list of codes, $(c_j, c_i) \in Beam_{l,1..b-1}$ is shorthand for checking that the code c_i and successor codes c_j match the one stored in any bucket smaller than b of $Beam_l$.

Improving Diversity in the Policy Adaptation. We refine beam NRPA by a reduction of elements eligible to be included in the beam. Therefore, we use $(c_j, c_i) \in Beam_{l,1..b-1}$ to denote that the best rollout code (defined by (c_j, c_i)) in a given level is already present in the prefix of the beam to bucket b in level l. This avoids overly stressing good solutions that have already influenced the policy to be learnt. We also do not want to update elements twice. The according code is shown in Fig. 5. The main function *Diversity-Adapt* calls the function *Other* which works as a filter, and collects the codes of moves that should be used to change the policy.

We used simple arrays for the data structure to check that a code and set of successor codes is contained in the beam and thus learnt already. Profiling revealed that a significant part of the running time is spent here. Surely, a hash map would be more efficient for checking $(c_j, c_i) \in Beam_{l,1..b-1}$. However, the algorithm has to be modified as the hash map then has to support deletion, given that elements in the buckets being dominated by incoming solutions are removed from the beam, and, thus, do no longer serve for duplicate detection in form of membership queries.

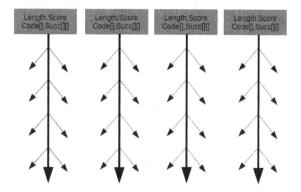

Fig. 6. Sketch of information that is stored in a beam of Diversity-NRPA; the buckets on top stand for the beam, thin arrows indicate successors (codes, stored in *Succ*), the thick arrow the best solution (codes, stored in *Code*). Duplicates are checked wrt. *forks* of state and set of successor states.

Given that the selection strategy of the successors does not prune away moves that are required to generate an optimal rollout sequence, NRPA and Beam-NRPA are *probabilistically complete* in the sense that an optimal solution can eventually be found. This, however, does not imply any performance quality like the ϵ-optimality of the resulting search algorithms.

5   Experiments

Same Game. The *same game* (Fig. 7) is an interactive game frequently played on hand-held devices. The input is an $n \times m$ board with tiles each of which

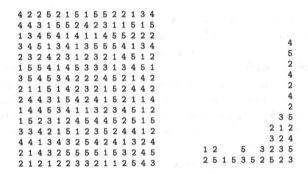

Fig. 7. Initial and terminal position in the *same game*.

having one (usually, $n = m = 15$ and $k = 5$). Tiles can be removed, if they form a connected group of $l > 1$ elements. The reward of the move is $(l-2)^2$ points. If a group of tiles is removed, others fall down. If a column becomes empty, others move to the left, so that all non-empty columns are aligned. The objective is to maximize the total reward until no more move is possible. Total clearance yields an additional bonus of 1,000 points.

The problem is known to be hard [1]. It is solvable in polynomial time for one column of tiles but NP-complete for two or more columns and five or more colors of tiles, or five or more columns and three or more colors of tiles.

Table 1 shows the scores in a level 4 (iteration 100) Diversity-NRPA and 30 × level 3 (iteration 100) Diversity-NRPA searches both obtained with beam width 10 and initial offset for learning 10. This is compared to NRPA and NMCS. An entire level 4 search takes about half a day of computation, while 30 level 3 searches finish in about two hours on our computer[1]. The sum of the high scores of Diversity-NRPA is 81706 (+144 if the 30 level 3 searches are included). While this is best wrt. all published results on the game, it is still inferior to the results published in the Internet[2]. Little is known about the holders of these records. However, we could exchange emails with a record holder who told us he is using beam search with a complex domain specific evaluation function.

We can see that improving the diversity generally gives better results than NMCS and NRPA, even though, through randomization, there are problem instances where the opposite is true.

Snake-in-the-Box. The *snake-in-the-box* problem is a longest path problem in a d-dimensional hypercube. The design of a long snake has impact for the genera-

---

[1] We used one core of an Intel® Core™ i5-2520M CPU @ 2.50 GHz × 4. The computer has 8 GB of RAM but all invocations of the algorithm to any problem instance used less than 10 MB of main memory. Moreover, we had the following software infrastructure. Operating system: Ubuntu 14.04 LTS, Linux kernel: 3.13.0-74-generic, the compiler: g++ version 4.8.4, and the compiler options: -O3 -march=native -funroll-loops -std=c++11 -Wall.

[2] http://www.js-games.de/eng/games/samegame.

Table 1. Results in the *same game.*

ID	NMCS(4)	NRPA(4)	Diversity-NRPA(4)	Diversity-NRPA(3)
1	3121	**3179**	3145	3133
2	3813	**3985**	**3985**	3969
3	3085	3635	**3937**	3663
4	3697	**3913**	3879	3887
5	4055	4309	**4319**	4287
6	4459	**4809**	4697	4663
7	**2949**	2651	2795	2819
8	**3999**	3879	3967	3921
9	4695	4807	**4813**	4811
10	**3223**	2831	3219	2959
11	3147	3317	**3395**	3211
12	3201	3315	**3559**	3461
13	3197	**3399**	3159	3115
14	2799	3097	**3107**	3091
15	3677	3559	**3761**	3423
16	4979	5025	**5307**	5005
17	4919	**5043**	4983	4881
18	5201	5407	**5429**	5353
19	4883	5065	**5163**	5101
20	4835	4805	5087	**5199**
Sum	77934	80030	**81706**	74753

tion of improved error-correcting codes. During the game the snake increases in length, but must not approach any of its previous visited vertices with Hamming distance 1 or less. The formal definition of the problem and its variants as well as heursitic search techniques for solving it are studied by [13]. Information on snake visits are kept in a perfect hash table of size 2^d.

Instead of having a Hamming distance of at least $k = 2$ for the incrementally growing head to all previous nodes of the snake (except the ones preceding the head), one may impose a minimal Hamming distance $k > 2$ to all previous nodes (inducing a Hamming sphere that must not be revisited). In Table 2 (left) we show the best-known solutions lengths for the (k, n) snake problem, where an asterisk (*) denotes that the optimal solution is known. The validation of the results in generating a solution with Diversity-NRPA is indicated with suffix v. For the first problem not solved, the best solutions are shown in brackets (all within one hour, $(11, 5) = 39$ within two days of computation in about 3.3 billion rollouts).

Table 2. Best known results in snakes-in-the-box and coil-in-the-box problems validated with Diversity-NRPA (approximate solutions are shown in brackets).

	2	3	4	5	6	7		2	3	4	5	6	7
3	4*v	3*v	3*v	3*v	3*v	3*v	3	6*v	6*v	6*v	6*v	6*v	6*v
4	7*v	5*v	4*v	4*v	4*v	4*v	4	8*v	8*v	8*v	8*v	8*v	8*v
5	13*v	7*v	6*v	5*v	5*v	5*v	5	14*v	10*v	10*v	10*v	10*v	10*v
6	26*v	13*v	8*v	7*v	6*v	6*v	6	26*v	16*v	12*v	12*v	12*	12*v
7	50*v	21*v	11*v	9*v	8*v	7*v	7	48*v	24*v	14*v	14*v	14*	14*v
8	98*(95)	35*v	19*v	11*v	10*v	9*v	8	96*(92)	36*v	22*v	16*v	16*	16*v
9	190	63(55)	28*v	19*v	12*v	11*v	9	188	64(55)	30*v	24v*	18*v	18*v
10	370	103	47*(46)	25*v	15*v	13*v	10	358	102	46*v	28v*	20*v	20*v
11	707	157	68	39*v	25*v	15*v	11	668	160	70(64)	40v*	30*v	22*v
12	1302	286	104	56(54)	33*v	25*v	12	1276	288	102	60(56)	36*v	32*v
13	2520	493	181	79	47(46)	31v	13	2468	494	182	80	50*v	36*v

Another variant asks for a closed cycle, by means that the snake additionally has to bite its own tail at the end of its journey. The algorithm's implementation has to take care that this is in fact possible. In Table 2 (right) the best-known solutions lengths and our validation results are given.

VRP. In the *vehicle routing problem* (VRP) we are given a fleet of vehicles, a depot, and a time delay matrix for the pairwise travel between the customers' locations, service times, time windows and capacity constraints, the task is to find a minimized number of vehicles with a minimized total distances that satisfies all the constraints. Clearly, by choosing only one vehicle, VRP extends the capacitated traveling salesman with time windows. We chose instances to the Solomon VRPTW benchmark for our experiments[3]. It containts a well-studied selection of (N=)100-city problem instances. Different solvers have contributed to the state-of-the-art.

Our implementation of the problem is based on the simple observation that a tour with V vehicles can be generated by a single vehicle, where the time (makespan) and the capacity of the vehicle are reset at each visit of the depot. Of course, in difference to all other cities the depot is allowed to be visited more times. In the implementation the i-th visit to the depot gets the ID i and has to be revisited. The tour again has size $N + V$ but the range of stored index of a city has increased. This imposes an order to set of depot IDs in every tour to $0, 1, \ldots, V - 1, 0$. This form of symmetry reduction saves about factor $V!$ for the permutations of the depot visits. The solver has the selective strategy that whenever a candidate city invalidates reaching another city it is discarded from the successor set. We selected a (Level 5, Iteration 50) Diversity-NRPA search with threshold $\Theta = 0$ to start learning.

---

[3] https://www.sintef.no/projectweb/top/vrptw/solomon-benchmark
http://web.cba.neu.edu/~msolomon/problems.htm.

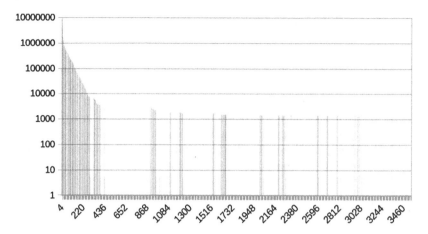

Fig. 8. Learning curve solving a VRP with Diversity-NRPA (y-axis shows the change in the score, x-axis denotes the number of completed level 4 search).

We could repeat the experiment of solving r101 in our implementation and found the optimal solution of cost 1650.79 in about 20 min after 625 thousand playouts. With 20 vehicles we found a slightly better solutions than this one, but the published results often assume a hierarchical objective of first reducing the number of vehicles, and only after that, reducing the score.

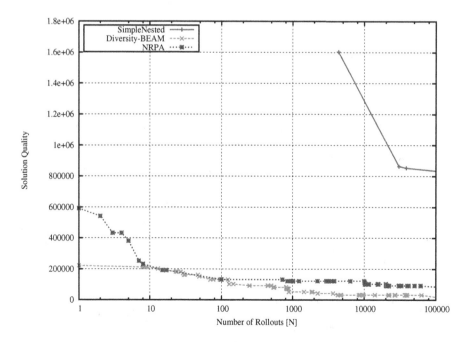

Fig. 9. Comparing the learning in VRP of Nested MCS, NRPA, and Diversity-NRPA.

With about 2.5 days of computation we could solve the r102 problem. After 215.125 million rollouts in total, we found a new high score 1486.664889, slightly improving the reported best solution[4].

In about a week of computation and more than 550 million rollouts we could not finish solving the r103 problem. Our best solution 1332.77670, while the best has value 1292.68. The learning process of the cost function is visualized in Fig. 8. We see that even after considerable time of no visible progress, there is continuation in the solving process. Figure 9 compares the different single-agent Monte Carlo search processes for the first 100 thousand playouts of the r101 problem. We see that Diversity-NRPA shows the fastest learning progress.

6   Conclusion

Nested Monte-Carlo tree search is a class of random search algorithms that has lead to a paradigm shift in AI game playing from enumeration to randomization, and NRPA has proven to be a viable option to solve hard combinatorial problems, combining random exploration with learning. In this paper we proposed to add more diversity to Beam-NRPA search. Together with a number of implementation refinements the algorithm performed convincingly in our benchmark domains.

References

1. Biedl, T.C., Demaine, E.D., Demaine, M.L., Fleischer, R., Jacobsen, L., Munro, J.I.: The complexity of clickomania. CoRR, cs.CC/0107031 (2001)
2. Bouzy, B.: An experimental investigation on the pancake problem. In: Cazenave, T., Winands, M.H.M., Edelkamp, S., Schiffel, S., Thielscher, M., Togelius, J. (eds.) CGW 2015/GIGA 2015. CCIS, vol. 614, pp. 30–43. Springer, Heidelberg (2016). doi:10.1007/978-3-319-39402-2_3
3. Browne, C.B., Powley, E., Whitehouse, D., Lucas, S.M., Cowling, P., Rohlfshagen, P., Tavener, S., Perez, D., Samothrakis, S., Colton, S.: A survey of Monte Carlo tree search methods. IEEE Trans. Comput. Intell. AI Games 4, 1–43 (2004)
4. Cazenave, T.: Nested Monte-Carlo search. In: IJCAI, pp. 456–461 (2009)
5. Cazenave, T.: Monte-Carlo beam search. IEEE Trans. Comput. Intell. AI Games 4(1), 68–72 (2012)
6. Cazenave, T., Teytaud, F.: Beam nested rollout policy adaptation. In: ECAI-Workshop on Computer Games, pp. 1–12 (2012)
7. Edelkamp, S., Gath, M., Rohde, M.: Monte-Carlo tree search for 3D packing with object orientation. In: Lutz, C., Thielscher, M. (eds.) KI 2014. LNCS, vol. 8736, pp. 285–296. Springer, Heidelberg (2014)

---

[4] The sequence of cities we found was 73, 22, 72, 54, 24, 80, 12, 0, 65, 71, 71, 20, 32, 70, 0, 92, 37, 98, 91, 16, 86, 85, 97, 13, 0, 83, 45, 61, 84, 5, 60, 89, 0, 94, 96, 99, 6, 0, 50, 33, 30, 51, 9, 67, 1, 0, 14, 44, 38, 43, 100, 95, 0, 27, 69, 76, 79, 68, 0, 52, 7, 11, 19, 49, 48, 82, 0, 28, 29, 78, 34, 35, 3, 77, 0, 62, 88, 8, 46, 17, 93, 59, 0, 36, 47, 18, 0, 39, 23, 67, 55, 4, 25, 26, 0, 63, 64, 90, 10, 31, 0, 87, 57, 2, 58, 0, 40, 53, 0, 42, 15, 41, 75, 56, 74, 21, 0.

8. Edelkamp, S., Gath, M.: Pickup-and-delivery problems with time windows and capacity constraints using nested Monte-Carlo search. In: ICAART (2014)

9. Edelkamp, S., Gath, M., Cazenave, T., Teytaud, F.: Algorithm and knowledge engineering for the TSPTW problem. In: IEEE SSCI (2013)

10. Gath, M., Herzog, O., Edelkamp, S.: Agent-based planning and control for groupage traffic. In: IEEE-CEWIT (2013)

11. Huang, S.-C., Arneson, B., Hayward, R.B., Müller, M., Pawlewicz, J.: MoHex 2.0: a pattern-based MCTS hex player. In: Herik, H.J., Iida, H., Plaat, A. (eds.) CG 2013. LNCS, vol. 8427, pp. 60–71. Springer, Heidelberg (2014)

12. Kocsis, L., Szepesvári, C.: Bandit based Monte-Carlo planning. In: Fürnkranz, J., Scheffer, T., Spiliopoulou, M. (eds.) ECML 2006. LNCS (LNAI), vol. 4212, pp. 282–293. Springer, Heidelberg (2006)

13. Palombo, A., Stern, R., Puzis, R., Felner, A., Kiesel, S., Ruml, W.: Solving the snake in the box problem with heuristic search: first results. In: Proceedings of the Eighth Annual Symposium on Combinatorial Search, SOCS 2015, 11–13 June 2015, Ein Gedi, The Dead Sea, Israel, pp. 96–104 (2015)

14. Rosin, C.D.: Nested rollout policy adaptation for Monte-Carlo tree search. In: IJCAI, pp. 649–654 (2011)

A Fast Elimination Method for Pruning in POMDPs

Selim Özgen[✉] and Mübeccel Demirekler

Department of Electrical and Electronics Engineering,
Middle East Technical University, Ankara, Turkey
seozgen@metu.edu.tr

Abstract. This paper aims to speed up the *pruning* procedure that is encountered in the exact value iteration in POMDPs. The value function in POMDPs can be represented by a finite set of vectors over the state space. In each step of the exact value iteration algorithm, the number of possible vectors increases linearly with the cardinality of the action set and exponentially with the cardinality of the observation set. This set of vectors should be pruned to a minimal subset retaining the same value function over the state space. Therefore, pruning procedure in general is the bottleneck of finding the optimal policy for POMDPs. This paper analyses two different linear programming methods, the classical Lark's algorithm and the recently proposed Skyline algorithm for detecting these useless vectors. We claim that using the information about the support region of the vectors that have already been processed, both algorithms can be drastically improved. We present comparative experiments on both randomly generated problems and POMDP benchmarks.

Keywords: Linear programming · POMDP · Pruning

1 Introduction

A Partially Observable Markov Decision Process (POMDP) models an agent acting in an uncertain environment with imperfect actuators and noisy sensors. For real life problems that require complex models, POMDPs have received much attention and applied in diverse areas such as radar resource management [11], scheduling in sensor networks [8], healthcare [7,9], collision avoidance [15], etc. Even though POMDPs provide the possibility for modeling various phenomena, the huge computational cost for coming up with an exact solution limits its use. Therefore last two decade research has focused on fast and approximate (heuristic) solvers for POMDPs over an infinite horizon [6,17]. These solvers put a trade-off between the liability of the final solution to the optimal one and the computational time.

Over a finite horizon, POMDPs can be solved by dynamic programming. The value function can be represented by a finite set of vectors over the belief state. During the dynamic programming update, the number of possible vectors, that

© Springer International Publishing AG 2016
G. Friedrich et al. (Eds.): KI 2016, LNAI 9904, pp. 56–68, 2016.
DOI: 10.1007/978-3-319-46073-4_5

model the problem, grows linearly with the cardinality of the action set and exponentially with the cardinality of the observation set [12]. Many of these vectors can be pruned without changing the exact value representation. The task of removing these useless vectors is typically known as pruning and is done by solving a number of linear programs (LPs).

Improving the scalability of solution methods for POMDPs is a critical research topic and have received much attention. There is a field of research that exploits the properties of the dynamic programming update steps to decrease the complexity of the LPs to be solved [2–4,16]. Yet, in all steps of the dynamic programming update, LPs are used to prune a set of given vectors, that takes the main computation. This paper presents an algorithmic improvement to speed up the pruning procedure.

The rest of the paper is organized as follows. In the next section, we briefly review the POMDP model and the properties of the optimal value function. Section 3 reviews the exact value iteration algorithm. Section 4 reviews two different pruning algorithms and discusses their linear programming implementation. Section 5 describes the revised counterparts. Section 6 gives the test results on benchmark and artificial problems. Section 7 concludes the paper.

2 Partially Observable Markov Decision Processes

The mathematical definition of a discrete time POMDP is a tuple composed of $(\mathcal{S}, \mathcal{A}, \Theta, \mathcal{T}, \mathcal{O}, \mathcal{R})$, where;

- $\mathcal{S}$ corresponds to a finite set of world states
- $\mathcal{A}$ is a finite set of actions the agent can execute
- $\mathcal{T} : \mathcal{S} \times \mathcal{A} \times \mathcal{S} \rightarrow [0,1]$ defines the transition probability distribution $P(s'|s,a)$ that describes the effect of actions on the state of the world. The transition function models the stochastic nature of the environment
- Θ is a finite set of observations
- $\mathcal{O} : \Theta \times \mathcal{S} \times \mathcal{A} \rightarrow [0,1]$ is the observation probability distribution, $P(o|s,a)$
- $\mathcal{R} : \mathcal{S} \times \mathcal{A} \times \mathcal{S} \rightarrow \mathbb{R}$ corresponds to the reward models that the agent receives for executing action a in state s.

For POMDPs, the aim is to maximize a function of its reward stream such as the sum of rewards, the average reward or, more often, the discounted reward. The standard approach to solving a POMDP is to convert it to a belief-state MDP. The belief state b is a probability distribution over the state space $b : S \rightarrow [0,1]$, such that $\sum_{s \in S} b(s) = 1$. For a given belief state b, b_o^a is the updated belief state after action a is executed and observation o is experienced. The calculation of b_o^a is given as follows:

$$b_o^a(s') = \frac{P(o|a,s')\sum_s P(s'|s,a)b(s)}{P(o|a,b)} \tag{1}$$

$$P(o|a,b) = \sum_{s,s''} P(o|a,s'')P(s''|s,a)b(s) \tag{2}$$

It has been shown that a belief state is a sufficient statistic that summarizes the entire history of the process. Using belief state as the sufficient statistic, the optimal value function for finite n-steps-to-go problems is obtained as follows:

$$V_n^*(b) = \max_{a \in \mathcal{A}} \left(\sum_{s \in \mathcal{S}} r(s,a)b(s) + \sum_{o \in \Theta} P(o|a,b)V_{n-1}^*(b_o^a) \right) \tag{3}$$

where n denotes time to reach to the final time (*time to go*), $r(s,a)$ is the state dependent reward function, V_n^* is the value function to be backed up at each time step and $P(o|b,a)$ is the probability of observing o for the belief state b when action a is executed.

Smallwood and Sondik [14] showed that the optimal finite horizon value function is piecewise linear and convex for any horizon T. This piecewise linear (PWLC) property is useful because it allows the value function to be represented using finite resources. Therefore, the value function V_n^* in Eq. 3 can be represented by a finite set of row vectors $\Gamma_n = \{\gamma_0, \gamma_1, \ldots, \gamma_k\}$ as follows:

$$V_n^*(b) = \max_{\gamma \in \Gamma_n} \gamma b \tag{4}$$

where $\gamma b = \sum_{s \in \mathcal{S}} \gamma(s)b(s)$ is the dot product of vector γ and belief state b.

3   Value Iteration

The dynamic programming approach to finding the optimal value policy in MDPs is referred to as *value iteration*. Value iteration means to compute V_n^* from V_{n-1}^*. It is beneficial to break down the optimal finite horizon POMDP value function into a series of related value functions. Value function given in Eq. 3 can be written in a series of related value functions [2];

$$V_n^*(b) = \max_{a \in \mathcal{A}} V_n^{*,a}(b) \tag{5}$$

$$V_n^{*,a}(b) = \sum_{o \in \Theta} V_n^{*,a,o}(b) \tag{6}$$

$$V_n^{*,a,o}(b) = \frac{1}{|\Theta|} r(b,a) + P(o|a,b)V_{n-1}^*(b_o^a) \tag{7}$$

As piecewise linearity assumption is preserved through the value iteration steps, the series of value functions can be written in terms of vector operations:

$$\Gamma_n = \mathbb{PR} \left(\bigcup_a \Gamma_n^a \right) \tag{8}$$

$$\Gamma_n^a = \mathbb{PR} \left(\bigoplus_o \Gamma_n^{a,o} \right) \tag{9}$$

$$\Gamma_n^{a,o} = \mathbb{PR}\left(\left\{\frac{1}{|\Theta|}r(a) + P^{a,o}\chi_{n-1} \mid \chi_{n-1} \in \Gamma_{n-1}\right\}\right) \tag{10}$$

The cross sum operator $\oplus$ in Eq. 9 is defined by $\mathcal{U} \oplus \mathcal{V} = \{u+v|u \in \mathcal{U}, v \in \mathcal{V}\}$. In Eq. 10, $P^{a,o}(s,s^{'}) := P(o|a,s^{'})P(s^{'}|s,a)$. Recall that in Eq. 7, we had to calculate b_o^a for each belief point to form the value function $V_n^{*,a,o}$. To avoid calculating updated belief states, batch enumeration algorithm constructs the Γ_n^a sets by constructing each possible $\gamma_n^a \in \Gamma_n^a$ as shown in Eq. 10. The algorithm prunes the useless ones in each step of the value iteration algorithm. The pruning operation is denoted by $\mathbb{PR}$.

In each iteration, the value function is updated across the entire belief space. As noted in [13], in Eq. 9, we create $|\Gamma|^{|\Theta|}$ new vectors for each action, with a complexity of $|\mathcal{S}|$ operations for each vector. There are $|\Gamma| \times |\mathcal{A}| \times |\Theta|$ vectors generated in Eq. 10 and computing each of these vectors takes $|\mathcal{S}|^2$ operations. Hence, the overall complexity of calculating all vectors for a single iteration is $O(|\mathcal{A}| \times |\mathcal{S}| \times |\Gamma|^{|\Theta|} + |\Gamma| \times |\mathcal{A}| \times |\Theta| \times |\mathcal{S}|^2)$.

4   Pruning

In each step of exact value iteration algorithm, the number of vectors increases exponentially with $|\Theta|$ and linearly with $|\mathcal{A}|$. Yet, not all these vectors are useful when determining the optimal value function V_n^*. Only those vectors that are maximal at some belief state are really necessary. In mathematical terms, when an arbitrary set of vectors $\bar{\Gamma}$ is given, the clean set Γ is defined as follows:

$$\gamma \in \Gamma \iff \exists b \in \mathcal{B} : \gamma b \geq \bar{\gamma}b, \quad \forall \bar{\gamma} \in \bar{\Gamma} \tag{11}$$

where $\mathcal{B}$ represents the infinite space of all belief states. In other words, $R(\gamma, \bar{\Gamma}) \neq \emptyset$, where R denotes the support region of this vector. Such γ vectors are called non-dominated vectors. Moreover, we will denote $\bar{\Gamma}$ as the dirty set and Γ as the clean set for the rest of the paper.

Obviously, if a vector $\bar{\gamma}$ is pointwise dominated, that is $\exists \gamma \in \bar{\Gamma} : \gamma(s) \geq \bar{\gamma}(s), \forall s \in \mathcal{S}$, then it can be easily pruned. Yet, eliminating vectors that are not pointwise dominated is not an easy task. Having a fast pruning procedure which can take an arbitrary set of vectors $\bar{\Gamma}$ and reduce it to a set of non-dominated vectors Γ, is the main concern for exact value iteration. We will explain two different pruning algorithms, namely Lark's algorithm and Skyline algorithm. For the rest of the paper we will denote $D = |\mathcal{S}|$, $N = |\bar{\Gamma}|$, and $n = |\Gamma|$. n is the number of vectors in the clean set at any time instant of the algorithm.

4.1   Lark's Algorithm

When an arbitrary set of vectors $\bar{\Gamma}$ is given, Lark's algorithm starts with an empty clean set Γ that holds the non-dominated vectors. The algorithm picks a vector $\gamma_i \in \bar{\Gamma}$ and tries to find a belief point b that satisfies $\gamma_i b > \gamma_j b, \forall \gamma_j \in \Gamma$, $j \neq i$. Such a belief point is found by the following LP:

$$\min \delta$$
$$(\gamma_i - \gamma_j)b + \delta > 0, \quad \forall \gamma_j \in \Gamma$$
$$\sum_{s \in S} b(s) = 1 \tag{12}$$
$$b(s) \geq 0, \quad \forall s \in S$$

If the optimal value of δ is less than 0, that means there is a vector in set $\bar{\Gamma}$ that gives a higher value for the belief state b_0 where the optimal solution occurs. For all vectors $\gamma_k \in \bar{\Gamma}$ the one which gives the highest value for $\gamma_k b_0$ is added to the clean set Γ and deleted from $\bar{\Gamma}$. If the optimal value of δ is greater than or equal to zero, the vector γ_i is dominated by the vectors in the clean set Γ and this vector is deleted from $\bar{\Gamma}$. The procedure continues until there are no vectors left in $\bar{\Gamma}$. Note that the number of constraints in the LP is n. Therefore, as the clean set, Γ, gets larger, the LP becomes harder to solve.

4.2 Skyline Algorithm

A recent alternative to the Lark's algorithm is the Skyline algorithm proposed by Raphael and Shani [13]. Skyline algorithm traces the upper envelope formed by the set of vectors. All vectors visited during this traversal are non-dominated, hence should be added to the clean set Γ, while vectors that can never be visited are pruned.

When an arbitrary set of vectors, $\bar{\Gamma}$, is given, it is possible to pick any vector γ_i and write the following equations for any belief state $b \in \mathcal{B}$;

$$\gamma_i b + x_i = \gamma_j b + x_j \quad \forall i, j \in \{1, \ldots, N\}$$
$$x_i \geq 0, \quad \forall i \in \{1, \ldots, N\} \tag{13}$$

where x_i, x_j are the slack variables. If we are at a belief state $b \in R(\gamma_i, \bar{\Gamma})$ where $x_i = 0$, then γ_i is a dominant vector. Therefore, if the algorithm reaches a belief state where $x_i = 0$ for the set of Equations given in 13, it concludes that vector γ_i is on the skyline.

The LP given in Eq. 14 is called iterative Skyline algorithm [13]. In the iterative version, Skyline algorithm starts with an empty set Γ that holds the non-dominated vectors. During the simplex iterations, if the algorithm discovers that a vector is on the skyline, adds it to Γ and discards it from $\bar{\Gamma}$. At the end of simplex iterations, if x_i is 0, then vector γ_i is added to Γ and discarded from $\bar{\Gamma}$. If x_i is greater than 0, vector γ_i is removed from $\bar{\Gamma}$. After the decision about vector γ_i is given, the algorithm picks one of the other vectors, say γ_k, from $\bar{\Gamma}$ and continues the procedure.

$$\min x_i$$
$$(\gamma_i - \gamma_j)b + x_i - x_j = 0, \quad \forall \gamma_j \in \bar{\Gamma} - \{\gamma_i\}$$
$$\sum_{s \in S} b(s) = 1 \tag{14}$$
$$b(s) \geq 0, \quad \forall s \in S$$
$$x_i \geq 0, \quad \forall i \in \{1, \dots, N\}$$

5 Revised Pruning Algorithms

As discussed above, both algorithms select one vector from the dirty set, $\bar{\Gamma}$, at each turn and try to make a decision about it. Raphael et al. discuss in detail the time complexity of both of the algorithms [13]. In this section, we propose different modifications to each algorithm and give the pseudocodes of the revised algorithms. The modified version of the Skyline algorithm, named as SM, is described in Algorithm 1 and Lark's algorithm, LRI, is described in Algorithm 2. The original algorithms will be mentioned as IS, for iterative Skyline algorithm and LR, for Lark's algorithm when needed. For the pseudocodes of the original algorithms, the reader can refer to [13].

5.1 Revisions to the Skyline Algorithm

Writing the LP. This LP is the same as the one given in Eq. 14 but written in a different format in which every hyperplane equation is written on its own. For this, variable $y > \gamma_i b, \forall i \in \{1, \dots, N\}$ is defined. This modification has no impact on the solutions, but makes the LP implementation easier.

$$\min x_i$$
$$\gamma_i b - y + x_i = 0, \quad \forall \gamma_i \in \bar{\Gamma}$$
$$\sum_{s \in S} b(s) = 1 \tag{15}$$
$$b(s) \geq 0, \quad \forall s \in S$$
$$x_i \geq 0, \quad \forall i \in \{1, \dots, N\}$$

Checking All the Vectors at Every LP Iteration. In a typical step to determine if a vector γ_i is in the clean set, we try to find the greatest improvement of this vector to the value function. This point b would always be a vertex. Therefore, if we are passing through a vertex which has not been visited before, we can check which of the vectors that are included in the simplex tableau have reached their optimal proximity to the skyline graph. We will demonstrate this with an example.

Suppose that the dirty set of vectors is $\bar{\Gamma} = \{[4\ 0]', [0\ 4]', [2\ 1.9]', [1\ 2.9]'\}$. Clearly, none of these vectors are pointwise dominated by another. In Table 1, the hyperplane equations for each vector is written in the first four rows and the fifth row corresponds to the simplex constraint. Assume that, we are trying to determine if vector $\gamma_3 = [2\ 1.9]'$ is in the clean set. That would mean minimizing the slack variable x_3. Notice that in this case, the objective function has a great similarity with the hyperplane equation for γ_3. The solution for the simplex tableau is also given in Table 1. As can be seen here, $x_3 = 0.05 > 0$ in the optimal point so γ_3 is not in the clean set. Moreover, γ_4 has also reached the optimal point as the coefficients of the non-basic variables are all negative (-0.263 for x_1 and -0.738 for x_2) and $x_4 = 0.05 > 0$. Therefore both hyperplane equations for γ_3 and γ_4 will be erased from the table in the following round. Using the similarity of the objective function to the hyperplane equations, by only doing a simple sign check for the coefficients of the undecided vectors in the simplex tableau, we can determine which of these vectors have reached their optimal point.

Table 1. Checking all vectors in $\bar{\Gamma}$, $|S| = D = 2$

	b_0	b_1	y	x_1	x_2	x_3	x_4	
γ_1	4	0	-1	1	0	0	0	0
γ_2	0	4	-1	0	1	0	0	0
γ_3	2	1.9	-1	0	0	1	0	0
γ_4	1	2.9	-1	0	0	0	1	0
S.C.	1	1	0	0	0	0	0	1
z	-2	-1.9	1	0	0	0	0	0

$\Longrightarrow$

	b_0	b_1	y	x_1	x_2	x_3	x_4	
γ_1	1	0	0	0.125	-0.125	0	0	0.50
γ_2	0	1	0	-0.125	0.125	0	0	0.50
γ_3	0	0	0	-0.513	-0.488	1	0	0.05
γ_4	0	0	0	-0.263	-0.738	0	1	0.05
S.C.	0	0	1	-0.500	-0.500	0	0	2.00
z	0	0	0	0.513	0.488	0	0	-0.05

5.2   Skyline Algorithm with Multiple Objective Functions

Algorithm 1 is the revised version of the Skyline algorithm. The main procedure is defined by SM, where we get an arbitrary set of vectors $\bar{\Gamma}$, and initialize an empty clean set Γ. LPINIT procedure writes the initial simplex tableau P defined by Eq. 15. Note that through LPINIT procedure, an equation is defined for each vector in the set $\bar{\Gamma}$. This set of equations, with the simplex constraint $\sum_{s \in S} b(s) = 1$, defines the simplex tableau. After this moment, the same simplex tableau is used to the end of the pruning procedure. After the simplex tableau is initialized, the objective function is selected as $\min x_i$, which is the slack variable of γ_i by the function LPOBJ. The objective function is important because it determines the direction of simplex iterations.

Yet for every simplex iteration, we call the function LPITER. LPITER is a simple simplex iteration followed by a check routine for the rows of the whole matrix at any point. With such a routine, we can detect which vectors from the dirty set $\bar{\Gamma}$ are at the belief point where they reached the closest to the skyline. As they can never get closer to the skyline, they can be discarded from the dirty set and also from the simplex tableau P. The algorithm continues until there are no vectors in the dirty set $\bar{\Gamma}$.

Algorithm 1. Skyline Algorithm with Multiple Objective Functions

---

1: **procedure** SM($\bar{\Gamma}$)
2:     $Q \leftarrow \emptyset$
3:     $F \leftarrow \{1, \ldots, N\}$
4:     $P \leftarrow \text{LPINIT}(\bar{\Gamma})$
5:     **while** $F \neq \emptyset$ **do**
6:         $i \leftarrow$ any element in F
7:         $P \leftarrow \text{LPOBJ}(P, i)$
8:         **while** $i \in F$ **do**
9:             $(P, F, Q) \leftarrow \text{LPITER}(P, F, Q)$
10:        **end while**
11:    **end while**
12:    **return** $\bar{\Gamma}(Q)$
13: **end procedure**
14: **procedure** LPINIT(Γ)
15:    write the initial tableau P
        variables: $y, x_i, b(s)\ \forall s \in S$
        $P(i,:) : \gamma_i b - y + x_i = 0,\ \forall \gamma_i \in \Gamma$
        $P(\text{N}+1,:) : \sum_{s \in S} b(s) = 1$
16:    set the objective function to zero

17:        **return** (P)
18: **end procedure**
19: **procedure** LPOBJ(P, i)
20:        set the objective function to min x_i
21:        **return** (P)
22: **end procedure**
23: **procedure** LPITER(P, F, Q)
24:        do one simplex iteration to P
25:        **for all** optimal $P(i,:), i \in F$ **do**
26:            **if** $x_i \neq 0$ **then**
                delete $P(i,:)$ from the tableau
                delete i from F
27:            **else**
                add i to Q
                delete i from F
28:            **end if**
29:        **end for**
30:        **return** (P, F, Q)
31: **end procedure**

5.3   Revisions to the Lark's Algorithm

Sorting the Vectors. As Lark's algorithm adds one vector to the constraint set at every LP, we want to define a measure which would help us to select the vector from the dirty set, $\bar{\Gamma}$, at each round. In two dimensional case, the belief state is parametrized as $b(\lambda) = [\lambda\ (1 - \lambda)]$. Assume that we have three non-dominated vectors as given in Fig. 1. For these vectors, it is possible to show the following relationship:

$$\begin{aligned}
\lambda = 0 &\implies \gamma_2^2 > \gamma_1^2 > \gamma_0^2 \\
\lambda = 1 &\implies \gamma_0^1 > \gamma_1^1 > \gamma_2^1
\end{aligned}$$
(16)

where γ_i^j denotes the jth element of vector γ_i. Therefore, $||\gamma_0 - \gamma_1|| < ||\gamma_0 - \gamma_2||$. Moreover, as γ_1 is neighbouring to γ_0 and γ_2 but γ_0 and γ_2 are not neighboring, $\forall b_i \in R(\gamma_i, \Gamma), i \in \{0, 1, 2\}$ we can assert $||b_0 - b_1|| < ||b_0 - b_2||$. Therefore non-neighbouring vectors have distant support sets compared to neighboring vectors in 2D.

To understand the importance of this relationship, assume that in Fig. 1, we only have two non-dominated vectors γ_0 and γ_1 in the clean set Γ, and we are trying to find if γ_2 is a non-dominated vector. If we start from any point in the support region of γ_0, we will first arrive at the vertex between γ_0 and γ_1, and then the Skyline algorithm would terminate at the maximal vertex between γ_1 and γ_2, and Lark's algorithm would come to an end at the point $b(s_0) = 0$. However, if we were to start from anywhere in the support region of γ_1, both of the pruning algorithms would arrive at the solution by visiting one vertex less.

Figure 1 shows that if we start the pruning algorithm for a selected vector from the support set of one of its neighbouring vectors, we would reach to the solution faster. Unfortunately, it is not easy to extend this idea to the vectors of dimension greater than two. Yet the experiments show that by sorting the vectors by using vector distance, Lark's algorithm benefit from not traversing the same paths again and again.

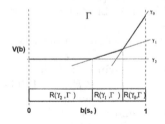

Fig. 1. Belief state partition

5.4   Lark's Algorithm with Initial Condition

Algorithm 2 is the revised version of the Lark's algorithm. The main routine is LRI, where we get an arbitrary set of vectors, $\bar{\Gamma}$, and initialize an empty clean set Γ. After a new vector, γ, is selected from the dirty set, the l_2 distance between this vector is compared to the vectors in the clean set Γ by the SORT routine and a vector $\hat{\gamma}$ is selected. Since we know a witness point of this vector, $b_0 = w(\hat{\gamma})$, we start the LP, discussed by the LPLARK procedure, from this belief state b_0. Notice the similarity of the LPLARK procedure with the structure of the LP for the Lark's algorithm discussed in Sect. 4.1. The major difference is the use of an initial condition b_0 in the algorithm.

Algorithm 2 also explains two other routines; PNTDOM and BEST. These two routines are used in the same fashion as the original algorithm. PNTDOM is used to prune, if possible, some of the dominated vectors without using linear programming and BEST is used to select one of the dominating vectors if a belief state is given. The symbol $<_{lex}$ in the pseudo-code denotes lexicographic ordering [10].

6   Experimental Results

In this section, we will present the result of the experiments with benchmark and artificial problems. All four of the algorithms (IS, SM, LR, LRI) were tested in all problems. We have written our own POMDP code for value iteration using batch enumeration in MATLAB environment. The tests are performed with a standard desktop computer (Intel Core i7-3770 3.4 GHz 8 GB RAM).

Algorithm 2. Lark's Algorithm with Initial Condition

1: **procedure** LRI($\bar{\Gamma}$)
2:     $\Gamma \leftarrow \emptyset$
3:     **while** $\bar{\Gamma} \neq \emptyset$ **do**
4:         $\gamma \leftarrow$ any element in $\bar{\Gamma}$
5:         $b_0 \leftarrow$ SORT(Γ, γ)
6:         **if** PNTDOM (γ, Γ) **then**
7:             $\bar{\Gamma} \leftarrow \bar{\Gamma} - \{\gamma\}$
8:         **else** $(\delta, b^*) \leftarrow$ LPLARK(γ, Γ, b_0)
9:             **if** $\delta < 0$ **then**
10:                 $\bar{\Gamma} \leftarrow \bar{\Gamma} - \{\gamma\}$
11:             **else**
12:                 $\gamma \leftarrow$ BEST($b, \bar{\Gamma}$)
13:                 $w(\gamma) \leftarrow b^*$
14:                 $\Gamma \leftarrow \Gamma \cup \gamma$
15:                 $\bar{\Gamma} \leftarrow \bar{\Gamma} - \{\gamma\}$
16:             **end if**
17:         **end if**
18:     **end while**
19:     **return** Γ
20: **end procedure**
21: **procedure** SORT(Γ, γ)
22:     $k = \infty$
23:     **for all** $\hat{\gamma} \in \Gamma$ **do**
24:         **if** $k > ||\gamma - \hat{\gamma}||$ **then**
25:             $k \leftarrow ||\gamma - \hat{\gamma}||$
26:             $b \leftarrow w(\hat{\gamma})$
27:         **end if**
28:     **end for**
29:     **return** b
30: **end procedure**
31: **procedure** PNTDOM(γ, Γ)
32:     **for all** $\hat{\gamma} \in \Gamma$ **do**

33:         **if** $\gamma(s) \leq \hat{\gamma}(s), \forall s \in S$ **then**
34:             **return** true
35:         **end if**
36:     **end for**
37:     **return** false
38: **end procedure**
39: **procedure** BEST($b, \bar{\Gamma}$)
40:     $\hat{\gamma} \leftarrow \emptyset$
41:     $k = -\infty$
42:     **for all** $\gamma \in \bar{\Gamma}$ **do**
43:         **if** $k < \gamma.b$ **then**
44:             $\hat{\gamma} \leftarrow \gamma$
45:         **else**
46:             **if** $k = \gamma.b$ & $\hat{\gamma} <_{lex} \gamma$
    then
47:                 $\hat{\gamma} \leftarrow \gamma$
48:             **end if**
49:         **end if**
50:     **end for**
51:     **return** $\hat{\gamma}$
52: **end procedure**
53: **procedure** LPLARK(γ, Γ, b_0)
54:     solve the following linear program
        start the linear program from b_0
        variables: $\delta, b(s) \ \forall s \in S$
        $\min \delta$ subject to
        $(\gamma - \hat{\gamma})b + \delta > 0 \quad \forall \hat{\gamma} \in \Gamma$
        $\sum_{s \in S} b(s) = 1$
        $b(s) \geq 0 \ \forall s \in S$
55:     **return** (δ, b)
56: **end procedure**

6.1   Benchmark Problems

We first tested the algorithms on a set of benchmark problems from [1]. As the proposed algorithms can be used for the general pruning procedure of any set of vectors, the operation in Eq. 8 will be targeted in these experiments. After action dependent vectors are calculated by the cross-sum step of the value iteration algorithm, $\mathbb{PR} (\bigcup_a \Gamma_n^a)$ operation is tested with different pruning algorithms.

Table 2 gives the specified time horizon for each problem, h, the number of non-dominated vectors at the end of the specified horizon, $|\Gamma|$, and the time spent in four algorithms in seconds. Different time horizons are chosen regarding the complexity of the specific benchmark problem. The time column consists of four results for IS, SM, LR, LRI from top to down. The discount factors specified for the benchmark problems in [1] are taken into consideration (0.75 for tiger, 0.95 for the other problems).

Table shows that for benchmark problems, modified versions of the algorithms prove beneficial. Benchmark problems with a large observation set are not suitable to deal with batch enumeration algorithm, because the number of vectors even for one step to go can

Table 2. Tests with benchmark problems in seconds

	Problem	h	$|\Gamma|$	Time	Problem	h	$|\Gamma|$	Time
IS	4 × 3	7	132	1.295	Cheese	15	14	0.0118
SM			132	0.760			14	0.0110
LR			132	3.722			14	0.115
LRI			132	1.371			14	0.0682
IS	Tiger	15	49	0.0596	Shuttle	7	411	8.010
SM			49	0.0150			408	6.918
LR			49	0.235			411	101.86
LRI			49	0.0826			397	4.342

increase dramatically. In our case, as we are aiming the pruning procedure of any set of linear vectors, we will strict our experiments with small benchmark problems and deal with randomly generated sets because it is easier to define any problem with a reasonable size.

The number of non-dominated vectors for different algorithms tends to alter due to the numerical errors in the LP. With the use of the discount factor for the benchmark problems, the vectors start converging to the optimal solution and getting closer to each other. Due to the computation precision, small roundoff errors can accumulate and get over a predetermined threshold causing some extraneous vectors to appear in the clean set. In our application, to assure numerical stability of the pivot operation, Harris ratio test is applied [5]. In the ratio test, the selection of the $\epsilon = 10^{-8}$ value is critical especially for almost-degenerate cases where the support region of some of the vectors becomes very small.

6.2   Pruning Performance of Randomly Generated Sets

To demonstrate the scalability of the proposed algorithms, we have also tested them with artificial problems. We first constructed a set of random vector sets $\{\Gamma_1, \ldots, \Gamma_k\}$. Random vectors in Γ_i are created by selecting D random numbers uniformly distributed between $(0, 200)$. Then, additional random vectors are generated and added to the set provided that they are not pointwise dominated. This process is repeated until the number of vectors in Γ_i reaches n. Then these vector sets are used to calculate $\mathbb{PR}\left(\bigoplus_{i=1}^{k} \Gamma_i\right)$ using different pruning algorithms. This operation corresponds to Eq. 9, which is the bottleneck of one step value iteration algorithm. Here, $k = |\Theta|$ is a substitute for the cardinality of the observation set. Increasing k means an exponential increase in the number of vectors as n^k.

Table 3. Time used by pruning algorithms for problems $(k, D, 5)$ in seconds

k	D	LR	LRI	IS	SM
2	5	0.2404	0.2726	0.0309	0.0369
3	5	1.0624	0.4438	0.3772	0.2544
4	5	8.0704	2.4245	10.687	5.4149
5	5	70.805	14.673	937.26	403.54
2	10	0.2161	0.1414	0.0298	0.0286
3	10	1.6880	0.7833	0.6329	0.4772
4	10	45.3547	4.9769	26.07	16.691
5	10	717.98	36.106	2800.9	1786.4
2	15	0.2271	0.1862	0.0299	0.0256
3	15	1.8488	1.1345	0.543	0.3865
4	15	139.21	7.859	27.838	18.280
5	15	980.21	73.330	2935.3	1875.1
2	20	0.2204	0.2828	0.0230	0.0207
3	20	2.0238	1.5664	0.4772	0.3323
4	20	155.60	10.915	22.928	13.166
5	20	1837.6	114.37	1929.3	880.54

A test problem is thus specified by the triple (k, D, n). The procedure for creating artificial vector sets is a simulation of Eq. 10. This procedure is logical, while in Eq. 10, the matrix $P^{a,o}$ is not a regular transition probability matrix; it can scale the vector from the set Γ_{n-1} to a completely different vector in $\Gamma_n^{a,o}$ for different observation probabilities $P(o|a, s')$.

Tests show that, when the number of vectors are small, Skyline algorithm outperforms the Lark's algorithm. Revision of the algorithms does not contribute much to the time complexity of these simple problems. However, as the number of vectors increase, the importance of using initial conditions is stressed. In all of the cases, the algorithms are strictly much more time consuming compared to their revised counterparts. Lark's algorithm becomes more advantageous among the revised algorithms, because it solves smaller LPs.

7   Conclusion

In the dynamic programming update of POMDPs, the number of vectors increase exponentially. Therefore, pruning this set of vectors to a minimal set becomes a major concern. This paper takes two pruning algorithms from the literature, Lark's and Skyline algorithms, and offers major revisions to these algorithms that decreases the time complexity of the pruning procedure drastically.

Our focus at this moment is on the comparison of the algorithms with their revised counterparts. For the Lark's algorithm we have used the optimization toolbox of MATLAB. However, for the Skyline algorithm, as we are considering the whole of the simplex tableau at each iteration, we have written our own simplex code. For this reason, the time disadvantage of the Skyline algorithm to the Lark's is not fair. The main result of this paper is to stress the effect of the revisions which can speed up the algorithm up to ten times as can be seen from Table 3. This manifests the importance of the revisions that have been made.

References

1. Cassandra, A.: Tony's POMDP file repository page (1999). http://www.cs.brown.edu/research/ai/pomdp/examples/index.html

2. Cassandra, A., Littman, M.L., Zhang, N.L.: Incremental pruning: a simple, fast, exact method for partially observable Markov decision processes. In: Proceedings of the Thirteenth Conference on Uncertainty in Artificial Intelligence, pp. 54–61. Morgan Kaufmann Publishers Inc. (1997)
3. Cassandra, A.R.: Exact and approximate algorithms for partially observable Markov decision processes. Brown University (1998)
4. Feng, Z., Zilberstein, S.: Region-based incremental pruning for POMDPs. In: Proceedings of the 20th Conference on Uncertainty in Artificial Intelligence, pp. 146–153. AUAI Press (2004)
5. Harris, P.M.: Pivot selection methods of the Devex LP code. Math. program. **5**(1), 1–28 (1973)
6. Hauskrecht, M.: Value-function approximations for partially observable Markov decision processes. J. Artif. Intell. Res. **13**, 33–94 (2000)
7. Hauskrecht, M., Fraser, H.: Planning treatment of ischemic heart disease with partially observable Markov decision processes. Artif. Intell. Med. **18**(3), 221–244 (2000)
8. Hero, A.O., Castanon, D., Cochran, D., Kastella, K.: Foundations and Applications of Sensor Management. Springer Science & Business Media, New York (2007)
9. Hoey, J., Poupart, P., von Bertoldi, A., Craig, T., Boutilier, C., Mihailidis, A.: Automated handwashing assistance for persons with dementia using video and a partially observable Markov decision process. Comput. Vis. Image Underst. **114**(5), 503–519 (2010)
10. Littman, M.L.: The Witness algorithm: solving partially observable Markov decision processes. Brown University, Providence (1994)
11. Mallick, M., Krishnamurthy, V., Vo, B.N.: Integrated Tracking, Classification, and Sensor Management: Theory and Applications. Wiley, Hoboken (2012)
12. Monahan, G.E.: State of the art - a survey of partially observable Markov decision processes: theory, models, and algorithms. Manage. Sci. **28**(1), 1–16 (1982)
13. Raphael, C., Shani, G.: The Skyline algorithm for POMDP value function pruning. Ann. Math. Artif. Intell. **65**(1), 61–77 (2012)
14. Smallwood, R.D., Sondik, E.J.: The optimal control of partially observable Markov processes over a finite horizon. Oper. Res. **21**(5), 1071–1088 (1973)
15. Temizer, S., Kochenderfer, M.J., Kaelbling, L.P., Lozano-Pérez, T., Kuchar, J.K.: Collision avoidance for unmanned aircraft using Markov decision processes. In: AIAA Guidance, Navigation, and Control Conference, Toronto, Canada (2010)
16. Zhang, N.L., Liu, W.: Planning in stochastic domains: problem characteristics and approximation. Technical report HKUST-CS96-31, Department of Computer Science, Hong Kong University of Science and Technology (1996)
17. Zhang, N.L., Zhang, W.: Speeding up the convergence of value iteration in partially observable Markov decision processes. J. Artif. Intell. Res. **14**, 29–51 (2001)

A Neural Field Approach to Obstacle Avoidance

Chun Kwang Tan[1]([✉]), Paul G. Plöger[1], and Thomas P. Trappenberg[2]

[1] University of Applied Science Bonn Rhein Sieg, Sankt Augustin, Germany
chunkwang.tan@smail.inf.h-brs.de
[2] Faculty of Computer Science, Dalhousie University, Halifax, NS, Canada

Abstract. Cognitive robotics aims at understanding biological processes, though it has also the potential to improve future robotics systems. Here we show how a biologically inspired model of motor control with neural fields can be augmented with additional components such that it is able to solve a basic robotics task, that of obstacle avoidance. While obstacle avoidance is a well researched area, the focus here is on the extensibility of a biologically inspired framework. This work demonstrates how easily the biological inspired system can be used to adapt to new tasks. This flexibility is thought to be a major hallmark of biological agents.

1 Introduction

Cognitive robotics has two main aims. One is to help understand biological processes as it is increasingly recognized that this requires the implementation of models in systems that interact with the real world. A second aim is the potential in improving some robotics solutions where biological system still outperform robotics systems. A good example of an area where humans performance is still superior is motor control such as grasping a objects with our hand. Another recognized challenge for robotic systems is their adaptability or better the lack thereof. While highly specialized systems can easily outperform humans in specific tasks, such as assembling a car, adapting these industrial robots to perform tasks typical for a service robot is now a major area of research.

In this paper we study a biologically inspired motor control system based on Dynamic Neural Fields (DNFs). Such models are derived from a macroscopic description of cortical tissue (Wilson et al. 1972, 1973; Amari 1977). The group around Bochum (Schöner et al. 1992, 1995; Sandamirskaya 2014) has developed this framework into a general language for cognitive neurorobotics, and several other authors applied them in the robotics domain such as in collaborative human-robot interaction (Bicho et al. 2010), rodent-inspired navigation and SLAM (Milford et al. 2004), human decision making (Strauss et al. 2012) and internal models for arm movements (Fard et al. 2015). (Engels et al. 1995) demonstrated that a DNF implementation is able to unify a planning and control process in a stable manner. DNF models can be augmented with a path integration mechanisms to enable dead reckoning (Stringer et al. 2002a,b; Connors et al. 2013). A specific model that can learn motor primitives has been

© Springer International Publishing AG 2016
G. Friedrich et al. (Eds.): KI 2016, LNAI 9904, pp. 69–87, 2016.
DOI: 10.1007/978-3-319-46073-4_6

proposed in (Stringer et al. 2003). Here we investigate the model by (Stringer et al. 2003) further and contribute in with two aspects, (1) we generalize this model to two dimensional neural fields appropriate for two dimensional movements, and (2) we show how this model can be augmented to implement obstacle avoidance in a robotics setting. While neural fields have been generalized to higher dimensions for some time, we are not aware of an implementation of the motor control model by (Stringer et al. 2003) in two dimensions. The second part is in particular an attempt to study how such a framework can be combined with other tasks specific modules.

Obstacle avoidance is related to path planing, though we distinguish here path planning that deals with generating a path prior to execution from obstacle avoidance that modifies an existing path during execution. Most methods of obstacle avoidance rely on a representation of the world, by a map, which is either provided by a human designers or obtained from sensor data. Most algorithm use some form of search algorithms on the representation of the environment to determine the movement of the robot. For example, some path planning methods, like the visibility graph, cell decomposition and Voronoi diagram method (Latombe 1991; Siegwart et al. 2011), represents the world as a graph to determine an optimal path to a goal by applying some mathematical algorithms. A method called Potential Field Path Planning applies a function to calculate the gradient towards a goal (Khatib 1985). A descending gradient would attract the robot towards a goal, while an ascending gradient, which indicates obstacles, would repel the robot. Obstacle avoidance methods like the Bug algorithm (Lumelsky et al. 1987) follow the contours of an obstacles and leaves the obstacle at a point where the distance is closest to the goal. Other methods like the Vector Field Histogram (Borenstein et al. 1991) employs histograms to represent obstacle density. The Curvature-Velocity method (Simmons 1996) formulates obstacle avoidance as a constrained optimization problem in the velocity space of the robot. Recently, novel methods are proposed. Some are based on reinforcement learning (Yang et al. 2004; Xia et al. 2015), some biologically-inspired (Montiel et al. 2015), and others, are based on a dynamic systems approach (Khansari-Zadeh et al. 2012). (Iossifidis et al. 2001) showed how a 8 degree-of-freedom arm can be controlled to perform obstacle avoidance in a reaching task. While obstacle avoidance is used here as an example application, the focus is not so much its comparative performance with these existing systems but rather the investigation of the adaptability of the biological framework. The long term goal here is to understand solutions found by nature and to see if such solutions can advance robotics systems in the future.

Related to our work is the paper by (Torta et al. 2012) who proposes a DNF framework to coordinate different competing behaviours in mobile robot in an obstacle avoidance task. While their methods selects a heading direction, our method is based on learned movement primitives. Also, their work does not use path integration as their work does not encode the workspace of the agent. In addition, the purpose of our work is less solving again obstacle avoidance but to show how a common robotics tasks can be integrated with a biologically inspired motor control framework.

In Sect. 2, we introduce the motor control model by (Stringer et al. 2003) and describe the augmentations to the model. Section 3 covers the training of the networks. Section 4 presents simulation results from three different test cases.

2 Model Specification

2.1 2-Dimensional DNF Program to Represent Motor Learning

(Stringer et al. 2003) introduced a generalized motor control model based on DNFs to present a dynamical systems approach to motor control. The model follows the framework proposed by (Schmidt 1987, 1988) which states that a generalized motor model controls a class of actions, instead of specific movements or sequences. It is also suggested that a particular class of actions has a common set of invariant features which defines that class. Common invariant features are: the relative timing of the components of the skill, the relative force used in performing the skill, and the sequencing of components.

In this paper, we extend the model by (Stringer et al. 2003) into a 2-dimensional (2D) form and introduced components necessary for the task of obstacle avoidance.

The basic model by (Stringer et al. 2003) is outlined in Fig. 1 with the solid boxes. The boxes with dashed lines are additions that will be described in the next section. The model has three components. The state network contain state cells that represent the postural state of the agent. The recurrent connections of the state network, w^S (Fig. 1), cause the state network to operate as a continuous attractor network and is able to maintain an activity region, which encodes the pose of the agent, in absence of external visual or proprioceptive inputs. The state network also operates as a movement path integrator, with inputs from the motor network. The motor network contains motor cells to represent motor activity. The motor network in the model represents the cortical motor command, and these neurons activate appropriate subcortical motor neurons that carry out a movement. The third component contains motor selector cells that represent prefrontal decision to perform a motor sequence.

This motor control model represents an internal model that can predict changes in pose with path integration (Stringer et al. 2003). More specifically, it is a forward model that is implemented with the weights from the motor network to the state network, w^{MS} (Fig. 1). This connection carries an efference copy from the motor command to the state network to update its positional state with path integration. The weights are learned with a traced Sigma-Pi learning rule, which describes the multiplicative interaction between neurons during learning. This learning rule allows a combination of the preceding position and motor command to be associated with the current positional state. Thus, in trained connections, for a particular combination of the agent's state and motor activity, the pattern of activity within the network of state cells should evolve continuously to express the changing state of the agent as it performs a motor sequence. Force can be controlled with the movement selector cells by varying their firing rates. An increase in firing rates of the movement selector cells would

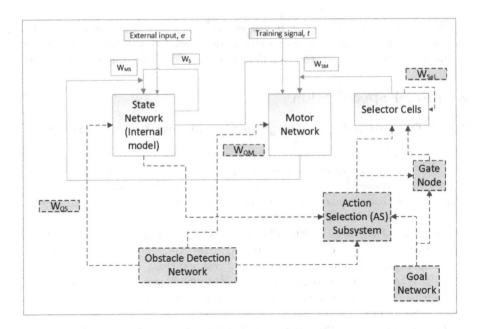

Fig. 1. Overview of the proposed system including the generalized original motor system by (Stringer et al. 2003) (solid lines) and the additional components for obstacle avoidance.

cause a corresponding increase in the size of the activity packet in the motor network, leading to an increase in force.

We extended the implementation of this model to 2-dimensions and use bold letters to indicate tensors. The activation $\mathbf{h}$ of the state network is governed by

$$\tau \frac{dh_{\mathbf{I}}^t(t)}{dt} = -h_{\mathbf{I}}^S(t) + \underbrace{(\frac{2\pi}{N})^2 \sum_{\mathbf{J}} w_{\mathbf{IJ}}^S r_{\mathbf{J}}^S(t)}_{\text{2nd term}} + \underbrace{e_{\mathbf{I}}}_{\text{3rd term}} + \underbrace{(\frac{2\pi}{N})^2 \sum_{\mathbf{J,K}} w_{\mathbf{IJK}}^{MS} r_{\mathbf{J}}^S r_{\mathbf{K}}^M}_{\text{4th term}} - \underbrace{\sum_{\mathbf{J}} w_{\mathbf{IJ}}^{OS} r_{\mathbf{J}}^{obs}}_{\text{5th term}},$$

(1)

where the second term on the right-hand side of the equation describes the effects of the firing of the state cells. The third term is an external input. The forth term described the coupled inputs from both the state cells and motor cells. Finally, the fifth term describes the inhibition by the detection network. N refers to the number of neurons in the network. The firing of the state network is monotonically related to the sigmoid activation,

$$r_{\mathbf{I}}^S(t) = \frac{1}{1 + e^{-2\beta^S (h_{\mathbf{I}}^S(t) - \alpha^S)}},$$

(2)

where α^S and β^S are the threshold and slope, respectively. The activation of the motor network is governed by

$$\tau \frac{dh_{\mathbf{I}}^M(t)}{dt} = -h_{\mathbf{I}}^M(t) + \underbrace{t_{\mathbf{I}}}_{\text{2nd Term}} + \underbrace{(\frac{2\pi}{N})^2 \sum_{\mathbf{J,K}} w_{\mathbf{IJK}}^{SM} r_{\mathbf{J}}^S r_{\mathbf{K}}^{MS}}_{\text{3rd Term}} - \underbrace{\sum_{\mathbf{J}} w_{\mathbf{IJ}}^{OM} r_{\mathbf{J}}^{obs}}_{\text{4th Term}}. \quad (3)$$

The second term on the right-hand side represents a training signal that models attention processes during learning. This input is set to zero during testing. The third term describes the contributions from the coupled state and motor selector cells. The fourth term describes the inhibition from the obstacle detection network. Finally, the firing of the motor network is similar to Eq. 2 (Replace the "S" superscript with "M") where α^M and β^M are again the threshold and slope, respectively. To stabilize the network against noise, the firing of the state and motor networks are modified such that they enhance the firing rate of the neurons that are already firing,

$$\alpha_i = \begin{cases} \alpha^{\text{HIGH}} & \text{if } r_i < \gamma \\ \alpha^{\text{LOW}} & \text{if } r_i \geq \gamma \end{cases} \quad (4)$$

This allows the activity packet within the networks to remain stable in presence of noise. Parameters of network used in the following simulations are summarized in tables below. All Gaussian profiles used for weights in the extended mode, be it 2D or 1D, have the same width, $\sigma = \frac{\pi}{8}$. Simulations of this basic 2D model have reproduced the findings of (Stringer et al. 2003).

2.2 Augmentations of the Model for Obstacle Avoidance

To allow obstacle avoidance we need to combine sensory components to this motor control framework. The goal is to show how learned actions can be selected with a combination of an intended goal, current state of the agent and presences of obstacles. Figure 1 provides a graphical overview of the complete model with the new components of this work depicted with dotted lines and boxes. These are the Obstacle Detection Network, the goal network, the gate node, and the action selection (AS) subsystem.

The Obstacle Detection network indicates the location of an obstacle in a 2D state space that is similar to the space that is represented by the state network. The activity of this network could be generated from sensor readings, but however, for the purpose of our simulations, the Obstacle Detection Network is modelled by a 2D Gaussian centred around an pre-defined location. Currently, this network assumes that only one obstacle is present in the state space. Inhibitory connections to the state and motor networks are provided by the connections with weights labelled w^{OS} and w^{OM}. The reason for these connections is that when an obstacle is present in the state space, the activity bubble representing the state and motor model of the agent should not enter the location of the obstacle. Thus, the obstacle network inhibits the neurons at the location where the obstacle is detected in the state and motor space. The weights w^{OS} and w^{OM} also perform the function of "expanding" the obstacle such that the agent does not physically touch the obstacle in the real world. This feature takes into consideration an aspect in robotics that physical contact with the robot and any obstacle should be avoided. Connections are provided to the AS subsystem without weights as the AS subsystem only needs to know the location of the obstacle.

The Goal network represents the location of the intended state that the agent wishes to achieve and is also modelled with a 2D Gaussian. The goal is assumed to be given by a high level executive functions, and is set manually during our simulations.

The Gate node consists of cells in this node are used to gate the action selection mechanism. The assumption is that in absence of a goal, the agent should not execute any actions in its memory. Gate cells have the additional function to stop motor commands once the agent is near the goal, hence the connection from the AS subsystem (Fig. 1). The activation of gate cells in our model depends on two factors, the existence of a goal and the closeness of a goal if there is one. The existence of a goal is checked by two subnodes, whose firing profile solely depends on the level of activity in the goal network. One subnode is always active, characterized by

$$r^{gate-ext} = \frac{1}{1 + e^{-2\beta^{gate-ext}\left(\sum_I r_I^{goal} - \alpha^{gate-ext}\right)}}, \tag{5}$$

and the other that is only active when a goal is present

$$r^{gate-inh} = \frac{1}{1 + e^{-2\beta^{gate-inh}\left(\sum_I r_I^{goal} - \alpha^{gate-inh}\right)}}, \tag{6}$$

These two subnodes are connected such that $r^{gate-inh}$ inhibits $r^{gate-ext}$ with postsynaptic inhibition. This is written as $r^{gate-ext} - r^{gate-inh}$.

A subnode calculates how much inhibition to send to the selector network. First, we calculate the distance to the goal,

$$r_I^{close} = r_I^{goal}(t) - r_I^{state}(t), \tag{7}$$

where negative values are removed by

$$\begin{cases} 0 & r_I^{close} \leq 0 \\ r_I^{close} & r_I^{close} > 0 \end{cases}. \tag{8}$$

This step is important because negative values will cause premature inhibition, as this subnode interprets any values below zero as "the current state is right on top of the goal". The activation and firing of this subnode is defined as

$$h^{inh} = \sum_I r_I^{goal} - \sum_I r_I^{close}, \tag{9}$$

with the firing given as

$$r^{inh} = \frac{1}{1 + e^{-2\beta^{inh}(h^{inh} - \alpha^{inh})}}. \tag{10}$$

The final output from the gate node is a sum of all the firing within the node,

$$r^{gate-final} = r^{inh} + (r^{gate-ext} - r^{gate-inh}). \tag{11}$$

AS Subsystem. Figure 2 gives a detailed view of the internals of the AS subsystem. Each sub node in the AS subsystem encodes the motor traces of a learned motor sequence, that is, these are copies of the trained weights of w_{SM}. Each sub node encodes a single motor action. In this paper, we are working with 3 actions for our simulations, hence there are only 3 sub nodes. Within each subnode, there are 4 more nodes that respond to the state, goal and obstacle inputs. The last node fires regardless of inputs, keeping the entire motor sequence active for further processing.

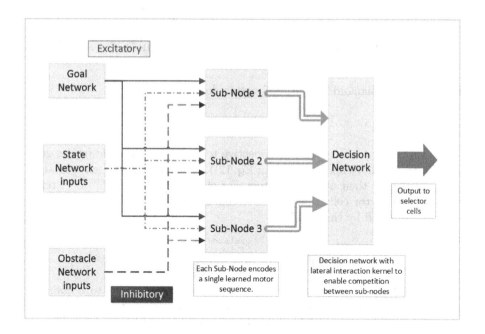

Fig. 2. AS subsystem

Excitatory inputs from the goal and state network are projected onto each motor sequence, activating only areas of the motor sequence that are close to the goal and current state. Similarly, inputs from the obstacle detection network is projected onto each motor sequence, but are inhibitory in nature, characterized by a negative value in simulation. This tells the nodes which area of the sequence is "blocked". Each subnode then sums up the total strength of response from all 4 elements and outputs them to a decision network. The decision network is trained to only respond to inputs at specific locations, hence each subnode can only activate cells that are associated with its own motor command on the decision network. These locations match locations that are activated in the selector network during training. A lateral interaction kernel allows the inputs to compete with each other via inhibition. Thereafter, the decision network sends its output to the selector cells.

Theoretically, the decision network is unnecessary, since the competition between nodes can actually occur in the selector network. However, since these nodes are dealing with the sum of responses from 4 different elements, the values of response can get very high. This would also cause the kernel parameter values for the selector network to be high as well, to handle these high value inputs. This would make it harder to tune during design. Hence, this decision network is more of design decision to normalize the values.

The activation of each subnodes are described by 2 sets of equations.

$$
\begin{aligned}
r_{\mathbf{I}}^{subnode} = & g^{state}\left(\sum_{\mathbf{J,K}} w_{\mathbf{IJK}}^{SM} r_{\mathbf{J}}^{S} r_{\mathbf{K}}^{subnode_{cmd}}\right) + g^{goal}\left(\sum_{\mathbf{J,K}} w_{\mathbf{IJK}}^{SM} r_{\mathbf{J}}^{goal} r_{\mathbf{K}}^{subnode_{cmd}}\right) + \\
& g^{trace}\left(\sum_{\mathbf{J,K}} w_{\mathbf{IJK}}^{SM}(1) r_{\mathbf{K}}^{subnode_{cmd}}\right) - g^{obs}\left(\sum_{\mathbf{J,K}} w_{\mathbf{IJK}}^{SM} r_{\mathbf{J}}^{obs} r_{\mathbf{K}}^{subnode_{cmd}}\right)
\end{aligned}
\tag{12}
$$

where $g^x(h)$ is a sigmoid activation function defined as

$$
r_{\mathbf{I}}^x = \frac{1}{1 + e^{-2\beta^x (h_i^x - \alpha^x)}}.
\tag{13}
$$

The superscript x denotes the respective terms in the subnode (state, goal, trace, obstacle (shortened to "obs" in Eq. 12)). Also, note that each activation function will have their own parameters. For clarity, the term $r_{\mathbf{K}}^{subnode_{cmd}}$ refers to the set of selector cells that are activated during training. Finally, negative values are removed by thresholding:

$$
\begin{cases}
0 & r_i^{subnode} \le 0 \\
r_i^{subnode} & r_i^{subnode} > 0
\end{cases}
\tag{14}
$$

To project the strength of responses from all the subnodes to a common network, the 2D firing responses will have to be "converted" into a 1D form to fit the decision network (1D because the selector network is also 1D). This is done by taking the sum of firing of the subnodes, then passing them through a 1D weight kernel that is only specific to their own motor sequence. Using the firing response from subnodes above (Eq. 12) this is expressed as

$$
h_i^{Decision} = \sum_j (w_j^{Decision} \sum_{\mathbf{I}} r_{\mathbf{I}}^{subnode})
\tag{15}
$$

$$
r_i^{Decision} = \frac{1}{1 + e^{-2\beta^{Decision}(h_i^x - \alpha^{Decision})}},
\tag{16}
$$

where the subscript j is an index represents the number of motor sequences and their associated motor commands. The weight kernel description is the same as Eq. 37, except that it is a 1D weight kernel instead of a 2D. The end result is a weight kernel, w_M^{cmd}, being a 1D centre-surround interaction kernel, with centres around their respective locations associated with motor commands. Note that the AS node is classic feed-forward network, and we assume in our simulations that the AS operates instantaneously. Therefore, there is no need to formulate them as dynamic systems. The sigmoid parameters for the "trace" subnetwork are adjusted so as the output strength of each subnetwork are relatively equal to each other.

Since the Selector Network is now a recurrent network, it is necessary to describe them formally. The activation of the Selector Network is given by:

$$\tau\frac{dh_i^{Selector}(t)}{dt} = -h_i^{Selector}(t) + r_i^{Decision} + \frac{2\pi}{N}\sum_j w_{ij}^{Selector}r_i^{Selector} \qquad (17)$$

and the firing of the selector network is governed by

$$r_i^{Selector}(t) = (\frac{1}{1 + e^{-2\beta^{Selector}(h_i^{Sel}(t)-\alpha^{Selector})}}) - r^{gate}, \qquad (18)$$

where $r_i^{Decision}$ represents input from the AS node. Inhibition from the gate cells are applied as postsynaptic inhibition on the entire network, as denoted by the r^{gate} in the firing equation.

Tables 1 and 2 below depicts the parameters used for our simulations

Table 1. Network firing profiles and dimensions

Network type (superscript)	α	β	α^{HIGH}	γ	X dimension	Y dimension
State (S)	−4.0	1	−0.25	0.5	20	20
Motor (M)	10.0	1	10.0	0.5	20	20
Selector	2	0.9			20	1
Gate (gate-ext) ·	−3	1			1	1
Gate (gate-inh)	3	1			1	1
Gate (inh)	3	1			1	1
AS subnode, state (state)	70	0.1			20	20
AS subnode, goal (goal)	50	0.1			20	20
AS subnode, obstacles (obs)	50	0.1			20	20
AS subnode, trace sequence 1	220	0.5			20	20
AS subnode, trace sequence 2	258	0.5			20	20
AS subnode, trace sequence 3	226	0.5			20	20
AS subsystem (decision)	95	1			20	1
Obstacle (obs)					20	20
Goal					20	20

Table 2. Weight scaling parameters of networks

Weight type	A^{net}	C^{net}
w^S	4	0.5
w^{SM}	12	0.2
w^{MS}	12	0.0
$w^{Selector}$	13	0.4
w^{OS}	1	0.3
w^{OM}	2	0.3
$w^{Decision}$	12	0.3

3   Training the Model

To speed up training, we chose to set the learning rate to $k = 1$ in Eqs. 23, 24, 27, 32, 33 and 34. This allows for 1 single training iteration.

Similar to the training phase in the original model (Stringer et al. 2003), we used a Gaussian training profile for the firing of the networks. However, in our case, the Gaussian is a 2D profile given as a multiplication of 2 Gaussians:

$$r_I^{2Dnet} = exp(-(s_{i_1}^{2Dnet})^2/2(\sigma^{2Dnet})^2) * exp(-(s_{i_2}^{2Dnet})^2/2(\sigma^{2Dnet})^2), \quad (19)$$

where $2Dnet = state, motor, obstacle, goal$. s is the absolute difference between the preferred firing state of the network and current firing state for each cell in the network. This is given as:

$$s_{i_1}^{2Dnet} = min(|x_i - x|, size_x - |x_i - x|)$$
$$s_{i_2}^{2Dnet} = min(|y_i - y|, size_y - |y_i - y|), \quad (20)$$

where the variables x and y describe the two dimensions of the network. The addition of the min function account for periodic boundary conditions. This form of equation apply to all 2D networks (state, motor, obstacle detection, goal) by changing the superscript net to reflect the firing profiles of the said network. Since these firing profiles are used to train weight kernels, it follows that all associated weight kernels have similar 2D profiles. As for the remaining networks, they are trained with 1D Gaussian profiles,

$$r_i^{1Dnet} = exp(-(s_i^{1Dnet})^2/2(\sigma^{1Dnet})^2) \quad (21)$$

and

$$s_i^{1DNet} = min(|x_i - x|, size_x - |x_i - x|)|x_i - x|. \quad (22)$$

Similar to the 2D Gaussian profile, the min function accounts for periodic boundary conditions. This form of the equation applies to the decision network in the AS subsystem and the selector cells.

All of the training rules used in the original model are extended to the 2D form. The training rule for the recurrent connections of the state network, $w_{\mathbf{IJ}}^{S}$ is given by

$$\delta w_{\mathbf{IJ}}^{S} = k^{S} r_{\mathbf{I}}^{S} r_{\mathbf{J}}^{S}, \tag{23}$$

and the connections from motor to state network is adjusted by

$$\delta w_{\mathbf{IJK}}^{MS} = k^{MS} r_{\mathbf{I}}^{S} \bar{r}_{\mathbf{J}}^{S} \bar{r}_{\mathbf{K}}^{M}, \tag{24}$$

where the bar over r denoting a memory trace of the firing over the state and motor activity. This trace value is given by

$$\bar{r}(t + \delta t) = (1 - \eta) r(t + \delta t) + \eta \bar{r}(t), \tag{25}$$

where η is a parameter which determines the contribution of the previous firing rate and current rate to the trace activity. For the purpose of our simulation, we set $\eta = 0.6$

Weights are normalized after the learning of each motor sequence. This is to ensure weights encoding each sequence are of the same relative strength,

$$w_{final}^{MS} = \sum_{M} ((w_{Seq} + \delta w_{Seq}) / max(w_{Seq})) \tag{26}$$

In our implementation, the weights for each sequence are normalized before combining them together.

The connection from state to motor network are changing according to

$$\delta w_{\mathbf{IJK}}^{SM} = k^{SM} r_{\mathbf{I}}^{M} r_{\mathbf{J}}^{S} r_{\mathbf{K}}^{Selector}. \tag{27}$$

A normalization of connection strength is performed after every learning of the motor sequence. This is to ensure that the weights encoding each motor sequence have the same relative strength, regardless of the length of the sequence. This is done by dividing the weight kernel with the its maximal value. They are combined together after normalization,

$$w_{final}^{SM} = \sum_{M} ((w_{Seq} + \delta w_{Seq}) / max(w_{Seq})), \tag{28}$$

where M denotes the number of motor sequences to be learned, and w_{Seq} denotes the current motor sequence is being trained. We defined three motor sequences for training by shifting a 2D Gaussian profile centred about the points listed below:

1st Motor Command: Diagonal movement

Sequence 1: X-direction $= [4, 5, 6, 7, 8, 9, 10, 11, 12, 13, 14, 15, 16]$

Sequence 1: Y-direction $= [4, 5, 6, 7, 8, 9, 10, 11, 12, 13, 14, 15, 16]$ $\tag{29}$

2nd Motor Command: Diagonal with a curve to the right

$$\text{Sequence 2: X-direction} = [4, 5, 6, 7, 8, 9, 10, 10, 11, 11, 12, 12, 13,$$
$$13, 14, 14, 15, 15, 16, 16, 16, 16, 16, 16]$$
$$\text{Sequence 2: Y-direction} = [4, 4, 4, 4, 4, 5, 5, 6, 6, 7, 7, 8, 8,$$
$$9, 9, 10, 10, 11, 11, 12, 13, 14, 15, 16] \tag{30}$$

3rd Motor Command: Right movement then straight up

$$\text{Sequence 3: X-direction} = [4, 5, 6, 7, 8, 9, 10, 11, 12, 13, 14, 14, 15,$$
$$15, 16, 16, 16, 16, 16, 16, 16, 16, 16, 16]$$
$$\text{Sequence 3: Y-direction} = [4, 4, 4, 4, 4, 4, 4, 4, 4, 4, 4, 5, 5,$$
$$6, 6, 7, 8, 9, 10, 11, 12, 13, 14, 15, 16] \tag{31}$$

Note that these motor sequences are deliberately chosen such that they are able to "cover" at least half of the locations in the motor network.

The connection from obstacle to state and motor network are modelled with the equations

$$\delta w_{IJ}^{OS} = k^{OS} r_I^{OS} r_J^{OS} \tag{32}$$

and

$$\delta w_{IJ}^{OM} = k^{OM} r_I^{OM} r_J^{OM} \tag{33}$$

respectively. These connections represent the effects of the obstacles on both the state and motor network. Although the learning rules are the same, the lateral interaction parameters given later would change their strength of inhibition to their respective networks.

Recurrent connections for selector network are trained with

$$\delta w_{ij}^{Selector} = k^{Selector} r_i^{Selector} l r_j^{Selector}. \tag{34}$$

This learning rule is similar, except that in the case of the selector network, it utilizes a 1D Gaussian profile for training. The weights from each subnode to the decision network is described by a 1D Gaussian profile.

$$w_i^{Decision} = exp(-(s_i^{Decision})^2 / 2(\sigma^{Decision})^2) \tag{35}$$

$$s_i^{Decision} = |x_i - x|, \tag{36}$$

where x_i is the centre of the Gaussian used for encoding motor commands. For our simulations, the centres of the Gaussians are used as indices of connections to the decision network. We associated $x_1 = 5$ with the 1st motor sequence, $x_2 = 10$ with the second motor sequence and $x_3 = 15$ with the 3rd motor sequence. Note that these values are arbitrarily chosen for the purpose of our simulations.

After training has been carried out, the weights kernels are adjusted with a scaling factor A and global inhibition constant C. This can be expressed as:

$$w^{net} = A^{net}((w^{net}/max(w^{net})) - C^{net}), \tag{37}$$

where the superscript net denotes the respective superscripts of the network where the weights belong to. Note that a normalization factor is also included, given by the division with the maximal value of trained weights, $max(w^{net})$. This help ensure that the relative strength of weights in the network are of similar magnitude. Also note that each network have their respective parameters A and C, which is listed below:

4   Simulations

In this section we demonstrate the abilities of the model in three scenarios. Model simulations are implemented in MATLAB R2015a (64 bits) on a system with Intel Core i7-4900MQ (2.8 GHz), with 16 GB memory running Windows 8.1 Pro (64 bits). For the numerical integration we use a simple Euler method with a time constant of $\tau = 1$ and an integration timestep of $\Delta t = 0.2$. Before the start of every simulation, we initialized our state network with an external input, e_I, at the location $(4, 4)$ for 100 timesteps. Then the external input is removed and the network is allowed to rest for another 30 timesteps to ensure that the activity region is stable. This location is assumed to be the agent's start position. Plots below show the activity of the networks consolidated over time.

Note that during simulation, no planning times were reported, as there is no planning, if viewed from a strict classic robotics planning context. Each state encoded by the state network is associated with a corresponding motor command and the next state of a sequence during training, thus allowing the agent to immediately move to the next state. This continues until the selector cells are inhibited, which stops the agent from moving.

4.1   Test Case 1: Goal State with No Obstacles

The first test case is similar to the original experiments by Stringer et al. except that it includes the goal network to automatically stop movements when the goal is reached. In this experiment we move the agent from its initial location at $(4, 4)$ to a goal at $(16, 16)$. The goal is communicated to the system by setting the goal network to a 2D Gaussian between $t = 50$ and $t = 180$. Figure 3 show the activities in the different subsystems.

The state activity moves from the initial state to the desired state (Fig. 3A), while the motor nodes and the selector network are only active during the movement (Fig. 3B and C). The AS subsystem (Fig. 3D) is inactive from $t = 0$ to $t = 50$ as there is no goal. Inhibition is strong from the beginning, preventing any movement. Inhibition is removed once a goal is detected at $t = 50$ and the gate node releases its inhibition on the selector cells. At about $t = 150$, the gate node begins to inhibit the selector network again, because of the proximity of the agent to the goal.

Figure 3F shows the Centre of Mass (CoM) of the activity packets within the motor network. This plot reveals that it took about 40 time steps before the agent started moving at $t = 90$ and stopped moving at $t = 174$. Furthermore,

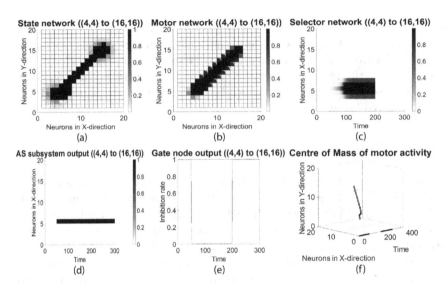

Fig. 3. Consolidated network activity trajectories over time (Test Case 1)

the motor network did not stop directly at point $(12, 12)$, but instead stopped near $(10,10)$. This is attributed to the "closeness" parameter within the gate node. However, since the width of the state activity packet is able to cover the goal, the agent is considered to have reached the goal.

4.2   Test Case 2: Static Obstacle

For the second test case, we presented a static obstacle to the model at location $(10, 10)$, while giving a goal of $(16, 16)$. This means that there is now an obstacle right in the path of the motor sequence executed in the first experiment. As shown in the corresponding Fig. 4, the agent avoids activating the motor command for the first motor sequence. Instead, the motor command for the second motor sequence is activated and the agent moves in a trajectory that avoids the obstacle. Interestingly, the output of the AS subsystem makes the decision to activate two motor commands together, the initial output at $t = 50$ is already stronger for the second motor command, thus selecting it. The recurrent connection of the selector network strengthens the decision output with a positive feedback loop, eventually activating the second motor command. As with test case 1, the inhibition is lifted once a goal is detected at $t = 50$.

The CoM analysis showed that needed just 21 time steps (from $t = 50$ when the goal is given) for the motor command to be activated at $t = 71$. This is because of the effects of inhibition from the obstacle caused the subnode for the first motor command to be weaker, hence reducing the amount of lateral inhibition on other motor commands. Since the competition is now between two motor commands, instead of three, the increase in speed for the decision makes sense.

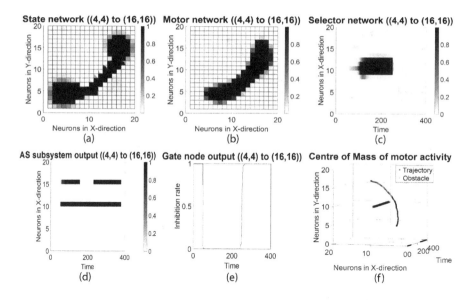

Fig. 4. Consolidated network activity trajectories over time (Test Case 2)

4.3   Test Case 3: Dynamic Obstacle

In this test case, we demonstrated that the agent can change motor commands dynamically when encountering an obstacle that is moving around. The obstacle is initially placed at location $(10, 10)$ at $t = 52$, then moved to location $(14, 9)$ at $t = 115$.

The shape of the activity trace extending outward to point $(10, 4)$ in Fig. 5(a) is the agent's attempt to move using the first motor command, switch to the second motor command, before finally deciding to activate the first motor command. This changing of decision is reflected in the plots of the selector network. Some signs of the decision making process can also be seen in the motor network, where motor activity dies off momentarily. This occurred between $t = 77$ to $t = 84$, where the agent switches from activating the first motor command to the second motor command after detecting an obstacle at $(10,10)$. The second occurrence of motor activity discontinuity is between $t = 127$ and $t = 142$, where the agent switches from the second motor command to the first motor command. However, the decision to execute a motor command is not clear from the perspective of the motor network, since motor commands will not be executed if the firing rates of the selector network is not high enough.

A step-by-step analysis of the AS subsystem output and selector network plots demonstrates the decision process. Right before the introduction of an obstacle at location $(10, 10)$ when $t = 52$, the selector network is about to activate the first motor sequence, as characterized by the increasing activity in the selector network. At the same time, the AS subsystem "notices" the introduction of the obstacle and changes its output. This causes the activity in the selector

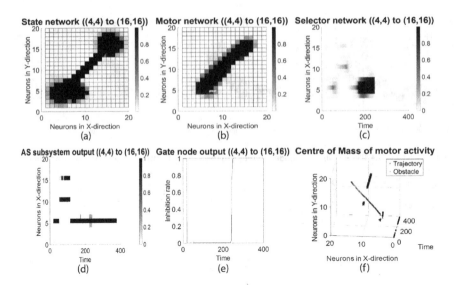

Fig. 5. Consolidated network activity trajectories over time (Test Case 3)

network to slowly decay, from $t = 53$ to $t = 77$. A point to note is that when the obstacle input is introduced to the state network, there is some excitation to the state network in areas far away from the obstacle location. Coupled with the slight activation of the motor network from the decaying selector inputs from $t = 53$ to $t = 77$, the state activity packet moves slightly to the right. The selector network then proceeds to build up activity to activate the second motor command, as per outputs from the AS subsystem. At $t = 115$, the obstacle changes location to $(14, 9)$, causing the AS node to immediately switch to the first motor command. At that time, the selector network is about to activate the second motor command, but is unable to maintain the current activity bubble, thus allowing it to decay. From $t = 130$ onwards, the selector network begins to activate the first motor command. Since there is no more change in the location of the obstacle, the first motor command will be fully activated and the agent moves towards the goal. Throughout the entire decision process, the agent only moved slightly to the right, which is partly due to the long-range excitation.

5   Discussions and Outlook

The model has been designed to show how an obstacle avoidance systems could be integrated with the original model that is able to learn motor sequences. We have demonstrated with simulations that the system is able to perform obstacle avoidance even when the initial learned motor sequences are initiated first. Although the current simulations only demonstrate movement towards a single direction, general movements would require additional networks to store movement sequences in different directions. This is described in detail in Experiment 4 in (Stringer et al. 2003). The addition of the AS subsystem is an improvement over Experiment 4 in (Stringer et al. 2003) in the sense that we do not require every single state to be associated with the motor networks, thus reducing learning time. It also made single trial learning possible, as described in the section on training above (setting of learning rate k to 1).

Currently, we demonstrated that single obstacles can be represented and used in the model. To extend the model to represent multiple obstacles, the obstacle network would have to be modified in such a way that it can properly encode multiple Gaussian profiles without interference. Weights from the obstacle network to the state and motor networks would also have to be modified such that the activity in the state and motor networks will not be completely inhibited. However, this would require further work to determine the effects of the extensions on the current model.

The original motor system by (Stringer et al. 2003) represents an internal model of an agent to represent the state or pose of the agent and to update this representation with specific motor commands. The work presented here shows that such an internal system can be easily interfaced with a sensory system and a goal system. We do not claim biological realism of this specific solution to obstacle avoidance, but our aim here was more to show that such solutions are possible with a biological inspired system. We used here obstacle avoidance as an example that requires the interaction of internal events with the internal planing or decision system. While the extensions look highly engineered for this specific part, the main message here is that it was easy to influence the original motor control system without major fine tuning of parameters.

We do not claim at this point that our method outperforms highly engineered solutions and think that new measures of robotics performance need to be introduced. Indeed, progress in the field of cognitive robotics is somewhat difficult with highly specialized benchmarks, and there is a real need to provide appropriate benchmarks that capture the difficulties that current robotic systems have, including the flexibility of the robotics system. For example, recall that there is no actual planning in this system. To use metrics in robotics like "planning time" makes it hard to quantify this system. Perhaps terms from neurophysiology could be borrowed, like "reaction time" to measure how fast can decisions that can arise from systems with a memory element. However, it is a question for further research to quantify the ability of such systems.

References

Amari, S.: Dynamics of pattern formation in lateral-inhibition type neural fields. Biol. Cybern. **27**(2), 77–87 (1977)

Bicho, E., Louro, L., Erlhagen, W.: Integrating verbal and nonverbal communication in a dynamic neural field architecture for human-robot interaction. Front. Neurorobot. **4**, 5 (2010). doi:10.3389/fnbot.2010.00005

Borenstein, J., Koren, Y.: The vector field historgram - fast obstacle avoidance for mobile robots. IEEE Trans. Robot. Autom. **7**(3), 278–288 (1991)

Connors, W., Trappenberg, T.: Improved path integration using a modified weight combination method. Cogn. Comput. **5**(3), 295–306 (2013)

Engels, C., Schöner, G.: Dynamic fields endow behavior-based robots with representations. Robot. Auton. Syst. **14**(1), 55–77 (1995)

Fard, F.S., Hollensen, P., Heinke, D., Trappenberg, T.P.: Modeling human target reaching with an adaptive observer implemented with dynamic neural fields. Neural Netw. **72**, 13–30 (2015)

Iossifidis, I., Steinhage, A.: Controlling an 8 DOF manipulator by means of neural fields. In: Proceedings of the International Conference on Field and Service Robotics. FSR 2001, Helsinki, Finland (2001)

Khansari-Zadeh, S.M., Billard, A.: A dynamical system approach to realtime obstacle avoidance. Auton. Robots **32**(4), 433–454 (2012)

Khatib, O.: Real-time obstacle avoidance for manipulators and mobile robots. In: Proceedings of the IEEE International Conference on Robotics and Automation, vol. 2, pp. 500–505 (1985)

Latombe, J.-C.: Robot Motion Planning. Kluwer Academic Publishers, New York (1991)

Lumelsky, V.J., Stepanov, A.A.: Path-planning strategies for a point mobile automaton moving amidst unknown obstacles of arbitrary shape. Algorithmica **2**(1), 403–430 (1987)

Milford, M.J., Wyeth, G.F., Prasser, D.: RatSLAM: a hippocampal model for simultaneous localization and mapping. In: 2004 IEEE International Conference on Robotics and Automation, Proceedings. ICRA 2004, vol. 1, pp. 403–408 (2004)

Montiel, O., Orozco-Rosas, U., Sepúlveda, R.: Path planning for mobile robots using bacterial potential field for avoiding static and dynamic obstacles. Experts Syst. Appl. **42**(12), 5177–5191 (2015)

Sandamirskaya, Y.: Dynamic neural fields as astep toward cognitive neuromorphic architectures. Front. Neurosci. **7**, 276 (2014). doi:10.3389/fnins.2013.00276

Schmidt, R.A.: Motor Control and Learning: A Behavioural Emphasis, 2nd edn. Human Kinetics, Champaign (1987)

Schmidt, R.A.: Motor and action perspectives on motor behaviour. In: Advances in Psychology, Volume 50, Complex Movement Behaviour: The Motor-Action Controversy, pp. 3-44. Elsevier, Science Publishers B.V., North Holland (1988)

Schöner, G., Zanone, P.G., Kelso, J.A.S.: Learning as change of coordination dynamics: theory and experiment. J. Motor Behav. **24**(1), 29–48 (1992)

Schöner, G., Dose, M., Engels, C.: Dynamics of behavior: theory and applications for autonomous robot architectures. Robot. Auton. Syst. **16**(2–4), 213–245 (1995)

Siegwart, R., Nourbakhsh, I.R., Scaramuzza, D.: Introduction to Autonomous Mobile Robots, 2nd edn. MIT Press, Cambridge (2011)

Simmons, R.: The curvature velocity method for local obstacle avoidance. In: Proceedings of the IEEE International Conference on Robotics and Automation, vol. 4, pp. 3375–3382 (1996)

Strauss, S., Heinke, D.: A robotics-based approach to modeling ofchoice reaching experiments on visual attention. Front. Psychol. **3**, 105 (2012). doi:10.3389/fpsyg.2012.00105

Stringer, S.M., Rolls, E.T., Trappenberg, T.P., de Araujo, I.E.T.: Self-organizing continous attractor networks and path integration: two-dimensional models of place cells. Netw.: Comput. Neural Syst. **13**(4), 429–446 (2002a)

Stringer, S.M., Trappenberg, T.P., Rolls, E.T., de Araujo, I.E.T.: Self-organizing continuous attractor networks and path integration: one-dimensional models of head direction cells. Netw.: Comput. Neural Syst. **13**(2), 217–242 (2002b)

Stringer, S.M., Rolls, E.T., Trappenberg, T.P., de Araujo, I.E.: Self-organizing continuous attractor networks and motor function. Neural Netw. **16**(2), 161–182 (2003)

Torta, E., Cuijpers, R.H., Juola, J.F.: Dynamic neural field as framework for behaviour coordination in mobile robots. In: World Automation Congress (WAC), pp. 1–6. IEEE (2012)

Wilson, H.R., Cowan, J.D.: Excitatory and inhibitory interactions in localized populations of model neurons. Biophys. J. **12**(1), 1–24 (1972)

Wilson, H.R., Cowan, J.D.: A mathematical theory of the functional dynamics of cortical and thalamic nervous tissue. Kybernetik **13**(2), 55–80 (1973)

Xia, C., El Kamel, A.: A reinforcement learning method of obstacle avoidance for industrial mobile vehicles in unknown environments using neural network. In: Proceedings of 21st International Conference on Industrial Engineering and Engineering Management, pp. 671–675 (2015)

Yang, G.-S., Chen, E.-K., An, C.-W.: Mobile robot navigation using neural Q-learning. In: Proceedings of International Conference of Machine Learning and Cybernetics, vol. 1, pp. 48–52 (2004)

Influence of ASP Language Constructs
on the Performance of State-of-the-Art Solvers

Richard Taupe[1,2(✉)] and Erich Teppan[1]

[1] Alpen-Adria-Universität Klagenfurt,
Universitätsstr. 65-67, 9020 Klagenfurt, Austria
erich.teppan@aau.at
[2] Siemens AG Österreich, Corporate Technology,
Siemensstr. 90, 1210 Vienna, Austria
richard.taupe@siemens.com

Abstract. Answer Set Programming (ASP) under the stable model semantics supports various language constructs which can be used to express the same realities in syntactically different, but semantically equivalent ways. However, these equivalent programs may not perform equally well. This is because performance depends on the underlying solver implementations that may treat different language constructs differently. As performance is very important for the successful application of ASP in real-life domains, knowledge about the mutual interchangeability and performance of ASP language constructs is crucial for knowledge engineers. In this article, we present an investigation on how the usage of different language constructs affects the performance of state-of-the-art solvers and grounders on benchmark problems from the ASP competition. Hereby, we focus on constructs used to express disjunction or choice, classical negation, and various aggregate functions. Some interesting effects of language constructs on solving performance are revealed.

Keywords: Answer set programming · Evaluation · ASP Competition

1 Introduction

In recent years, Answer Set Programming (ASP) under stable model semantics [13] has evolved to an extremely powerful approach to represent and solve even industrial-sized combinatorial problems in real-life application domains [1,10,12]. There are mainly two reasons for these significant advancements: First, the performance of state-of-the-art ASP systems has tremendously improved, e.g. by the incorporation of conflict-driven search [11], portfolio solving [9], lazy grounding [5], or the inclusion of powerful heuristics like berkmin or vsids [17]. Second, the language itself has been extended by expressive constructs like disjunction, choice rules, aggregates, weak constraints or optimization statements

---

This article summarizes the key findings of Richard Taupe's master's thesis [21]. Erich Teppan provided the idea for the topic and supervised the thesis. Both authors contributed equally to this paper.

© Springer International Publishing AG 2016
G. Friedrich et al. (Eds.): KI 2016, LNAI 9904, pp. 88–101, 2016.
DOI: 10.1007/978-3-319-46073-4_7

[8,14,16,20]. As a consequence, various language features allow to express the same thing in different ways and thus to produce syntactically different, but semantically identical problem encodings.

For this reason, a line of research has emerged that focuses on different aspects of automatic code rewriting. For example, [6] discusses the theoretical aspects of different equivalence-preserving rewritings under uniform and strong equivalence. The authors of [15] propose an extended calculus for ASP in order to add additional redundant rules for increasing solving performance. In [18], the effects of an automatic rule decomposition approach are discussed. In opposition to this line of research that concentrates on the background of a solving system itself, this paper focuses on how to write user programs (cf. [7], for example).

Taking up the point of view of domain engineers, we are concerned with (1) which language constructs can easily by changed by engineers without changing program size significantly, and (2) how the changes influence time and memory requirements of state-of-the-art grounders and solvers. The solvers are hereby seen as black boxes.

In particular, we present the setup and most important results of an extensive empirical evaluation. The experiments were conducted using the benchmark problems from the ASP competitions 2013[1] and 2014[2]. For each of these problems, several encodings were produced. It was made sure that the different encoding versions for a particular problem were equivalent, i.e. produced the same solutions. Furthermore, the program differences introduced were kept small and modular so that any change in time or memory consumption could be attributed to the usage of a certain language construct. All programs have been tested on a number of randomly drawn test instances from the ASP competition by running them on different combinations of state-of-the-art grounders and solvers. Statistical analysis of the experimental data revealed interesting dependencies between the usage of certain language constructs, problems, grounders and solvers in terms of memory and time consumption.

The remainder of this article is structured as follows. Section 2 refreshes the most important concepts of ASP, in particular syntax and semantics of the ASP language constructs treated in this article. Those who are totally unfamiliar with ASP might want to consult additional literature, e.g. [2,4,7,8]. Section 3 describes the experimental setup. Section 4 discusses the most interesting results of our evaluations. Finally, Sect. 5 briefly concludes the article.

2   Background

A *term* is either a *variable* or a *constant*. Strings starting with upper-case letters denote variables. Constants are represented by strings starting with lower-case letters, by quoted strings or by integers. An *atom* is either a *classical atom*, a *cardinality atom* or an *aggregate atom*. A classical atom is an expression $p(t_1, \ldots, t_n)$

---

[1] https://www.mat.unical.it/aspcomp2013.
[2] https://www.mat.unical.it/aspcomp2014.

where p is an n-ary predicate and $t_1, \ldots, t_n$ are terms. A *classical literal* is a classical atom α or its negation $\neg\alpha$. A *negation as failure (NAF) literal* is either a classical literal λ or its negation *not* λ. A cardinality literal is either a cardinality atom ψ or its negation *not* ψ. A *cardinality atom* is of the form

$$l \prec_l \{a_1 : l_{1_1}, \ldots, l_{1_m}; \ldots; a_n : l_{n_1}, \ldots, l_{n_o}\} \prec_u u$$

where

- $a_i : l_{i_1}, \ldots, l_{i_m}$ represent *conditional literals* in which a_i (the heads of the cardinality atom) constitute classical literals and l_{i_j} are NAF literals
- l and u are terms representing non-negative integers and
- $\prec_l$ and $\prec_u$ are comparison operators.

An aggregate literal is either an aggregate atom φ or its negation *not* φ. An *aggregate atom* is of the form

$$l \prec_l \#op\{t_{1_1}, \ldots, t_{1_m} : l_{i_1}, \ldots, l_{i_o}; \ldots; t_{n_1}, \ldots, t_{n_p} : l_{i_1}, \ldots, l_{i_q}\} \prec_u u$$

Most syntactical parts of aggregate literals are the same as with cardinality atoms, except that

- the heads $t_{i_1}, \ldots, t_{1_m}$ of conditional literals are tuples of terms
- and $\#op$ is an aggregate function from $\{\#min, \#max, \#count, \#sum\}$.

Generally, a *rule* is of the form

$$h_1; \ldots; h_d \leftarrow b_1, \ldots, b_m, not\ b_{m+1}, \ldots, not\ b_n.$$

where

- $h_1, \ldots, h_d$ and $b_1, \ldots, b_m$ are positive literals (i.e. atoms),
- *not* $b_{m+1}, \ldots, not\ b_n$ are negative literals,
- $H(r) = \{h_1, \ldots, h_d\}$ is called the *head* of the rule,
- $B(r) = \{b_1, \ldots, b_m, not\ b_{m+1}, \ldots, not\ b_n\}$ is called the *body* of the rule,
- $B^+(r) = \{b_1, \ldots, b_m\}$ is the positive body and
- $B^-(r) = \{not\ b_{m+1}, \ldots, not\ b_n\}$ is the negative body of the rule.

A rule r with $H(r)$ consisting of a cardinality atom is called *choice rule*. A rule r with a head consisting of more than one classical atom (i.e. $|H(r)| > 1$) is called *disjunctive rule*. A rule r with a head consisting of at most one classical atom is a *normal rule*. A normal rule r where $B(r) = \{\}$, e.g. 'a $\leftarrow$' is called *fact*. A normal rule r where $H(r) = \{\}$, e.g. '$\leftarrow b$', is called *integrity constraint*, or simply *constraint*.

We allow the typically built-in arithmetic functions $(+, -, *, /)$ and comparison predicates $(=, \neq, <, >, \leq, \geq)$. For example, $A = B + C$ could also be rewritten as $= (A, +(B, C))$.

2.1 Semantics of ASP

The semantics of a non-ground program is defined w.r.t. its *grounding*. A program's grounding can be defined in terms of its Herbrand universe and base. The *Herbrand universe* HU_P of a program P is the set of all constants appearing in P.

The grounding for a rule r without cardinality atoms and aggregates is the set of rules obtained by applying all possible substitutions of variables in r with constants in HU_P. The grounding of a rule which contains cardinality or aggregate literals is defined by the two-step instantiation described in [19]: first produce a set of partially grounded rules by substituting variables occurring outside the cardinality/aggregate literal and then, within each partially grounded rule, substitute each conditional literal by a set of ground conditional literals by substituting the remaining variables inside the cardinality or aggregate literal.

The *grounding* P_G of a program P is the union of all rule groundings. The *Herbrand base* HB_P w.r.t P is the set of all positive NAF literals (i.e. classical literals) that occur in P_G. An *interpretation* $I \subseteq HB_P$ w.r.t P is *consistent* iff there are no complementary classical literals, i.e. $\alpha \in I \implies \neg\alpha \notin I$ and (equivalently) $\neg\alpha \in I \implies \alpha \notin I$. For the remainder of this article we always assume interpretations to be consistent.

An interpretation I satisfies a (ground) positive NAF literal λ (written as $I \vDash \lambda$) iff $\lambda \in I$. A positive cardinality literal is satisfied by I iff the number of satisfied head literals in the cardinality atom satisfies the lower and upper bounds l and u w.r.t. the order relations $\prec_l$ and $\prec_u$. Both bounds and comparison symbols are optional. By default, $0 \leq$ is used for the lower and $\leq \infty$ for the upper bound. A choice rule is said to have trivial bounds if both default bounds are used and to have explicit bounds otherwise. In the latter case, we also call it *bounded*. A positive aggregate literal is satisfied iff the value returned by the aggregate function $\#op$ applied on the set of term tuples fulfilling its conditions does not violate the lower and upper bounds. Here, $\#count$ counts the number of distinct term tuples fulfilling the related conditions, and $\#min, \#max$ and $\#sum$ calculate the minimum, maximum or sum of the first terms in the distinct term tuples fulfilling the related conditions. A negative literal *not* ω is satisfied (written as $I \vDash not\ \omega$) iff ω is not satisfied. A set of literals, in particular the body B, the positive body B^+ or the negative body B^-, is satisfied if every literal in B, B^+ respectively B^- is satisfied.

A ground rule r is satisfied by I (written as $I \vDash r$) iff the head is satisfied or the body is not. In particular, an empty body is always satisfied and integrity constraints are satisfied iff the body is not satisfied, i.e. the constraint is not violated. The head of a rule is satisfied iff at least one of the literals in it is satisfied. A program P is satisfied by an interpretation I iff all rules in its grounding P_G are satisfied.

An answer set for a program can be defined on the basis of the program's *reduct* [13,19]. The reduct P^I of a ground program P relative to an interpretation $I \subseteq HB_P$ is defined as $P^I := \{H(r) \leftarrow B^+(r) : r \in P, I \vDash B^-(r)\}$.

An interpretation $I \subseteq HB_P$ (which may be empty) is an *answer set* for a program P not containing choice rules iff

- I satisfies all rules r in P^I, i.e. $\forall r \in P^I \colon I \vDash r$ and
- I is subset-minimal, i.e. there is no $I' \subset I$ so that I' satisfies all rules in $P^{I'}$.

Choice rules can produce answer sets that are not subset-minimal, which leads to a slight change of semantics when such rules are present. For example, the program consisting only of the choice rule $\{a\}$. possesses the two answer sets $\{\}$ and $\{a\}$. In order to be in line with the original semantics and thus to restore subset-minimality, an equivalent program can be produced by extending the program as follows:

For every head a_i within a cardinality atom of a choice rule, a new atom a_i' is introduced that does not occur anywhere else in the program. Furthermore, additional rules are added that assure that either a_i or a_i' but not both are in an answer set. Thus, informally speaking, a_i' expresses that a_i is not in the interpretation. This way, the choice rule $\{a\}$. equivalently produces the two answer sets $\{a'\}$ and $\{a\}$, i.e. one answer set contains a_i while the other does not. For details, consult [8].

An ASP program is *unsatisfiable* iff it has no answer sets and *satisfiable* otherwise.

2.2 ASP Coding Practices and Equivalence

It is common practice in ASP to encode the generic problem specification and instance data as two separate programs. We call them *encoding* and *instance*, respectively. While the encoding always stays the same, it can be solved together with different instance programs to solve different problem instances [3,8].

An instance typically contains only facts involving certain predicates. We call this set of predicates the program's *input signature*. On the other hand, solutions to the problem are also encoded by a specific set of predicates, which we call the program's *output signature*. Given an answer-set program Π, we denote by $in(\Pi)$ its input signature and by $out(\Pi)$ its output signature [3].

As the rule transformations discussed in this paper often change the program's predicates, we use the concept of *output-equivalence* [3]:

For a set X of atoms and a set P of predicate symbols[3], let $X_{|P}$ be the subset of X that only contains the atoms whose predicate symbols are in P. Furthermore, let $AS(\phi)$ denote the set of answer sets for ϕ.

Two *encodings* Π and Π' are output-equivalent, if and only if

1. their input and output signatures coincide, i.e. $in(\Pi) = in(\Pi') \wedge out(\Pi) = out(\Pi')$, and
2. for each *instance* I, i.e. a set of facts of predicates in $in(\Pi)$, it holds that:
   - For each answer set $X \in AS(\Pi \cup I)$ there exists an answer set $X' \in AS(\Pi' \cup I)$ such that $X_{|out(\Pi)} = X'_{|out(\Pi')}$ and vice versa.

---

[3] To distinguish predicates with the same symbol but different arities, identifiers like p/n can be used.

3   Experimental Setup

In order to test whether and how the inclusion or exclusion of certain language constructs influences solving performance, we tested variations of problem encodings on a set of state-of-the-art grounders and solvers. In these experiments, we focused on the language constructs for expressing disjunction, classical negation and the aggregate functions *count*, *min* and *max*. An overview on the experimental setup is given in Fig. 1.

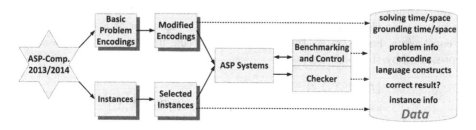

Fig. 1. Experimental setup

3.1   Problems and Encodings

All problems that appeared in the ASP competitions 2013 and 2014 were used for our experiments[4], except for *Chemical Classification, Reachability* and *Strategic Companies*, for which no alternative encodings could be produced. At least one of the official encodings provided for each problem was used as a basis. From this basis, variations were produced by making small changes where special language constructs were used. For the 24 problems that were used in our experiments, 223 different problem encodings were produced, i.e. 9.3 encodings per problem on average (not every language construct was applicable to every problem). Many of these 223 encodings had to be additionally adapted for grounders accepting different dialects of ASP[5].

In many cases, classical negation can be replaced by introducing a new predicate. Take, for example, the following rule from an encoding of the *Bottle Filling* problem:

$$filled(X, Y); \neg filled(X, Y) \leftarrow bottle(B, X, Y).$$

If the negated version of the *filled* predicate is not used anywhere else, the disjunction is only used to guess whether *filled*(X, Y) is present or not. In this case, the following rule without classical negation is equivalent to the one stated above:

$$filled(X, Y); unfilled(X, Y) \leftarrow bottle(B, X, Y).$$

---

[4] Please find datasets and additional information at https://www.mat.unical.it/aspcomp2013 and https://www.mat.unical.it/aspcomp2014.

[5] Encodings can be downloaded from http://isbi.aau.at/hint/misc.

If the whole program is head-cycle free[6] w.r.t. this disjunctive rule, the disjunction can be *shifted* into the body, i.e.

$$filled(X, Y) \leftarrow bottle(B, X, Y), not\ unfilled(X, Y).$$
$$unfilled(X, Y) \leftarrow bottle(B, X, Y), not\ filled(X, Y).$$

or be replaced by the following choice rule:

$$1\{filled(X, Y); unfilled(X, Y)\}1 \leftarrow bottle(B, X, Y).$$

Furthermore, a choice rule with explicit bounds can often be expressed as an unbounded choice rule, which may require the addition of a small number of constraints. For example, the bounded choice rule from above can as well be represented by the following rules:

$$\{filled(X, Y)\} \leftarrow bottle(B, X, Y).$$
$$unfilled(X, Y) \leftarrow bottle(B, X, Y), not\ filled(X, Y).$$

If *unfilled* is not used anywhere else, the latter of these two rules can even be omitted.

Disjunction, shifted disjunction, choice rules and bounded choice rules are also referred to as *guessing constructs*.

Rules with counting aggregates where the lower and upper bounds are constants (and the difference between the lower and upper bound is small) can be replaced by a small set of normal rules without aggregates. Take, for example, the following (simplified) integrity constraint from an encoding of *Knight Tour with Holes*:

$$\leftarrow cell(X, Y), not\ \#count\{X1, Y1 : move(X1, Y1, X, Y)\} = 1.$$

This constraint enforces that for each $cell(X, Y)$ there must be exactly one other cell from which it is visited. This can also be expressed by the introduction of two new predicates *e1* and *e2* reflecting whether there is exactly one or at least two moves entering from different cells and a constraint stating that the first one must hold:

$$\leftarrow cell(X, Y), not\ e1(X, Y).$$
$$e1(X, Y) \leftarrow move(X1, Y1, X, Y), not\ e2(X, Y).$$
$$e2(X, Y) \leftarrow move(X1, Y1, X, Y), move(X2, Y2, X, Y), X1 <> X2.$$
$$e2(X, Y) \leftarrow move(X1, Y1, X, Y), move(X2, Y2, X, Y), Y1 <> Y2.$$

Min and *max* aggregates can be replaced by rules which check whether there is a smaller respectively greater element. Take, for example, the following rule from an encoding of *Graceful Graphs*:

$$next(X, Y) \leftarrow pair(X, Y), Y = \#min\{Z : pair(X, Z)\}.$$

---

[6] Please find more information about head-cycles in [16].

This rule can be replaced by the following rules:

$$existsSmaller(X, Y) \leftarrow pair(X, Y), pair(X, S), S < Y.$$
$$next(X, Y) \leftarrow pair(X, Y), not\ existsSmaller(X, Y).$$

These examples show that rules that use special language constructs are often interchangeable. When doing this, attention has to be paid to producing *equivalent* encodings. In our setting, encodings are considered as equivalent, iff they are output-equivalent (as defined in Sect. 2.2).

3.2 Benchmarking

We tested our encodings on different grounders and solvers in various configurations that already proved a certain stability in the ASP competitions or in our own evaulations. Table 1 gives an overview on the grounders and solvers used. They were used in all combinations (henceforth called *systems*) where the solver was compatible to the grounder's output format. Grounders produce the grounding of a program and solvers search for solutions of a ground program.

Table 1. Used ASP systems

Solvers	Grounders
clasp 3.1.0	gringo 3.0.5
claspfolio 2.0.0	gringo 4.4.0
cmodels 3.85	dlvg (29-09-2014)
dlv	
GnT 2.1	
lp2bv	
lp2sat	
lp2normal2 1.7	
MinisatID 3.9.3	
smodels 2.34	
wasp 1.0	
wasp 2.0	

Some of the mentioned solvers were additionally used in several configurations, e.g. clasp was used with varying heuristics. For each problem we randomly selected four test instances. As there were 223 encodings, 73 systems in different configurations and 4 test instances for each problem, there were 65,116 different test cases. As it was known beforehand that the monolithic system dlv was not able to digest the encodings containing choice rules, the actual number of test cases was 63,884. Experiments were run on four virtual machines running Ubuntu 14.04.1 LTS trusty. Each machine had exclusive access to one processor with 2.53 GHz and 7.8 GB of RAM. The RAM available to ASP grounders and solvers was limited to 6 GB. Furthermore, there were time limits of 60 min for grounding and of 10 min for solving.

RunLim[7] was used to measure use of time and space during the execution of grounders and solvers. The correctness of the produced answer sets was verified by checkers provided by the ASP competition 2014. For each test case, we recorded information on the involved systems, grounding and solving time and space, information about the problem and its encoding (including which language constructs were present), the problem instance, and the verification results of the checker.

Of the 63,884 test cases, 25,913 produced a valid solution or proved to be unsatisfiable. In 16,774 cases the solver ran out of time and in 4695 cases it ran out of memory. In 1449 cases the grounder ran out of memory and in 552 cases it ran out of time. In the remaining 14,501 cases, the solver had problems with some language constructs which could be identified post-hoc, produced an incorrect answer or aborted out of unknown reasons. Those were excluded from analysis.

4   Results

For reasons of readability we use short names in the tables within this section in order to refer to the different types of language constructs. The meaning should be clear from the context and the textual explanations.

Tables 2 and 3 list the median values for grounding and solving time and space for all systems and gringo4/clasp respectively w.r.t. classical negation as well as *count*, *min* and *max* aggregates. Please note that the median of the total time (i.e. grounding + solving) is not the same as the median of grounding + the median of solving. For all constructs, only those problems were included in the analysis where the respective language construct could be varied, i.e. where there were encodings with and without the language construct. The number of these problems is given as *#probs*. The given number of *cases* indicates how often an encoding with (*yes*) or without (*no*) the respective language construct was used by a system.

It can be seen that the inclusion of classical negation slightly increases required space and grounding time but decreases solving time which results in a lower total time. The differing case numbers are due to the fact that, in contrary to other guessing constructs, for unbounded choice rules no encodings including classical negation could be produced (in a natural and intuitive way). As our measurements also showed that unbounded choice rules overall had a slight positive influence but was not used with classical negation, the positive influence of classical negation can be seen as even stronger.

Aggregates with *count* function decreased the grounding size and time significantly, but solving was much harder compared to the cases where this construct was not present. As the effort for grounding can be neglected in these

---

[7] http://fmv.jku.at/runlim/.

Table 2. Medians for non-guessing constructs: space in MB, time in secs

All systems		Cases	grd-space	slv-space	grd-time	slv-time	Total
negation (#probs = 22)	No	29, 513	8.00	150.80	0.29	87.33	182.13
	Yes	17, 856	8.10	161.25	0.39	72.83	145.21
aggrcount (#probs = 9)	No	12, 914	7.20	160.80	0.86	99.39	241.26
	Yes	12, 358	6.70	103.85	0.18	128.32	285.22
aggrmin (#probs = 1)	No	1605	8.80	144.60	0.09	Timeout	Timeout
	Yes	1603	8.80	148.80	0.09	Timeout	Timeout
aggrmax (#probs = 2)	No	3796	0.00	25.35	0.00	16.63	16.83
	Yes	3796	0.00	25.50	0.00	16.56	16.95

Table 3. Medians for non-guessing constructs: space in MB, time in secs

gringo4/clasp		Cases	grd-space	slv-space	grd-time	slv-time	Total
negation (#probs = 22)	No	3629	7.20	45.30	0.09	43.03	49.78
	Yes	2306	7.20	48.90	0.09	25.42	27.51
aggrcount (#probs = 9)	No	1645	6.50	43.90	0.09	92.07	92.15
	Yes	1686	6.50	31.30	0.08	125.11	155.31
aggrmin (#probs = 1)	No	168	1.30	55.45	0.04	527.01	527.01
	Yes	168	0.00	54.05	0.00	339.56	339.56
aggrmax (#probs = 2)	No	476	0.00	5.70	0.00	1.46	1.46
	Yes	476	0.00	5.70	0.00	1.46	1.46

cases, aggregates with *count* function had a negative overall effect. Since there were only very few problems which allowed encodings with and without *min* and *max* aggregates, the results are only representative for the problems where these constructs were varied. These were *Labyrinth* and *Weighted Sequence* for *max* aggregates and *Graceful Graphs* for *min* aggregates. Instances of *Graceful Graphs* were not hard to ground but very hard to solve such that the all-systems median of the solving time (and consequently of the total time) was a timeout. The combination of gringo 4 and clasp performed much above average. Clasp showed significantly smaller solving times in cases with *min* aggregates. The presence/absence of *max* aggregates effected only negligible differences over all systems and no differences at all for the combination of gringo 4 and clasp.

Tables 4 and 5 show the measured median values w.r.t. the different guessing constructs for all systems and gringo4/clasp respectively. Here, only those 19

Table 4. Medians for guessing constructs (#probs = 19): space in MB, time in secs

All systems	Cases	grd-space	slv-space	grd-time	slv-time	Total
Choice	6198	7.40	135.00	0.27	84.65	178.40
Bounded choice	7589	7.20	98.90	0.09	147.72	260.95
Disjunction	13,735	8.90	166.90	0.57	77.51	171.90
Shifted disjunction	12,503	7.80	168.50	0.48	95.07	186.96

Table 5. Medians for guessing constructs (#probs = 19): space in MB, time in secs

gringo4/clasp	Cases	grd-space	slv-space	grd-time	slv-time	Total
Choice	861	7.00	35.30	0.09	76.70	91.45
Bounded choice	1134	4.00	38.55	0.06	76.98	77.07
Disjunction	1918	7.60	48.00	0.09	40.54	42.67
Shifted disjunction	1742	7.00	40.10	0.09	58.63	73.11

Table 6. Problem-dependent medians: total time in secs

Problem	Encoding	Constructs	All systems	gringo4/clasp
Bottle filling	1	Shifted disjunction	66.44	0.83
	2	Choice	17.57	0.47
	3	Disjunction	26.08	0.57
	4	Disjunction, negation	26.83	1.06
	5	Shifted disjunction, negation	54.70	0.89
	6	Bounded choice	45.25	1.19
	7	Bounded choice, neg	43.14	1.26
Labyrinth	1	Shifted disjunction	Timeout	85.13
	2	Bounded choice	Timeout	98.47
	3	Disjunction	261.68	42.43
	4	Shifted disjunction, aggrmax	Timeout	85.51
	5	Bounded choice, aggrmax	Timeout	99.48
	6	Disjunction, aggrmax	261.61	42.46
Partner units	1	Disjunction, negation	149.09	580.67
	2	Disjunction	148.08	540.89
	3	Shifted disjunction, negation	156.76	572.88
	4	Shifted disjunction	155.97	561.26
	5	Choice	154.51	575.20
	6	Bounded choice	595.23	405.73

problems were included for which there were encodings for all guessing constructs and each encoding included exactly one of them. Furthermore, only those systems were taken into account which could deal with all four guessing constructs. It can be seen that over all systems, bounded choice rules led to smaller space usage. The combination of gringo 4 and clasp showed a similarly efficient space usage for all four constructs. Disjunction showed best solving and total times in the view on all systems as well as in the one on gringo 4 and clasp.

Although some general tendencies can be seen in the results, on the problem level there are more fine-grained influences, partially working in the opposite direction. Table 6 shows some examples. Although disjunction showed the best performance over all problems, for the *Bottle Filling* problem, unbounded choice rules (encoding 2) outperformed disjunction. On the other hand, for *Labyrinth* the median values for encodings without disjunction over all systems were time-outs. For *Labyrinth*, also gringo4 + clasp performed best on encodings with disjunction. For the *Partner Units* problem, gringo4 + clasp performed above average with encoding 6 that includes bounded choice rules, but below average with all other encodings.

5   Conclusions

Answer Set Programming (ASP) under the stable model semantics constitutes an extremely powerful approach to solve hard combinatorial problems. One reason for the success of ASP is the high performance of state-of-the-art solvers harness-ing sophisticated conflict-driven search methods. Also, ASP provides superior problem encoding capabilities as ASP is declarative in nature and even provides language features beyond first order.

As a consequence of the broad problem representation capabilities, there are many elegant ways to express the same issue differently. In particular, for most problems various encodings of similar readability including different language constructs can be created quite naturally. However, even if logically equivalent, the performance of different encodings may vary significantly, depending on the language constructs involved. The reason for that is clearly that different con-structs are processed differently by the solver implementations.

The main goal of this work is to answer the question whether there is a relevant non-negligible impact of the used language constructs on runtime and space consumption and, if so, whether general tendencies can be identified. Our results suggest that the runtime and space consumption heavily depends on the used constructs in some cases and is never to be neglected. Furthermore, some general tendencies were identified in our experiments. For example, normal disjunction had a positive overall effect on the solving speed compared to the other guessing constructs. A more fine-grained analysis revealed that, although there are general tendencies, the presence of positive or negative effect is highly dependent on the problem at hand and the ASP system used.

An important conclusion with respect to the implementation of an ASP solu-tion for a real-life problem is that a small investment in producing various slightly differing problem encodings may pay off with remarkable performance gains. An interesting direction for future work is automatic code rewriting, similarly to query optimization for relational databases.

Acknowledgements. The research for this paper was conducted in the scope of the project *Heuristic Intelligence (HINT)* funded by the Austrian research fund FFG under grant 840242.

References

1. Balduccini, M.: Industrial-size scheduling with ASP+CP. In: Delgrande, J.P., Faber, W. (eds.) LPNMR 2011. LNCS, vol. 6645, pp. 284–296. Springer, Heidelberg (2011)
2. Brewka, G., Eiter, T., Truszczyński, M.: Answer set programming at a glance. Commun. ACM **54**(12), 92–103 (2011)
3. Buddenhagen, M., Lierler, Y.: Performance tuning in answer set programming. In: Calimeri, F., Ianni, G., Truszczynski, M. (eds.) LPNMR 2015. LNCS, vol. 9345, pp. 186–198. Springer, Heidelberg (2015)
4. Calimeri, F., Faber, W., Gebser, M., Ianni, G., Kaminski, R., Krennwallner, T., Leone, N., Ricca, F., Schaub, T.: ASP-Core-2 input language format. Technical report, ASP Standardization Working Group, version 2.03b, December 2012
5. Dal Palù, A., Dovier, A., Pontelli, E., Rossi, G.: GASP: answer set programming with lazy grounding. Fundam. Informaticae **6**(3), 297–322 (2009)
6. Eiter, T., Fink, M., Tompits, H., Woltran, S.: Simplifying logic programs under uniform and strong equivalence. In: Lifschitz, V., Niemelä, I. (eds.) LPNMR 2004. LNCS (LNAI), vol. 2923, pp. 87–99. Springer, Heidelberg (2003)
7. Eiter, T., Ianni, G., Krennwallner, T.: Answer set programming: a primer. In: Tessaris, S., Franconi, E., Eiter, T., Gutierrez, C., Handschuh, S., Rousset, M.-C., Schmidt, R.A. (eds.) Reasoning Web. LNCS, vol. 5689, pp. 40–110. Springer, Heidelberg (2009)
8. Gebser, M., Kaminski, R., Kaufmann, B., Schaub, T.: Answer Set Solving in Practice. Synthesis Lectures on Artificial Intelligence and Machine Learning. Morgan and Claypool Publishers, San Rafael (2012)
9. Gebser, M., Kaminski, R., Kaufmann, B., Schaub, T., Schneider, M.T., Ziller, S.: A portfolio solver for answer set programming: preliminary report. In: Delgrande, J.P., Faber, W. (eds.) LPNMR 2011. LNCS, vol. 6645, pp. 352–357. Springer, Heidelberg (2011)
10. Gebser, M., Kaminski, R., Schaub, T.: Complex optimization in answer set programming. Theory Pract. Logic Program. **11**, 821–839 (2011)
11. Gebser, M., Kaufmann, B., Schaub, T.: Conflict-driven answer set solving: from theory to practice. Artif. Intell. **187–188**, 52–89 (2012)
12. Gebser, M., Kaminski, R., Kaufmann, B., Ostrowski, M., Schaub, T., Thiele, S.: Engineering an incremental ASP solver. In: Garcia de la Banda, M., Pontelli, E. (eds.) ICLP 2008. LNCS, vol. 5366, pp. 190–205. Springer, Heidelberg (2008)
13. Gelfond, M., Lifschitz, V.: The stable model semantics for logic programming. In: Kowalski, R., Bowen, K. (eds.) Proceedings of the Fifth International Conference and Symposium of Logic Programming (ICLP 1988), pp. 1070–1080. MIT Press, Cambridge (1988)

14. Gelfond, M., Lifschitz, V.: Classical negation in logic programs and disjunctive databases. New Gener. Comput. **9**(3–4), 365–385 (1991)
15. Järvisalo, M., Oikarinen, E.: Extended ASP tableaux and rule redundancy in normal logic programs. In: Dahl, V., Niemelä, I. (eds.) ICLP 2007. LNCS, vol. 4670, pp. 134–148. Springer, Heidelberg (2007)
16. Leone, N., Pfeifer, G., Faber, W., Eiter, T., Gottlob, G., Perri, S., Scarcello, F.: The DLV system for knowledge representation and reasoning. ACM Trans. Comput. Logic **7**(3), 499–562 (2006)
17. Lewis, M.D.T., Schubert, T., Becker, B.W.: Speedup techniques utilized in modern SAT solvers. In: Bacchus, F., Walsh, T. (eds.) SAT 2005. LNCS, vol. 3569, pp. 437–443. Springer, Heidelberg (2005)
18. Morak, M., Woltran, S.: Preprocessing of complex non-ground rules in answer set programming. In: Dovier, A., Costa, V.S. (eds.) Technical Communications of the 28th International Conference on Logic Programming (ICLP'12). Leibniz International Proceedings in Informatics (LIPIcs), vol. 17, pp. 247–258. Schloss Dagstuhl-Leibniz-Zentrum fuer Informatik, Dagstuhl, Germany (2012)
19. Syrjänen, T.: Cardinality constraint programs. In: Alferes, J.J., Leite, J. (eds.) JELIA 2004. LNCS (LNAI), vol. 3229, pp. 187–199. Springer, Heidelberg (2004)
20. Syrjaenen, T.: Logic programming and cardinality constraints: theory and practice. Ph.D. thesis, Helsinki University of Technology (2009)
21. Taupe, R.: Einfluss von Sprachkonstrukten auf die Lösbarkeit von Answer-Set-Programmen: Eine empirische Untersuchung aktueller ASP-Systeme. Masterarbeit, Alpen-Adria-Universität, Klagenfurt (2015)

A Robotic Home Assistant with Memory Aid Functionality

Iris Wieser[⊠], Sibel Toprak, Andreas Grenzing, Tobias Hinz,
Sayantan Auddy, Ethem Can Karaoğuz, Abhilash Chandran,
Melanie Remmels, Ahmed El Shinawi, Josip Josifovski,
Leena Chennuru Vankadara, Faiz Ul Wahab, Alireza M. Bahnemiri,
Debasish Sahu, Stefan Heinrich, Nicolás Navarro-Guerrero,
Erik Strahl, Johannes Twiefel, and Stefan Wermter

Department of Informatics, Knowledge Technology (WTM),
University of Hamburg, Vogt-Kölln-Straße 30, 22527 Hamburg, Germany
{4wieser,heinrich}@informatik.uni-hamburg.de

Abstract. We present the robotic system IRMA (*Interactive Robotic Memory Aid*) that assists humans in their search for misplaced belongings within a natural home-like environment. Our stand-alone system integrates state-of-the-art approaches in a novel manner to achieve a seamless and intuitive human-robot interaction. IRMA directs its gaze toward the speaker and understands the person's verbal instructions independent of specific grammatical constructions. It determines the positions of relevant objects and navigates collision-free within the environment. In addition, IRMA produces natural language descriptions for the objects' positions by using furniture as reference points. To evaluate IRMA's usefulness, a user study with 20 participants has been conducted. IRMA achieves an overall user satisfaction score of 4.05 and a perceived accuracy rating of 4.15 on a scale from 1–5 with 5 being the best.

Keywords: Robotic home assistant · Human-robot interaction · Social robotics · Memory service system · Speech recognition · Natural language understanding · Object detection · Person detection

1 Introduction

Trying to find misplaced belongings may be time consuming and might end in frustration. A study about domestic assistive systems has shown that older adults would prefer robotic assistance over human help to support them in finding lost objects at home [3].

One assistive system developed for this task is the *Home-Explorer* presented by Guo and Imai [16]. It locates objects, that are equipped with smart sensors, in an indoor environment and is operated by a search interface. Deyle et al. [10] use a similar approach by attaching RFID (*Radio-Frequency Identification*) tags to household objects, which can then be found by a robot. Another example is

ⓒ Springer International Publishing AG 2016
G. Friedrich et al. (Eds.): KI 2016, LNAI 9904, pp. 102–115, 2016.
DOI: 10.1007/978-3-319-46073-4_8

the robotic home assistant *Care-O-bot 3* presented by Graf et al. [15], that can execute fetch and carry tasks on objects. The user selects the object using a touch screen attached to the robot.

For such robots to be incorporated into everyday life, however, additional aspects beyond functionality need to be considered. Foster et al. [13], for example, present a robot bartender that can operate in dynamic social environments. They identify both task success and dialogue efficiency as the main factors contributing to user satisfaction. Fasola and Matarić [11] present a robotic system that engages elderly people in physical exercise and conclude that users strongly prefer a physical robot embodiment instead of a computer simulation. To our knowledge, no working object finding system exists that provides a physical robot embodiment, offers a natural and intuitive interaction, and is independent of external sensors (e.g. on objects).

In a student project, we developed the stand-alone robotic system IRMA (*Interactive Robotic Memory Aid*) that can help users find various objects in an indoor home-like environment. IRMA integrates the required functionalities in a stable and robust manner, aims for a more intuitive and natural interaction, and is capable of learning the position of objects without the support of external hardware. This paper presents system details and the scores IRMA received in a user study. Also, the aspects of the system that have an impact on the users' opinions as well as further insights gained in the study are discussed here.

2   The IRMA System

IRMA is a domestic robotic system that assists people in their search for misplaced belongings.[1] It provides help in two ways, either by *moving* to the position of the requested object or by *describing* the requested object's position using other objects in the scene as reference points. The robotic system is able to navigate through the home environment in a collision-free manner. To do so, the robot creates a map beforehand. Knowledge about the current positions of all objects is acquired by performing an initial exploration run through the environment, during which the objects are detected and located on the map.

2.1   Architecture

We implemented IRMA as a distributed system in ROS (Indigo) [25]. As shown in Fig. 1, the overall system is decomposed into eight modules which can be grouped into four categories:

– **Communication:** There are three communication-related modules in the system. The *Speech Recognition* module recognizes human speech and converts the audio input into a string representation. The *Natural Language Understanding* module takes the string as input and identifies the desired

---

[1] A video showing the robot's performance is presented in the video session of the IEEE RO-MAN 2016 conference [29].

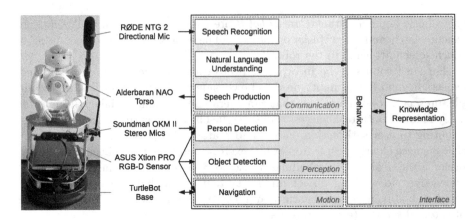

Fig. 1. An overview of the IRMA system: A picture of the robotic platform is shown in addition to a list of the used hardware components *(left)* and the decomposition of the IRMA system *(right)*. The arrows depict the data flow.

object and type of action, which can be either "move" or "describe". The *Speech Production* module allows the output of generated natural language descriptions, e.g. to describe an object's position.

- **Perception:** Two modules provide the required perceptual capabilities. The *Object Detection* module uses visual input to detect and locate relevant objects in the scene. The *Person Detection* module uses both visual and audio input to do the same for persons.
- **Motion:** *Navigation* performs exploration in an environment, maps it and uses the map to navigate through the environment without any collisions.
- **Interface:** The *Behavior* module realizes the interface between all modules. It is the core of the system and contains the control of the robot's behavior. For storing knowledge it relies on the *Knowledge Representation* module that provides a database. It is also responsible for generating natural language descriptions of an object's position relative to other objects in the scene.

2.2 Robot Platform

IRMA's robotic platform is composed of different hardware components, shown in Fig. 1. The base component is a NAO torso. It offers a significant number of in-built functionalities such as turning text into speech used by the *Speech Production* module. Also, its appearance is very likely to make the overall system look more approachable, as shown in [26]. The NAO torso is mounted on a TurtleBot platform. The TurtleBot is accessed and controlled by the *Navigation* module. To get both, depth information and high quality RGB images, an Xtion camera is used, which is attached to the TurtleBot. The Xtion camera is used by the *Object Detection*, *Person Detection* and *Navigation* modules. The robotic platform is also equipped with a directional microphone and stereo microphones. As the robot faces the human during a conversation, a directional microphone enables a more robust speech recognition by reducing the noise from different directions. The stereo microphones are used to perform sound source localization to determine the position of the person relative to the robot [24].

2.3   Methods

Speech Recognition: To convert speech signals to textual transcriptions the speech recognition framework DOCKS (*Domain and Cloud-based Knowledge for Speech recognition*) [27] is adapted. The concept behind DOCKS is to combine the recognition advantages of large-scale ASR (*Automatic Speech Recognition*), here Google ASR, with phoneme-based post-processing techniques. This restricts the very general cloud-ASR results to a more specific, domain-based language.

To generate the domain-based language, user data has been collected via an online form. The users were asked to write down sentences to make the robot execute a task-object combination. These phrases are used as domain-specific hypotheses. The hypothesis with the lowest phonetic Levenshtein distance [19] to any of the cloud-ASR results is selected as the final textual transcription.

Natural Language Understanding: To understand the user command, the following semantic words need to be identified: The requested action, the object of interest and corresponding attributes (e.g. "find", "ball", "red"). Filtering keywords is straightforward and fast, but it is restricted to specific words and is highly error-prone (e.g. "I will find the ball" has a different meaning than "Can you find the ball?"). Other known approaches, such as semantic role labeling [23], rely on hardly accessible corpora that do not focus on the grammatical constructions required in our scenario (e.g. direct and indirect questions).

Thus, a combination of bi-gram scoring, an ESN (*Echo State Network*) based on Hinaut et al. [17], and a filter is utilized, see below. The ESN has been modified to extract also attributes and special "clues". The clues are important to differentiate the meaning of sentences like "Tell me the *color* of the ball" and "Tell me the *location* of the ball". Thus, the roles extracted by our modified ESN are `predicate(object,clue)` and `object(attribute)`, e.g. `tell(ball,location)`, `ball(red)`. We chose to use an ESN with 750 reservoir units and a leak rate of 0.2 after empirically evaluating different numbers of reservoir units and different leak rates in a 6-fold cross-validation. In a preprocessing step, collocated words are detected using bi-gram scoring and joined to provide only a one-word representation to the ESN (e.g. "milk carton" to "milkcarton"). The filter that is additionally applied to the output of the ESN serves two purposes: The assurance that only context-relevant verbs and objects are extracted (e.g. "Where is my love?" is beyond the scope) and the recognition of predefined synonyms.

As each sentence is processed individually by the ESN, the system is not able to recognize context spanning more than one sentence. Also, it cannot handle collocations consisting of more than two words or anaphora. Despite that, with the proposed approach, IRMA is capable of recognizing a substantial number of different grammatical constructions. Compared to grammar-based approaches, the user is not limited to a specific set of commands, but can use various sentences such as direct and indirect questions as well as imperative statements. This gives the user freedom in formulating a request intuitively and naturally. While the false negative rate lies above 93 %, it achieves a true positive accuracy rate of 82 % on an independently collected test set.

Object Detection: A pipelined approach with classical image processing techniques is used to detect and locate objects in real-time: First, region proposals are extracted. Mean shift filtering [8] is used to smoothen the image. The image is then binarized using adaptive thresholding and contours are extracted. The bounding boxes around the contours define our ROIs (*Regions Of Interest*). Due to the nonparametric nature of the segmentation pipeline, detections are independent of specific scenarios and objects.

In the next stage, SIFT (*Scale-Invariant Feature Transform*) [21] features are extracted from each ROI and BoW models (*Bag of Visual Words*) are created for each ROI [12]. These are vectors counting the occurrence of certain groups of features that are listed in a codebook. The codebook is constructed beforehand by extracting SIFT features on all training images and performing k-means clustering on the concatenation of the features. BoW models destroy the spatial structure of the features that constitute an object, therefore we employ a spatial pyramid-based ROI representation [18] to partially retain that structure: Each ROI is recursively decomposed into four cells, where the depth of the recursion is three. For the cells on the same layer, the BoW models are constructed and are concatenated to obtain a layer-based intermediate representation. The final ROI representation is then obtained by concatenating the vectors for all layers.

In the final stage, the ROI representations of all training images are used to train K-SVM (*Kernel Support Vector Machine*) classifiers [9]. To deal with the high-dimensionality in the histograms representing the ROIs, Histogram Intersection was used as a kernel distance metric [1].

To reduce the number of false positives caused by a noisy background, "object background classes" are created. These classes act as a buffer between the object and the background class in the dataset. This approach is combined with median filtering on the list of detections.

Person Detection: To detect and then locate human presence in the robot's surroundings, visual as well as audio input is used. A pre-trained OpenCV Haar features-based cascade classifier is applied to the image for frontal face detection [28]. This classifier can yield multiple face candidates, among which the one with the largest bounding box area is selected. As the visual field alone is limited, sound source localization is additionally performed on audio input coming from the stereo microphones. The implementation is based on Parisi et al. [24], where the angle of the sound source relative to the robot is estimated using TDOA (*Time Difference Of Arrival*) [22]. While it is not possible to distinguish between a sound source that is located in the front or in the back, it can be determined whether the sound source is located to the left or to the right, in a range of ±90°. This was taken into consideration when implementing person tracking: If no face is detected in the visual field, but a sound is located, IRMA is turned towards the sound source incrementally based on the sign of the angle value. It stops turning once a face has been detected or a maximum number of turns has been performed.

Navigation: Robot localization and exploration of the environment rely on the `navigation` stack of the ROS middleware. Robot localization is achieved using the `amcl` stack, which uses a particle filter to track the pose of a robot against a known map (Adaptive Monte Carlo Localization [14]). The robot explores its environment by navigating in a collision-free manner to a sequence of waypoints distributed throughout the room. If a particular waypoint is unreachable (e.g. because of an obstacle), the robot drops the unreachable waypoint and carries on to the next. The aim of exploration is to identify known objects and locate their positions on a two-dimensional map of the environment. To do so, the robot first identifies objects using the *Object Recognition* module. The centroid of the object in the depth image is utilized to calculate the three-dimensional coordinate of the object with respect to the robot's reference frame. This 3D coordinate is converted to a 2D coordinate and stored in the knowledge database for later usage. To allow the robot to continuously move and, at the same time, process a given frame for the object recognition task, timestamps are used to query caches of transformations and depth information.

In order to move to a particular object, the object's position needs to be retrieved from the knowledge base and a valid path needs to be calculated. However, as objects are usually placed on or even inside furniture (e.g. in a shelf), the object's position itself cannot always be chosen as the final destination point for the robot. To overcome this problem, goal rectification was implemented. This process results in a new goal, which is as close as possible to the original goal (if the original goal is within an obstacle), and ensures that the goal is reachable for the robot. The final orientation of the robot is chosen so that it faces the object when it reaches its goal.

Knowledge Representation: Knowledge about the environment (e.g. object positions) is stored in the RDF (*Resource Description Framework*) format. The description of an object's position is generated with respect to the robot's viewpoint. This verbal description is calculated in two steps.

At first, the reference objects that are closest to the requested object are determined based on the Euclidean distance. If the two closest reference objects have approximately the same distance to the requested object and it lies within their convex hull, the requested object is considered to be "in between" both.

If there is no such relation, the direction ("right", "left", "front", "behind") of the closest reference object needs to be computed. Initially, the perspective is normalized so that the requested object becomes the center of the new coordinate system and the y-axis corresponds to the robot's viewing angle. The Cartesian quadrant, in which the reference object (that is, its representative point) is, determines two possible directions. In Fig. 2 (left) for example, the representative point is in Quadrant I, so the directions are "front" and "left". The reference object's bounding box is used and a 45°-diagonal is computed through the corner that points towards the opposite quadrant. The side of the diagonal, on which

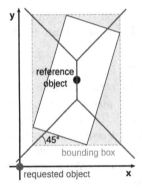
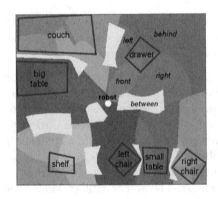

Fig. 2. *Left:* Determining the spatial relations between objects. Here, the requested object is "in front of" the reference object. *Right:* The descriptions produced for a test environment (the robot in the center). Each colored area has the same reference object and the intensity corresponds to one of the four spatial relations, which are only shown for the drawer. Gray stands for "in between".

the requested object is, determines the actual direction. In the example, it is below the diagonal, and thus the requested object is "in front" of the reference object. In Fig. 2 (right) a visualization of generated descriptions is shown.

Behavior: The desired system behavior was modeled with SMACH [4], which is a library for designing complex task-level executives. SMACH is faster than other imperative scripting approaches or model-based task planners [5] and can be used by a task planning system as a procedure definition architecture. Here, four parallel state machine containers were implemented. Each container performs one of the following tasks: *Exploration, Object and Person Detection, Person Tracking* and *Object Finding.* Among the termination policies that SMACH provides to overrule an active state machine container by another one, preemption is used.

3 Evaluation

To evaluate the usability of IRMA, we conducted a user study[2] with 20 participants (8 female, 11 male, 1 not specified) of different nationalities and ages ranging from 20 to 50 years. The participants were proficient in English and their previous experience with robots varied significantly: 5 did not have any experience with robots, 10 had little experience and 5 were familiar with robots.

3.1 Experimental Setting

The user study took place in a living room environment, shown in Fig. 3. It consists of a couch, a table, a drawer and a shelf placed along walls and a setting of two chairs with a coffee table between them. The setting covered $3.7\,\text{m} \times 4.8\,\text{m}$.

---

[2] Our dataset is available at https://figshare.com/s/d949d3410df8db468f77 [30].

Fig. 3. *Left:* Setting and used objects. *Right:* Schematic map of all four object configurations used in the user study. The circle marked with the letter 'T' indicates the *trash can* and the circle marked with 'M' indicates the *milk carton*.

To provide consistent lighting conditions, all windows were shaded and artificial light was used. The room was mapped a priori to provide information about the layout and positions of static objects (i.e. furniture). Two objects, a *milk carton* and a *trash can*, can be moved within the environment.

The participants were introduced to the environment and the robot IRMA. After being informed about the available objects and tasks that can be requested, they were asked to interact with the robot. In particular, the participants were asked to speak in a moderately loud voice and to repeat their command if IRMA does not react within 5–10 s.

In each user study session, a participant performed 8 runs in total, where each run ends with the robot performing the command. After the first 4 runs, the placement of the objects within the room was changed. All object configurations used in the study are shown in Fig. 3 (right). After each run, the participants were asked to rate how satisfied they were with the performed action and how accurate the system was in their opinion. After the complete session, the participant filled out a questionnaire comprised of three parts: (1) the SUS questionnaire [6], which measures overall usability, (2) the GODSPEED questionnaire [2], which measures five key HRI aspects, namely *Anthropomorphism, Animacy, Likeability, Perceived Intelligence*, and *Perceived Safety*, and (3) additional questions regarding the overall performance of the system that were answered on a 5-point Likert scale [20].

3.2   Results

Overall, IRMA correctly understood the requested type of help in 82.9 % and the requested object in 92.1 % of all runs performed during the user study. We did not consider two runs that had to be aborted and six runs that were not performed due to network issues. The response time, which was measured for each individual run, is the time between the end of the user's request until IRMA finishes its task, i.e. either having moved in front of the object or having finished its verbal description. For all runs without repetitions, the average response time for the task *describe* is 10.1 s, whereas the average response time for the task *move* is 36.8 s. For the *move*-task the robot did not move in 19.5 % of the runs since it was already positioned close enough to the requested object. In the other cases the distance to the object was reduced, except for one run (out of 82 in total). The results of the user feedback are summarized in Table 1. IRMA achieves a mean SUS score of 77.3, which translates to a C on the *Grade Scale* and to a *Good* on the *Adjective Rating Scale* according to [7]. The achieved GODSPEED scores, which evaluate key HRI aspects, are shown in Table 1. IRMA was perceived as likeable by the participants (4.28). However, it received a comparatively low score for antropomorphism (2.95).

Table 1. User study results including the SUS score (on a scale 0–100 with 100 being the best), the GODSPEED scores, and the scores computed from the additional questions on a scale of 1–5 with 5 being the best score

SUS	Mean (±StD)	**Additional Questions**	Mean (±StD)
Score	77.3 (±15.3)	*Average over all runs*	
GODSPEED	Mean (±StD)	User Satisfaction	4.05 (±0.56)
Anthropomorphism	2.95 (±0.66)	Perceived Accuracy	4.15 (±0.56)
Animacy	3.19 (±0.70)	*Average over all sessions*	
Likeability	4.28 (±0.57)	Usefulness for Elderly	4.15 (±1.19)
Perceived Intelligence	3.61 (±0.69)	Intuitiveness	4.25 (±0.94)
Perceived Safety	3.86 (±0.48)	Enjoyment	4.21 (±0.83)

The mean user satisfaction is little correlated with the perceived quickness of response (correlation value of 0.35). No correlation could be found between the final distance of the robot from the queried object and the satisfaction (0.0) or accuracy (-0.13) perceived by the user for a *move*-task.

The users' satisfaction and assessment of accuracy are consistent for all four object configurations used, as shown in Fig. 4 (left). The standard deviation for the settings are roughly the same and they overlap across all settings. This indicates further that no setting was significantly better or worse than the others. The slightly lower value in the accuracy rating for Config 4 is most likely due to the central position of the milk carton, see Fig. 3 (right). The central position of the *milk carton* might make the usefulness of the system seem less valuable due to the obvious placement of the object. Also, after completion of the *move*-task, the robot was on average further away from the milk carton, whereas it got very close to the trash can. This interpretation can be justified by Fig. 4 (right) which shows lower accuracy ratings for the runs including the *milk carton* compared to the runs including the *trash can*, especially for the *move*-task.

Although the participants were informed in advance about the possible tasks IRMA can perform, in 5.2 % of all runs users used commands like "bring" or "get me" to instruct the robot. 3.6 % of all sentences include other object references (e.g. "Is the milk carton left or right from you?" or "Is the milk

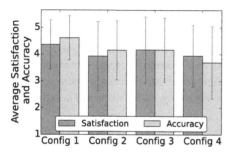 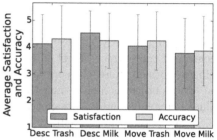

Fig. 4. *Left*: User satisfaction and accuracy scores for each object configuration *Right*: User satisfaction and accuracy scores for each individual task in Config 4

box on the table?"). Also, in 1.3 % two tasks were requested within one sentence and in 1.9 % anaphora were used. In total, in 13.5 % of all sentences, the user asked IRMA for something that it was not able to understand or perform.

The number of times a user had to repeat a phrase until IRMA understood the command had a negative impact on his satisfaction, as shown in Fig. 5 (left). IRMA understood 50.7 % of the instructions on the first try, while only 11.4 % of the instructions had to be repeated more than two times. However, the assessment of accuracy does not seem to be affected by the number of repeats.

Figure 5 (right) shows that the subjective rating of IRMA's intuitiveness as well as the user's enjoyment increased with how often the robot identified the task and object requested by the user correctly. The relation between the number of utterances that IRMA misinterpreted and the resulting intuitiveness (significantly worse only for 3 sentences) and enjoyment scores can be seen in this plot. The number of misinterpreted commands is correlated with intuitiveness and enjoyment, with the correlation coefficients being -0.54 and -0.51 respectively. It also turns out that the correct object being identified by the robot is more important for the satisfaction of the users than the intended task being

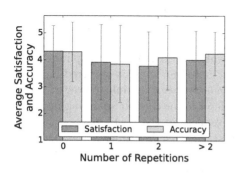 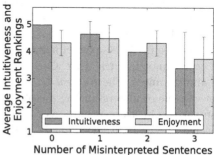

Fig. 5. *Left*: User satisfaction and accuracy scores versus the number of times a user had to repeat himself until a reaction of the robot was observed *Right*: The number of sentences misunderstood by IRMA versus the intuitiveness and enjoyment scores

performed by the robot. While the correlation coefficient for user satisfaction and correct object is 0.57, the correlation for user satisfaction and correct task is only 0.29. Similarly, the users perceive the performance of the robot as more accurate if the correct object is being identified compared to the correct task being performed. Here, the correlation coefficient for the perceived accuracy and the correct object is higher than the one for accuracy and correct task, with the values being 0.56 and 0.25 respectively.

Table 2 shows that all subjective factors obtained in the user study, such as satisfaction and accuracy, are uncorrelated to the previous experience the participants have had with robotics. The highest correlation value with experience with robots exists for a GODSPEED aspect, namely animacy, with still a low value of −0.29.

Table 2. Results of the correlation between the users' prior experience with robots and SUS, GS (GODSPEED) and additional subjective factors

Correlation	Experience		
		User Satisfaction	−0.28
SUS:Score	0.22	Perceived Accuracy	−0.25
GS:Anthropomorphism	0.02	Usefulness for Elderly	0.06
GS:Animacy	−0.29	Intuitiveness	0.08
GS:Likeability	0.10	Enjoyment	0.09
GS:Perceived Intelligence	−0.20	Perceived Quickness	−0.09
GS:Perceived Safety	0.02	Time Acceptable	0.00

4   Discussion

In general, IRMA performs well and achieves a high user satisfaction. However, there are certain parts of the system that can still be improved in future studies. The rotation of the robot was confusing to many participants. Firstly, *Person Detection* sometimes recognized false positives in a very cluttered environment and thus, the robot stopped rotating at the wrong time. Secondly, participants were not aware that the robot is trying to locate the user and sometimes misinterpreted this behavior as a "reaction" to their request.

Also, sometimes participants used sentences containing anaphora (e.g. "I still cannot find the milk. Can you show *it* to me?"). This occurred in 1.9 % of all utterances. The *Natural Language Understanding* module, however, is not yet capable of understanding anaphoric references or context spanning multiple sentences. On average only every second request of the participants was performed by the IRMA system. In many cases, *Speech Recognition* was not able to recognize the sentence correctly. This might be due to the microphone not being clearly directed towards the user, as person tracking stopped too early. Moreover, in 21 % of all recognized sentences, the sentences contained either an object or a task that was different from what was actually requested by the user. The results show that a wrongly understood object has more impact on the user satisfaction than a wrongly chosen task (*describe* or *move*). This is because the position of the wrong object is not of interest to the user, while performing the wrong task with the correct object is still helpful.

Most people preferred one of the capabilities over the other (40 % *move*, 55 % *describe*, 5 % neither-nor), which shows that it is useful to have both capabilities in our scenario. However, the fact that users often expected the robot to interact more with the environment and bring the object directly to them, indicates that this additional task might be a more helpful form of assistance to the user when compared to the *move*-task alone. The assistance could further be enhanced by other tasks, e.g. with a reminder functionality for taking medicine. One reason for the higher preference of the *describe*-task might be that the average response time for the *describe*-task took only about 25% of the time required for the completion of the *move*-task. Additionally, description tasks were rated with a higher accuracy (4.3) compared to movement tasks (4.02).

The results of our user study show that the previous experience of the users with robots has little influence on how they rated the system. In combination with a relatively high satisfaction score of 4.05 (on a scale from 1–5 with 5 being the best), this indicates that our system is intuitive to use. Moreover, the average response time for a *describe*-task only takes 10.1 s. Assuming that a search by the user without external help would take longer than 10 s, IRMA can save valuable time and effort of the user locating misplaced belongings.

5   Conclusion

IRMA is a stand-alone robotic system designed to help people in finding lost objects. Several state-of-the-art methods and frameworks have been integrated to enable an easy, robust and natural human-robot interaction. IRMA has the ability to explore the environment, detect objects and remember their positions. It can also describe the location of objects using natural language and is able to move to a specified object, when the user asks to do so using natural phrases (e.g. direct and indirect questions as well as imperative statements).

The results of our user study with 20 participants show that the system is able to accomplish its task to an average satisfaction rate of the user of 4.05 on a scale from 1–5 with 5 being the best. IRMA is able to identify the intention of the user for every second sentence that has been naturally uttered by the participants, and perform the corresponding task successfully. As the average response time for a successful description of the object's position is 10.1 s on average, IRMA can save time for users, especially elderly, finding a misplaced belonging. IRMA has also shown to be intuitive to use, as the user's previous experience with robots has no influence on the subjective evaluation of the system.

Acknowledgments. The authors gratefully acknowledge partial support from the German Research Foundation DFG under project CML (TRR 169), the European Union under project SECURE (No 642667), and the Hamburg Landesforschungsförderungsprojekt.

References

1. Barla, A., Odone, F., Verri, A.: Histogram intersection kernel for image classification. In: International Conference on Image Processing (ICIP), vol. 3, pp. 513–516. IEEE (2003)
2. Bartneck, C., Kulić, D., Croft, E., Zoghbi, S.: Measurement instruments for the anthropomorphism, animacy, likeability, perceived intelligence, and perceived safety of robots. Int. J. Social Robot. **1**(1), 71–81 (2008)
3. Beer, J.M., Smarr, C.A., Chen, T.L., Prakash, A., Mitzner, T.L., Kemp, C.C., Rogers, W.A.: The domesticated robot: design guidelines for assisting older adults to age in place. In: Annual ACM/IEEE International Conference on Human-Robot Interaction, HRI 2012, pp. 335–342. ACM/IEEE (2012)
4. Bohren, J., Cousins, S.: The SMACH high-level executive. IEEE Robot. Autom. Mag. **17**(4), 18–20 (2010)
5. Bohren, J., Rusu, R.B., Jones, E.G., Marder-Eppstein, E., Pantofaru, C., Wise, M., Mösenlechner, L., Meeussen, W., Holzer, S.: Towards autonomous robotic butlers: lessons learned with the PR2. In: IEEE International Conference on Robotics and Automation (ICRA), pp. 5568–5575. IEEE (2011)
6. Brooke, J.: SUS - a quick and dirty usability scale. In: Usability Evaluation in Industry, pp. 189–194. Taylor & Francis (1996)
7. Brooke, J.: SUS: a retrospective. J. Usability Stud. **8**(2), 29–40 (2013)
8. Cheng, Y.: Mean shift, mode seeking, and clustering. IEEE Trans. Pattern Anal. Mach. Intell. **17**(8), 790–799 (1995)
9. Cortes, C., Vapnik, V.: Support-vector networks. Mach. Learn. **20**(3), 273–297 (1995)
10. Deyle, T., Reynolds, M.S., Kemp, C.C.: Finding and navigating to household objects with UHF RFID tags by optimizing RF signal strength. In: 2014 IEEE/RSJ International Conference on Intelligent Robots and Systems, pp. 2579–2586, September 2014
11. Fasola, J., Mataric, M.: A socially assistive robot exercise coach for the elderly. J. Hum.-Robot Interact. **2**(2), 3–32 (2013)
12. Fei-Fei, L., Perona, P.: A Bayesian hierarchical model for learning natural scene categories. In: IEEE Computer Society Conference on Computer Vision and Pattern Recognition (CVPR), vol. 2, pp. 524–531. IEEE (2005)
13. Foster, M.E., Gaschler, A., Giuliani, M., Isard, A., Pateraki, M., Petrick, R.P.: Two people walk into a bar: dynamic multi-party social interaction with a robot agent. In: ACM International Conference on Multimodal Interaction, pp. 3–10. ICMI, ACM (2012)
14. Fox, D.: Adapting the sample size in particle filters through KLD-sampling. Int. J. Robot. Res. **22**(12), 985–1003 (2003)
15. Graf, B., Reiser, U., Hägele, M., Mauz, K., Klein, P.: Robotic home assistant care-O-bot 3 - product vision and innovation platform. In: IEEE Workshop on Advanced Robotics and its Social Impacts, pp. 139–144. IEEE (2009)
16. Guo, B., Imai, M.: Home-explorer: search, localize and manage the physical artifacts indoors. In: International Conference on Advanced Information Networking and Applications (AINA), pp. 378–385. IEEE (2007)
17. Hinaut, X., Petit, M., Pointeau, G., Dominey, P.F.: Exploring the acquisition and production of grammatical constructions through human-robot interaction with echo state networks. Front. Neurorobotics **8**, 16 (2014)

18. Lazebnik, S., Schmid, C., Ponce, J.: Beyond bags of features: spatial pyramid matching for recognizing natural scene categories. In: IEEE Computer Society Conference on Computer Vision and Pattern Recognition (CVPR), vol. 2, pp. 2169–2178. IEEE (2006)
19. Levenshtein, V.: Binary codes capable of correcting deletions, insertions and reversals. Sov. Phys. Dokl. **10**, 707 (1966)
20. Likert, R.: A Technique for the Measurement of Attitudes. Archives of Psychology (1932)
21. Lowe, D.G.: Distinctive image features from scale-invariant keypoints. Int. J. Comput. Vis. **60**(2), 91–110 (2004)
22. Murray, J., Wermter, S., Erwin, H.: Auditory robotic tracking of sound sources using hybrid cross-correlation and recurrent networks. In: IEEE/RSJ International Conference on Intelligent Robots and Systems (IROS), pp. 3554–3559. IEEE (2005)
23. Palmer, M., Gildea, D., Xue, N.: Semantic role labeling. Synth. Lect. Hum. Lang. Technol. **3**(1), 1–103 (2010)
24. Parisi, G.I., Bauer, J., Strahl, E., Wermter, S.: A multi-modal approach for assistive humanoid robots. In: Workshop on Multimodal and Semantics for Robotics Systems (MuSRobS), vol. 1540, pp. 10–15. CEUR Workshop Proceedings (2015)
25. Quigley, M., Gerkey, B., Conley, K., Faust, J., Foote, T., Leibs, J., Berger, E., Wheeler, R., Ng, A.: ROS: an open-source robot operating system. In: ICRA Workshop on Open Source Software, vol. 3, p. 6 (2009)
26. Rosenthal-von der Pütten, A.M., Krämer, N.C.: How design characteristics of robots determine evaluation and uncanny valley related responses. Comput. Hum. Behav. **36**, 422–439 (2014)
27. Twiefel, J., Baumann, T., Heinrich, S., Wermter, S.: Improving domain-independent cloud-based speech recognition with domain-dependent phonetic post-processing. In: AAAI Conference on Artificial Intelligence, vol. 28, pp. 1529–1535. AAAI Press (2014)
28. Viola, P., Jones, M.: Rapid object detection using a boosted cascade of simple features. In: IEEE Computer Society Conference on Computer Vision and Pattern Recognition (CVPR), vol. 1, pp. 511–518. IEEE (2001)
29. Wieser, I., Toprak, S., Grenzing, A., Hinz, T., Auddy, S., Karaoğuz, E.C., Chandran, A., Remmels, M., El Shinawi, A., Josifovski, J., Vankadara, L.C., Ul Wahab, F., Bahnemiri, A.M., Sahu, D., Heinrich, S., Navarro-Guerrero, N., Strahl, E., Twiefel, J., Wermter, S.: A Robotic Home Assistant with Memory Aid Functionality, video. IEEE RO-MAN 2016. https://www.informatik.uni-hamburg.de/wtm/videos/VideoSubmission_UniHamburgWTM_RO-MAN2016.mp.4. Accepted May 2016
30. Wieser, I., Toprak, S., Grenzing, A., Hinz, T., Auddy, S., Karaoğuz, E.C., Chandran, A., Remmels, M., El Shinawi, A., Josifovski, J., Vankadara, L.C., Ul Wahab, F., Bahnemiri, A.M., Sahu, D., Heinrich, S., Navarro-Guerrero, N., Strahl, E., Twiefel, J., Wermter, S.: Dataset for "A Robotic Home Assistant with Memory Aid Functionality", May 2016. https://figshare.com/s/d949d3410df8db468f77

Technical Communication

Using Ontological Knowledge About Active Pharmaceutical Ingredients for a Decision Support System in Medical Cancer Therapy

Christoph Beierle[1(✉)], Lewin Eisele[1], Gabriele Kern-Isberner[2],
Ralf Georg Meyer[3], and Mathias Nietzke[3]

[1] Department of Computer Science, University of Hagen, 58084 Hagen, Germany
christoph.beierle@fernuni-hagen.de
[2] Department of Computer Science, TU Dortmund, 44221 Dortmund, Germany
[3] St.-Johannes-Hospital Dortmund, 44137 Dortmund, Germany

Abstract. The number of parameters leading to a defined medical cancer therapy is growing rapidly. A clinical decision support system intended for better managing the resulting complexity must be able to reason about the respective active ingredients and their interrelationships. In this paper, we present a corresponding ontology and illustrate its use for answering queries relevant for clinical therapy decisions.

1 Introduction

For the medicamentous therapy of cancer, a large variety of different active pharmaceutical ingredients is available. Typically, several of these ingredients are combined in a therapy and are applied to the patient according to a given temporal scheme. For determining a patients's therapy, several important aspects originating from different information resources have to be taken into account. In particular, this includes the current medical guidelines regarding the present cancer type, the individual situation of the patient, and the molecular factors of the tumor.

The parameters leading to a defined therapy are rapidly changing for multiple reasons. Many new drugs representing new therapeutic strategies have come to the clinic during the last five years and their number is constantly increasing. In addition, the knowledge of individual properties of each individual tumor is facilitated by new molecular technologies. These developments lead to a rapid diversification and individualization of tumor therapy. Many attempts are undertaken to manage this ongoing informational diversification. Over the last 15 years, the pharmaceutical department together with the clinic of Oncology of the St.-Johannes-Hospital Dortmund has developed an electronic support system containing treatment plans for more than 2.300 individual treatment situations. These plans are provided together with all necessary information on co-medication, behavioral rules and explanations for the patient. In addition, the system documents all therapies of more than 40.000 therapeutical cycles with the information of actual application, dose modifications, and tumor-board

© Springer International Publishing AG 2016
G. Friedrich et al. (Eds.): KI 2016, LNAI 9904, pp. 119–125, 2016.
DOI: 10.1007/978-3-319-46073-4_9

decisions. In an ongoing project, these data together with advanced knowledge representation and reasoning methods from computer science are the basis of an approach for the development of a comprehensive AI-based tool to support decision making taking into account all available clinical as well as molecular information of each patient and his tumor. Part of this project is the development of an ontology providing general knowledge about active ingredients and their interrelationships in medical cancer therapy that can be used by such a clinical decision support system. The purpose of this paper is to give a short overview of the ontology OCTA (Ontology for Cancer Therapy Application) we have developed and implemented. We will also illustrate how OCTA, whose current focus is the therapy of breast cancer, can be used to answer queries relevant for clinical therapy decisions.

This paper is organized as follows: We first present the requirements guiding the development of OCTA and describe its main concepts and roles in Sect. 2, deal with answering queries in Sect. 3, and discuss related work, conclude, and point out further developments in Sect. 4.

2   Ontology Development

OCTA was developed in OWL using Protégé http://protege.stanford.edu, and for reasoning, Pellet was used [10].

2.1   Requirements

The overall objective of the ontology to be developed is to provide general knowledge about active ingredients and their interrelationships in medical cancer therapy that can be used by a clinical decision support system. Therefore, the ontology should enable the answering of the following kinds of queries:

- Which active ingredients belong to a particular therapy regimen? What is the administered dose of the active ingredients?
- Which therapy regimens contain a particular active ingredient? Which therapy regimens contain an active ingredient from a particular class of active ingredients?
- What are the regular doses of the active ingredients of a particular therapy regimen, given the patient's body surface area?
- Which therapy regimens contain active ingredients within a specific toxicity profile?
- What is the cumulative dose of an active ingredient that has been administered to the patient within the treatment?
- How much of the maximal cumulative dose of an active ingredient has been administered to a patient within the treatment?

2.2   Core Concepts and Roles

The active ingredients employed in medical cancer therapy can be classified in different ways. There are cytotoxic substances that disturb physiological processes of the cell, thus influencing other somatic cells. On the other hand, specific cell structures of the tumor are attacked by so-called *targeted therapies*. For instance, there is an increased occurrence of the protein HER2/neu in the cell membrane of the tumor cells in a subset of patients suffering from breast cancer [7],[1] and the monoclonal antibody trastuzumab is a targeted therapy that interferes with the HER2/neu receptor. A further therapy category is given by the anti-hormonal therapy. Within the different therapy categories, further subcategories can be identified. For instance, cytostatic drugs can be differentiated according to their mechanism of action, and targeted therapies can be categorized by the target structures of the cell. Furthermore, the active ingredients used in cancer therapy may have severe adverse effects regarding e.g. the cardiovascular system or the neurological system. Thus, the toxicity of an active ingredient can be subcategorized according to its toxicity with respect to the particular organ systems. We

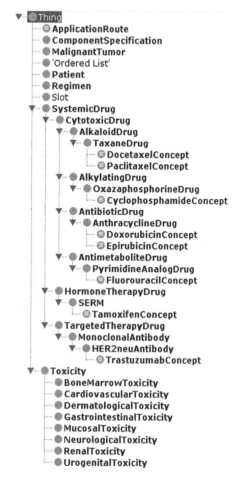

Fig. 1. Part of the concept hierarchy of the ontology OCTA

developed the concept hierarchy in the ontology OCTA along these lines. Part of the resulting concept hierarchy is shown in Fig. 1.

When a malignant tumor is diagnosed and indication for medical cancer therapy is given, the patient is administered drugs with the corresponding active ingredients. These drugs are associated with the treatment of the given tumor type. Accordingly, the classes *Patient* and *MalignantTumor* were defined, together with the relation *diagnosedWith*.

---

[1] All examples in this paper will focus on the treatment of breast cancer.

2.3 Therapy Regimens

In medical cancer therapy, usually a combination of active ingredients, called a *therapy regimen* , is administered. Particular therapy regimens are employed for specific tumor entities, where the dose of each active ingredient mainly depends on the body surface area of a patient. Figure 2 illustrates the FEC regimen which is used for the treatment of breast cancer [4]; it contains three different cytotoxic substances.

Typically, therapy regimens are administered in cycles. For instance, according to the FEC regimen, the cytotoxic substances are administered on day 1 of a cycle. Thus, for a cycle of 21 days, the 22nd day will be the first day of the next cycle. The dose of each active ingredient has to be computed at the beginning of each cycle since the body surface area of the patient may have changed.

For modelling therapy regimens in the ontology, the class [2] *Regimen* is introduced. Via the property *hasComponent*, each of its instances may be connected to one or to several instances of the class *ComponentSpecification*. Using the property *hasDrug*, each instance of *ComponentSpecification* can be connected to the corresponding active ingredient. Figure 3 shows (part of) the resulting ontology representation of the FEC regimen.

active ingredient	day	dose	route of administration	infusion time
cyclophosphamide	1	500 mg/m^2	intravenous	1h
epirubicin	1	100 mg/m^2	intravenous	15min
5-fluorouracil	1	500 mg/m^2	intravenous	1h

Fig. 2. Example of a therapy regimen: the FEC regimen

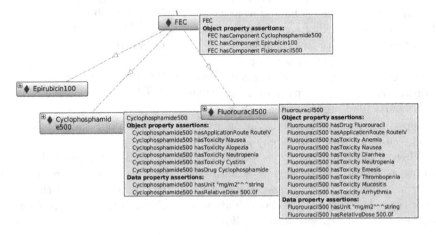

Fig. 3. Ontology representation of the FEC regimen

---

[2] In the OWL context, often the terms *class* and *property* are used instead of *concept* and *role*. In the following, we will often adopt this wording.

In order to model the fact that if an active ingredient being connected to a component via *hasDrug* it should also be considered to be connected to the *Regimen* instance having a *hasComponent* property with respect to this component, OWL *propertyChain* axioms are used. E.g., in the presence of the triples[3]

```
ctx:FEC ctx:hasComponent ctx:Cyclophosphamide500.
ctx:Cyclophosphamide500 ctx:hasDrug ctx:Cyclophosphamide.
```

a reasoner will be able to infer that the FEC regimen contains the active ingredient cyclophosphamide although this is represented only indirectly.

For modelling that specific toxicities are typical for an active ingredient or a class of active ingredients, the property *hasToxicity* is used. *hasRelativeDose* indicates the dose with respect to the body surface area, and *hasApplicationRoute* points to the route of application, e.g., *RouteIV* for intravenous (cf. Fig. 3). The cumulative dose of a certain active ingredient administered to a patient must not be higher than a certain maximal level. For instance, for doxorubicin the maximal cumulative dose is $550\,mg/m^2$, and for epirubicin it is $850\,mg/m^2$ [2]; thus, a patient with body surface area $1.7\,m^2$ must not be administered more than $550\,mg \times 1.7 = 935\,mg$ doxorubicin. This is modelled using the property *hasCumulativeDose* connecting an active ingredient to the corresponding maximal cumulative dose.

3   SPARQL Queries

For answering the kind of questions outlined in Sect. 2.1, SPARQL (http://www. w3.org/TR/rdf/sparql-query/) is used. Factual evidence was added to the ontology OCTA as facts represented by RDF triples. The facts are expressed in a separate name space with prefix `joho:`, while the prefix `ctx:` is used for the original ontology. For combining factual and ontological knowledge, we used the semantic web framework Jena together with the reasoner Pellet. For executing SPARQL queries the ARQ application API provided by the Jena framework was employed. In the following, we present some SPARQL queries along with the computed answers as obtained as output from a Java test program.

For illustration purposes, we assume that there are just two (fictitious) patients Testpat1 and Testpat2. Testpat1 has been administered a single cycle of the TAC regimen, while Testpat2 has been diagnosed with two malignant tumors and has been administered two cycles of the FEC regimen and a single cycle of the TAC regimen. The SPARQL query shown in Fig. 4(a) asks for all patients that have been administered alkaloids. While no information about alkaloids is present in the factual knowledge, the reasoner is able to infer that the TAC regimen contains docetaxel (cf. the chain axioms in Sect. 2.3). From the concept hierarchy, the reasoner infers that docetaxel belongs to the group of taxanes, and that taxanes are alkaloids. Thus, since both patients have been administered the TAC regimen, they are both returned in the result of the query.

---

[3] For the representation of RDF triples we use the turtle syntax, cf. http://www.w3. org/TR/turtle.

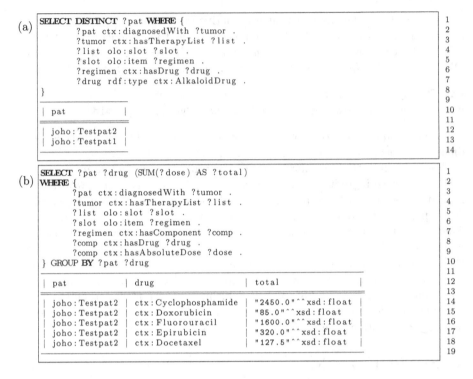

Fig. 4. Queries (a) asking for all patients having been administered alkaloids, and (b) asking for the cumulative dose for patients diagnosed with a tumor.

The query in Fig. 4(b) asks for the cumulative dose of the active ingredients administered to patients diagnosed with a tumor, returning the absolute doses. For patients that have been administered anthracyclines in the past and that are intended to be administered a therapy regimen containing anthracyclines, the remaining admissible dose must be computed, taking into account the current cumulative doses of all kinds of anthracycline. Our system is also able to determine this information. For instance, for a corresponding query, the system might answer that Testpat2 has already been administered 31.2 % of the maximal cumulative dose of anthracyclines. Similarly, all other question types sketched in Sect. 2.1 can be processed by the system.

4   Related Work, Conclusions, and Further Development

There are several ontologies related to OCTA. The objective of the ontology GO [1] is to provide a standardized vocabulary for the annotation of genes. The ontology ChEBI [3] classifies biologically interesting molecules, focussing on chemical, biochemical, and structural properties of the molecules. The NCI thesaurus [9] is a controlled vocabulary aiming at the support of adiministrative and scientific activities. SNOMED CT [5,6] and GALEN [8] also provide standardized terminologies for medical terms. Whereas all these ontologies cover various aspects belonging to the area of medical cancer therapy, none of them addresses the specific point of view of clinical therapy decisions as in OCTA.

We presented the main features of the OCTA ontology and illustrated its use for answering queries relevant for clinical therapy decisions. The development of OCTA is part of an ongoing project aiming at the realization of a clinical decision support system in medical cancer therapy. While the current focus of OCTA is the therapy of breast cancer, further tumor entities are addressed in our ongoing work. Another aspect of further work is the investigation of how modifications of the ontology induced e.g. by a newly developed active ingredient can be adequately supported.

References

1. Ashburner, M., Ball, C.A., Blake, J.A., Botstein, D., Butler, H., Cherry, J.M., Davis, A.P., Dolinski, K., Dwight, S.S., Eppig, J.T., Harris, M.A., Hill, D.P., Issel-Tarver, L., Kasarskis, A., Lewis, S., Matese, J.C., Richardson, J.E., Ringwald, M., Rubin, G.M., Sherlock, G.: Gene ontology: tool for the unification of biology. Nat. Genet. **25**(1), 25–29 (2000)
2. Berger, D., Engelhardt, R., Mertelsmann, R.: Das Rote Buch. Eco-med Medizin (2010)
3. de Matos, P., Alcántara, R., Dekker, A., Ennis, M., Hastings, J., Haug, K., Spiteri, I., Turner, S., Steinbeck, C.: Chemical entities of biological interest: an update. Nucleic Acids Res. **38**(Database–Issue), 249–254 (2010)
4. French Adjuvant Study Group. Benefit of a high-dose epirubicin regimen in adjuvant chemotherapy for node-positive breast cancer patients with poor prognostic factors: 5-year follow-up results of French Adjuvant Study Group 05 randomized trial. J. Clin. Oncol. **19**(3), 602–611 (2001)
5. Lee, D., Cornet, R., Lau, F., De Keizer, N.: A survey of SNOMED CT implementations. J Biomed. Inf. **46**(1), 87–96 (2013)
6. Lee, D., De Keizer, N., Lau, F., Cornet, R.: Literature review of SNOMED CT use. J. Am. Med. Inf. Assoc. **21**, e11–e19 (2014)
7. Ménard, S., Tagliabue, E., Campiglio, M., Pupa, S.: Role of HER2 gene overexpression in breast carcinoma. J. Cell Physiol. **182**(2), 150–162 (2000)
8. Rector, A.L., Nowlan, W.A., Glowinski, A.: Goals for concept representation in the GALEN project. In: Proceedings of the Annual Symposium on Computer Application in Medical Care, pp. 414–418 (1993)
9. Sioutos, N., de Coronado, S., Haber, M.W., Hartel, F.W., Shaiu, W.-L., Wright, L.W.: NCI Thesaurus: a semantic model integrating cancer-related clinical and molecular information. J. Biomed. Inf. **40**(1), 30–43 (2007)
10. Sirin, E., Parsia, B., Grau, B.C., Kalyanpur, A., Katz, Y.: Pellet: a practical OWL-DL reasoner. J. Web Sem. **5**(2), 51–53 (2007)

Solving Negotiation Problems Against Unknown Opponents with Wisdom of Crowds

Siqi Chen[1(✉)], Gerhard Weiss[2], and Shuang Zhou[2]

[1] School of Computer and Information Science,
Southwest University, Chongqing, China
siqi.chen09@gmail.com
[2] Department of Knowledge Engineering,
Maastricht University, Maastricht, The Netherlands
{gerhard.weiss,shuang.zhou}@maastrichtuniversity.nl

Abstract. For a successful automated negotiation, a vital issue is how well the agent can learn the latent preferences of opponents. Opponents however in most practical cases would be unwilling to reveal their true preferences for exploitation reasons. Existing approaches tend to resolve this issue by learning opponents through their observations during negotiation. While useful, it is hard because of the indirect way the target function can be observed as well as the limited amount of experience available to learn from. This situation becomes even worse when it comes to negotiation problems with large outcome space. In this work, a new model is proposed in which the agents can not only negotiate with others, but also provide information (e.g., labels) about whether an offer is accepted or rejected by a specific agent. In particular, we consider that there is a crowd of agents that can present labels on offers for certain payment; moreover, the collected labels are assumed to be noisy, due to the lack of expert knowledge and/or the prevalence of spammers, etc. Therefore to respond to the challenges, we introduce a novel negotiation approach that (1) adaptively sets the aspiration level on the basis of estimated opponent concession; (2) assigns labeling tasks to the crowd using online primal-dual techniques, such that the overall budget can be both minimized with sufficiently low errors; (3) decides, at every stage of the negotiation, the best possible offer to be proposed.

1 Introduction

Negotiation has traditionally been investigated in game theory [17,18], and in previous years it has also developed into a core topic of multiagent systems [1,5,15,16,20]. Generally speaking, it is a process by which parties of conflicting interests try to reach a mutually acceptable agreement [13]. In many cases, it is however expensive and low efficient mainly because humans find the activity challenging, stressful as well as time-consuming. Thus, to alleviate huge negotiation efforts of humans, autonomous agents are proposed that perform, on behalf of humans, complicated negotiation tasks in a efficient manner. Automated negotiation also provides one of the most fundamental and powerful mechanisms for

© Springer International Publishing AG 2016
G. Friedrich et al. (Eds.): KI 2016, LNAI 9904, pp. 126–133, 2016.
DOI: 10.1007/978-3-319-46073-4_10

intelligent systems, e.g., managing inter-agent dependencies, coordination and cooperation. With the rapid development of automated negotiation in recent decades, it has successfully gained a broad spectrum of applications in industrial and commercial domains [6,10,19,20].

The driving force of negotiating agents is governed by its (hidden) preferences through its (hidden) negotiation strategy [4]. By exploiting the preferences and/or strategy of opposing agents, better final (or cumulative) agreement terms can be reached [3]. Existing literature [7–9,11] attempts to achieve that by means of learning the behavior/preferences of opponents through observations of opponent negotiation moves. Although useful, learning an opposing agent's model is not efficient, mainly because: (1) the opponent preference can only be observed indirectly through offer exchanges (e.g., our rejected offers and opponent counter offers), (2) the absence of prior information about opponent strategy/preferences, and (3) the confinement of the interaction number/time in single negotiation sessions. Apparently, this kind of learning methods somehow restrict agents' learning ability.

Thus, we consider a general negotiation model in which automated agents not only carry out negotiation with others, but also provide advice (e.g., in terms of binary label) on whether an offer is accepted or rejected by a specific agent in a ongoing negotiation, according their knowledge and experience. Each label on offers from the crowd is associated with a certain (but low) cost, while the overall budget is limited; moreover, the collected labels are assumed to be noisy, due to labeling agents' lack of expert knowledge regarding negotiation problems or the target agents, and the prevalence of spam, etc. That is to say, each agent may have different and unknown reliability. Therefore to infer the true labels from the non-expert crowd, an assignment strategy is needed to allocate tasks to the crowd, to minimize the labeling budget, while guaranteeng sufficiently low errors. With the labels in hand, the negotiating agent is more likely to make decisions toward reaching efficient agreements.

2   Negotiation Approach

The actions of the agent at each time point should take into account, (1) the aspiration level, which governs the minimum amount of expected satisfaction from negotiation at a time point, and (2) what offer to accept or reject given that. The decision-making process is decomposed into two stages – aspiration setting (AS) component and offer responding (OR) component, which are essential and vital for the agent to operate successfully. The aspiration setting (AS) component is described. It adopts a non-parametric and computationally efficient regression technique in order to approximate the opponent's negotiation strategy. This allows the agent to have accurate estimates that are used to adjust its own aspiration level. The second stage of the approach (i.e., the offer responding (OR) component) deals with how to respond to those counter-offers and determines what counter-offer to send out if not satisfied with proposals from opponents.

When selecting offers of interest, the agent adopts an adaptive assignment strategy to ask information from the crowd so that the preferences of opponents over offers could be well learnt. Next, each of the above components is detailed.

2.1 Aspiration Setting Component

As opponent strategies are unavailable to the agent, it may be beneficial to adaptively set aspiration level R(t) according to negotiation dynamics, which specifies the lowest utility expectation of the agent. Toward this end, we adopt Gaussian process to obtain opponent strategy in terms received concession, which is proved to be successful in a variety of negotiation scenarios [4,8], while we refine a simplified version here to get rid of tuning a bunch of parameters (overfitting).

The agent uses the expected received utility $E_{(}t)$ in its decision making. This utility, which corresponds to the expectation of how much profit can be received from an opponent at some future time $t_\star$, is defined by:

$$E(t_\star) = \frac{t_\star}{NC} \int_{-\infty}^{+\infty} u \cdot f(u; \mu_\star, \sigma_\star) du \qquad (1)$$

where NC is a constant called normalizing constant, f is the probability density function of Gaussian distribution, and $\mu_\star$ and $\sigma_\star$ are the mean and standard deviation (both obtained from GPs) at $t_\star$. Unlike the approach described in [21], which truncates the probability distribution to $[0,1]$, the agent preserves the probability distribution by introducing the normalizing constant C.

$$R(t) = u_{\text{res}} + (U_{\max} - u_{\text{res}})(1 - t)^\beta \qquad (2)$$

where $u_{\text{res}} = \min(\theta, \xi)$ (with ξ the maximal received concession), and concession coefficient controlling the concession rate is given by,

$$\beta = 1 - (\frac{E(t_\star)}{U_{\max}})^2 \qquad (3)$$

where $U_{\max}$ is the possible maximum utility in the scenario.

2.2 Offer Responding Component

Having obtained the aspiration level, the agent then needs to decide acceptance or rejection of opponent offers. If the opponent offer can provide a utility higher (or at least equal to) than the R(t), the agent agrees with the offer and the negotiation is finished successfully; otherwise, the agent should prepare a counter offer to continue the negotiation. The two steps are detailed next.

Negotiation Decision-Making. Given the expected utility of $R(t)$, the agent needs to examine one of two conditions in response to the opponent. In the first the agent has to validate whether the utility of the counter-offer $U(O_{opp})$ is better than u', while in the second the agent has to determine whether the opponent had already proposed this offer earlier in the negotiation process. If either one of these two conditions is satisfied, the agent accepts it and terminates the session as shown in line 12 of Algorithm 1.

Otherwise, if none of them are met, the agent proposes a new offer depending on an λ-greedy strategy. That is to select either a greedy action (i.e., exploit) with λ probability or to select a random action with a $1 - \lambda$ probability ($0 \leq \lambda \leq 1$). The greedy action is determined based on the advice of crowds, that is, labels of acceptance or rejection on offers provided by a large amount of related agents. Those agents either have negotiation experience with the agent's opponents or have certain domain knowledge. Unfortunately, the labels may be noisy due to the lacking expertise and/or different reliability among them. It usually makes labels generated by crowd suffer from low quality. Moreover, each label is produced at certain cost. In the next subsection, we will dive into details of how to adaptively assign tasks to crowded agents. With a probability λ, agent then picks the offer whose gets the best negotiation value.

In the case of the random action (probability $1 - \lambda$), the agent constructs a new offer which has an utility within some range around u'. The main motivation behind this choice is twofold: (1) it is possible, for multi-issue negotiations, to generate a number of offers whose utilities are the same or very similar to the offering agent, with granting the opposing negotiator different utilities, and (2) it is sometimes not possible to find an offer whose utility is exactly u'. Thus it is reasonable that an agent selects an offer whose utility is in the narrow range $[(1 - 0.005)u', (1 + 0.005)u']$. If no such solution can be found, the agent repeats sending the latest bid in the next round.

Adaptive Assignment Strategy. Crowdsourcing services, as a remedy for noisy labels, usually resort to labeling redundancy – collecting labels from different workers for each item [14,22]. A fundamental issue for crowdsourcing in negotiation is then raised: how to make crowdsourced task assignments such that it can output desired labels with sufficiently low error, while requesting as few labels from workers as possible. Toward this end, we apply the technique proposed in [2,12] to solve crowdsourced task assignment for automated negotiation setting. Prior to task assignment, the agent first decides upon which part of the outcome space to explore via crowdsourcing. In our approach, the exploration zone first excludes offers of utility below reservation value (θ) and offers of first K highest values (by sorting the possible outcomes according to our agent's own preferences), and then selects offers randomly from the remaining offers according to the given budget. When having collected enough opponent responses (i.e., gold standard tasks) placed by Algorithm 1, the agent begins online crowdsourcing task assignment (e.g., each agent's reliability is unknown). The main steps of assignment strategy is given below.

Before diving into details of the assignment strategy, we introduce a simple model to capture workers' reliability: each worker (agent) w_j is characterised by a reliability $p_{i,j} \in [0,1]$ for task t_i, and workers answer each question correct independently. Since errors are common among the low-paid workers, majority

Algorithm 1. Adaptive assignment strategy for negotiation tasks. s is the number of gold standard tasks. m is the number of workers, with n the number of tasks.

1: *Require:* $s, \overline{q}^*_{\min}, m, n$
2: **while** $K < s$ **do**
3:     *collect more offer responses;*
4:     *recordOffers(t_c, O_{opp});*
5: **end while**
6: pick up random γ percentage workers from m
7: calculate $\hat{q}_{i,j}$ for each agent in γ m
8: calculate $C_{\epsilon'}$ and obtain estimated task wight $\hat{x}^*$
9: **for** each agent j **do**
10:     calculate $\hat{q}_{i,j}$ using s gold standard tasks
11:     run primal approximation algorithm with $\hat{q}_{i,j}$ and $\hat{x}^*$
12:     assign agent j to tasks i if $y_{i,j} = 1$
13: **end for**
14: aggregate labels using weighted majority voting.
15: return labels

voting should be applied to their advice for a target reliability. Next, we show the error bound under this model using majority voting. Assume J_i is the set of workers assigned to task t_i, $X_{i,j}$ a random variable which represents the weighted label, with $w_{i,j}$ being the weight. Given a positive label (e.g., the value is 1), we have

$$X_{i,j} = \begin{cases} w_{i,j} & \text{with probability } p_{i,j}, \\ -w_{i,j} & \text{with probability } 1 - p_{i,j} \end{cases} \tag{4}$$

and $X_i = \Sigma_{j \in J_i} X_{i,j}$.

If $X_i \geq 0$ the task is predicted to have a label of 1, and 0 otherwise. Assume the true label is 1, bounding $P(X_i \geq 0)$ would give us a bound on the probability of an error. The expectation of X_i can be expressed as below,

$$\begin{aligned} E[X_i] &= \Sigma_{j \in J_i} E[X_{i,j}] \\ &= \Sigma_{j \in J_i} (p_{i,j} w_{i,j} - (1 - p_{i,j}) w_{i,j}) \\ &= \Sigma_{j \in J_i} (w_{i,j} (2p_{i,j} - 1)) \end{aligned} \tag{5}$$

Applying Hoeffding's inequality, we have

$$\begin{aligned} P(X_i \leq 0) &\leq exp(-\frac{2(E[X_i])^2}{\Sigma_{j \in J_i} (2w_{i,j})^2}) \\ &= exp(-\frac{(\Sigma_{j \in J_i} w_{i,j} (2p_{i,j} - 1))^2}{2\Sigma_{j \in J_i} w_{i,j}^2}) \end{aligned} \tag{6}$$

Obviously, this error bound is maximized when the right side of Eq. 6 is minimized. So, we set the gradient of this expression to 0.

Then, let $y_{i,j}$ be a variable to indicate the assignment of task t_i to worker w_j, with 1 representing positive and 0 negative. The requirement can be expressed as a linear constraint of these variables. This allows us to express the optimal assignment strategy as an integer linear program,

$$\min \ \sum_{i=1}^{n}\sum_{j=1}^{m} y_{i,j} \cdot \eta \qquad \qquad \text{(LP1)}$$

$$\text{s.t.} \ \sum_{i=1}^{n} y_{i,j} \leq M_j$$

$$\sum_{j=1}^{m} q_j y_{i,j} \geq C_\epsilon$$

$$y_{i,j} \in 0,1 \qquad \qquad \forall (i,j)$$

where η is the cost for each task. However, solving integer linear program requires the values q_j for each worker. It will be convenient to work with the dual of the linear program,

$$\max \ C_\epsilon \sum_{i=1}^{n} x_i - \sum_{j=1}^{m} M_j z_j - \sum_{i=1}^{n}\sum_{j=1}^{m} t_{i,j} \qquad \qquad \text{(LP2)}$$

$$\text{s.t.} \ 1 - q_{i,j} x_i + z_j + t_{i,j} \geq 0 \qquad \qquad \forall (i,j)$$

$$x_i, z_j, t_{i,j} \geq 0 \qquad \qquad \forall (i,j)$$

$$\tag{7}$$

Suppose that we were given access to the task weights x_i for each task i and the values $q_{i,j}$. Then we could use the following algorithm to approximate the optimal primal solution. Then, the agent should choose the offer whose utility not smaller than the utility indicated by $R(t_c)$, and whose label is positive, When needing to propose a counter-offer. If no such an offer can be found, the offer with the minimal utility (but not smaller than the utility indicated by $R(t_c)$) is proposed for greedy offer selection.

3   Conclusions

This work introduced a novel automated negotiation approach on the basis of opponent behavior prediction and crowdsourcing services. Opponent behavior prediction is captured by Gaussian processes to estimate future received concession, thereby governing the aspiration level function in an adaptive way. The deployment of crowdsourcing mechanism provides the agent with the wisdom of the noisy crowd, and using the assignment strategy, the labeling budget can be both minimized, while guaranteeing sufficiently low errors. It is clear that the agent is more efficient than the others due to a more advanced technical framework.

Acknowledgements. This work is supported by Southwest University and Fundamental Research Funds for the Central Universities (Grant number: SWU115032, XDJK2016C042). Special thanks also go to the anonymous reviewers of this article for their valuable comments.

References

1. Baarslag, T., Fujita, K., Gerding, E.H., Hindriks, K.V., Ito, T., Jennings, N.R., Jonker, C.M., Kraus, S., Lin, R., Robu, V., Williams, C.R.: Evaluating practical negotiating agents: results and analysis of the 2011 international competition. Artif. Intell. **198**, 73–103 (2013)
2. Buchbinder, N., Naor, J.: Online primal-dual algorithms for covering and packing. Math. Oper. Res. **34**(2), 270–286 (2009)
3. Chen, S., Ammar, H.B., Tuyls, K., Weiss, G.: Optimizing complex automated negotiation using sparse pseudo-input Gaussian processes. In: Proceedings of the 12th International Joint Conference on Autonomous Agents and Multi-agent Systems, Saint Paul, Minnesota, USA, pp. 707–714. ACM (2013)
4. Chen, S., Ammar, H.B., Tuyls, K., Weiss, G.: Using conditional restricted Boltzmann machine for highly competitive negotiation tasks. In: Proceedings of the 23th International Joint Conference on Artificial Intelligence, pp. 69–75. AAAI Press (2013)
5. Chen, S., Hao, J., Zili, Z., Weiss, G., Zhou, S.: Toward efficient agreements in real-time multilateral agent-based negotiations. In: 27th IEEE International Conference on Tools with Artificial Intelligence, pp. 896–903. IEEE Computer Society (2015)
6. Chen, S., Weiss, G.: An efficient and adaptive approach to negotiation in complex environments. In: Proceedings of the 20th European Conference on Artificial Intelligence, Montpellier, France, pp. 228–233. IOS Press (2012)
7. Chen, S., Weiss, G.: An efficient automated negotiation strategy for complex environments. Eng. Appl. Artif. Intell. **26**(10), 2613–2623 (2013)
8. Chen, S., Weiss, G.: An intelligent agent for bilateral negotiation with unknown opponents in continuous-time domains. ACM Trans. Auton. Adapt. Syst. **9**(3), 16:1–16:24 (2014)
9. Chen, S., Weiss, G.: An approach to complex agent-based negotiations via effectively modeling unknown opponents. Expert Syst. Appl. **42**(5), 2287–2304 (2015)
10. Duan, L., Dogru, M.K., Ozen, U., Beck, J.: A negotiation framework for linked combinatorial optimization problems. Expert Syst. Appl. **25**(1), 158–182 (2012)
11. Hao, J., Song, S., Leung, H.-F., Ming, Z.: An efficient and robust negotiating strategy in bilateral negotiations over multiple items. Eng. Appl. Artif. Intell. **34**, 45–57 (2014)
12. Ho, C.-J., Jabbari, S., Vaughan, J.W.: Adaptive task assignment for crowdsourced classification. In: Proceedings of the 30th International Conference on Machine Learning (ICML 2013), pp. 534–542 (2013)
13. Jennings, N.R., Faratin, P., Lomuscio, A.R., Parsons, S., Sierra, C., Wooldridge, M.: Automated negotiation: prospects, methods and challenges. Eng. Appl. Artif. Intell. **10**(2), 199–215 (2001)
14. Karger, D.R., Oh, S., Shah, D.: Iterative learning for reliable crowdsourcing systems. In: Advances in Neural Information Processing Systems, pp. 1953–1961 (2011)
15. Lopes, F., Wooldridge, M., Novais, A.: Negotiation among autonomous computational agents: principles, analysis and challenges. Artif. Intell. Rev. **29**, 1–44 (2008)

16. Mor, Y., Goldman, C.V., Rosenschein, J.S.: Learn your opponent's strategy (in polynomial time)!. In: Weiss, G., Sen, S. (eds.) IJCAI-WS 1995. LNCS, vol. 1042, pp. 164–176. Springer, Heidelberg (1996)

17. Osborne, M., Rubinstein, A.: A Course in Game Theory. MIT Press, Cambridge (1994)

18. Raiffa, H.: The Art and Science of Negotiation. Harvard University Press, Cambridge (1982)

19. Sanchez-Anguix, V., Julian, V., Botti, V., García-Fornes, A.: Tasks for agent-based negotiation teams: analysis, review, and challenges. Eng. Appl. Artif. Intell. **26**(10), 2480–2494 (2013)

20. Weiss, G. (ed.): Multiagent Systems, 2nd edn. MIT Press, Cambridge (2013)

21. Williams, C.R., Robu, V., Gerding, E.H., Jennings, N.R.: Negotiating concurrently with unkown opponents in complex, real-time domains. In: Proceedings of the 20th European Conference on Artificial Intelligence, pp. 834–839 (2012)

22. Zhang, Y., Chen, X., Zhou, D., Jordan, M.I.: Spectral methods meet EM: a provably optimal algorithm forcrowdsourcing. In: Advances in Neural Information Processing Systems, pp. 1260–1268 (2014)

Declarative Decomposition and Dispatching for Large-Scale Job-Shop Scheduling

Giacomo Da Col[✉] and Erich C. Teppan

Alpen-Adria-Universität Klagenfurt, Universitätsstr. 65-67,
9020 Klagenfurt, Austria
{giacomo.da,erich.teppan}@aau.at

Abstract. Job-shop scheduling problems constitute a big challenge in nowadays industrial manufacturing environments. Because of the size of realistic problem instances, applied methods can only afford low computational costs. Furthermore, because of highly dynamic production regimes, adaptability is an absolute must. In state-of-the-art production factories the large-scale problem instances are split into subinstances, and greedy dispatching rules are applied to decide which job operation is to be loaded next on a machine. In this paper we propose a novel scheduling approach inspired by those hand-crafted scheduling routines. Our approach builds on problem decomposition for keeping computational costs low, dispatching rules for effectiveness and declarative programming for high adaptability and maintainability. We present first results proving the concept of our novel scheduling approach based on a new large-scale job-shop benchmark with proven optimal solutions.

Keywords: Job-shop scheduling · Problem decomposition · Declarative programming

1   Introduction

The scheduling of jobs [6] is an important task in almost all production systems in order to optimize various objectives such as the makespan, i.e. the time needed to perform all the job operations. In general, jobs are structured into operations, which must be allocated to resources such that various manufacturing constraints are satisfied and in addition an objective function is minimized. The job-shop scheduling problem (JSP) and variants like the flexible job-shop problem (FJSP) are among the most famous $\mathcal{NP}$-hard [10] and longest studied combinatorial problems (e.g. [4]).

State-of-the-art search algorithms for JSP and FJSP are local search methods like tabu search [15] or large-neighborhood search [17]. However, without

The research for this paper was conducted in the scope of the project *Heuristic Intelligence (HINT)* in cooperation with Infineon Technologies Austria AG and Siemens AG Österreich funded by the Austrian research fund FFG under grant 840242. Authors are given in alphabetical order and contributed equally to this paper.

© Springer International Publishing AG 2016
G. Friedrich et al. (Eds.): KI 2016, LNAI 9904, pp. 134–140, 2016.
DOI: 10.1007/978-3-319-46073-4_11

equipping the search approaches with sophisticated domain specific heuristics the performance is quite limited [1,7,8]. Furthermore, for large-scale problems, problem decomposition is absolutely needed [5]. When applying problem decomposition, a problem instance is partitioned into subinstances which are solved independently. The subsolutions are then combined again to form the overall solution.

Daily scheduling routines in semi-conductor factories like those of our project partner Infineon Technologies also build on problem decomposition on the one hand and heuristics on the other hand for producing scheduling solutions. The problem decomposition is hereby realized by partitioning the machines into so called workcenters. Each workcenter is responsible only for a fraction of operation types, i.e. job operations are assigned to workcenters rather than actual machines. The production plan is made for each workcenter independently based on dispatching rules, a widely employed state-of-the-art technique for dealing with large and complex scheduling problems in nowadays manufacturing environments [13]. Dispatching rules are greedy heuristics for step-wise deciding which is the operation to be processed next by a machine. Simple examples for dispatching rules are first-come-first-serve, i.e. the preference of the longest waiting operation, or shortest-job-first. One of the most effective dispatching rules for minimizing the makespan is the most-total-work-remaining (MTWR) rule [16]. According to MTWR, the next operation to be dispatched belongs to a job such that the sum of lengths of all remaining operations is maximal.

One big advantage of dispatching rules is that they can be computed typically in linear time. Another big advantage is their flexibility. Dispatching rules can be changed, adapted or combined easily in order to react on changing order situations as well as changing product portfolios. This is crucial for modern manufacturing regimes like mass customization [9], just-in-time or lean production [14]. Moreover, almost every real-world scheduling problem has specific constraints regarding the manufacturing processes. Consequently, in order to be successfully applied in real-life production environments, an approach for automatic decomposition and dispatching must be easily adaptable. In particular, it must be possible to implement different decomposition methods and dispatching rules in a compact but well-maintainable form.

One way of achieving high adaptability and maintainability is declarative programming. Declarative programming approaches such as answer set and constraint programming [2,11] provide high-level language representation features. Encodings specify the problem to be solved rather than how it is to be solved, which leads to short and well-maintainable code. A general problem solver is then responsible for finding a consistent solution for the encoded problem. Although declarative approaches have already been often applied to scheduling problems (e.g. [3]), their direct applicability on large-scale problems is limited. For example, incremental scheduling problem instances (a variant of FJSP) used in the answer set programming competition[1] do not comprise more than 120 job operations on max 7 machines. Also constraint programming approaches cannot be

---

[1] https://www.mat.unical.it/aspcomp2014/.

directly applied on problems like investigated in this paper. This is due to the fact that otherwise well-applicable global constraints[2] possess quadratic complexities which, in the light of instances comprising up to 10000 job operations and 100 machines, can already be too much.

In this paper we present a novel scheduling approach building on declarative programming in order to benefit from the high-level and compact knowledge representation and combine it with problem decomposition and dispatching rules in order to ensure adaptability and maintainability, low computational costs and effectiveness.

2   A Novel Scheduling Approach

Figure 1 shows the general architecture of our scheduling approach. Conforming to our proposed architecture, a scheduler is build upon a general purpose declarative problem solver. This can be - but is not limited to - constraint solvers like Gecode[3] or Jacop[4], answer set solvers like Clingo[5] or hybrids like proposed in [2,12].

Our first proof-of-concept prototype is implemented in Java incorporating ASCASS, a constraint answer set programming (CASP) solver [18]. ASCASS follows the idea given in [2], i.e. answer set programming (ASP) is used for specification of constraint satisfaction problems (CSPs). The CSPs are solved by the constraint solver Jacop. CASP approaches have proven to be highly effective for problems with very large domains, like industrial sized scheduling problems [3]. This is due to the combination of the high-level knowledge representation features of ASP and the possibility of stating the variable domains as intervals by means of constraint variables. Since the scheduling problems usually present large domains for the time representation, CASP suits well our needs.

Two declarative programs written in the language of the solver are responsible to define the scheduling behavior. In particular, *decompose.prg* specifies

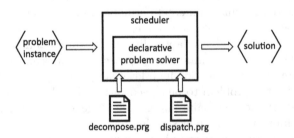

Fig. 1. General architecture of the scheduler

---

[2] http://sofdem.github.io/gccat/.

[3] http://www.gecode.org/.

[4] http://jacop.osolpro.com/.

[5] http://potassco.sourceforge.net/.

the strategy for the problem decomposition, i.e. the method for splitting the problem instance into subinstances, which are then treated independently. How those subinstances are processed is determined by a dispatching rule defined in *dispatch.prg*.

As a first decomposition strategy we currently split the input instance based on the predefined machine and workcenter information so that every subinstance comprises a single machine of each workcenter. This makes sure that it is possible to process every operation type in every subinstance. In order to balance the workload, the set of jobs is equally divided among the subinstances.

Concerning the dispatching rule implemented in *dispatch.prg*, we currently rely on the most-total-work-remaining (MTWR) rule for makespan optimization. In our encoding, this rule can easily be expressed as a logic predicate specifying the operation priorities in a recursive manner, i.e.

```
opPriority(J,L):-
  op(J), opLength(J,L), not precedes(J,_).
opPriority(J,P2+L):-
  op(J), op(J2), precedes(J,J2), opPriority(J2,P2), opLength(J,L).
```

The declarative solver (ASCASS) processes the operations conforming the stated priorities, behaving in accordance to the MTWR rule.

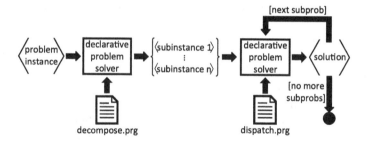

Fig. 2. Data flow of the scheduling process

Figure 2 shows the data flow of the scheduling process. First, the solver combines the instance with the decomposition program, that divides it into a number of subinstances. Both the number of subinstances and the decomposition strategy are determined by *decompose.prg*. Once the subinstances have been created, they are processed sequentially by the declarative solver following the dispatching rule defined in *dispatch.prg*. The dispatching process is incremental. Thus, the solution of one subinstance is forwarded as an additional input to the next subinstance in line until no more subinstances are left. The overall solution is the composition of all the subsolutions.

3   Proof of Concept

In this section we discuss the impact of problem decomposition on our large-scale scheduling benchmark. The purpose of the presented experiment is not to investigate the performance of different dispatching rules. Instead, we want to show that dispatching rules in general can be successfully exploited in the context of declarative programming and problem decomposition.

We tested our prototype against a new large scale benchmark instances comprising up to 10000 job operations to be performed on 100 machines[6]. All the instances are solved once with the decomposition approach described in the last section and once without decomposition. In both cases, we used the most-total-work-remaining (MTWR) dispatching rule. The experiment was conducted on a system with Intel i7-3930K CPU (3.20 GHz), 64 Gb of RAM. The timeout for the computation of the complete schedule for each instance was set to 4000 s. This time frame would allow a frequent recalculation in a weekly or bi-weekly scheduling scenario.

3.1   Results

Table 1 shows the percentage of solved instances for the different machines/operation settings. The first column distinguishes between the approaches with decomposition (dec) and without decomposition (no dec). The results are given grouped by the different flexibility factors, i.e. the number of possible machines for each operation. It gets obvious that the sizes of the job-shop in terms of number of machines/operations as a big impact in the number of solved instances. In particular, less instances can be solved without producing a timeout in larger job-shops. On the other hand, also the increase of the flexibility factor negatively impacts on the number of solved instances. A particular result is the case with flexibility of 5, where in the approach without decomposition it was possible to solve 66.7 % of the 100/1000 instances, but 0 % of the 10/1000 instances. The reason behind this behavior is the ratio between the number of operations and the number of machines. In the case with 100 machines and 1000 operations the ratio is 10, meaning that in a perfectly balanced schedule, where all

Table 1. Comparison of percentage of solved instances of the approaches with and without decomposition

	#mach/#ops	JSP	FJSP-2	FJSP-5	FJSP-10	FJSP-20	FJSP-50	FJSP-100	total
No dec	10/100	100 %	100 %	100 %	0 %	-	-	-	75 %
Dec	10/100	100 %	100 %	100 %	100 %	-	-	-	100 %
No dec	10/1000	100 %	100 %	0 %	0 %	-	-	-	50 %
Dec	10/1000	100 %	100 %	100 %	100 %	-	-	-	100 %
No dec	100/1000	100 %	100 %	66.7 %	0 %	0 %	0 %	0 %	38 %
Dec	100/1000	100 %	100 %	100 %	100 %	100 %	100 %	100 %	100 %
No dec	100/10000	83.3 %	0 %	0 %	0 %	0 %	0 %	0 %	11.9 %
Dec	100/10000	83.3 %	100 %	100 %	100 %	100 %	100 %	100 %	97.6 %
No dec	Total	95.8 %	75 %	58.4 %	0 %	0 %	0 %	0 %	38.6 %
Dec	Total	95.8 %	100 %	100 %	100 %	100 %	100 %	100 %	99.2 %

---

[6] Benchmark and prototype at http://isbi.aau.at/hint/scheduling-prototype.

the machines get the same amount of operations, there are 10 operations per machine. In the case of 10 machines and 1000 operations the ratio is 100 operations per machine. An increased number of operations per machine leads to a longer constraint propagation in the general declarative problem solver.

Concerning the instances with 10 machines and 1000 operations, 12 out of 24 (50 %) were solved. In the set of instances with 100 machines and 1000 operations, the number of solved instances was 16 out of 42 (38 %). Note, the varying number of total instances (24 vs. 42) is due to the varying number of machines in the different settings. A greater number of machines naturally allows more flexibility factors. The total number of solved instances of the approach without decomposition is 51 out of 132, which corresponds to 38.6 % of the benchmark.

In comparison, the decomposition approach showed better results. With respect to the JSP, the results are the same as in the approach without decomposition, because the JSP corresponds to a FJSP with flexibility of 1. Consequently, no decomposition occurs, as the workcenters cannot be split any further. In all the other cases the decomposition plays a crucial role in the solvability, since it was possible to solve all the FJSP instances with any size of the problem. The only unsolved case is a JSP instance with 100 machines and 10000 operations, where the decomposition is not applied. Overall it was possible to solve 131 out of 132 (99.2 %) instances, proving the effectiveness of the decomposition approach.

Table 2. Comparison of the makespan results (in seconds) of the two approaches

	#mach/#ops	JSP	FJSP-2	FJSP-5	FJSP-10	FJSP-20	FJSP-50	FJSP-100
No dec	10/100	855350	712685	645226	t/o	-	-	-
Dec	10/100	855350	1067370	1093303	1014521	-	-	-
No dec	10/1000	780589	696931	t/o	t/o	-	-	-
Dec	10/1000	780589	995531	1083530	995953	-	-	-
No dec	100/1000	933775	754580	670931	t/o	t/o	t/o	t/o
Dec	100/1000	933775	1170844	1426045	1451335	1686282	1418501	1193235
No dec	100/10000	767278	t/o	t/o	t/o	t/o	t/o	t/o
Dec	100/10000	767278	1035810	1225529	1295864	1353059	1365883	1236629

Table 2 shows the makespans produced by MTWR with and without decomposition. The term t/o indicates where the instances reached the timeout. It is to be noticed that, when it is possible to find a solution, the approach without decomposition presents a lower makespan. This is due to the fact that the decomposition program used in our experiment aims to distribute the job equally among the subinstances. However, the number of operations per job varies in the benchmark. Thus, an equal number of jobs in the subinstances does not necessarily correspond to an equal number of operations. Consequently, the total workload to be processed in the subinstances is not perfectly balanced. Opportune tuning of the decomposition program may lead to better results in terms of makespan. This will be investigated in future work.

References

1. Azi, N., Gendreau, M., Potvin, J.Y.: A dynamic vehicle routing problem with multiple delivery routes. Ann. Oper. Res. **199**(1), 103–112 (2012)
2. Balduccini, M.: Representing constraint satisfaction problems in answer set programming. In: ICLP09 Workshop on Answer Set Programming and Other Computing Paradigms (ASPOCP 2009) (2009)
3. Balduccini, M.: Industrial-size scheduling with ASP+CP. In: Delgrande, J.P., Faber, W. (eds.) LPNMR 2011. LNCS, vol. 6645, pp. 284–296. Springer, Heidelberg (2011)
4. Bellman, R.: Mathematical aspects of scheduling theory. SIAM J. Soc. Ind. Appl. Math. **4**, 168–205 (1956)
5. Bent, R., Van Hentenryck, P.: Spatial, temporal, and hybrid decompositions for large-scale vehicle routing with time windows. In: Cohen, D. (ed.) CP 2010. LNCS, vol. 6308, pp. 99–113. Springer, Heidelberg (2010)
6. Blazewicz, J., Ecker, K., Pesch, E., Schmidt, G., Weglarz, J.: Handbook on Scheduling: Models and Methods for Advanced Planning (International Handbooks on Information Systems). Springer, Secaucus (2007)
7. Carchrae, T., Beck, J.C.: Principles for the design of large neighborhood search. J. Math. Model. Algorithms **8**(3), 245–270 (2009)
8. Easton, T., Singireddy, A.: A large neighborhood search heuristic for the longest common subsequence problem. J. Heuristics **14**(3), 271–283 (2008)
9. Fogliatto, F.S., Da Silveira, G.J.C., Borenstein, D.: The mass customization decade: an updated review of the literature. Int. J. Prod. Econ. **138**(1), 14–25 (2012)
10. Garey, M.R., Johnson, D.S.: Computers and Intractability. A Guide to the Theory of NP-Completeness. W. H. Freeman and Company, New York (1979)
11. Gebser, M., Kaminski, R., Kaufmann, B., Schaub, T.: Answer Set Solving in Practice Synthesis Lectures on Artificial Intelligence and Machine Learning. Morgan and Claypool Publishers, San Rafael (2012)
12. Gebser, M., Ostrowski, M., Schaub, T.: Constraint answer set solving. In: Hill, P.M., Warren, D.S. (eds.) ICLP 2009. LNCS, vol. 5649, pp. 235–249. Springer, Heidelberg (2009)
13. Hildebrandt, T., Goswami, D., Freitag, M.: Large-scale simulation-basedoptimization of semiconductor dispatching rules. In: Proceedings of the 2014 Winter Simulation Conference, WSC 2014, pp. 2580–2590. IEEE Press, Piscataway (2014). http://dl.acm.org/citation.cfm?id=2693848.2694175
14. Holweg, M.: The genealogy of lean production. J. Oper. Manag. **25**(2), 420–437 (2007). Special Issue Evolution of the Field of Operations Management SI/ Special Issue Organisation Theory and Supply Chain Management
15. Hurink, J., Jurisch, B., Thole, M.: Tabu search for the job-shop scheduling problem with multi-purpose machines. Oper.-Res.-Spektrum **15**(4), 205–215 (1994)
16. Kaban, A.K., Othman, Z., Rohmah, D.S.: Comparison of dispatching rules in job-shop scheduling problem using simulation: a case study. Int. J. Simul. Model. **11**(3), 129–140 (2012)
17. Pacino, D., Van Hentenryck, P.: Large neighborhood search and adaptive randomized decompositions for flexible jobshop scheduling. In: Proceedings of the International Joint Conference on Artificial Intelligence (2011)
18. Teppan, E.C., Friedrich, G.: Heuristic constraint answer set programming. In: Proceedings of the 6th International Workshop on Combinations of Intelligent Methods and Applications (CIMA16 at ECAI16) (2016)

A Multi-Objective Approach for both Makespan- and Energy-Efficient Scheduling in Injection Molding

Klaas Dählmann$^{(\boxtimes)}$ and Jürgen Sauer

Department of Computing Science, University of Oldenburg,
Uhlhornsweg 84, 26129 Oldenburg, Germany
{klaas.daehlmann,juergen.sauer}@uni-oldenburg.de

Abstract. Recent sustainability efforts require machine scheduling approaches to consider energy efficiency in the optimization of schedules. In this paper, an approach to reduce power peaks while maintaining the makespan is proposed and evaluated. The central concept of the approach is to slowly equalize highs and lows in the energy input of the schedule without affecting the makespan through an iterative optimization. The approach is based on the simulated annealing algorithm to optimize machine schedules regarding the makespan and the energy input, using the goal programming method as the objective function.

Keywords: Energy efficiency · Goal programming · Multi-objective optimization · Scheduling · Simulated annealing

1 Introduction

Large-scale facilities and devices such as industrial machines, air-condition, as well as computer and server systems may unnecessarily load the power grid if they are operated in parallel and especially if they have unsteady power consumption. Temporarily switching off one or many appliances not essential to the business processes may be one option to solve this problem. But, if the power consumption of the individual is known or well documented, the appliances may instead be parallelized in such a way that unnecessary peak loads can be avoided altogether without severely affecting the business processes. Especially with regard to the scheduling of industrial machines, this concept may already be utilized at a predictive planning level to generate energetically ideal schedules without sacrificing an already good makespan.

This paper therefore presents an approach for the optimization of the total energy input while maintaining a near-optimal makespan using the example of discontinuous plastics processing via injection molding machines. The approach is then examined through a combinatorial evaluation, describing, testing, and assessing different, plausible parameter settings.

The challenge herein is that the injection molding cycles of different products and machines do not have the same duration and power consumption throughout

© Springer International Publishing AG 2016
G. Friedrich et al. (Eds.): KI 2016, LNAI 9904, pp. 141–147, 2016.
DOI: 10.1007/978-3-319-46073-4_12

the cycle as well as the fact that the highs and lows of the energy input are not equally spaced and symmetrical.

The different injection molding machines considered for this paper are shown in Table 1. The steps *cooling* and *melting* start at the same time and run in parallel.

Table 1. Individual steps, durations and power consumption of the injection molding cycles of the machines considered.

Step	Engel victory 750/140 tech		Engel ES 2550/400 HL		KraussMaffei KM420-2700C1	
	Duration	Power	Duration	Power	Duration	Power
Clamping	3 s	1.8 kW	7 s	14.08 kW	5 s	14.85 kW
Nozzle	1 s	1.2 kW	1 s	9.39 kW	1 s	9.9 kW
Injecting	3 s	7.2 kW	6 s	56.31 kW	6 s	59.4 kW
Dwelling	3 s	1.2 kW	5 s	9.39 kW	5 s	9.9 kW
Cooling	11 s	4.22 kW	29 s	32.98 kW	27 s	34.79 kW
Melting	7 s	5.98 kW	20 s	46.8 kW	22 s	49.37 kW
Opening	3 s	0.32 kW	6 s	2.48 kW	7 s	2.62 kW
Ejecting	1 s	0.4 kW	3 s	3.13 kW	0 s	3.3 kW
Demolding	2 s	0.17 kW	0 s	1.34 kW	0 s	1.41 kW
Set-up	25 min	-	60 min	-	150 min	-

These issues, both machine scheduling and energy-efficient production, have had increased recent consideration: Multi-objective optimization approaches for job and flow shop problems have been sucessfully used to either create the pareto front of possible solutions for an a posteriori evaluation [3,5] or to compare the results of different local search heuristics for the special case of no-wait scheduling [10]. Holistic simulation and forecasting systems have been employed to examine mutual dependencies and reciprocal effects regarding the energy efficiency of the appliances [4,6] while evolutionary/genetic algorithms have been successfully utilized for energy optimization within the context of parallel machines and cloud service scheduling [9,11, pp. 191–224].

2   Approach

As the scheduling of injection molding machines and jobs is based on combinatorial and $\mathcal{NP}$-hard optimization problems [1, p. 51], the trajectory-based simulated annealing algorithm [2,7] instead of a mathematically exact method is chosen. The initial solution is constructed while attempting to balance production jobs on the available machines, thereby minimizing the total makespan. The main objective of the optimization is to reduce the power peaks within the initial solution without negatively affecting the makespan while doing so.

Minimizing the makespan by parallelizing as many jobs as possible increases the total energy input and may cause unwanted power peaks. However, trying to minimize energy consumption means to run as few machines as possible in parallel. In this paper, this dilemma will be counteracted by using the goal programming objective function to define aspiration levels or goals for each objective and subsequently attempting to find solutions to the scheduling problems considered that reach these goals with the least deviation. As simulated annealing only genereates a single solution, a posteriori objective functions are not suited for further consideration. Goal programming on the other hand is an a priori objective function that permits an equal examination of all objectives [8]. The goal factors are relative to the initial solution, e.g. a goal factor of 1 describes a goal value that is identical to the initial solution while goal factor of 1.5 and 0.5 means a goal value that is 50 % larger or smaller respectively and a goal factor of 0 describes a utopian zero value. Because the objectives considered in multi-objective decision making are often measured on different scales (in this case time in seconds and energy input in watts), a subsequent standardization of the scales is necessary to make them comparable. The solution is then rated using a distance function to determine the deviation between the current and the goal values.

The neighborhood function used for the simulated annealing algorithm selects a random, active machine at the instant of time of a random power peak to shift the current and all future jobs one time unit towards the end, slowly resolving power peaks originating from unfavorable parallelization in the process.

3   Evaluation

The aim of the evaluation is twofold: On the one hand, different distance functions are evaluated in their applicability for bi-objective optimization regarding time-based and energy-based objectives. On the other hand, as energy-efficient optimization is a rather recent consideration, utopian and realistic goals for the power peak are compared with regard to their feasibility. The underlying idea of the evaluation is to systematically observe the behavior of the power peaks of the resulting schedules and to describe their dependency on the makespan, the objective function as well as the structure of the initial solution.

3.1   Method

To mimic the layout of the local company the machine data of which was obtained from, two machines of each type shown in Table 1 will be assumed for the following evaluation, making a total of six machines. The simulated annealing parameters remain unchanged for the entire evaluation. The algorithm starts at an initial temperature of 1 and is iteratively cooled by 1 % until it reaches or falls below the minimal temperature of 0.01. Two different initial solutions are examined in the evaluation. The first solution assumes constant production on all machines after an initial setup time while the second solution consists of two to four equidistant changeovers to alternative product variants on each machine during the observation period, depending on the size of the machine. The observation period itself is a single work shift of 8 h for all experiments. Three common distance functions are individually examined as objective functions for the goal programming method: The euclidean distance, the manhattan/taxicab distance, or the maximum/Chebyshev/chessboard distance. Moreover, six different goals regarding the makespan are set and analyzed. A utopian goal with a makespan of zero as well as five further goals, starting at a goal identical to the initial solution's makespan and increasing in 5 % steps up to 20 % more makespan. The last parameter of the evaluation is the goal factor for the power peak, with two different goals being compared. The first goal is the utopian goal as well while the second, realistic goal is calculated based on the average power peaks of the first set of evaluations using the utopian goal. These parameters and their assignments make a total of 72 different combinations. Each combination is then independently run 20 times to avoid some statistical deviation due to the random simulated annealing and neighborhood function.

3.2   Results

The results of the evaluation are divided into four categories, one for each combination of changeovers in the initial solution (with or without) and power peak goal factor (utopian or realistic). For reference, both initial solutions, with or without changeovers, have a duration of 8 h and a power peak of 348.3 kW.

Without Changeover and Utopian Power Peak Goal Factor. A utopian goal for the makespan results in a plan that has only little improvement on the power peak but also does not increase the makespan at all. Results from makespan goal factor 1 depend on the chosen distance function: For the euclidean distance, the average power peak is identical to the solution using a utopian makespan goal while the makespan is slightly longer. For the manhattan distance, the results are identical to the utopian makespan goal. For the maximum distance, the results are located in the same value range as those for makespan goal factor 1.1 to 1.2, as further described below. For the euclidean and the manhatten distance, a makespan goal factor of 1.05 creates solutions that have their power peaks reduced by 20 to 15 kW and are approximately 2 min longer than the initial solution. For the maximum distance, the results are again in the same value range as those with from goal factor 1.1 to 1.2. Makespan goal factors 1.1, 1.15, and 1.2 generate results that decrease the power peak by roughly 30 to 40 kW while increasing the makespan by about 3 min.

With Changeover and Utopian Power Peak Goal Factor. For the utopian makespan goal factor 0, the results for the euclidean and manhattan distance have their power peak reduced by about 30 kW peak without affecting the makespan, while for the maximum distance, the power peak does not change much at all. Regarding the solutions for makespan goal factor 1, these are, in case of the manhattan distance, either identical to those obtained with a goal factor of 0, in case of the euclidean distance slightly longer but with identical power peak, or, in case of the maximum distance, located in the same value range as all further goal factors. The average results for makespan goal factors 1.05 to 1.2 have their power peaks reduced between 50 and 60 kW while having their makespan increased by almost 2 min.

Without Changeover and Realistic Power Peak Goal Factor. When setting realistic goals for the power peak, the results of the euclidean distance are similar to those of the manhattan distance throughout all makespan goal factors. For goal factors 0 and 1, the results again show just little improvement of the power peak but do not increase the makespan. For the euclidean and manhattan distance, goal factor 1.05 results in solutions that have a roughly 10 kW reduced power peak, just slightly better than those generated with goal factors 0 and 1, but have their makespan increased by about 2 min. Results generated by makespan goal factors 1.1 to 1.2 have their power peaks reduced by 25 to 30 kW while simultaneously having their makespan increased by about 3 min. The results when using the maximum distance are significantly different from those described above. A utopian makespan goal creates almost no change at all for both the power peak and the makespan. Results from goal factors 1 to 1.2 have their power peaks reduced by roughly 20 to 30 kW but at the same time have their makespan increased by up to 7 min.

With Changeover and Realistic Power Peak Goal Factor. The results for the euclidean and the manhattan distance are again comparable. Makespan goal factors 0 and 1 generate solutions with almost 30 kW smaller power peaks while not increasing the makespan of the results. Goal factors 1.05 to 1.2 reduce the power peaks of the results even further by 55 to almost 60 kW, but increase the makespan by 2 min. The results generated using the maximum distance are again different from those using the euclidean or manhattan distance. For a utopian makespan goal there is again no change for neither the power peak nor the makespan. For all other evaluated goal factors, the power peak is reduced by about 55 to 60 kW, but the makespan progressively increases from 1 min at goal factor 1 to 9 min increase at goal factor 1.2.

3.3   Discussion

Several different properties and behaviors can be derived from the evaluation: Regarding the behavior of the three distance functions examined, it is evident that there is no direct linear dependency between the makespan and the power peak. Allowing for an increase in makespan does not automatically imply a proportional reduction of the power peak. Instead, the power peaks of the solution become more balanced and equalized with every iteration of the optimization, resulting in plans that cannot be further improved within the up to 20 % makespan increase considered in the evaluation. This power peak limit is reached when using a makespan goal factor of 1.1 or higher, in some cases even earlier.

Continuing on to the individual analysis of the distance functions, the behavior of the euclidean and manhattan distance is comparable while the results generated using the maximum distance differ significantly. In general, when comparing the results of the euclidean and manhattan distance, using a utopian power peak goal causes the individual solutions scatter more around the average solutions than they do when using a realistic power peak goal. When setting a utopian makespan goal, the euclidean and manhattan distance can create results that have a reduced power peak without affecting the makespan at all. The actual amount of improvement depends on the initial solution with just a slight improvement using a plan without changeovers to a more significant improvement when starting from a solution with frequent changeovers. This is because it is more difficult to move power peaks to phases of low energy input when using a plan with constantly operating machines than it is when working with a plan that already has long phases of low energy input due to changeovers.

In contrast, the results of the maximum distance differ greatly from those described above. When setting a utopian makespan goal, only the makespan will be considered. But, as the initial solution is makespan-optimal already, the makespan cannot be further reduced, resulting in solutions that do not differ much from the initial solution. When using a non-utopian goal for the makespan with a utopian goal for the power peak, it is the other way around. As a utopian power peak goal attempts to reduce the energy input by 100 %, the mere 0 to 20 % goals set by the makespan goal factors 1 to 1.2 are never taken into account, resulting in virtually identical average solutions for all makespan goal factors. The third and last case when using the maximum distance is the setting of realistic, attainable goals for both the makespan and the power peak. For these settings, the general characteristic of the maximum distance, as described above, becomes apparent. Contrary to the euclidean and manhattan distance, the maximum distance attempts to reach all different makespan goals, even if it does not provide any improvement for the power peak.

4   Conclusion

This paper presented and evaluated an approach and its parameters to retroactively optimize machine schedules, improving their energy efficiency without significantly worsening the already optimal makespan. As apparent from the results and the subsequent discussion, there is no consistently and uniformly best setting for all situations. Rather, the decision maker setting up the optimization and its goals needs to know the desired extent of the results. If small improvements of the power peak suffice, using the euclidean or manhattan distance with utopian goals for both makespan and the power peak creates plans with unchanged makespan. If extending an 8-h work shift by just a few minutes is acceptable, better results can be achieved by increasing the makespan goal. If a suitable makespan goal is not known, using the maximum distance together with virtually any non-utopian makespan goal and a utopian power peak goal may also be an option.

References

1. Brucker, P.: Scheduling Algorithms, 5th edn. Springer, Heidelberg (2007)
2. Černý, V.: Thermodynamical approach to the traveling salesman problem: an efficient simulation algorithm. J. Optim. Theor. Appl. **45**(1), 41–51 (1985)
3. Geiger, M.J.: Multikriterielle Ablaufplanung. Deutscher Universitäts-Verlag (2005)
4. Haag, H.: Eine Methodik zur modellbasierten Planung und Bewertung der Energieeffizienz in der Produktion. Ph.D. thesis, Universität Stuttgart (2013)
5. Henning, A.: Praktische job-shop scheduling-probleme. Ph.D. thesis, Universität Jena (2002)
6. Junge, M.: Simulationsgestützte Entwicklung und Optimierung einer energieeffizienten Produktionssteuerung. Ph.D. thesis, Universität Kassel (2007)
7. Kirkpatrick, S., Gelatt, C.D., Vecchi, M.P.: Optimization by simulated annealing. Science **220**(4598), 671–680 (1983)
8. Miettinen, K.: Introduction to multiobjective optimization: noninteractive approaches. In: Branke, J., Deb, K., Miettinen, K., Słowiński, R. (eds.) Multiobjective Optimization. Interactive and Evolutionary Approaches. LNCS, vol. 5252, pp. 1–26. Springer, Heidelberg (2008)
9. Rager, M.: Energieorientierte Produktionsplanung. Gabler (2008)
10. Schuster, C.: No-wait Job-Shop-Scheduling: Komplexität und Local Search. Ph.D. thesis, Universität Duisburg-Essen (2003)
11. Tao, F., Zhang, L., Laili, Y.: Configurable Intelligent Optimization Algorithm. Springer, Heidelberg (2015)

Learning Event Time Series
for the Automated Quality Control of Videos

Stefan Edelkamp[1]([✉]) and Fritz Jacob[2]

[1] Fachbereich Mathematik und Informatik, Universität Bremen,
Am Fallturm 1, 28359 Bremen, Germany
edelkamp@tzi.de

[2] Cube-Tec International GmbH, Anne-Conway-Strasse 1, 28359 Bremen, Germany

Abstract. In this work, several approaches to feature extraction on sets of time-based events will be developed and evaluated. On the one hand, these sets of events will be extracted from video files and on the other hand it will be manually annotated. By using methods of supervised machine learning the two sets of events will be mapped onto each other. After that, per time slot and requested event type, a binary classification will be applied. Thus aspects of data mining and media technology will be discussed and combined with the goal to reach a reasonable reduction of the input-set by projecting it on an output-set. This will save operator-time in an automated process environment for quality control of audiovisual files. It can be shown, that this objective can be achieved by applying the developed methods. In addition to that, further results and limitations will be presented.

1 Introduction

To meet the aspects of quality assurance in media industry available analysis tools are integrated in the process flow to support decisions. One question is, if a video file meets all relevant requirements in order to be broadcast, or whether further processing steps are needed.

Analysis tools rate the audio-visual material at different levels in the process [1]. The analysis of what is heard or seen, however, remains a major challenge [8], because the results of the various tools are always coupled with uncertainty. In addition, the accuracy, the recall and the precision in individual analysis tools are often insufficient. Furthermore, tools from the professional sector are black boxes and provide no insight into their internal workings. Another problem is the syntax of the analytical results, because there is no standardized notation being accepted among all tool manufacturers, e.g. MPEG 7 [4]. This fact makes it difficult to make the right decisions in the process flow. Also, the prediction quality of the events varies not only from tool to tool, but also between different analysis focuses. After passing through an analysis tool it is, therefore, necessary to interrupt the process flow and evaluate the results manually. Based on these inspections, decisions for the course of actions are made.

ⓒ Springer International Publishing AG 2016
G. Friedrich et al. (Eds.): KI 2016, LNAI 9904, pp. 148–154, 2016.
DOI: 10.1007/978-3-319-46073-4_13

The demanding question is whether there is a way through which a manual intervention could be accelerated by intelligent filtering the analytical results, and to what extent an added-value from supposedly independent results from multiple analysis tools with respect to the same audio-visual file can be obtained. Machine learning by data mining the tools' analyses can provide a basis for improved decisions. However, as the frame-based data is a time series of many even noisy events, the choice of features is not immediate, so that novel discrete approaches for feature extraction are derived.

2   Problem Formulation

In the broadest sense, we aim at a mapping between two sets of temporally correlated events in order to detect patterns in one of the events sets. For fast storage of and access to events, they are stored in an interval tree [2].

Definition 1 (Event, Domain). *An* event *e* *is a tuple* $e =$ (start, end, type, conf) *with* start, end $\in \mathbb{N}$, type $\in C$, *where C is a set of event types and* conf $\in [0,1]$ *a confidence value. The set of all events is denoted by $\mathcal{E}$. A domain $D \in \mathcal{D}$ is a pair* (length, E) *containing its duration* length *and a set of events $E \subseteq \mathcal{E}$.*

Definition 2 (Automated and Manual Events). *The set of events in a domain $D =$ (length, E) partitiones into sets of* automated events $A \subseteq E$ *and* manual events $B \subseteq E$ *with $E = A \cup B$ and $A \cap B = \emptyset$. Furthermore, for domains $D_1, \ldots, D_n$ with $D_i =$ (length$_i$, E_i) classes $\mathcal{A}$ and $\mathcal{B}$ are defined as $\mathcal{A} = A_1 \cup \ldots \cup A_n$ with $A_i \in E_i$ and, similarly, for $\mathcal{B}$ we have $\mathcal{B} = B_1 \cup \ldots \cup B_n$ with $B_i \in E_i, i \in \{1, \ldots, n\}$. If $D =$ (length, E) and $E = A \cup B$, we impose that for all $e =$ (start, end, type, conf) $\in E$ we have $1 \leq$ start $<$ end $\leq$ length; and for all $e =$ (start, end, type, conf) $\in A$, and $e' =$ (start', end', type', conf') $\in B$ we have* conf' $= 1$ *and* type $\neq$ type'.

Definition 3 (Types, Events, Evaluation). *The Function* types : $\mathcal{E} \to C$ *maps events to their according types, the function* events : $C \times D \to \mathcal{E}$ *projects domains to ones of the chosen type. Function* types (events) *naturally extends to sets of events (sets of domains). The evaluation function* eval$_{A,b}$: $\mathbb{N} \to \mathbb{B}$ *is a mapping indexed by a set of events $(A, b) \in 2^A \times B$ used for binary classification.*

Definition 4 (Event Learning Task). *Given a domain set $\mathcal{D} = \{D_1, \ldots, D_n\}$ inducing sets of automated events $\mathcal{A} = \{A_1, \ldots, A_n\}$ and manual events $\mathcal{B} = \{B_1, \ldots, B_n\}$, the* event learning task *is to find a binary classifier* eval$_{A,b}$ *that for set $A_i \in \mathcal{A}$ determines the existence of $b \in$ types$(B_i), B_i \in \mathcal{B}$, in a given time step $t, i \in \{1, \ldots, n\}$.*

Definition 5 (Slice, Probe, Pattern). *An event $e =$ (start, end, type, conf) $\in A$ is* sliced *by event $e' =$ (start', end', $\cdot$, 1) $\in B$ into event $e'' =$ (start'', end'', type, conf) if* start'' $=$ max{start, start'}, *and* end'' $=$ min{end, end'}. *Function* probe$_{A,b}$: $B \to E$ *is a* slice *of $A \subseteq E$ wrt. event*

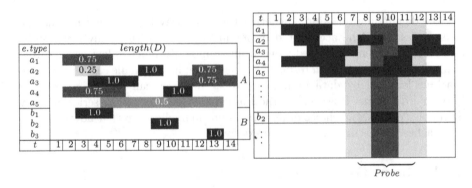

Fig. 1. Domain and pattern (wrt. event $(9, 10, b_2, 1)$ and $r = 2$).

$b \in B$. Let $\mathcal{P}$ be the set of all probes b. Then, function $\text{pattern}_{A,r} : B \to \mathcal{P}$ denotes a pattern to select a probe in set A wrt. event $b \in B$ and radius $r \in \mathbb{N}$.

Figure 1 (left) shows a sample domain D. In the upper part we see the temporally correlated occurrence of the events in A, and in the lower part the the occurrence of the events from B. Each event contains its confidence parameter, which is also reflected in its gray scale (e.g., event $(2, 5, a_1, 0.75)$ can be found). In addition, we see that there are a total of eight different types of events in this image. Several events of the same type may co-exist in one domain (e.g. for a_2). The intersection of events of the same type, however, is prohibited. For the events $e = (start, end, type, conf) \in A$ we have $type \in \{a_1, \ldots, a_5\}$, and for the events $e' = (start', end', type', conf') \in B$ we have $type' \in \{b_1, \ldots, b_3\}$. Moreover, $types(A) = \{a_1, \ldots, a_5\}$, $events(a_3, D) = \{(4, 7, a_3, 1), (11, 14, a_3, 0.75)\}$, and $eval_{A,b_1}$ is the following mapping from $\mathbb{N}$ to $\mathbb{B}$:

t	1	2	3	4	5	6	7	8	9	10	11	12	13	14
$eval\,(A, b_1)$	0	0	1	1	1	0	0	0	0	0	0	0	0	0

Figure 1 (right) highlights $probe_{A,2}$ in dark and $pattern_{A,2}(9, 10, b_2, 1)$ in light gray.

3   Feature Extraction

The learning problem is a classification of multi-variate time series, where for all types c individual event sets are considered. To reduce the dimensionality of the learning vector, feature extraction is recommended. In the following, we propose two different approaches: *fingerprints* and *event correlation*. Two more statistics are gererated from the event data stream: *relevance* and *event parallelism* [5].

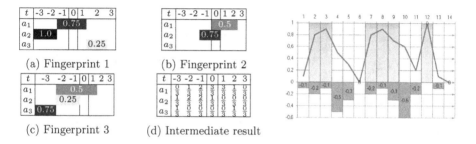

(a) Fingerprint 1   (b) Fingerprint 2

(c) Fingerprint 3   (d) Intermediate result

Fig. 2. Superposition of and *score* function for fingerprints.

A *fingerprint* is a data structure related to a probe, for which repeating combinations of events are generalized and used for classification.

Definition 6 (Fingerprint). *A fingerprint $f_{A,c,r}: \mathbb{N} \to \mathcal{E}$ wrt. radius $r \in \mathbb{N}$ is a slice of A wrt. a time interval, defined through an event type $c \in$ types(B), $B \in \mathcal{B}$. It consists of a radius r which defines the extension to both sides of its current median time point t. The set of all fingerprints is denoted by F. The function radius $: F \to \mathbb{N}$ can be used to access the extension of the fingerprint, while the length $|f|$ of the fingerprint $f \in F$ is defined as $1 + 2 \cdot$ radius(f).*

For matching fingerprints f of set A we call *performMatch* that loops on t (to the length of A) and k (to the radius of f). In the inner loop for each c in the slice wrt. k and t that is touched the evaluation h is incremented by the weight w of k and t, times a certain combination of probability and confidence.

The *superposition* of the fingerprints $f_1 \ldots, f_k$ wrt. events $a_1 \ldots, a_l$ operates in two phases. The relative occurence of the events is determined, followed by the multiplication with the confidence value average $conf_f(a)$. For the example of Fig. 2 we have $conf_f(a_1) = 0.58$. To raise the influence of values closer to the middle of the fingerprint, we apply Gaussian decay: the *weight* of time step t and radius r is defined as $weight(t,r) = e^{-4 \cdot (t/r)^2}$.

For scoring we apply procedure *performMatching* to a set of manual events B. For each $b \in B$ an individual score is computed and the predicted values v are normalized to $[0, 1]$. Finally, we add the distance values between the predicted and the manual annotation u, so that $score(u, v) = \sum_{1 \leq t \leq length} -|u_t - v_t|$. For the example we have $score([0.1, 0.8, 0.9, 0.5, 0.3, 0, 0.8, 0.9, 0.7, 0.6, 0.2, 1, 0.1, 0]$, $[0, 1, 1, 0, 0, 0, 1, 1, 1, 0, 0, 1, 0, 0]) = -2.7$.

Another aspect for the extraction of features for a set of annotated videos is based on the following observation. Suppose an event of type $c \in$ types$(\mathcal{B})$ frequently occurs at the same time as $c' \in$ types$(\mathcal{A})$, with high probability the interval of a c' event has to be anotated with c. Therefore, we use an event (correlation) matrix that denotes statistical relations between events.

Definition 7 (Event Matrix, Score). *Let $k = |$types$(\mathcal{A}) \cup$ types$(\mathcal{B})|$, the event matix M of size k^2, is defined as $M = \{R_c \in \mathbb{R}^k \mid c \in$ types$(\mathcal{A}) \cup$ types$(\mathcal{B})\}$, where each R_c is a row in M and each colum of R_c contains a pair*

Fig. 3. Video annotation.

of values (c', z) *with* $c' \in$ types$(\mathcal{A}) \cup$ types$(\mathcal{B})$, $c \neq c'$ *and* $z \in \mathbb{R}$. *Assuming function* occur$_{\mathcal{D}}(c) : C \to \mathbb{N}$ *that counts the number of events of a given type, and* matches$_{D,q} : C \times C \to \mathbb{N}$ *that returns how often two types are present at the same time and q to be threshold parameter for tolerance, we have* $z = \sum_{D \in \mathcal{D}}$ matches$_{D,q}(c, c')/$occ$_{\mathcal{D}}(c')$. *The score of M wrt. event set A and* $b \in$ types$(\mathcal{A})$ *is a function* score$_{A,M,b}(t) = \prod_{e=(\text{start,end,type,conf})\in\text{slice}_A(t)} 1 +$ relOcc$_M(b, \text{type})$ *where* relOcc$_M(c) : C \times C \to \mathbb{N}$ *is the relative occurence of accessing event c wrt. event c'.*

4   Evaluation

We first copied all video test data (with and without audio) to a Digital Betacam tape. Then the tape was physically manipulated to enforce errors in the replay. Especially, we used diagonal bendings that were efficient to generate *dropout* artefacts. Horizonal bendings yield the loss of audio signal. Stronger manipulations yield to problems in the recorder, while perforation let to no significant change to the video (in the *BlackmagicDeckLink Studio 4K* capture card).

Given that the video data was uncompressed, we converted it to IMX MPEG 50 and stored it into MXF containers. For audioanalysis-only we also exported audio in WAV-format. The MXF data was forwarded to the different tools for push-botton analysis. Manual annotation has been done via the cutting program *Sony Vegas Pro 13* (see Fig. 3). Similar to other tools like *Adobe Premiere* or *Final Cut ProX* it features annotations via *markers*, linking a text to a frame or sequence of frames in an easy to handle manner.

First, we separated start from end fingerprints. For *constant color frames* we get a picture shown in Fig. 4 (left). For the learning process we use a set of annotated files and generate the following six different feature graphs for each of the file to be analyzed: *single-frame fingerprint, start-fingerprint, end-fingerprint, event matrix, accumulated relevance* and *parallel events*. Every graph consists of a time series of discrete values for each frame. Based on the large amount of noise, we avoid thresholding, but instead take these as features to train a classificator (random forest) using the WEKA machine learning library [3,6]. If *g* is the

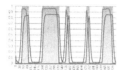

Event Type	Number	Accuracy	F_1
Macro Blocking	199	0.79	0.58
Digibeta Drop Outs	135	0.91	0.76
Stripe Blocking	84	0.85	0.35
Edge Blocking	81	0.84	0.43
Border Blocking	41	0.81	0.3

Fig. 4. Effect of *start-end* fingerprints to detect constant color frames (start blue, end red, manual shaded); and overall learning results.

number of feature graphs and r is the radius of the frame to be classified we obtain $3g + (2r + 1)g + 1$ attributes. For the six graphs above and a radius of 30 frames this results in 385 attributes.

As a feature of our algorithm we learn different parameters for each of the five error types. Moreover, to control the experiment, we used 10-fold crossvalidation already on the file layer (to avoid inter-dependency of the features collected), and the standard statistical quality measures (accuracy, error rate, precision, recall, F1-measure). As the parameter space, we had 6 feature graphs (fingerprints, result correlation matrix, etc.), 4 analytical tools, n as the frame radius, together with $6k$ model-specific parameters for the fingerprints and l model-specific parameters for the result correlation matrix. As $n = 50$, $k = 20$ and $l = 10$ yield 56.7 million combinations, we performed the experiments in stages. (1) For the 5 event types (macro blocking, digibeta drop outs, stripe blocking, edge blocking, and border blocking) 35 configurations were tested each (30 for finger prints and 5 for event matrix correlation). (2) The frame radius for the best 3 configuration for each type is varied, yielding 75 further configurations. (3) Additional feature graphs for the best 3 configurations are chosen yielding 15 further configurations. (4) For each event type we drop tools in their best setting, yielding 40 further configurations.

For each of the steps we obtain a certain parameterization. For the quality of the overall learning process, we obtain the data shown in Fig. 4 (right).

If we relate this to the saving in operator time for 1 min video, than this leads to significant advance. For pure manual quality constrol we have an average analysis, we measured 30 min working time and about 18 events. This is compared to the results of the four professional tools that in summary yield 671 events in about 15 min. Checking one event might consume 3 s, so that again 30 min working time is needed. Our learning scheme, however, resulted in a reduction to only 22 events, which contained 66 % of the manually annotated ones. This reduces the working time to about 1 min. Note that the input set of the professional tools is also incomplete and contains errors. While the training process consumes considerable time, classification is immediate.

5   Conclusion

This work improved automated quality control of audio-visual inputs by classifying event data of different analysis tools. This way, an increase in the degree of automation could be obtained that is able to deal with uncertain and imprecise analysis results. The amount of the automatic analysis results depends on the (manually defined) event types. In principle an arbitrary reduction is possible. Compared to the state of the art for quality assurance in the media industry, the presented system provides a significant relief of the employees by reducing the event diversity and given the fact that virtually no prior knowledge about the analysis tools has been assumed. The ultimate goal is an unsupervised learning algorithm with early results to be found in [7].

References

1. AMWA and EBU. Framework for interoperable media services (FIMS). Technical report, Advanced Media Workflow Association and European Broadcasting Union (2011). FIMS Media SOA Framework 1.0
2. Cormen, T.H., Leiserson, C.E., Rivest, R.L.: Introduction to Algorithms. MIT Press, Cambridge (2009)
3. Hall, M., Frank, E., Holmes, G., Pfahringer, B., Reutemann, P., Witten, I.H.: The weka data mining software: an update. SIGKDD Explor. Newsl. 11(1), 10–18 (2009)
4. ISO. Information technology - multimedia content description interface. ISO 15938–3, International Organization for Standardization (2002)
5. Jacob, F.: Ereignis-basierte Analyse von Mediendaten mit Methoden des maschinellen Lernens. Master's thesis, Universität Bremen (2015)
6. Marsland, S.: Machine Learning: An Algorithmic Perspective. Chapman & Hall/CRC Machine Learning & Pattern Recognition Series, vol. 2. Taylor & Francis, Abingdon-on-Thames (2014)
7. Mörchen, F.: Time series knowledge mining. Citeseer (2006)
8. Schallauer, P., Bailer, W., Morzinger, R., Furntratt, H., Thallinger, G.: Automatic quality analysis for film and video restoration. In: IEEE International Conference on Image Processing, ICIP 2007, vol. 4, pp. IV9–IV12 (2007)

Solving the Physical Vehicle Routing Problem for Improved Multi-robot Freespace Navigation

Stefan Edelkamp[✉], Denis Golubev, and Christoph Greulich

Fachbereich Mathematik und Informatik, Universität Bremen,
Am Fallturm 1, 28359 Bremen, Germany
edelkamp@tzi.de

Abstract. Freespace navigation for autonomous robots is of growing industrial impact, especially in the logistics and warehousing domain. In this work, we describe a multiagent simulation solution to the *physical vehicle routing problem*, which extends the *physical traveling salesman problem* —a recent benchmark used in robot motion planning research— by considering more than one concurrent vehicle.

For the interaction of vehicles, we compute the collision of physical bodies and then apply the impact resulting from the elastic collision. A multi-threaded controller is implemented which forwards the proposed actions from each individual robot's controller to the environment real-time simulator. For computing an optimized assignment of the pickup and delivery tasks to the vehicles we apply nested Monte-Carlo tree search.

In the experiments, we study the problem of robot navigation for automated pickup and delivery of shelves to and from picking stations.

1 Introduction

The market for consumer goods which are ordered in online shops is continuously growing. Companies store large amounts of goods in distribution warehouses. Several optimization tasks have to be solved, including the selection of the most appropriate warehouse, the proper choice of the delivery point (e.g., packing station), the distribution of goods to the vehicles, and their respective best tour.

Within warehouses, an increased level of automatism takes place. Companies like Amazon Robotics[1] employ hundreds of autonomous robots to improve the transport of shelves from and to picking stations. So far, these robots (also called *autonomous vehicles, carriers,* or *forklifts*) operate on an underlying grid of floor cells. This eases some of the navigation aspects, but neglects the dynamics of the moving robots. In larger environments, including vehicle dynamics and freespace navigation, however, is inevitable.

In alignment with the terms *physical traveling saleman problem* (PTSP) (which has been invented for a competition for solving single-vehicle TSP problems [18]) and *vehicle routing problem* (VRP) (which is used for the distribution

---

[1] Previously KIVA Systems.

© Springer International Publishing AG 2016
G. Friedrich et al. (Eds.): KI 2016, LNAI 9904, pp. 155–161, 2016.
DOI: 10.1007/978-3-319-46073-4_14

of goods with several vehicles [20]), we introduce the *physical vehicle routing problem* (PVRP) in this paper. In addition to the static vehicle routing problem, the vehicle model in the PVRP includes orientation and speed, as well as friction and acceleration.

The challenge of the PTSP is to visit a number of waypoints in the best possible order, where *best* is expressed in a cost function that reflects the travel time (number of ticks) in the simulation. In the multi-objective PTSP, the cost function has been extended to include other factors like minimized damage and fuel consumption. The number of actions for steering options has been discretized. In the real-time simulation, an obstacle-avoiding dynamically-feasible trajectory is executed. While the benchmark is bound to a bitmap representation of the environment and its obstacles, it has been shown that solutions valid for the PTSP translate to more complex robot motion planning problems, including 2D and 3D environmental models, robots with higher degree of freedom and nonlinear, high-dimensional, nonholonomic system dynamics [10]. The challenge for the PVRP besides the computation of valid low-cost solution trajectories are often long and that, after some precomputations, a simulation operates in real-time: only a few milliseconds are available to select the next possible steering and forward the action vector to the simulator. In the PVRP we assume three possible waypoint types (colors): the location to pickup a shelf, the picking station, and the location to store the shelf.

To model collisions properly in real-time, we use a refined physical model with bounding spheres which eases the computation of the intersection of every two polygonial vehicle objects (the robots), and, if required, computes the impact of the elastic collision. For tour optimization we apply *Nested Rollout Policy Adaptation* (NRPA) [19], an extension to nested Monte-Carlo search [4]. It computes a possible assignment of waypoints to the vehicles and the order in which a vehicle will traverse the waypoints. As NRPA can be parameterized, we will study the change of parameters in this work.

2   Physical TSPs and VRPs

The classic vehicle routing problem (VRP) [2] is a well-studied problem in Operations Research. It extends the traveling salesman problem (TSP) from one to several vehicles. Often constraints are added to the problem, like pickup-and-deliveries, time-windows, and/or capacity constraints. For the sake of simplicity and driven by the application, we assume the stacker-crane scenario where each vehicle carries at most one object (shelf).

There are different formalizations for the VRP. The most prominent one is mathematical programming model with 0-1 variables for choosing tour edges. This formalization, however, includes subtour elimination constraints that our solver does not need, as it will create complete (sets of) tours. Let $G = (V, E, w)$ be a weighted graph with $V = \{0, 1, \ldots, n\}$ being the nodes set, $E = \{e_{i,j} \mid 0 \leq i, j \leq n, i \neq j\}$ being the edge set, and w being a weight function that models the cost (time, distance) to travel from one node to another. The graph may be constructed by compressing a larger graph (the map) using calls to a shortest path algorithm, so that the input of a VRP often operates on a cost matrix. Each node i represents a customer that has a demand (in our case 1) for his goods and a time window (in our case maximal), during which service must take place. Let $R = \{V_1, \ldots, V_r\}$ be the set of all vehicles. The available fleet is homogeneous and each vehicle has a known capacity (in our case 1). A valid solution S consists of a set of non-vertex-intersecting vehicle routes $S = \{S_1, \ldots, S_r\}$ that visit all customer nodes. Usually, all routes start and end in the common depot 0, but in an *Open VRP* that we consider, all vehicles start in an individual position, and end in some arbitrary destination (often the last customer visited), resulting in a cost matrix of size $n \cdot r \times n \cdot r$.

In continous space $\mathcal{S}$ and $\mathcal{U}$ denote the state and control spaces of the robots, respectively. The equations of motions are given by a set of differential equations $f : \mathcal{S} \times \mathcal{U} \to \dot{\mathcal{S}}$, where $\dot{\mathcal{S}}$ denotes the tangent space of $\mathcal{S}$. A trajectory $\lambda : [0, T] \to \mathcal{S}$ is a continuous function, parametrized by the time duration $T \in \mathbb{R}^{\geq 0}$. Trajectories are obtained by applying a control function $u : [0, T] \to U$ starting from some state $s \in \mathcal{S}$ and integrating f, i.e., $\forall t \in [0, T] : \lambda(t) = s + \int_0^t f(\lambda(h), u(h)) dh$.

Let $\mathcal{W}, \mathcal{O} = \{O_1, \ldots, O_m\}, \mathcal{P} = \{P_1, \ldots, P_n\}$ denote the workspace, obstacles, and waypoint regions, respectively, where $O_i \subseteq \mathcal{W}$ and $P_j \subseteq \mathcal{W}, 1 \leq i \leq m, 1 \leq j \leq n$. A function VALID : $\mathcal{S} \to \{\top, \bot\}$ is used to determine whether a state is valid or not. Such function typically checks whether the robot is in collision with obstacles and that state values are within desired bounds. A trajectory λ is considered valid if every state along the trajectory is valid, i.e., for all $t \in [0, T]$: VALID$(\lambda(t)) = \top$. Let WAYPOINT : $\mathcal{S} \to \{P_1, \ldots, P_n, \bot\}$ determine which waypoint, if any, a state $s \in \mathcal{S}$ satisfies. For a trajectory $\lambda : [0, T] \to \mathcal{S}$, let WAYPOINTS$(\lambda)$ denote the waypoints satisfied by λ, i.e., WAYPOINTS$(\lambda) = \mathcal{P} \cap \left(\bigcup_{t=0}^{T} \text{WAYPOINTS}(\lambda(t)) \right)$.

Let $\mathcal{C} = \{C_1, C_2, C_3\}$ denote a partition of $\mathcal{P}$ into three groups, i.e., $\mathcal{P} = \bigcup_{i=1}^{3} C_i$ and for all $i, j \in \{1, \ldots, 3\}, i \neq j : C_i \cap C_j = \emptyset$. Let COLOR : $\mathcal{P} \to \mathcal{C}$ return the color assignment, i.e., COLOR$(P_i) = C_j \iff P_i \in C_j$. For a trajectory $\lambda : [0, T] \to \mathcal{S}$, let COLORS$(\lambda)$ denote the color set associated with the waypoints satisfied by λ, i.e., COLORS$(\lambda) = \bigcup_{P_i \in \text{WAYPOINTS}(\lambda)} \text{COLOR}(P_i)$. The objective is then for each robot to compute a valid trajectory that (a) in combination visits all waypoints, (b) reaches the colors in the order C_1, C_2, C_3 (as imposed by task, station and delivery sets).

The PVRP framework origins in the PTSP competition [18] with its main purpose to provide a benchmark for combined task and motion planning. As an input the framework takes different sets of two-dimensional bitmaps of blocking and non-blocking cells with colored waypoints (see Fig. 1)[2].

Within the framework, vehicles move autonomously and freely through an environment by applying thrust and rotation, with up to six different *macro*

---

[2] A video animation of the solution process is avaialble at https://bitbucket.org/ Denis_Golubev/pvrp/src.

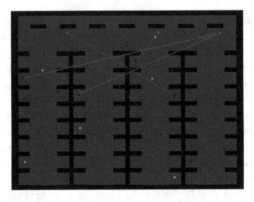

Fig. 1. A warehouse-inspired physical vehicle routing problem (robots are yellow, picking stations are green, empty spots are purple, and occupied spots are blue, and orders are indicated with red lines; figure best viewed in colors on screen) (Color figure online).

actions. The former can be seen as a boolean input (either the vehicle accelerates or not), while the latter is an integer value to indicate rotation to the left, to the right or no rotation at all. All actions are applied to the vehicle as forces which update its position, orientation and velocity at each time step. The environment itself is modeled as map of pixel cells. The crucial parts of the software framework are the *controller* and the *solver*. The controller adapts the map to a proper world model and determines the shortest path from the current position of the vehicle towards every available waypoint. The solver then calculates a route based on the shortest paths provided by the controller and reports it back. Based on the solution, the controller navigates the vehicle.

We extended both, controller and solver, to find solutions for the PVRP. In the default controller, each map is approximated by a weighted graph (every 64 cells are merged into one graph node), in which A* is called to compute pairwise shortest paths between the start location and each of the waypoints. These distances are then fed as a matrix into a VRP solver, and –utilizing the imposed schedule of waypoints– the controller software performs a random search on macros. As part of the framework, besides computer play, the interface allows replay of preceding games and human players to participate in solving the problem using interactive steering. The execution model of the framework is real-time: actions have to be committed at a rate of about 40 ms. The startup time is 0.1 s for each waypoint.

The shortest path implementations of [9,17] (one based on flood-fill the other on radix heaps, respectively) are more efficient, so that pixel-precise shortest-paths distance computation from every waypoint to every pixel cell could be performed within setup time. Besides adding more vehicles, we are solving PTSPs with colored waypoints. In the general PTSP a node of each color has to be visited at least once within a tour, so that all colors but not necessarily all waypoints are visited. In a *Clustered PTSP*, we have to visit every waypoint in a pre-defined cluster before approaching the next. Our quest is a mixture, requesting to visit shelf locations (one color), bringing them to the picking station (second color) and back to empty spots (third color). There is even dynamics that can be considered, as empty spots are generated during the time the shelves are transported. The changes to include colored waypoints in the PTSP software framework were rather small: for waypoints we included colors as member variables that were randomly assigned. For debugging the controller, we also added waypoint IDs.

3   Implementation

The implementation in Java uses design patterns [11]. For the test of collision, we model the robot as a convex polygon and add a bounding sphere to it, the latter to filter the intersection tasks by looking at the sum of the radii.

2D intersection is computed by evaluating the normals [1], resulting in the minimum translation [3,8] for a collision to be avoided. If the two vehicles intersect, an elastic collision is performed: based on the angle of the collision, the speed and acceleration of the two vehicles [6] are computed [7].

NRPA by [19] has been applied to two puzzles. For tour generation the recursion looks as follows (parameters *level* & *iteration*, and calls to *rollout* & *adapt*).

```
public Tour nrpa(final int level, final Policy policy) {
  if (level == 0) return rollout(policy);
  Tour bestTour = Tour.worst();
  Policy currentPolicy = policy;
  for (int i = 0; i < iterations; ++i) {
   Tour resultingTour = nrpa(level - 1, currentPolicy);
   if (resultingTour.cost() < bestTour.cost())
     bestTour = resultingTour;
     currentPolicy.adapt(initialSimulation, bestTour);
   return bestTour
  }
}
```

We parallelized the controller by using threads [16]. Each agent gets an own controller thread, which is synchronized by communication to the multicontroller. The multicontroller sends action information to and receives the outcome from the server. In every simulation step, the agents have to make a number of decisions:

1. After reaching a delivery stop, a next pickup is visited, or stop.
2. After a pickup, one station initiating the order has to be visited.
3. After visiting a station, every possible delivery waypoint is available.

A list of decisions together with the according cost is maintained and performed in the simulation engine.

Table 1. Simulation and running time for different NRPA parameters.

	Simulation time		CPU time	
	Mean	Std-dev	Mean	Std-dev
Initial (level 2, 100 iterations)	4354.17	90,89	$2.91\,s$	$0.13\,s$
Initial (level 3, 100 iterations)	4260.78	1.46	$286.63\,s$	$28.17\,s$
Random (level 2, 100 iterations)	4576.62	104.37	$0.9\,s$	$0.03\,s$
Random (level 3, 100 iterations)	4299.23	40.43	$88.46\,s$	$9.5\,s$

4   Results

We extended the parser to process maps with annotations of the form
$tasks : (x_1, y_1) \rightarrow (x_2, y_2), (x_3, y_3), \rightarrow (x_4, y_4), \ldots, (x_n, y_n) \rightarrow (x_{n+1}, y_{n+1})$ and
$deliveries : (x_1, y_1) \rightarrow (x_2, y_2), (x_3, y_3) \rightarrow (x_4, y_4), \ldots, (x_n, y_n) \rightarrow (x_{n+1}, y_{n+1})$.
The task parsing part uses regular expressions. The map viewer visualizes the
problem including task and delivery task (used to produce Fig. 1).

The simulation time and CPU time results are shown in Table 1. We used
Linux Kernel: 4.4.1, Java-Version: 1.8.0_74 Intel Xeon E3-1230 v3 CPU, 3.3 Ghz

Reducing the iteration width from 100 to 75 of the NRPA solver with level 3
search gave one more solution, namely 4260.49. We also implemented an optimal
solver based on depth-first search, which found the best solution 4260.49 in 48 s.
It generated 15'114'240 tours compared to the 421'875 playouts in the best
NRPA setting. Using one more station, 46'125'000 and 2 m 24 s were needed by
the optimal solver, whereas NRPA's performance remained fixed.

5   Conclusion

In this paper we have illustrated a novel scientific challenge with high relevance
in the logistics domain: the optimized freespace navigation of multiple robots
in warehouses with obstacles. The dynamics of the robots as well as pairwise
intersections are handled properly without affecting real-time constraints. In the
long term, we envision applications, where extended PVRP controllers navigate
autonomous robots in the real-world.

In pick-pack-and-ship warehouses hundreds of small autonomous robots lift
movable storage shelves. By bringing the product to the worker, productivity is
increased by a factor of two or more, while simultaneously improving account-
ability and flexibility. The ultimate goal of KIVA [22] goes back to Alphabet
Soup [12], a testbet for assembling words with robots that —in contrast to the
currently implemented solutions— operate in freespace instead of a grid.

References

1. allegro.cc: 2D concave polygon collision detection (2009). https://www.allegro.cc/forums/thread/598784
2. Applegate, D.L., Bixby, R.E., Chvtal, V., Cook, W.J.: The Traveling Salesman Problem: A Computational Study. Princeton University Press, New Jersey (2006)
3. Bittle, W.: SAT (Separating Axis Theorem) (2010)
4. Cazenave, T.: Nested Monte-Carlo search. In: Proceedings of the Twenty-First International Joint Conference on Artificial Intelligence, Universit Paris-Dauphine, Paris (2009)
5. Cordeau, J.-F., Laporte, G., Savelsbergh, M.W., Vigo, D.: Vehicle routing. In: Handbooks in Operations Research and Management Science, vol. 14, pp. 367–428. Elsevier B.V (2007). Chapter 6
6. Cornelsen: Das große Tafelwerk: Formelsammlung für die Sekundarstufen I und II. Berlin: Cornelsen (2010). (German)
7. Craver, W.: Elastic Collisions (2016)
8. Eberly, D.: Intersection of Convex Objects: The Method of Separating Axes. Geometric Tools, LLC (2008)
9. Edelkamp, S., Greulich, C.: Solving physical traveling salesman problems with policy adaptation. In: IEEE Conference on Computational Intelligence in Games (CIG), pp. 1–8 (2014)
10. Plaku, E., Sarah, R., Stefan, E.: Observation of strains: multi-group motion planning in virtual environments. Comput. Animation Virtual Worlds (2011)
11. Gamma, E., Helm, R., Johnson, R.E., Vlissides, J.: Design Patterns: Elements of Reusable Object-Oriented Software. Addison-Wesley, Boston (1995)
12. Hazard, C.J., Wurman, P.R., Soup, A.: A testbed for studying resource allocation in multi-vehicle systems. In: AAAI-Workshop on Auction-Based Robot Coordination (2006)
13. Landau, L.D., Lifshitz, E.M.: Mechanics. Course of Theoretical Physics, vol. 1. Pergamon Press, Oxford (1969)
14. Mitchell, T.M.: Machine Learning. McGraw-Hill, New York (1997)
15. Neward, T.: Java 8: Lambdas, Part 1. Oracle (Java Mag.) (2013)
16. Oracle: Java Platform Standard 8th edn. Documentation (2016)
17. Perez, D., Powley, E.J., Whitehouse, D., Rohlfshagen, P., Samothrakis, S., Cowling, P.I., Lucas, S.M.: Solving the physical travelling salesman problem: tree search and macro-actions. IEEE Trans. Comput. Intell. AI Games (2013)
18. Perez, D., Rohlfshagen, P., Lucas, S.M.: The physical travelling salesman problem: WCCI 2012 competition (2012)
19. Rosin, Christopher D.: Nested rollout policy adaptation. In: IJCAI, USA (2011)
20. Tzoreff, T.E., Granot, D., Granot, F., Soic, G.: The vehicle routing problem with pickups and deliveries on some special graphs. Discrete Appl. Math. **116**(3), 139–229 (2002)
21. Urma, R.-G.: Processing data with Java SE 8 streams, Part 1. Oracle (Java Mag.) (2014)
22. Wurman, P.R., D'Andrea, R., Mountz, M.: Coordinating hundreds of cooperative, autonomous vehicles in warehouses. AI Mag. **29**(1), 9 (2008)

Trending Topic Aggregation
by News-Based Context Modeling

Sebastian Fuchs[1], Damian Borth[2], and Adrian Ulges[1(✉)]

[1] RheinMain University of Applied Sciences (HSRM), 65195 Wiesbaden, Germany
`sebastian.b.fuchs@student.hs-rm.de`, `adrian.ulges@hs-rm.de`
[2] German Research Center for Artificial Intelligence (DFKI),
67663 Kaiserslautern, Germany
`damian.borth@dfki.de`

Abstract. We tackle social media analysis based on trending topics like
"super bowl" and "oscars 2016" acquired from channels such as Twitter or Google. Our approach addresses the identification of semantically
related topics (such as "oscars 2016" and "leonardo dicaprio") by enriching trends with textual context acquired from news search and applying a clustering and tracking in term space. In quantitative experiments
on manually annotated trends from Feb–Mar 2016, we demonstrate this
approach to work reliably (with an F_1-score of > 90%) and to outperform
several baselines, including knowledge graph modelling using DBPedia
as well as a direct comparison of articles or terms.

Keywords: Trending topics · Social media analysis · Text mining

1 Introduction

Social media provide a rich repository of people's opinion about a broad spectrum
of topics, extracting which is the challenge of *multimedia opinion mining* [1–3].
One task in this area is the detection of topics of general interest the very
moment they occur. Such *trending topics* (related to natural disasters, sports
events, etc.) are usually derived from spikes in search frequency, and are highly
useful indicators of user interest.

Often, the same event is represented by different topic titles. Sometimes these
may be similar, in which case a simple string matching may suffice (e.g. "oscars"
vs. "oscars 2016"). In other cases, semantic relatedness may be more difficult to
uncover (e.g., "oscars 2016" vs. "leonardo dicaprio"). We refer to the challenge of
identifying and grouping semantically identical topics as *aggregation* (see Fig. 1
for an example). Aggregation is supposed to merge topics from different channels
("patriots" on Twitter, "super bowl" on Wikipedia) as well as topics over time
("paris bombing" in Nov 2015, changing into "isis" the next days).

To do so, we enrich trending topics with news context: Given a topic title, we
retrieve news articles from the corresponding day and use simple models of text
statistics to cluster and track trending topics in term space. The approach is

© Springer International Publishing AG 2016
G. Friedrich et al. (Eds.): KI 2016, LNAI 9904, pp. 162–168, 2016.
DOI: 10.1007/978-3-319-46073-4_15

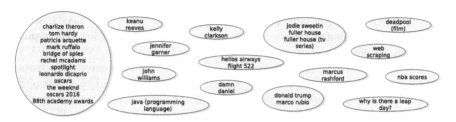

Fig. 1. Aggregating trending topics of Feb 29 2016.

plugged into an end-to-end system for trending topic understanding, including the acquisition from various social media channels, aggregation, and in-depth inspection of trends[1]. We demonstrate on a dataset crawled in Feb–Mar 2016 covering about 800 trending topics and 10 K topic pairs labeled by a human expert that this approach outperforms several baselines, including knowledge graph modelling (DBPedia), a string matching comparison of trending topic titles, as well as the comparison of articles acquired by a search engine.

2 Related Work

Detecting and tracking topics in broadcast media has been studied for about two decades (including the mapping of television and radio sources) [4]. Over the last decade, work on trend discovery has focused on blogs and Twitter content [5,6], where approaches employ aggregated trends provided by the platform itself [6] or perform trend analysis on the raw data [2,5]. Similar to the former, we utilize platform provided lists of trends to form clusters, contextualize those trending topics, and arrange them around real-world events.

In this context, Benhardus et al. [7] employ uni- and bigrams in tf-idf space. Temporal characteristics of trending topics were studied by Li et al. [8], where topic clusters were tracked over time by comparing topic centroids representing *stories* to newly emerging topics. Semantic similarity based on synonyms were also utilized in the context of trending topic clustering [9]. In this work, we combine all three approaches together to improve clustering performance within one day and inbetween multiple days capturing topic shift over time.

3 Approach

This section outlines our approach towards trending topic aggregation and explanation. We first discuss the acquisition of trending topics from social media channels, followed by the aggregation of trends over different channels (*clustering*) and over time (*tracking*).

Acquisition of Trending Topics and Context Data. We crawl the top trends from three major online media channels (Twitter, Google, and

---

[1] A demo is available at http://multimedia-opinion-mining.appspot.com.

Wikipedia), covering different aspects of people's communication needs, search patterns, and information demand. We retrieve daily ranked lists of popular terms from 10 different sources: 5 Google channels (Search and News for USA and Germany as well as the "Trends"s feed), 3 Twitter channels (daily trends for USA and Germany as well as the "Daily Trends" feed), and two Wikipedia channels (popular articles in English or German). For each feed we retrieve 10–20 ranked topics (110 topics per day). In total our dataset covers the observation period Feb 02 2016–Mar 09 2016.

Given a trending topic title (such as "super bowl"), we retrieve news articles as a context. As a news source, we use the Bing Search API[2], which can be queried for news from certain regions and dates. Each retrieved article contains a headline (consisting of about 5–10 terms) and a short description (consisting of about 20–30 terms). We obtain about 44 articles per trending topic on average, after removing duplicates from Bing's result list. We preprocess each article by lowercasing, removing non-alphabetic characters (incl. numbers), tokenization, stopword removal, and stemming (using the Porter stemmer for English and the Snowball stemmer for German).

Clustering. We first focus on aggregating trending topics from a single day. Hereby, a *trending topic* refers to a short 1–3 words title (such as "super bowl" or "oscars 2016"). From several social media channels, we obtain a set of such trending topics that may contain duplicates, near-duplicates (such as "super bowl" vs. "super bowl L") or different but semantically related topics (such as "super bowl L" vs. "broncos"). Our goal is to *cluster* the set of trending topics into semantically coherent groups. Thereby, two topics should be assigned to the same cluster if they refer to the same specific news event, not if they bare some general semantic resemblance (e.g., both covering sports). We refer to the resulting clusters as **trends**.

We discuss two approaches. The first considers two topics similar if their news context contains similar terms. The other exploits a structured knowledge representation, i.e. topics are considered similar if they are closely connected in the DBPedia knowledge graph.

The first approach collects terms for each trending topic from all its news articles (using both the title and description, both preprocessed) and derives a bag-of-words representation. Each trending topic (or *document*) is represented by a tf-idf vector (we use all terms appearing at least once on the day in question). To estimate a similarity between two trending topics, the cosine measure is applied to their tf-idf vectors. Based on these similarity values, the trending topics are clustered using an agglomerative clustering with single linkage. The resulting dendrogram is transformed into a set of flat clusters by cutting it off at a threshold similarity α.

Our second approach is based on linked data: As an alternative to unstructured text (which comes with well-known caveats such as context dependence, synonymy and polysemy, etc.), useful indicators for topic relatedness can be

---

[2] https://datamarket.azure.com/dataset/bing/search.

derived from large-scale knowledge graphs: For example, in DBPedia[3] the Oscar nominees "leonardo dicaprio" and "mark ruffalo" share the (dct:subject) links 21th-century_American_ male_actors or American_male_film_actors. Our approach replaces the news statistics similarity with one derived from the DBPedia knowledge graph. Given two trending topics t_1, t_2, we use SPARQL queries with the bif:contains operator to conduct a full text search for both topics' titles. We obtain two sets of entry nodes in the DBPedia knowledge graph and collect the nodes' subjects in two sets $S(t_1)$ and $S(t_2)$. Our similarity measures the normalized overlap of those subjects:

$$sim(t_1, t_2) := \frac{1}{2} \cdot \left(\frac{\#\left(S(t_1) \cap S(t_2) \right)}{\#S(t_1) + 1} + \frac{\#\left(S(t_1) \cap S(t_2) \right)}{\#S(t_2) + 1} \right). \tag{1}$$

The above normalization is used because the distribution of subjects may be highly imbalanced between different nodes: Some nodes like "super bowl" come with 378 subjects, while others like "oscars" display only 8 subjects. Given this similarity measure, we apply the same single-linkage agglomerative clustering as with the text statistics approach and cut-off at a threshold α.

Tracking. While the above approach focuses on grouping topics within a single day, trending topics in practice keep emerging and evolving over time. New (clusters of) trending topics need to be matched to existing trends, which may shift as new events occur (think of "paris attacks" on Nov. 13 2015, leading to a terrorist hunt in "brussels" a few days later).

Our approach is based on the news statistics representation. We represent each cluster of trending topics (or *trend*) by a centroid in term space. When a new trend T is initialized as a cluster of trending topics, we compute the centroid by averaging the trending topics' tf-idf representations. As time progresses, new topics $t_1, ..., t_N$ emerge and need to be matched against existing trends $T_1, T_2, ..., T_K$. To do so, we compute each trending topic's tf-idf similarity to each trend, $cos(v_{tf-idf}(t), v_{tf-idf}(T))$. We assign the topic to the closest trend if at least a minimum similarity γ is measured. The remaining new topics – which seem to fit no existing trend – are clustered using the above approach. The resulting clusters are added to the set of current trends. We further assume trends to expire when not matched to any trending topics for a subsequent period of days.

As a set of new trending topics T' is assigned to a trend T, we expect the trend to evolve over time as new events and developments are added. Therefore, we adapt T's centroid using exponential decay, i.e. we update:

$$v_{tf-idf}(T) := (1 - \lambda) \cdot v_{tf-idf}(T) + \lambda \cdot \frac{1}{\#T'} \sum_{t \in T'} v_{tf-idf}(t)$$

---

[3] The *Live* endpoint (http://live.dbpedia.org/sparql) which syncs with Wikipedia continuously.

4   Experiments

We evaluated topic clustering and tracking on a set of trending topics acquired between Feb. 02 2016–Mar. 09 2016 for the regions "US" and Germany ("DE") from Google, Wikipedia and Twitter. A human expert grouped each day's topics to clusters. Two topics were assigned to the same cluster when related to the *same event*: For example, "Hillary Clinton" and "Donald Trump" (both presidential candidates in the US pre-elections 2016) would be considered similar, but not "Hillary Clinton" and "Angela Merkel" (both famous female politicians and both subject to current news, but due to different events). The resulting dataset contains 805 trending topics grouped into 530 clusters, with $4,749$ (DE) and $5,760$ (US) topic pair annotations. As an evaluation measure, we use the well-known F_1-score derived from precision and recall over all topic pairs' cluster annotations.

Clustering. We first evaluate the text statistics approach from Sect. 3. News articles were acquired from Bing, preprocessed and represented by tf-idf vectors (whereas the inverse document frequency was computed over all articles of a day). Figure 1 illustrates a sample result of clustering from Feb 29, with a major cluster covering the Oscar awards. We compared several approaches and baselines:

- **Our Approach:** The above approach based on news statistics using tf-idf representations. α was set to 0.03 for German and 0.05 for US topics (we found accuracy to be quite stable within a range of $[0.03, 0.05]$).
- **DBPedia:** The *Linked Data* approach from Sect. 3, deriving a trending topic similarity from the DBPedia knowledge graph. Like for the tf-idf representation, the α parameter was derived using grid search.
- **String Matching:** Our prior work [1] conducted a simple fuzzy string matching between the topic titles: Given two trending topic titles t_1 and t_2, we compute their Levenshtein distance $dist_L(t_1, t_2)$ and define the similarity as $sim(t_1, t_2) := 1 - dist_L(t_1, t_2)/max(length(t_1), length(t_2))$ This similarity measure is used in standard single-linkage clustering (α optimized via grid search).
- **Article Matching:** Obviously, our approach relies heavily on the quality of its news context. In our evaluation, we acquire such context from Bing, whose internal statistical models and optimizations are not publicly revealed. To evaluate the extent to which our approaches' success is due to the "black box" Bing, we compare our approach to a baseline that defines semantic relatedness based not on *article content* but *article identity*. Let $A(t)$ be the set of articles retrieved by our news source for a trending topic t. Then we employ the similarity measure from Eq. 1, only measuring the overlap in Bing articles instead of DBPedia `subjects`. Accordingly, two topics are considered "similar" if Bing retrieves the same articles for them. We use standard single-linkage clustering (α determined via grid search).

Approach	F_1-Score	
	US	DE
our approach	**94.4**	**92.8**
DBPedia	41.3	50.0
string matching	61.2	65.9
article matching	89.3	89.7
word matching	87.5	80.2

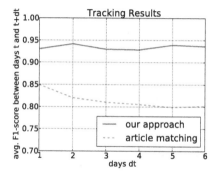

Fig. 2. Left: results of topic clustering for different approaches. Right: results of tracking, comparing our approach vs. the 'article matching' baseline.

- **Word Matching:** Finally, we use another baseline comparing news titles: For each topic, we collect all terms from all its articles' titles. Then we measure the overlap in those terms as a similarity between topics (again, using Eq. 1 but replacing DBPedia `subjects` with title terms).

We observe (Fig. 2) that our approach yields the highest accuracy, outperforming string matching significantly (by about 30 % on average). A detailed inspection revealed that most remaining errors occurred in cases where a Bing news search yielded no context articles ("unix-shell", "hilbert-transformation", or "mansplaining", which are all not in the core focus of "regular" news articles). The DBPedia approach worked well in *some* cases. For example, the topics "leonardo dicaprio" (with 151 subjects in total) and "mark ruffalo" (with 120 subjects in total) share 22 subjects, which leads to a relatively high similarity of about 16 %. In contrast, "bridge of spies" (with 26 subjects in total) and "jodie sweetin" (with 39 subjects in total) share only 1 common subject and are not grouped. Overall, the DBPedia similarity is outperformed significantly by all news-based approaches. This is because (1) we found the acquisition of suitable DBPedia entry nodes by text tricky (think of topics like "why is there a leap day"), and (2) DBPedia links express a general semantic relatedness not necessarily a relatedness to current events (think of "Hillary Clinton" vs. "Angela Merkel").

The *article matching* baseline yields a high accuracy, which indicates that our approach heavily depends on the quality of Bing's news context. However, we also see that adding a statistical text modelling by tf-idf on top improves performance further (by about 4 %). Finally, we observe that the word matching baseline performs well too, but that modelling context in its entirety via tf-idf outperforms a mere keyword matching (consider a topic like "super bowl" where tf-idf can exploit contextual terms like "inning" or "stadium" for a more accurate matching).

We also compare the *tracking* accuracy of our approach (α adopted from Sect. 4, λ set to 0.5) with the Bing article matching baseline. When progressing to the next day, we replace a trend's Bing articles with all its articles from the last day it has been observed. The similarity threshold γ is adopted from the clustering experiment.

For any day t in the observation period, we track trending topics from day t to day $t + dt$ and compare our tracking results to manual annotations over all pairs of trending topics between the two days. Figure 2 displays the F_1-score, averaged over all trending topics and all start days t and grouped by the difference dt. The resulting plot indicates the average tracking accuracy dt days into the future. We observe that our approach yields an accurate tracking and outperforms article matching significantly.

5   Conclusion

We have presented an approach towards trending topic aggregation based on news context modeling and text mining. The approach was demonstrated to yield accurate clusters (with an F_1-score of $> 90\%$) and outperform several baselines that use the DBPedia knowledge graph, article identity, or plain string matching on topic titles.

Our remaining key challenge – and basis of future work – is the integration of other appropriate context sources. Trending topics are diverse, covering anything that causes spikes in user interest, and we found some of these spikes to be poorly covered by news, such as "unix-shell" or "mansplaining". Other issues might be the exploitation of additional information sources such as topic popularity for an improved tracking or prediction [1].

References

1. Althoff, T., Borth, D., Hees, J., Dengel, A.: Analysis and forecasting of trending topics in online media streams. In: Proceedings of ACM International Conference on Multimedia (ACM MM), pp. 907–916, October 2013
2. Becker, H., Naaman, M., Gravano, L.: Beyond trending topics: real-world event identification on Twitter. In: Proceedings of AAAI International Conference on Weblogs and Social Media (ICWSM), July 2011
3. Borth, D., Ji, R., Chen, T., Breuel, T., Chang, S.F.: Large-scale visual sentiment ontology and detectors using adjective noun pairs. In: Proceedings of ACM International Conference on Multimedia (ACM MM), pp. 223–232, October 2013
4. Allan, J.: Introduction to topic detection and tracking. In: Allan, J. (ed.) Topic Detection and Tracking, vol. 12, pp. 1–16. Springer, New York (2002)
5. Glance, N., Hurst, M., Tomokiyo, T.: Blogpulse: automated trend discovery for weblogs. In: Workshop on the Weblogging Ecosystem: Aggregation, Analysis and Dynamics (2004)
6. Kwak, H., Lee, C., Park, H., Moon, S.: What is Twitter, a social network or a news media? In: Proceedings of ACM International Conference on World Wide Web (WWW), April 2010
7. Benhardus, J., Kalita, J.: Streaming trend detection in Twitter. Int. J. Web Based Communities 9(1), 122–139 (2013)
8. Li, B., Li, W., Lu, Q.: Enhancing topic tracking with temporal information. In: Proceedings of ACM SIGIR Conference on Research and development in Information Retrieval, pp. 667–668 (2006)
9. Kumar, S.: Semantic clustering of index terms. J. ACM 15(4), 493–513 (1968)

Image-Based Identification of Plant Species Using a Model-Free Approach and Active Learning

Jonatan Grimm[1(✉)], Mark Hoffmann[1], Ben Stöver[2], Kai Müller[2], and Volker Steinhage[1]

[1] Institute of Computer Science IV, Bonn University, Bonn, Germany
grimm@informatik.uni-bonn.de
[2] Institute for Evolution and Biodiversity and Botan. Garden, Münster University, Münster, Germany

Abstract. Collection and maintenance of biodiversity data is in need for automation. We present first results of an automated and model-free approach to the species identification from herbarium specimens kept in herbaria worldwide. Methodologically, our approach relies on standard methods for the detection and description of so-called interest points and their classification into species-characteristic categories using standard supervised learning tools. To keep the approach model-free on the one hand but also offer opportunities for species identification even in very challenging cases on the other hand, we allow to induce specific knowledge about important visual cues by using concepts of active learning on demand. First encouraging results on selected fern species show recognition accuracies between 94 % and 100 %.

1 Introduction

The automated collection and integration of botanical observation data is crucial for the sustainable conservation and documentation of biodiversity. Moreover, the fields of systematics, evolutionary biology and ecology would generally benefit from the greater throughput and repeatability achieved by such automation. The classical representation of a conserved botanical sample is the herbarium specimen - dried plants or plant parts mounted on herbarium sheets and stored and organized in herbaria. Millions of these specimens have already been digitized and are available online as digital images. However, these images are highly underutilized, because analytic tools for the extraction and analysis of morphological data are lagging behind, while techniques for the acquisition and analysis of molecular data have been universally adopted. Most image-based identification methods proposed in the past were so far based on leaf images (e.g. in Backes et al., 2009 [2], Belhumeur et al., 2008 [3], Goëau et al., 2011a [5], 2011b [6]). Kadir et al. [9] give a comprehensive survey on methods to identify plants by classifying their leaves. Only few approaches focused on flower's images as in Nilsback and Zisserman (2008) [13]. But while leaves are far from being the only

© Springer International Publishing AG 2016
G. Friedrich et al. (Eds.): KI 2016, LNAI 9904, pp. 169–176, 2016.
DOI: 10.1007/978-3-319-46073-4_16

discriminant visual key for species identification, they have the advantage to be easily observed, captured and described due to their shape and size.

These methods are model-based, i.e., they are customised to the specific application or specific plant parts, e.g., leaves. Model-free approaches do not employ application-specific knowledge and therefore promise a higher degree of generalisation onto different plants and plant parts. One approach to model-free methods in computer vision uses so-called interest points (IPs) and their descriptors. These IP descriptors are based on the image gradient information within their local pixel neighbourhood. Informally, IPs are showing high contrast in their local neighbourhood thereby identifying object edges or object corners. A comprehensive survey and performance evaluation of keypoint descriptors is given by Mikolajczyk and Schmid [11]. In an interdisciplinary project between biologists of Münster University and computer scientists of Bonn University, we are working on an automatic approach to species identification of plants conserved in herbarium specimens. Due to the huge variety, we are aiming for a model-free approach to species identification.

2   A Model-Free Approach to Identification of Species from Herbaium Specimens

The image data used are scanned herbarium specimens of ferns depicting dried plants or plant parts (cf. Fig. 1). The example scans of herbarium specimens used in this contribution are from the collection of the *Muséum national d'histoire naturelle* in Paris [12]. Specimens of fern represent a very difficult application example due to different sizes, orientations and (partially filigree) shapes. Additionally, the plant parts are bended in different ways. For finding IPs in multiple levels of detail, we employ the *Scale Invariant Feature Transform* (SIFT) introduced by David Lowe in 2004 [10]. SIFT detects IPs and describes them with

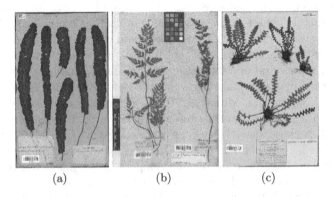

(a)   (b)   (c)

Fig. 1. Three herbarium specimens of fern species (a) *Asplenium scolopendrium* (P01515633), (b) *Asplenium andantium-nigrum* (P00636536), (c) *Asplenium ceterach* (P01560771).

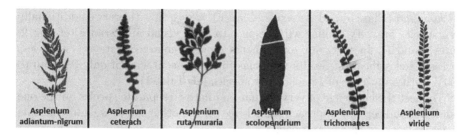

Fig. 2. Six fern species used in our experiments. From left to right: (a) *A. adiantum-nigrum*, (b) *A. ceterach*, (c) *A. ruta-muraria*, (d) *A. scolopendrium*, (e) *A. trichomanes*, (f) *A. viride*.

a gradient magnitude and direction based descriptor. Furthermore, SIFT has shown to perform superior in a performance evaluation of IP descriptors by Mikolajczyk and Schmid [11]. The SIFT-based descriptor vectors of the IPs are used within a supervised classification approach to species identification from the herbarium specimens using a Support Vector Machine (SVM) approach.

We used scans of four different fern species resulting in four classes for SVM learning: Class 1 = *Asplenium adiantum-nigrum*, Class 2 = *Asplenium ceterach*, Class 3 = *Asplenium ruta-muraria*, and Class 4 = *Asplenium scolopendrium*. For training and parameter optimization of the SVM, we used 18 scans per species resulting in our evaluation on 4 species in 72 scans. For the evaluation, we operated a leave-one-out cross-validation. This first approach shows very promising identification results, i.e., classification accuracies of at least 96 % up to 100 %. It must be stressed that these identification results have been obtained without any explicit modelling and customization.

But we still have not reached the end of the road. As Fig. 2 shows, the four fern species used in that approach so far (*A. adiantum-nigrum, A. ceterach, A. ruta-muraria, A. scolopendrium* (cf. Fig. 2, parts a, b, c and d)) show a sufficient amount of specific characteristic visual features to identify these species with the given accuracies. Adding in our evaluation two additional fern species, i.e., *A.*

Table 1. Results of the cross-validation for six classes

	Class 1	Class 2	Class 3	Class 4	Class 5	Class 6
True positive	18	17	16	18	12	10
True negative	83	90	85	90	88	87
False positive	7	0	5	0	2	3
False negative	0	1	2	0	6	8
Recall	1,00	0,94	0,89	1,00	0,67	0,56
Precision	0,72	1,00	0,76	1,00	0,86	0,77
Accuracy	0,94	0,99	0,94	1,00	0,93	0,90

trichomanes (Class 5) and *A. viride* (Class 6), we see that these two additionally fern species are very similar with respect to their visual appearance (cf. Fig. 2, parts e and f). In fact, our experiments on this enlarged data set show less successful classification results with classification accuracies of only 90 % up to 100 % with a data set of 18 scans per species (cf. Table 1).

To meet the challenge of very similar and hard to separate species on the one hand, but to keep our approach model-free on the other hand, we add concepts of active learning to our approach.

3   A Model-Free Approach to Species Identification Including Concepts of Active Learning

To discriminate very similar species, we propose a hierarchical approach to our project of species identification. In the initial level, our pure model-free approach summarized in Sect. 2 is used to identify as many species as possible. In following levels, we interactively query the human expert to define image templates of significant and characteristic plant features of her choice for such species showing insufficient identification accuracies in the initial level. Since the user is able to decide, which characteristic part to select, the approach is still model-free. We implemented this approach for species identification of ferns within a two level hierarchy. We will now explain the complete processing chain of this implementation that is summarized in Fig. 3. The input is formed by images of plants, i.e., scans of the herbarium specimens that are preprocessed by contrast stretching and downsampling to a fixed resolution to have keypoints in comparable detail levels for each scan. In the first step of our processing chain, we use the SIFT detector to detect IPs in the scans (1). For these IPs, we derive the SIFT descriptors (2). The SIFT descriptors are numeric vectors used as training and test data for the SVM classification (3). For four of our six species *A. adiantum-nigrum*, *A. ceterach*, *A. ruta-muraria* and *A. scolopendrium*, we have good recognition accuracies. So, scans of these species already are identified after step 3. For *A. trichomanes* and *A. viride*, the recognition accuracies of this step are not sufficient. Therefore we proceed with step 4 by using a template matching approach to discriminate these very similar species (4). Image templates depict small, but very characteristic plant parts like lobes in our implementation and therefore serve to select species-characteristic regions. The expert user is asked to select interactively these species-characteristic regions in an easy understandable and operable way by drawing bounding boxes around these regions. The generated templates are then matched with the detected IPs (5) and described by a well established shape based image descriptor (6), namely the HOG descriptor [4]. Now these HOG descriptors are used in a SVM-based classification to identify the very similar species of A. trichomanes and A. viride (7). For the active learning approach in step 4, we employ the average margin in a threshold-based minimum marginal hyperplane strategy for SVMs (cf. Settles [17], Tong and Koller [18]).

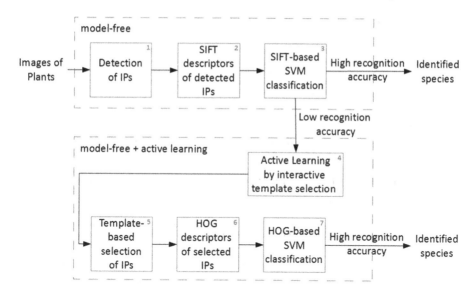

Fig. 3. The processing chain of the two-level approach to species identification from herbarium specimens of fern species.

4   Evaluation

We implemented the complete processing chain in Java as a plug-in for ImageJ [15]. For the SIFT method, we employ an implementation of Saalfeld [16]. For the SVM, we chose SVM^{light} (cf. [7,8]). For the HOG descriptor, we use the implementation of Anzivino and Spampani [1] and for the Template matching, we utilise an implementation of O'Dell [14].

We proceed with the scans of the six mentioned fern species (cf. Fig. 2) as described in Sect. 3 . Low identification rates are predicted by a threshold-based minimum marginal hyperplane strategy for SVMs for the two species *A. trichomanes* and *A. viride*. Therefore, in this evaluation templates of their lobes are selected. Using these templates, such SIFT points are identified that are positioned on such lobes. Their HOG descriptors are now used in the second level of our identification approach to identify scans of the species *A. trichomanes* and *A. viride* again by using an SVM.

For the evaluation, we operate a leave-one-out cross-validation on a separate test data set of so far unseen for the SVM. The results are shown in Table 2. We now see classification accuracies of 96 % and 94 % for the difficult to separate species *A. trichomanes* and *A. viride*, respectively, compared to the results given in Table 1 that show identification accuracies of only 93 % and 90 %. Again, we stress that our complete approach is in general still model-free but allows to incorporate application-specific models in terms of templates on demand by using concepts of active learning.

Table 2. Results of the cross validation for six classes (cf. Sect. 4).

	Class 1	Class 2	Class 3	Class 4	Class 5	Class 6
True positive	18	17	16	18	14	12
True negative	83	90	85	90	90	89
False positive	7	0	5	0	0	1
False negative	0	1	2	0	4	6
Recall	1, 00	0, 94	0, 89	1, 00	0, 78	0, 67
Precision	0, 72	1, 00	0, 76	1, 00	1, 00	0, 92
Accuracy	0, 94	0, 99	0, 94	1, 00	0, 96	0, 94

5   Conclusion and Future Work

In this contribution, we proposed a model-free approach to the image-based identification of plant species. Our processing chain shows two identification levels.

In the first level, we combine a standard approach (SIFT) to the detection and description of interest points (IPs) with a standard approach to supervised learning (SVM) to identify plant species. For species that can be identified in this first level with only low identification accuracy, we employ a concept of active learning by interactively querying the expert user for domain-specific models in terms of templates. The templates specify meaningful plant parts like lobes and are used to select those interest points positioned at this plant parts within a second identification level. In the second level, a shape descriptor (HOG) is used for an SVM-based identification for the difficult to separate species.

We employed this approach to scans of herbarium specimens from fern species that show challenging variations with respect to their visual appearance and are difficult to identify. This first evaluation shows encouraging results in terms of classification accuracies between 94 % and 100 %. By applying concepts of active learning, we advocate that our approach is still free of predefined models. Domain-specific models are only generated on demand by interactively querying the expert user for domain-specific models in terms of templates. These templates can be selected by the user in an easy understandable and operable way by drawing bounding boxes around characteristic plant parts.

Based on these promising results, we will investigate additional feature descriptors in both levels of our image-based approach to species identification from herbarium specimens. As suggested by Mikolajczyk and Schmid [11] we will compare for the first level the SIFT approach for IP description with its GLOH variant that uses a larger neighbourhood region to describe an IP compared to SIFT, but also a reduction of dimensions by PCA yielding higher computational costs. For the shape-based description of the IP selected by the templates in the second level, we want to investigate the combination of the HOG descriptor with the LBP descriptor since Wang et al. [19] reported that this combination of LBP with HOG improves the detection performance considerably on some datasets.

We will also investigate the generalisation capacity of our approach by applying it to herbarium specimens of other plant groups. Thereby, our hierarchical approach that shows currently two processing levels, could easily be extended by adding more levels that offer the inclusion of taxon-specific knowledge and methods on demand using again concepts of active learning.

References

1. Matteo Spampani Alessio Anzivino: Hog-processing. http://hogprocessing. altervista.org. Accessed 15 Mar 2016
2. Backes, A.R., Casanova, D., Bruno, O.M.: Plant leaf identification based on volumetric fractal dimension. Int. J. Pattern Recogn. Artif. Intell. **23**(06), 1145–1160 (2009)
3. Belhumeur, P.N., et al.: Searching the world's Herbaria: a system for visual identification of plant species. In: Forsyth, D., Torr, P., Zisserman, A. (eds.) ECCV 2008, Part IV. LNCS, vol. 5305, pp. 116–129. Springer, Heidelberg (2008)
4. Dalal, N., Triggs, B.: Histograms of oriented gradients for human detection. In: IEEE Computer Society Conference on Computer Vision and Pattern Recognition, 2005, CVPR 2005, vol. 1, pp. 886–893. IEEE (2005)
5. Goëau, H., Bonnet, P., Joly, A., Boujemaa, N., Barthélémy, D., Molino, J.-F., Birnbaum, P., Mouysset, E., Picard, M.: The imageclef 2011 plant images classi cation task. In: ImageCLEF 2011 (2011)
6. Goëau, H., Joly, A., Selmi, S., Bonnet, P., Mouysset, E., Joyeux, L., Molino, J.-F., Birnbaum, P., Bathelemy, D., Boujemaa, N.: Visual-based plant species identification from crowdsourced data. In: Proceedings of the 19th ACM International Conference on Multimedia, pp. 813–814. ACM (2011)
7. Joachims, T.: Making large scale svm learning practical. Technical report, Universität Dortmund (1999)
8. Joachims, T.: Svm^{light} (2008). http://svmlight.joachims.org/. Accessed 14 Nov 2015
9. Kadir, A., Nugroho, L.E., Susanto, A., Santosa, P.I.: Leaf classification using shape, color, and texture features (2013). arXiv preprint arXiv:1401.4447
10. David, G.: Lowe: distinctive image features from scale-invariant keypoints. Int. J. Comput. Vision **60**(2), 91–110 (2004)
11. Mikolajczyk, K., Schmid, C.: A performance evaluation of local descriptors. IEEE Trans. Pattern Anal. Mach. Intell. **27**(10), 1615–1630 (2005)
12. Muséum national d'Histoire naturelle, Paris (France). Collection: Vascular plants (P). Specimens
13. Nilsback, M.-E., Zisserman, A.: Automated flower classification over a large number of classes. In: Sixth Indian Conference on Computer Vision, Graphics and Image Processing, ICVGIP 2008, pp. 722–729. IEEE (2008)
14. O'Dell, W.: Imagej plugins: Template-matching. http://rsb.info.nih.gov/ij/ plugins/template-matching.html. Accessed 15 Mar 2016
15. Rasband, W.S.: Imagej. U. S. National Institutes of Health, Bethesda, Maryland, USA (2015). http://imagej.nih.gov/ij/. Accessed 14 Nov 2015
16. Saalfeld, S.: Javasift (2015). https://github.com/axtimwalde/mpicbg. Accessed 14 Nov 2015

17. Settles, B.: Active learning literature survey. Computer Sciences Technical report 1648, University of Wisconsin-Madison (2010)
18. Tong, S., Koller, D.: Support vector machine active learning with applications to text classification. J. Mach. Learn. Res. **2**(Nov), 45–66 (2001)
19. Wang, X., Han, T.X., Yan, S.: An hog-lbp human detector with partial occlusion handling. In: 2009 IEEE 12th International Conference on Computer Vision, pp. 32–39. IEEE (2009)

Using a Deep Understanding of Network Activities for Workflow Mining

Mona Lange[1]([⊠]), Felix Kuhr[2], and Ralf Möller[1]

[1] Universität zu Lübeck, Lübeck, Germany
{lange,moeller}@ifis.uni-luebeck.de
[2] Hamburg University of Technology, Hamburg, Germany
felix.kuhr@tuhh.de

Abstract. Workflow mining is the task of automatically detecting work-flows from a set of event logs. We argue that network traffic can serve as a set of event logs and, thereby, as input for workflow mining. Networks produce large amounts of network traffic and we are able to extract sequences of workflow events by applying data mining techniques. We come to this conclusion due to the following observation: Network traffic consists of network packets, which are exchanged between network devices in order to share information to fulfill a common task. This common task corresponds to a workflow event and, when observed over time, we are able to record sequences of workflow events and model workflows as Hidden Markov models (HMM). Sequences of workflow events are caused by network dependencies, which force distributed network devices to interact. To automatically derive workflows based on network traffic, we propose a methodology based on network service dependency mining.

Keywords: Workflow mining · Hidden Markov model · Network dependency analysis

1 Introduction

Workflow and business process models have recently gained a lot of traction in the cyber security community. This is due to the fact that they can be used as a foundation for operational impact assessment within a security information and event management system, or as a foundation for process-aware information systems. Workflows are often not documented and there have been reoccurring issues [16] with manually designed workflows. It is a very time consuming process to design hand-made workflow models and, thereby, expensive. Hand-made work-flows are idealized descriptions of the process at hand and often describe more what should be done, than the actual process. Additionally, with a hand-made workflow it difficult to detect when concept drifts have occurred and the work-flow model needs to be updated. Hence, the data mining community has paid a lot of attention to the automated acquisition of workflow models [5,13,14,17,18]. Based on event logs, workflow mining methods automatically deduce sequences of workflow events.

© Springer International Publishing AG 2016
G. Friedrich et al. (Eds.): KI 2016, LNAI 9904, pp. 177–184, 2016.
DOI: 10.1007/978-3-319-46073-4_17

Currently, workflow mining is dependent on event logs and research in this domain can be divided into three topics: discovery, conformance and enhancement of workflows [15]. As we focus on workflow discovery in the context of this work, we list workflow discovery techniques in the following. A lot of workflow mining methods [5,13,14,17,18] rely on Petri nets, due to their similarities to workflow models established in business science. Other workflow mining methods [2,11] rely on HMMs, which are statistical models. Unlike Petri nets, HMMs are able to model properties such as the transition probability between workflow events. However, Petri nets can be efficiently mapped to HMMs [9,10]. Event logs are the basis for all previously listed techniques and are supposed to contain workflow data. Obtaining workflow information is not as easy and often experiments are conducted based on synthetic data sets [11]. A common limitation that all previously listed techniques have is that they rely on event logs containing workflow data, a data source that is hard to come by in every day enterprise networks.

Network traffic contains traces of communicating network services, which interact to fulfill a higher mission. This communication leads to indirect dependencies, which are clues for a data-communication networks workflow. To achieve the goal of mining workflows based on network traffic, we rely on network service dependency discovery to identify workflow events. This is why we rely on an automatic network service dependency methodology called Mission Oriented Network Analysis (MONA) [7]. MONA was compared to three state of the art network service dependency discovery methodologies: NSDMiner [8], Sherlock [1] and Orion [3]. MONA was compared via F-measures to all these state of the art methodologies and was shown to have a better performance.

2   Network Service Dependency Discovery

In the following, we will only use the term workflow, however it should be noted that earlier publications use the terms workflow and business process models interchangeably [5]. Companies, organizations and enterprises have a workflow, which translates into network activities within their data communication network. Workflows often cause reoccuring network activity patterns. We understand these network activity patterns as workflows and network service dependency analysis has the purpose of detecting workflow events. and we rely on an automatic network service dependency methodology called Mission Oriented Network Analysis (MONA) [7]. In the following, we thus rely on the same network model introduced by MONA.

2.1   Indirect Dependencies

In the context of this work, we introduce network dependency analysis as a basis for workflow mining. For this purpose, indirect dependencies correspond to workflow events. Similarly to previous work, we distinguish remote-remote (RR)

(a) Remote-remote indirect dependency.   (b) Local-remote indirect dependency.

Fig. 1. Example for indirect dependencies.

dependencies and local-remote (LR) dependencies [3]. Examples for both dependency types are shown in Fig. 1. For a remote-remote (RR) dependency, first one remote host must be contacted before issuing a request to another remote host. Figure 1a shows an RR dependency $ISDEP_{RR}$ and Fig. 1b shows and LR dependency $ISDEP_{LR}$. The set of all RR and LR dependencies is defined as $ISDEP = \{ISDEP_{LR}, ISDEP_{RR}\}$. Following MONA [7], normalized cross correlation provides us with a heuristic for learning indirect dependencies $ISDEP$. An indirect dependency event $\iota_i = \{\delta(s_i^j, s_k^l), \delta(s_m^j, s_o^n)\}$ is based on direct dependency events δ. The set of all indirect dependencies $ISDEP$ translates into a set of indirect dependency events $\Omega = \{\iota_0, \ldots, \iota_n\}$. MONA creates probabilities $\varrho(\tau_{delay}) \in P_\varrho$ ranging between $\varrho(\tau_{delay}) = [0, \ldots, 1]$ and provides a set of observed workflow events $F \subseteq \Omega$.

$$p\big(\iota_{hg}(\delta_h(s_i^j, s_k^l), \delta_g(s_m^j, s_o^n)) \mid \delta_h(s_i^j, s_k^l) \wedge \delta_g(s_m^j, s_o^n)\big) = \varrho_{r,s}(\tau_{delay}) \qquad (1)$$

Obviously, there is a level of uncertainty associated with detected indirect dependencies. By understanding indirect dependencies as indirect dependency events, we are able model the probability of uncertain event by relying on Kolmogorov axioms of probability theory [6]. An example for this probability space is illustrated in Fig. 1a and contains a set of workflow events $F \subseteq \Omega$, showing an RR dependency and consists of a client d_c sending an HTTP request to a load balancing server d_{lbs}. The load balancing server d_{lbs} then sends an HTTP request to a webserver d^{ws}. The RR dependency, shown in Fig. 1a, can be written as $\iota_{01}\big(\delta_0(s_*^c, s_{80}^{lbs}), \delta_1(s_*^{lbs}, s_{80}^{ws})\big)$. Figure 1b shows an LR dependency, where the client d_c sends a request to a DNS server d_{DNS}. Afterwards, the client d_c sends a load balancing server d_{lbs}. The LR dependency, shown in Fig. 1b, can be written as $\iota_{23}\big(\delta_2(s_*^c, s_{53}^{DNS}), \delta_3(s_*^c, s_{80}^{lbs})\big)$.

3 Workflow Mining

Normalized cross correlation provides an heuristic approach for estimating workflow events and the result is described by a probability space (Ω, F, P_ϱ) described in Sect. 2. Based on the probability space, we define the problem of mining workflows as detecting the most likely sequence of hidden states. This is a problem often associated with HMMs. Using HMMs, it is possible to identify the probability whether a specific workflow is in place or not. We are interested in the most likely sequence of workflows in a given communication data network. The most likely sequence of hidden states can be calculated using the dynamic programming Viterbi algorithm [4]. An HMM $\lambda = (a_{ij}, e_{\iota_{kl}}, \pi)$ representing a workflow is defined as follows:

- n states $\Omega = \{\iota_0, \ldots, \iota_{n-1}\}$,
- an alphabet $\Delta = \{\delta_0, \ldots, \delta_{m-1}\}$ of m symbols,
- a transition probability matrix $a_{ij} = \iota_i \times \iota_j$,
- emission probabilities $e_{\iota_{kl}}(\delta_l)$ representing the probability of a state ι_{kl} emitting symbol δ_l and
- initial state distribution vector $\pi = \pi_o$.

We refer to a sequence of observed symbols as $O = \delta_0, \delta_1, \delta_2, \ldots$ and a sequence of states as $Q = \iota_0, \iota_1, \iota_2, \ldots$. Based on tumbling windows $w_{t_i} \in W$

$$W = w_{t_0}, \ldots, w_{t_i}, \ldots, w_{t_{n-1}} \tag{2}$$

with a shift Δ_t, we derive indirect dependency events based on observed direct dependencies. Direct dependencies imply that network packets are exchanged between two network services. Normalized cross correlation is a heuristic approach, hence observed workflow events can be untrue and existing indirect dependencies might not be detected. However, repeatedly reoccurring workflow events are very likely to be actual workflow events.

The parameters of a_{ij} and $e_{\iota_{kl}}(\delta_l)$ the HMM $\lambda = (a_{ij}, e_{\iota_{kl}}, \pi)$ can be learned over multiple tumbling windows $w_{t_i} \in W$ and $t_i \in [t_0, \ldots, t_p]$ by:

$$a_{ij} = \frac{A_{ij}}{\sum_{q=\{0,\ldots,p\}} A_{iq}}, \tag{3}$$

where A_{ij} is the number of observed state transitions from state ι_i to ι_j over p tumbling windows and it is normalized over all of ι_i's outgoing state transitions. An emission probability $e_{\iota_{kl}}(\delta_l)$ is derived as

$$e_{\iota_{kl}}(\delta_l) = \frac{E_{\iota_{kl}}(\delta_l)}{\sum'_{\forall \iota_{xl}, \delta_l \subset \iota_{xl}} E_{\iota_{xl}}(\delta_l)}, \tag{4}$$

where $E_{\iota_{kl}}(\delta_l)$ is the number of times that state ι_{kl} is observed, when symbol δ_l is emitted. This is normalized over the number of occurances of all states $\iota_{xl} \subset \delta_l, \iota_{xl} \in F$, which also emit symbol δ_l. By observed network traffic within an monitored network traffic, this HMM allows us to automatically derive workflows based on network service dependency analysis. This introduced methodology is applied to a real-life network and the results of this experimental evaluation are shown in the next section.

4   Experimental Evaluation

The disaster recovery site of an energy distribution network, provided an Italian water and energy distribution company, was available for non-invasive experimentation. We integrate our framework into this test network to test the ability of our newly introduced workflow mining approach to rediscover workflows based on network traffic. The implementation of our introduced methodology works online and continuously analysis network traffic, which is mirrored by routers and switches in the test environment. Based on this set-up, we are able to analyze detected network service dependencies, which constitute workflow events and evaluate, whether our novel workflow mining approach is able to rediscover workflows. Figure 2 shows all network service dependencies detected by MONA. Based on Supervisory Control and Data Acquisition (SCADA) protocols, remote terminal units TTY-T116 to TTY-T164 in substations of medium voltage and high voltage, acquire data from electrical devices (e.g., programmable logic

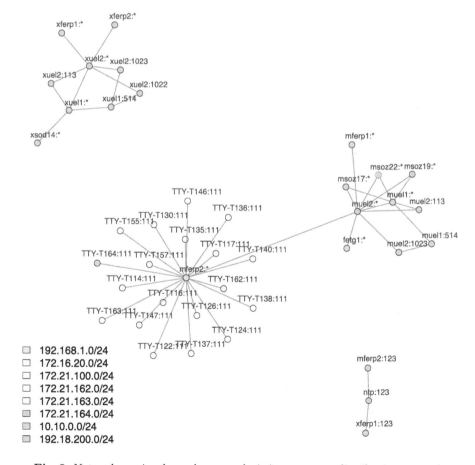

Fig. 2. Network service dependency analysis in an energy distribution network.

controllers, sensors, etc.), and send them via front end servers mferp1, mferp2 to the supervisory scada servers muel1 and muel2 of the power grids main office. These network service dependencies were classified as complete and correctly identified by network operators.

Figure 3 shows an excerpt of workflows derived based on network service dependencies. These workflows are plotted in BPMN 2.0 [12]. To point out work-flows spanning multiple subnetworks, we model subnetworks as swimlanes. Our experimental analysis consists of comparing automatically derived workflows to workflows provided by network operators beforehand. Based on this analysis, we conclude whether our introduced online workflow mining approach is able to rediscover workflows. This experimental evaluation showed that our introduced workflow mining approach is able to rediscover workflows based on network traffic.

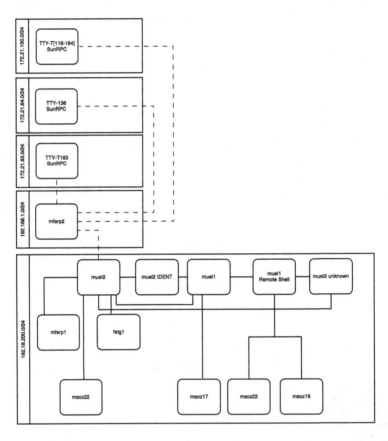

Fig. 3. Excerpt of workflows derived from network traffic in an energy distribution network.

5 Conclusion

We introduced an approach to mine workflows online, based on network traffic via network service dependency discovery. To the best of our knowledge this is the first workflow mining approach, which is able do deduce a HMM based workflow model by analyzing network traffic. We integrate this online workflow mining approach into the data-communication network of an energy distribution network. In the context of our experimental evaluation, we came to the conclusion that network operators have a high level understanding of workflows in their monitored network. However, they lack a detailed understanding on what applications and network services are involved. This was generally due to this network relying heavily on third party software that are often also updated and maintained by the third party. Thus, we concluded that deriving manual workflow models is costly and requires specialist know how. Luckily, network traffic based workflow mining support network operators in understanding workflows in their monitored network on application layer level.

Acknowledgments. This work was partly supported by the Seventh Framework Programme (FP7) of the European Commission as part of the PANOPTESEC integrated research project (GA 610416).

References

1. Bahl, P., Chandra, R., Greenberg, A., Kandula, S., Maltz, D.A., Zhang, M.: Towards highly reliable enterprise network services via inference of multi-level dependencies. In: ACM SIGCOMM Computer Communication Review, vol. 37, pp. 13–24. ACM (2007)
2. Blum, T., Padoy, N., Feußner, H., Navab, N.: Workflow mining for visualization and analysis of surgeries. Int. J. Comput. Assist. Radiol. Surg. **3**(5), 379–386 (2008)
3. Chen, X., Zhang, M., Mao, Z.M., Bahl, P.: Automating network application dependency discovery: experiences, limitations, and new solutions. OSDI **8**, 117–130 (2008)
4. Forney, G.D.: The viterbi algorithm. Proc. IEEE **61**(3), 268–278 (1973)
5. Herbst, J.: A machine learning approach to workflow management. In: Lopez de Mantaras, R., Plaza, E. (eds.) ECML 2000. LNCS (LNAI), vol. 1810, pp. 183–194. Springer, Heidelberg (2000)
6. Kolmogorov, A.N.: Foundations of the Theory of Probability. Chelsea publishing company, New York (1950)
7. Mona Lange, R.M.: Time Series data mining for network service dependency analysis. In: The 9th International Conference on Computational Intelligence in Security for Information Systems. Springer, Heidelberg (2016)
8. Natarajan, A., Ning, P., Liu, Y., Jajodia, S., Hutchinson, S.E.: NSDMiner: automated discovery of network service dependencies. IEEE (2012)
9. Priyadharshini, V., Malathi, A.: Analysis of process mining model for software reliability dataset using HMM. Indian J. Sci. Technol. 9(4), 1–5 (2016)
10. Rozinat, A., Veloso, M., van der Aalst, W.M.: Using hidden markov models to evaluate the quality of discovered process models. Extended Version. BPM Center Report BPM-08-10, BPMcenter. org (2008)

11. Silva, R., Zhang, J., Shanahan, J.G.: Probabilistic workflow mining. In: Proceedings of the Eleventh ACM SIGKDD International Conference on Knowledge Discovery in Data Mining, pp. 275–284. ACM (2005)

12. Silver, B., Richard, B.: BPMN Method and Style, vol. 2. Cody-Cassidy Press, Aptos (2009)

13. Aalst, W., et al.: Process mining manifesto. In: Daniel, F., Barkaoui, K., Dustdar, S. (eds.) BPM 2011. LNBIP, vol. 99, pp. 169–194. Springer, Heidelberg (2012). doi:10.1007/978-3-642-28108-2_19

14. Aalst, W.M.P.: Business process management demystified: a tutorial on models, systems and standards for workflow management. In: Desel, J., Reisig, W., Rozenberg, G. (eds.) ACPN 2003. LNCS, pp. 1–65. Springer, Heidelberg (2004). doi:10.1007/978-3-540-27755-2_1

15. Van Der Aalst, W.M.: Process Mining: Discovery, Conformance and Enhancement of Business Processes. Springer, Heidelberg (2011)

16. Van Der Aalst, W.M., van Dongen, B.F., Herbst, J., Maruster, L., Schimm, G., Weijters, A.J.: Workflow mining: a survey of issues and approaches. Data Knowl. Eng. 47(2), 237–267 (2003)

17. Van Der Aalst, W.M., Weijters, T., Maruster, L.: Workflow mining: discovering process models from event logs. IEEE Trans. Knowl. Data Eng. 16(9), 1128–1142 (2004)

18. Dongen, B.F., Aalst, W.M.P.: Multi-phase process mining: building instance graphs. In: Atzeni, P., Chu, W., Lu, H., Zhou, S., Ling, T.-W. (eds.) ER 2004. LNCS, pp. 362–376. Springer, Heidelberg (2004). doi:10.1007/978-3-540-30464-7_29

Using Modelica Programs for Deriving Propositional Horn Clause Abduction Problems

Bernhard Peischl[✉], Ingo Pill, and Franz Wotawa

Institute for Software Technology, Graz University of Technology, Graz, Austria
{bpeischl,ipill,wotawa}@ist.tugraz.at

Abstract. Despite ample advantages of model-based diagnosis, in practice its use has been somehow limited to proof-of-concept prototypes. Some reasons behind this observation are that the required modeling step is resource consuming, and also that this step requires additional training. In order to overcome these problems, we suggest to use modeling languages like Modelica that are already established in academia and industry for describing cyber-physical systems as basis for deriving logic based models. Together with observations about the modeled system, those models can then be used by an abductive diagnosis engine for deriving the root causes for detected defects. The idea behind our approach is to introduce fault models for the components written in Modelica, and to use the available simulation environment to determine behavioral deviations to the expected outcome of a fault free model. The introduced fault models and gained information about the resulting deviations can be directly mapped to horn clauses to be used for diagnosis.

1 Introduction

Formalizing and automating diagnosis, i.e., the identification of root causes for observed, but unwanted or unexpected effects, are tasks that have a long tradition in Artificial Intelligence. Based on experience gained from classical rule-based expert systems, Davis [4], and later on Reiter [13] as well as De Kleer and Williams [7] introduced the concept of model-based diagnosis (MBD). With MBD the idea is to use a sytem model for localizing faulty components in the actual system directly from its model and some observations. Due to its flexibility, this "reasoning from first principles" is very appealing. The only thing that we have to provide is a system's model, ideally comprised of interconnected components. When using such component-connection models, changes in the system can be easily incorporated in the model, thus making also a system's diagnosis much more convenient and flexible since changes are kept local. Due to these advantages, one would expect a high adoption of model-based diagnosis in practice. Indeed, many prototypical implementations have been proposed and numerous case studies have been published, all showing that model-based diagnosis can be used in practice, see, e.g., [10,12,14,16]. Unfortunately, however, the current use of model-based diagnosis methods and techniques in practice is rather limited.

© Springer International Publishing AG 2016
G. Friedrich et al. (Eds.): KI 2016, LNAI 9904, pp. 185–191, 2016.
DOI: 10.1007/978-3-319-46073-4_18

There are several reasons that lead to this observation. Some major issues are connected to the fact that, indeed, modeling a system has turned out not to be that easy, if we are not lucky enough that the "system" itself provides a model, like for behavioral diagnosis of specifications [11]. Moreover, modeling requires tools that have to be integrated into the development process, which often requires us to change this process. Hence, there is a need for tools and techniques that (1) make modeling more easy, and (2) seamlessly integrate into a development process. In this paper, we contribute to these goals, and introduce a method that makes use of the modeling language Modelica [6]. Modelica is used in academia and industry for modeling systems as complex as cyber-physical ones, and we show in this paper how to extract models via Modelica that then can be used for model-based reasoning. In contrast to classical consistency-based diagnosis, e.g., [13], we suggest to use abductive diagnosis [2,3]. The proposed approach allows one for automating the modeling step and thus for an easy integration into any existing development process.

In [1], the authors introduced a methodology of how to use abductive diagnosis in practice. This work relies on earlier work [17] where Wotawa explained the use of tables comprising information about component fault modes and their effects for abductive diagnosis. In our paper, we rely on these previous research, but extend it such that we are able to extract abductive models from Modelica programs directly, without the need of generating fault-effect tables manually. For this article to be self-contained, we briefly discuss the definitions of abductive diagnosis from Friedrich et al. [5] first.

Definition 1 (PHCAP).   *Given a knowledge base (A, Hyp, Th), where $A \subseteq PROPS$ denotes a set of propositional variables, $Hyp \subseteq A$ a set of hypotheses, and $Th \subseteq HC$ a set of horn clause sentences over A, and a set of observations $Obs \subseteq A$, the tuple (A, Hyp, Th, Obs) forms a propositional horn clause abduction problem (PHCAP).*

Given a PHCAP and a set of concrete observations, we are interested in finding the reason for the observations, i.e., the diagnosis or solution of a PHCAP.

Definition 2 (Diagnosis; Solution of a PHCAP).   *Given a PHCAP (A, Hyp, Th, Obs), a set $\Delta \subseteq Hyp$ is a solution if and only if $\Delta \cup Th \models Obs$ and $\Delta \cup Th \not\models \bot$. A solution Δ is parsimonious or minimal if and only if no set $\Delta' \subset \Delta$ is a solution.*

In Definition 2, diagnoses need not be minimal or parsimonious. In most practical cases, however, only minimal diagnoses or minimal explanations for given effects are of interest. Hence, from here on, we assume that all diagnoses are minimal ones if not specified explicitly.

In the remainder of this paper, we introduce our model generation process, discuss related research, and finally conclude this paper.

2 Model Generation Approach

In a nutshell, our approach works as follows: First, we extend the Modelica program with fault modes for individual components and describe their corresponding behavior. Those modes can then be invoked at any point during simulation. Second, we enable the individual faults in the Modelica program and simulate the resulting faulty program versions together with the correct variant for certain inputs. The fault modes leading to a deviation between the output behavior are then the causes for the deviations, i.e., the effects. Third, we store the fault modes together with the corresponding deviations as cause-effect rules in an abductive knowledge base. These three initial steps lead to the computation of a knowledge base, where this process can be automated and executed before deploying the diagnosis system. In the final step we use this knowledge base together with obtained observations, i.e., deviations and inputs obtained from the observed system for diagnoses. For computing possible root causes for the unexpected or unwanted effects we make use of abductive reasoning.

Let us explain our approach using a voltage divider as an example. In Fig. 1, you can find the schematics of a voltage divider circuit comprising a battery BAT and two resistors R1, R2. The voltage drops v_1 and v_2 of resistors R1 and R2 with respective resistances of 100 Ω and 50 Ω can be computed as follows: $v1 = v2 \cdot \frac{r_1}{r_2}$. Furthermore, according to Kirchhoff's circuits' law, we know that we have $v = v_1 + v_2$, where v is the voltage of the battery BAT. Hence, in our example, v_1 has to be 8 V and v_2 4 V, summing up to the 12 V delivered by the battery.

For obtaining a diagnosis model, we have to introduce fault modes for the different components written in Modelica. For a resistor's extended model we introduce three modes *ok*, *short*, and *broken* as shown in Fig. 1 (the latter mode only indirectly used for going to the else branch). Here we see that all the modes have their corresponding behaviors attached. When specifying these behaviors it is necessary to avoid specifications that do not hold always. For example, there will never be a current flowing through a broken resistor. However, there might be a voltage drop. For a resistor that is a short, i.e., that has a value of 0 Ω, the voltage drop is always 0 V but there might situations (like the one in the example) where a current flows through it. As suggested, this faulty behavior is implemented in Modelica. In addition to a resistor's extended model, we also introduce an extended Modelica model for batteries delivering 12 V in case of it working correctly, and 0 V in case of an *empty* battery.

In total, the set of fault modes for the components $COMP = \{BAT, R1, R2\}$ in our example is: $FM = \{short, broken, empty\}$. Hence, we call the simulator for all components and all fault modes (the latters enabled individually). Figure 1 outlines some of the results where the outcomes, i.e., simulation results, for empty batteries or a short in resistor R2 at time 0.5 s are depicted. In summary, we obtain the following results for the individual fault modes:

In the table given above, we also state the deviations (or effects e_1, e_2) of the individual modes to values v_1 and v_2, which should be 8 V and 4 V respectively. What we also see is that the values obtained when simulating our extended

Component	Mode	v_1	v_2	e_1	e_2
BAT	*empty*	0	0	smaller	smaller
R1	*short*	0	12	smaller	larger
R1	*broken*	12	0	larger	smaller
R2	*short*	12	0	larger	smaller
R2	*broken*	0	12	smaller	larger

Modelica program do not necessarily guarantee that we are able to distinguish between all diagnoses. For example, both, a *broken* R1 and a *short* R2 would produce the same values for v_1 and v_2.

Using the conversion of tables into abductive diagnosis models from [17], we obtain the following rules for the knowledge base for our example:

$$empty(\text{BAT}) \rightarrow smaller(v1) \quad empty(\text{BAT}) \rightarrow smaller(v2)$$
$$short(\text{R1}) \rightarrow smaller(v1) \quad short(\text{R1}) \rightarrow larger(v2)$$
$$broken(\text{R1}) \rightarrow larger(v1) \quad broken(\text{R1}) \rightarrow smaller(v2)$$
$$short(\text{R2}) \rightarrow larger(v1) \quad short(\text{R2}) \rightarrow smaller(v2)$$
$$broken(\text{R2}) \rightarrow smaller(v1) \quad broken(\text{R2}) \rightarrow larger(v2)$$

The hypotheses $\{empty(\text{BAT}), short(\text{R1}), broken(\text{R1}), short(\text{R2}), broken(\text{R2})\}$ together with propositions $\{smaller(v1), larger(v1), smaller(v2), larger(v2)\}$ form the set of propositions, which completes our knowledge base for the voltage divider example. Note that in addition, we might also want to specify that some values cannot occur at the same time. For example, a voltage drop cannot be larger *and* smaller at the same time. Such background knowledge can be added easily to the knowledge base via stating $smaller(v1) \wedge larger(v1) \rightarrow \perp$ and $smaller(v2) \wedge larger(v2) \rightarrow \perp$. Furthermore, any such information can be easily added automatically to some knowledge base in a similar way.

3 Related Research

Regarding related research, we focus on publications related to Modelica and model-based diagnosis. In the context of Modelica, we found three main approaches for diagnosis making use of model-based reasoning as underlying diagnosis technique.

Lunde [8] discussed the capabilities of the tool RODON that uses an extended version of the language Modelica for diagnosis. In particular, RODON makes use of some extensions to Modelica in order to deal with unknown behavior and also fault models directly. In contrast to this approach, we rely on pure Modelica and do not require modifications or adaptations.

Minhas and colleagues [9] discussed an approach for diagnosis using Modelica that is based on fault augmented model extensions. There, the underlying idea is to introduce fault models into the Modelica models in an automated way.

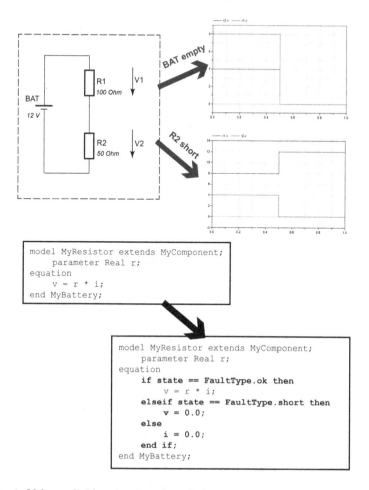

Fig. 1. Voltage divider circuit and its fault modes represented in Modelica.

These fault models are then used to identify a fault for some observations. In particular, a Bayesian approach is used for comparing the simulation results with the given observations. In case of a small enough distance between the observed and simulated data based on a fault model, the corresponding fault model can be given back as result. Minhas et al.'s work is very close to ours. However, in our method introduced in this paper, we make all simulations *before* deployment of the diagnosis system. Moreover, we assume that the observations are already provided in a qualitative form, i.e., either as deviations from expected values or as some qualitative value representing a set of concrete values. Furthermore, we make use of abduction as logical foundation for diagnosis.

In [15], Sterling et al. introduced a model-based diagnosis approach that is coupled with Modelica in the following way. For each used basic Modelica component model there is a qualitative representation. When using an hierarchical model based on the component library, the qualitative component models are used for diagnosis. The authors also present the application of the proposed technique to Air Handling Units. Sterling et al.'s work focuses more on an integration of diagnosis into well established model-based system development processes. The approach of Sterling et al. is different to ours in the way models are generated. We obtain the abductive diagnosis model directly from the simulation whereas in [15] it is assumed that a qualitative representation of component models already exists.

4   Conclusion

In this paper, we focused on modeling for diagnosis based on abduction. The idea was to make use of models that are usually written as part of a development process for verification and validation purposes. In order to allow obtaining an abductive diagnosis model, we introduce fault modes to be incorporated into these models. This way, the model can be simulated with disabled or individually enabled faults, such that we compare the respective values and derive an abductive knowledge base comprising horn clause rules of the form "causes implies effects". In particular, we assume our models to be written in the object-oriented modeling language Modelica. In the paper, we used a small case study for explaining the different steps through the process.

The advantage of the introduced method is that we are able to obtain models requiring an additional overhead only for specifying the incorrect behavior. The rule extraction process can be automated and thus allows one for an easy integration of model-based diagnosis into the development process of cyber-physical systems. There are of course also limitations to the proposed approach. Currently, we only consider single fault simulation and corresponding single fault diagnoses. However, this limitation can be lifted easily, if we consider a combination of fault modes for multiple components when simulating the Modelica model and creating the knowledge base.

Another challenge is the mapping of concrete quantities to their qualitative representation. In this paper, we made use of the concept of deviations between the expected and the observed values. However, there might also be other qualitative representations that can be used in the context of this work. More and larger case studies have to be carried out in order to obtain experience in corresponding classifications and the mapping of quantitative values to their qualitative representation as then used for diagnosis.

Acknowledgement. The work presented in this paper has been supported by the FFG project Applied Model Based Reasoning (AMOR) under grant 842407. We would further like to express our gratitude to our industrial partner, Uptime Engineering GmbH.

References

1. Gray, C.S., Koitz, S.P. R., Wotawa, F.: An abductive diagnosis and modeling concept for wind power plants. In: 9th IFAC Symposium on Fault Detection, Supervision and Safety of Technical Processes (2015)
2. Console, L., Dupré, D.T., Torasso, P.: On the relationship between abduction and deduction. J. Logic Comput. **1**(5), 661–690 (1991)
3. Console, L., Torasso, P.: Integrating models of correct behavior into abductive diagnosis. In: Proceedings of the European Conference on Artificial Intelligence (ECAI), pp. 160–166. Pitman Publishing, Stockholm, August 1990
4. Davis, R.: Diagnostic reasoning based on structure and behavior. Artif. Intell. **24**, 347–410 (1984)
5. Friedrich, G., Gottlob, G., Nejdl, W.: Hypothesis classification, abductive diagnosis and therapy. In: Gottlob, G., Nejdl, W. (eds.) Expert Systems in Engineering. LNCS, vol. 462, pp. 69–78. Springer, Heidelberg (1990)
6. Fritzson, P.: Object-Oriented Modeling and Simulation with Modelica 3.3–A Cyber-physical Approach, 2nd edn. Wiley-IEEE Press, Hoboken (2014)
7. de Kleer, J., Williams, B.C.: Diagnosing multiple faults. Artif. Intell. **32**(1), 97–130 (1987)
8. Lunde, K.: Object oriented modeling in model based diagnosis. In: 2000 Proceedings of the Modelica Workshop, pp. 111–118 (2000)
9. Minhas, R., de Kleer, J., Matei, I., Saha, B.: Using fault augmented modelica models for diagnostics. In: Proceedings of the 10th International Modelica Conference. Lund, Sweden, 10–12 March 2014
10. Pell, B., Bernard, D., Chien, S., Gat, E., Muscettola, N., Nayak, P., Wagner, M., Williams, B.: A remote-agent prototype for spacecraft autonomy. In: Proceedings of the SPIE Conference on Optical Science, Engineering, and Instrumentation, Volume on Space Sciencecraft Control and Tracking in the New Millennium. Society of Professional Image Engineers, Bellingham (1996)
11. Pill, I., Quaritsch, T.: Behavioral diagnosis of LTL specifications at operator level. In: International Joint Conference on Artificial Intelligence, pp. 1053–1059 (2013)
12. Rajan, K., Bernard, D., Dorais, G., Gamble, E., Kanefsky, B., Kurien, J., Millar, W., Muscettola, N., Nayak, P., Rouquette, N., Smith, B., Taylor, W., Tung, Y.: Remote agent: an autonomous control system for the new millennium. In: Proceedings of the 14th European Conference on Artificial Intelligence (ECAI), Berlin, Germany, August 2000
13. Reiter, R.: A theory of diagnosis from first principles. Artif. Intell. **32**(1), 57–95 (1987)
14. Sachenbacher, M., Struss, P., Carlén, C.M.: A prototype for model-based on-board diagnosis of automotive systems. AI Commun. **13**(2), 83–97 (2000). Special Issue on Industrial Applications of Model-Based Reasoning
15. Sterling, R., Struss, P., Febres, J., Sabir, U., Keane, M.M.: From modelica models to fault diagnosis in air handling units. In: Proceedings of the 10th International Modelica Conference, Lund, Sweden, 10–12 March 2014
16. Struss, P., Rehfus, B., Brignolo, R., Cascio, F., Console, L., Dague, P., Dubois, P., Dressler, O., Millet, D.: Model-based tools for the integration of design and diagnosis into a common process - a project report. In: Proceedings of the Thirteenth International Workshop on Principles of Diagnosis, Semmering, Austria (2002)
17. Wotawa, F.: Failure mode and effect analysis for abductive diagnosis. In: Proceedings of the International Workshop on Defeasible and Ampliative Reasoning (DARe-14) (2014)

Symbolic Robot Commanding Utilizing Physical Properties - System Overview

Michael Spangenberg$^{(\boxtimes)}$ and Dominik Henrich

Chair for Applied Computer Science III, Robotics and Embedded Systems,
University of Bayreuth, 95440 Bayreuth, Germany
{michael.spangenberg,dominik.henrich}@uni-bayreuth.de

Abstract. One long term goal of artificial intelligence and robotics research is the development of robot systems, which have approximately the same cognitive, communicational, and handling abilities like humans. This yields several challenges for future robot systems. For instance in the field of communicational abilities, future robot systems have to bridge between natural communication methods of the human, primarily utilizing symbols like words or gestures, and the natural communication methods of artificial systems, primarily utilizing low-level subsymbolic control interfaces. In this work, we outline a system which utilizes physical properties, respectively physical effects for the mapping between a high-level symbolic user interface and a low-level subsymbolic robot control interface.

1 Introduction

There are several long term goals in current robotic research. One is the development of robot systems, which have approximately the same cognitive, communicational, and handling abilities like humans. As part of this ongoing development, application domains for robot systems shall be expanded, from industrial settings with separated working cells, fixed object positions, and preprogrammed motions towards a flexible usage in small or medium-sized enterprises (SMEs) or private households. This sets additional requirements to the abilities of future robot systems. In the field of cognitive abilities, future robot systems must utilize appropriate sensors to extract information from the environment. In the field of handling abilities, future robot systems need action representations, which allow a flexible parameterization and execution of a specific task. In the field of communicational abilities, future robot systems must provide an intuitive and symbolic user interface.

The interaction between cognitive, communicational, and handling abilities is crucial for future robot systems. In Fig. 1, potential tasks in SMEs or private households are visualized. Such tasks typically require the definition of sensor-based actions, which are defined utilizing a subsymbolic robot control interface like iTaSC [1] or manipulation primitives [2]. The definition of sensor based actions require expert knowledge in the domain of robotics, since the programmer must define subsymbolic parameters like positions, forces, setpoints, or control

© Springer International Publishing AG 2016
G. Friedrich et al. (Eds.): KI 2016, LNAI 9904, pp. 192–199, 2016.
DOI: 10.1007/978-3-319-46073-4_19

Fig. 1. Typical applications in SMEs or private households which require the execution of sensor based motions. From left to right: Drilling, Paletting, Pouring.

strategies. In SMEs or private households, it cannot be assumed that this expert knowledge in robotics is available. Therefore, future robot systems must provide an intuitive user interface, which allows a symbolic communication. Such a robot system needs information about the semantics of the used symbols, for example executable actions or manipulable objects. Furthermore, the robot system must be able to extract the needed subsymbolic information from the environment, utilizing appropriate software components and sensors.

In the following sections, we give an overview of our system, which utilizes physical effects, respectively physical properties for the grounding of symbols and parameterization of subsymbolic sensor-based motions.

The remainder of the work is organized as follows: The related work is described in the next section. Here, an overview of robot systems utilizing a symbolic user interface is given. In Sect. 3, we give an overview of our system, outline the action representation based on verbalized physical effects, and describe the relations between the used symbols, physical parameters, and components for the extraction of the needed subsymbolic parameters from given symbolic instructions. At last, we describe our future work in Sect. 4.

2   Related Work

The problem of assigning semantics to symbolic tokens like words is known as the symbol grounding problem and was described by Harnad [3] with aspects from psychology and artificial intelligence. Since practical applications of artificial intelligence, for example in form of robots and intelligent systems, become more complex, also researchers from these domains have to consider about the problem of symbol grounding [4]. The grounding of symbols can be organized into two subtopics, physical symbol grounding [5], and social symbol grounding [6]. While social symbol grounding focuses on sharing symbols in populations of agents, physical symbol grounding focuses on building relations between sensor values and symbols. Since we want to extract subsymbolic physical parameters, we focus on physical symbol grounding in more detail. There are already systems, which can be operated utilizing symbolic commands. In general, such robot systems are either used within navigational [7–10] or handling tasks [11–16]. These systems can be categorized according to the extractable subsymbolic information.

The first category of systems allows *no extraction* of subsymbolic information, i.e. they can only execute predefined instructions. The second category of systems is able to extract *geometric* information from known object identifiers utilizing an object database and an object recognition system. Systems of the third category can additionally extract *spatial relations* from symbolic instructions.

Because all of the described systems are based on action representations, which utilize geometric information, they do not need to extract *kinematic* and *dynamic* parameters like forces, torques, or energies. Our system is based on an action representation utilizing verbalized physical effects and manipulation primitive nets [17], which is parameterized by geometric, kinematic, and dynamic parameters, therefore we need to specify how to extract these quantities from a symbolic representation.

3   System Overview

An overview of our system architecture is shown in Fig. 2. The system is build according to the 3T architecture [18], a common architecture for systems which have to transform between different types of representations. In case of our system, we need to transform a high-level symbolic user representation into a low-level subsymbolic robot control representation. Typically, these high-level representations cannot be mapped directly to a low-level robot control representation. Therefore, such systems consists of an additional transformation layer, which describes the mapping between the high-level user interface and the low-level robot control interface. In the following subsections, we outline the realization of the three tiers of our system.

3.1   User Layer

The main function of this layer is to provide high-level user interfaces, which allow the usage of the robot system by non-experts. Therefore, we focus on intuitive symbolic representations like a domain specific language (DSL) or a natural language interface. We introduced a domain-specific language for sensor-based actions in [19]. In the DSL, executable actions are described by verbal expressions, and parameterized by phrases. For instance, the DSL provides a sensor-based action shove, which takes a *noun phrase* and a *prepositional phrase* as parameter. This allows the user to specify an instruction like shove("the red cube", "towards the gray box"). Users are able to instruct executable actions to the robot system, without specifying low-level control parameters. Since these parameters are required for the execution, the robot system must be able to extract low-level parameters utilizing additional components like a knowledge base, action skeletons, or environment information gathered by sensors.

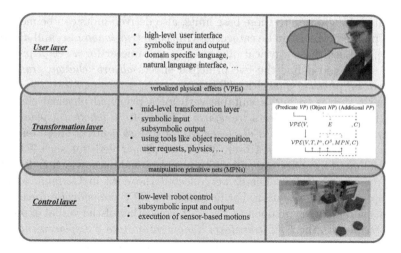

Fig. 2. Overview of the system architecture.

3.2   Transformation Layer

The next step is to transform the high-level user input into a suitable representation for the low-level robot control. The robot control typically consists of subsymbolical interfaces, which require the definition of parameters like set points, control strategies, or task frames. These parameter are not specified explicitly by the user, therefore this information must be specified implicitly based on the context, respectively based on the semantics of the used symbols. This information must be grounded to the robot system.

The main idea of our symbol grounding approach is based on the working hypothesis that object manipulation tasks consist of mechanical operations and can be described using the laws of physics, especially from the field of mechanics. If we analyze the function of a specific symbol, it represents either an executable action or a parameter for an action. Therefore, we describe the grounding of actions and parameters in the following paragraphs.

Action Grounding. The concept of verbalized physical effects $\mathcal{VPE}$s is used to describe executable actions in terms of physical effects. This representation is utilized for the linkage of symbolic instructions and sensor based motions, and the calculation of subsymbolic parameter from a given symbolic instruction. Furthermore, this concept is used for the identification of needed information and the automatic generation of temporal states, since instructions typically specify only the goal state of a task. In this subsection, we give an overview of the used physical quantities, principal physical effects $\mathcal{PPE}$s, and the mapping of a verbal expression to an specific $\mathcal{PPE}$.

Generally, seven base units are defined in ISO 30-0 [20]. Within an object manipulation task, mechanical base units *length L*, *mass M* and *time T* are manipulated. In addition to these base units, also derived units can be measured and manipulated, which can be categorized in *geometric*, *kinematic*, and *dynamic* units [21]. We use these physical quantities as parameter for a set of principal physical effects and define the five principal effects *absorb*, *change*, *transform*, *merge*, *split* on physical quantities ($\mathcal{PPE}$s).

The next step is to find a suitable verb for a principal physical effect, for example for the physical effects *transform a force into a length (displacement)*, *transform a momentum into a displacement*, or *absorb a force*. These terms are not intuitive to verbalize for a user. The most proper verb for each $\mathcal{PPE}$ can only be evaluated by collecting and analyzing empirical data, which is described in our previous work [22]. There, we collected the data in German, and use here an appropriate translation. For instance, the $\mathcal{PPE}$ *transform a force into a length (displacement)* is mapped to the $\mathcal{VPE}$ consisting of the verbal expression *to shove (schieben)*, the $\mathcal{PPE}$ *transform a momentum into a displacement* to the $\mathcal{VPE}$ consisting of the verbal expression *to push (stoßen)*, and the $\mathcal{PPE}$ *absorb a force* to the $\mathcal{VPE}$ consisting of the verbal expression *to touch (berühren)*. More details about the concept of verbalized physical effects are presented in [17].

Parameter Grounding. Besides executable actions, the semantics of the symbolic parameters have to be grounded to the robot system. These parameters are applied to the defined verbalized physical effects, therefore it is necessary to describe the semantics of the parameters in terms of physical properties. Based on an analysis of symbols, we introduced a physical dictionary for the grounding of symbols based on physical properties in [23].

The first task of the physical dictionary is to ground information about the symbol class and syntactic function of a specific symbol. This information is used to determine coherence between different symbols. Let a user instruct the natural language instruction *Stack the red cylinder on the blue cube!* With the grounded information, we can determine that the determiner *the* and the adjective *red* relates to the noun *cylinder*.

The second task of the dictionary is to ground information about the manipulated properties of a specific symbol. We analyzed that symbols can affect various properties, which can be specified in different degrees of determination. In general, a symbol describes either an object, a process, a relation, or a property. For instance, the class of adjectives describe properties of objects or the class of prepositions describe relations between objects. The degree of determination can be for example exact or within an interval. For instance, a symbol of type numeral describes a property exact, while an adjective describes a property typically by an interval.

Parameter Extraction. The next step towards an robotic execution of the instructed symbolic command is the subsymbolic parameter extraction, dependent on the actual context, respectively environment of the robot system. The extraction of the subsymbolical information is done by specific software components, which utilize the sensors of the actual robot system. Therefore, we expand our knowledge base with a component and a sensor submodule. The component submodule stores information about available extraction methods for physical quantities, and the sensor submodule stores information about the sensors utilized by the specific extraction method. All components share the same interface, which on the one hand allows us to integrate existing approaches in the overall system. On the other hand, the extraction of subsymbolical information is decoupled from the overall functionality and new components or sensors can easily be integrated in the knowledge base. Since there are typically more components and sensors for the extraction of a physical quantity available, we can define a criteria which describes the most suitable component for the actual situation of the environment. An evaluation of the symbol grounding and subsymbolical parameter extraction is described in [23].

3.3   Control Layer

As low-level robot control interface, we use manipulation primitives [2], respectively manipulation primitive nets [24]. In general, a manipulation primitive net is a graph representation of an sensor-based task, consisting of manipulation primitives as nodes and stopping criteria as edges. The definition of a manipulation primitive consists of a hybrid motion, a set of tool commands, and a set of termination criteria.

The hybrid motion describes the executable sensor-based motion based on a local coordinate system, called the task frame. For this task frame, a control strategy for each degree of freedom must be specified. Valid control strategies are for instance position or force control. The set of tool commands holds information about the used tool and the state of the tool. For instance, a gripper shall be opened or closed during the execution of the sensor-based motion. The set of termination criteria is a set of Boolean conditions, which are checked during the execution of a manipulation primitive. The execution of the actual manipulation primitive is stopped, when at least one termination criteria is fulfilled.

The relations between verbalized physical effects, effect parameters, and the mapping and parameterization of the appropriate manipulation primitive net is describe in [17] in more detail.

4   Conclusion and Future Work

In this work, we gave a conceptual overview of our robot system. We outlined the different approaches from a symbolic user interface towards a subsymbolical robot control interface. The transformation between the symbolical and subsymbolical representation is done utilizing physical effects, respectively physical properties.

Our future work mainly focuses on extending the supported vocabulary, which includes on the one hand more complex executable actions, and on the other hand a more flexible parameterization of the actions. Furthermore, we will extend the toolbox of components, which are available for the extraction of subsymbolic information from the environment.

References

1. De Schutter, J., De Laet, T., Rutgeerts, J., Decré, W., Smits, R., Aertbeliën, E., Claes, K., Bruyninckx, H.: Constraint-based task specification and estimation for sensor-based robot systems in the presence of geometric uncertainty. Int. J. Robot. Res. **26**(5), 433–455 (2007)
2. Finkemeyer, B., Kroger, T., Wahl, F.M.: The adaptive selection matrix a key component for sensor-based control of robotic manipulators. In: IEEE International Conference on Robotics and Automation (ICRA), pp. 3855–3862. IEEE (2010)
3. Harnad, S.: The symbol grounding problem. Phys. D Nonlinear Phenom. **42**(1), 335–346 (1990)
4. Coradeschi, S., Loutfi, A., Wrede, B.: A short review of symbol grounding in robotic and intelligent systems. KI-Künstliche Intelligenz **27**(2), 129–136 (2013)
5. Vogt, P.: The physical symbol grounding problem. Cogn. Syst. Res. **3**(3), 429–457 (2002)
6. Cangelosi, A.: Grounding language in action and perception: from cognitive agents to humanoid robots. Phys. life Rev. **7**(2), 139–151 (2010)
7. Lauria, S., Bugmann, G., Kyriacou, T., Klein, E.: Mobile robot programming using natural language. Robot. Auton. Syst. **38**(3), 171–181 (2002)
8. Kemke, C.: "From Saying to doing"- Natural Language Interaction with Artificial Agents and Robots. INTECH Open Access Publisher (2007)
9. Matuszek, C., Herbst, E., Zettlemoyer, L., Fox, D.: Learning to parse natural language commands to a robot control system. In: Desai, J.P., Dudek, G., Khatib, O., Kumar, V. (eds.) Experimental Robotics. STAR, vol. 88, pp. 403–415. Springer, Heidelberg (2013)
10. Kollar, T., Tellex, S., Roy, D., Roy, N.: Grounding verbs of motion in natural language commands to robots. In: Khatib, O., Kumar, V., Sukhatme, G. (eds.) Experimental Robotics. STAR, vol. 79, pp. 31–47. Springer, Heidelberg (2012)
11. Laengle, T., Lueth, T.C., Stopp, E., Herzog, G., Kamstrup, G.: Kantra-a natural language interface for intelligent robots. In: Intelligent Autonomous Systems (IAS 4), pp. 357–364 (1995)
12. Knoll, A., Hildenbrandt, B., Zhang, J.: Instructing cooperating assembly robots through situated dialogues in natural language. In: IEEE International Conference on Robotics and Automation, vol. 1, pp. 888–894. IEEE (1997)
13. Pires, N.: Robot-by-voice: experiments on commanding an industrial robot using the human voice. Ind. Robot Int. J. **32**(6), 505–511 (2005)
14. Tenorth, M., Nyga, D., Beetz, M.: Understanding and executing instructions for everyday manipulation tasks from the world wide web. In: IEEE International Conference on Robotics and Automation (ICRA), pp. 1486–1491. IEEE (2010)
15. Stenmark, M., Nugues, P.: Natural language programming of industrial robots. In: 44th International Symposium on Robotics (ISR), pp. 1–5. IEEE (2013)
16. Misra, D.K., Sung, J., Lee, K., Saxena, A.: Tell me dave: context-sensitive grounding of natural language to manipulation instructions. In: Proceedings of Robotics: Science and Systems (RSS), Berkeley, USA (2014). doi:10.15607/RSS.2014.X.005
17. Spangenberg, M., Henrich, D.: Grounding of actions based on verbalized physical effects and manipulation primitives. In: IEEE/RSJ International Conference on Intelligent Robots and Systems (IROS), pp. 844–851. IEEE (2015)
18. Bonasso, R.P., Firby, R.J., Gat, E., Kortenkamp, D., Miller, D.P., Slack, M.G.: Experiences with an architecture for intelligent, reactive agents. J. Exp. Theor. Artif. Intell. **9**(2–3), 237–256 (1997)

19. Spangenberg, M., Henrich, D.: Towards a domain specific language for sensor-based actions. Appl. Mech. Mater. **840**, 42–49 (2016)
20. International Organization of Standardization: ISO Standards Handbook: Quantifies and Units (1993)
21. Awrejcewicz, J.: Classical Mechanics: Kinematics and Statics. Advances in Mechanics and Mathematics. Springer, New York (2012)
22. Spangenberg, M., Henrich, D.: Towards an intuitive interface for instructing robots handling tasks based on verbalized physical effects. In: RO-MAN: The 23rd IEEE International Symposium on Robot and Human Interactive Communication, pp. 79–84. IEEE (2014)
23. —: Symbol grounding for symbolic robot commands based on physical properties. In: IEEE International Conference on Information and Automation. IEEE (2016, accepted, to appear)
24. Thomas, U., Wahl, F.M.: Planning sensor feedback for assembly skills by using sensor state space graphs. In: Su, C.-Y., Rakheja, S., Liu, H. (eds.) ICIRA 2012, Part II. LNCS, vol. 7507, pp. 696–707. Springer, Heidelberg (2012)

Personalization of Gaze Direction Estimation with Deep Learning

Zoltán Tősér[1]([✉]), Róbert A. Rill[1,3], Kinga Faragó[1], László A. Jeni[2], and András Lőrincz[1]

[1] Faculty of Informatics, Eötvös Loránd University, Budapest, Hungary
zoltan.toser@gmail.com
[2] Robotics Institute, Carnegie Mellon University, Pittsburgh, PA, USA
[3] Faculty of Mathematics and Informatics, Babes-Bolyai University,
Cluj-napoca, Romania

Abstract. There is a growing interest in behavior based biometrics. Although biometric data has considerable variations for an individual and may be faked, yet the combination of such 'weak experts' can be rather strong. A remotely detectable component is gaze direction estimation and thus, eye movement patterns. Here, we present a novel personalization method for gaze estimation systems, which does not require a precise calibration setup, can be non-obtrusive, is fast and easy to use. We show that it improves the precision of gaze direction estimation algorithms considerably. The method is convenient; we exploit 3D face model reconstruction for the enrichment of a small number of collected data artificially.

1 Introduction

With the advance of facial expression recognition and animation technologies (see, e.g., [8] and the references therein) biometric information is becoming more and more ambiguous and imitable by computer graphics. Behavior based biometric may serve us as a rescue. It was shown more than a decade ago that facial expressions and head movements provide as relevant recognition cues as the face itself [22]. From both practical and theoretical point of views, imitation of such behavioral patterns will also be feasible in the near future, but – as argued many years ago – the more behavioral information is available, the better the chances are for the identification of anomalies and malicious episodes [18]. IoT and smart tools provide novel means for such characterization. On the other hand, remote identification of a person may not use IoT tools and only visible behavioral patterns may serve us. Eye movement pattern is one of the suggested components [1] and it may be used both in task oriented [2] and task independent settings [6,12,17]. Precision of the measurement is critical.

Another application field is gaze-based control, e.g., for special needs, since it may replace the need for wearable tools [24].

Here, we put forth a personalization method that can work with a small number of labeled samples, since we increase the number of samples artificially:

© Springer International Publishing AG 2016
G. Friedrich et al. (Eds.): KI 2016, LNAI 9904, pp. 200–207, 2016.
DOI: 10.1007/978-3-319-46073-4_20

we fit the mentioned 3D face model (i.e., [8]) to the image, rotate the model to different head poses and increase our dataset with the 2D projections of the 3D data. Otherwise, the method would be of limited use, as we discuss it later.

The paper is organized as follows. We review the related gaze direction estimation works (Sect. 2) followed by the section on the databases and the estimation methods. The methods include deep learning, supervised descent, Support Vector Regression (SVR) that we use for the estimation of the facial mesh, positions of eye marker points, the head pose, and the gaze direction and we are searching for a good combination (Sect. 3). Results can be found in Sect. 4. Conclusions are drawn in the last section (Sect. 5).

2   Related Works

Gaze estimation systems are generally classified into two types: model-based and appearance-based methods. Our work is concerned with the latter.

In recent years, numerous papers have been published on appearance-based gaze estimation systems. Lu et al. [13,14] described a method using Adaptive Linear Regression (ALR). They manually designed a feature descriptor based directly on normalized pixel intensities of the preprocessed eye region. They estimate the gaze positions by finding the best subset of the training samples, which linearly reconstructs the feature descriptor of the actual test sample. The estimated gaze position is computed with a linear regression on the selected subset.

Instead of regression, Smith et al. [20] solve a classification problem: they classify images to detect "gaze locking" i.e. direct eye contact with the camera. They also start from raw pixel intensities of a masked area on the image, but they apply principal component analysis and multiple discriminant analysis to achieve dimensionality reduction. Their classifier is a linear support vector machine.

Using the same dataset, Schneider et al. [19] compared various feature descriptors such as Histogram of Oriented Gradients (HOG) [5], Local Binary Patterns (LBP) [16] and raw pixel intensities in combination with different regression algorithms, such as k-Nearest-Neighbours and Support Vector Regression. They report that a multi-level HOG with LBP features and SVR make the best combination.

Sato et al. [23] presented a unique solution to enrich their training database for gaze estimation. They created a setup with multiple 2D cameras and reconstructed a 3D model of the subject's face. Given this 3D model they synthesised 2D images from multiple views thus increasing the variation coverage of the head pose. For regression, they used random forests on the image features combined with the data on the 3D head poses.

To our best knowledge Zhang et al. [26] were the first to use convolutional neural networks for gaze estimation. Alike Sato et al. [23], they also appended the head pose to the convolutional feature descriptor. They achieved slightly better results than Schneider et al. [19]. For more details, on this subject, the interested reader is referred to the paper of Zhang et al. [26].

3   Databases and Methods

3.1   Databases

Several datasets are publicly available for training gaze estimation systems, including the EYEDIAP [15], the MPIIGaze [26] and the UT Multi-view [23] sets. Among these, the full face is visible only in the EYEDIAP dataset. Since we extend our training dataset by fitting a 3D model of the head to images and we want to rotate the heads, our method requires the whole face. We used two datasets in our studies; the dataset from Columbia and our own dataset.

The 'Columbia Gaze Data Set' (CGDS) [20] consists of 5880 images from 56 subjects. The head of each subject was stabilized with a chin rest. The authors used multiple, carefully aligned cameras and gaze targets to record various head poses and gaze directions. The resolution of the images is high: they use 5184 × 3456 pixels. A sample image is shown in Fig. 1(a).

Our dataset (ELTE dataset) consists of recorded videos of 19 subjects (4 females and 15 males) taken in more realistic scenarios. Subjects were instructed to gaze directly into the camera and rotate their heads in different directions while keeping their gaze locked at the camera. We used a HD webcam, uniform lighting conditions, and a white canvas as background during data collection (Fig. 1(a)).

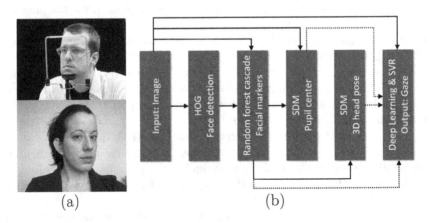

(a)   (b)

Fig. 1. (a) Datasets. Top: chins are stabilized and subjects look at predefined gaze targets [20]. Bottom: gazes are locked at the camera and head poses are changed. (b) Gaze estimation pipeline. Solid lines: used in all cases, dotted lines: used in some of the experiments. Marker positions are used for image normalization (not shown).

3.2   Methods

In our gaze estimation pipeline presented on Fig. 1(b) we use non-linear regressions at multiple stages that we review below.

As the first step of our pipeline, we estimate a bounding box around the face. The method we used is a linear support vector machine on Histogram of Oriented Gradients (HOG) features, similar to [5]. We used the open source implementation together with the available trained model from the *dlib library* [10]. Once the face has been detected, we estimate 2D facial landmarks from a small subset of pixel intensities, using a cascade of random forests [9].

The visual features used for gaze estimation were extended with the 3D head pose data. We used 49 pieces of 2D facial markers as the inputs to the Supervised Descent Method (SDM) [25] and estimated the head pose as follows: we constructed a 3D mean shape, rotated it, and successively minimized the angular error using the 2D reprojection error.

The position of the pupil center was also estimated and served as an optional additional feature. We used the facial marker positions of the SDM regressor, normalized our training images by converting them to grayscale, scaling them to a predefined intercanthal distance (ICD) and by rotating them in 2D to horizontal intercanthal direction. We also flipped each training image horizontally to increase the variance of our training data. The initial estimation was the centroid of the eye corners. We used HOG features with 9 signed bins.

The last step in our pipeline is the gaze estimation. We compared two variants: a Support Vector Regressor-based estimator (SVR) with HOG features as a baseline and a convolutional neural network (CNN) as the state-of-the-art. In both cases, we tried if additional features can improve the quality of the estimation, such as (i) the 3D head pose and (ii) the position of the 2D eye and pupil markers. In both cases, images were scaled to a predefined ICD.

We used both LIBLINEAR [7] and the LIBSVM [3] libraries for SVR estimations, both of which are publicly available. Details of these well-performing algorithms are well described in the literature [4].

We implemented a convolutional neural network similar to [26] in Lasagne. There are two main differences between the original implementation and ours: (i) we use dropout [21] and (ii) rectified linear units in all layers except for the output. Image patches were cut for both eyes with the centroid of the eye corners at the center. Adamax [11] and early stopping were used for network training.

Our architecture was composed of two convolutional and max pooling layer pairs, and 2 dense layers. The first four layers had 2×2 filters, except for the first convolutional one, which had 3×3. The optional head pose and pupil position were concatenated to the convolutional features. We used 1024 units in both fully connected layers. The dropout probability was 10% for the last pooling layer and for the first dense layer.

Beyond our pipeline, we included the ZFace tool [8], an SDM application. ZFace starts with an SDM based generic tracker that locates the 2D and 3D coordinates of main fiducial landmarks in each image. It then reconstructs a high resolution 3D mesh of 512 points. We generated new, realistic 2D projections of the face by mapping the texture to the 3D mesh and rotating it. Although ZFace could be used in the gaze estimation pipeline, due to time considerations, we inserted the cascade of random forests into that.

3.3 Personalization

The personalization method requires only a handful of images, yet it may decrease gaze estimation error by more than 40 %.

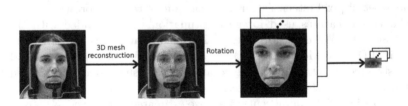

Fig. 2. Personalization pipeline on a CGDS image: input → reconstruct the 3D mesh → generate new training samples by rotating it.

Our algorithm works as follows.

1. Get 'personalization images' of the subject with known gaze vectors and various head positions, e.g., when both components of the gaze vector is 0, i.e. the subject is looking directly into the camera.
2. Fit a 3D mesh to each personalization image. We used ZFace [8] in this step.
3. Rotate the estimated 3D meshes in random directions and generate 2D projections. Calculate the gaze vectors in accordance with these rotations.
4. Improve the gaze estimation model with the generated 2D projections.

The method is sketched in Fig. 2. We explored different algorithmic combinations to be detailed in the following section (Sect. 4).

4   Results

We studied the performance of three algorithms, namely, LIBLINEAR, LIBSVM and CNN in the absence of personalization. We evaluated these algorithms on our own database and on the CGDS database. After reconstructing the 3D meshes on both of them, we first rotated them back to a frontal view, then we rotated them with angles drawn randomly from the uniform distributions in the ranges $[-30°, 30°]$ and $[-15°, 15°]$ for the yaw and pitch angles, respectively. We evaluated the gaze algorithms with leave-one-subject-out cross-validation. LIBSVM is somewhat better than LIBLINEAR, but in some cases we used the latter as our baseline due to computer time requirements; scaling characteristics of LIBSVM can be prohibitive for large sample sizes. In LIBLINEAR we used the solver for the dual problem and also employed a bias term. Results are shown in Table 1.

We evaluated the performance of the personalization pipeline for different algorithms and ICDs. We extended the visual features both with the head pose, the eye and pupil marker positions in all cases. Images used for personalization

Table 1. Comparisons of performances for the two databases ELTE and CGDS [20] and for the three algorithms LIBSVM (LSVM), LIBLINEAR (LLIN), and CNN. 32 and 96 in the table header denote the ICD we used for scaling. The table shows mean angular errors in degrees.

Additional	ELTE LSVM		ELTE LLIN		ELTE CNN		CGDS CNN	
features	32	96	32	96	32	96	32	96
None	6.89	7.11	6.69	7.06	5.98	5.06	10.37	8.62
Pupil	4.88	7.69	5.20	5.36	5.64	5.07	10.11	8.53
Head pose	6.17	**6.35**	6.05	6.06	3.92	**3.85**	**8.07**	**6.97**
Pupil + h.pose	**3.78**	7.96	**5.07**	**5.27**	**3.82**	3.86	8.28	7.12

Table 2. Comparisons of personalization performances for the two databases ELTE and CGDS [20], for the the three algorithms LIBSVM (LSVM), LIBLINEAR (LLIN), CNN, and for different number of personalization images. All runs had both pupil and head pose data as inputs. For each personalization image 10 rotated samples were generated. Notation: augmented database is (a): trained from scratch, (b): added as a single mini batch at the end of training. The displayed values are mean angular errors in degrees.

Pers	ELTE	ELTE	ELTE CNN 32 ICD		ELTE CNN 96 ICD		CGDS CNN 96 ICD	
images	LSVM	LLIN	(a)	(b)	(a)	(b)	(a)	(b)
0	3.78	5.07	3.82	3.83	3.86	3.89	7.12	7.09
5	2.81	3.71	2.91	3.06	2.45	3.29	6.13	6.47
10	2.56	3.45	2.61	2.75	2.24	3.24	5.59	6.27
15	2.36	3.13	2.34	2.26	2.02	2.28	4.98	5.33
20	2.22	3.08	2.21	2.04	1.80	1.93	4.61	4.59

were randomly selected from the samples of each subject. The images were pre-processed the same way as in the evaluation of gaze estimation algorithms. We show our results on Table 2. By using the personalization pipeline, performace increases gradually. For 20 personalization images rotated to 10 different head poses, the mean gaze error fell down to less than two third of its original value (from 100 % to 58 %) on the average.

5   Summary

We have presented a non-obtrusive method together with a learning architecture for gaze direction estimation in a considerable range of head pose angles. Such estimations have a number of applications from the medical field, to remote surveillance systems and also computer assisted education. The special feature of our method is the personalization capability that does not require a complicated calibration setup, yet improves precision considerably.

Acknowledgements. This work was supported in part by EIT Digital under grant No. 16257. The authors thank the contributions of Tamás Nyíri who ran the numerical studies.

References

1. Bednarik, R., Kinnunen, T., Mihaila, A., Fränti, P.: Eye-movements as a biometric. In: Kalviainen, H., Parkkinen, J., Kaarna, A. (eds.) SCIA 2005. LNCS, vol. 3540, pp. 780–789. Springer, Heidelberg (2005)
2. Cantoni, V., Galdi, C., Nappi, M., Porta, M., Riccio, D.: Gant: gaze analysis technique for human identification. Pattern Recogn. **48**(4), 1027–1038 (2015)
3. Chang, C.C., Lin, C.J.: Libsvm: a library for support vector machines. ACM Trans. Intell. Syst. Technol. (TIST) **2**(3), 27 (2011)
4. Cortes, C., Vapnik, V.: Support-vector networks. Mach. Learn. **20**(3), 273–297 (1995)
5. Dalal, N., Triggs, B.: Histograms of oriented gradients for human detection. In: IEEE Computer Society Conference on Computer Vision and Pattern Recognition (CVPR 2005), vol. 1, pp. 886–893. IEEE (2005)
6. Eberz, S., Rasmussen, K.B., Lenders, V., Martinovic, I.: Preventing lunchtime attacks: fighting insider threats with eye movement biometrics. In: NDSS (2015)
7. Fan, R.E., Chang, K.W., Hsieh, C.J., Wang, X.R., Lin, C.J.: Liblinear: a library for large linear classification. J. Mach. Learn. Res. **9**, 1871–1874 (2008)
8. Jeni, L.A., Cohn, J.F., Kanade, T.: Dense 3d face alignment from 2d videos in real-time. In: 2015 11th IEEE International Conference and Workshops on Automatic Face and Gesture Recognition (FG), vol. 1, pp. 1–8. IEEE (2015)
9. Kazemi, V., Sullivan, J.: One millisecond face alignment with an ensemble of regression trees. In: Proceedings of the IEEE Conference on Computer Vision and Pattern Recognition, pp. 1867–1874 (2014)
10. King, D.E.: Dlib-ml: a machine learning toolkit. J. Mach. Learn. Res. **10**, 1755–1758 (2009)
11. Kingma, D., Ba, J.: Adam: a method for stochastic optimization. arXiv preprint (2014). arXiv:1412.6980
12. Kinnunen, T., Sedlak, F., Bednarik, R.: Towards task-independent person authentication using eye movement signals. In: Proceedings of the 2010 Symposium on Eye-Tracking Research & Applications, pp. 187–190. ACM (2010)
13. Lu, F., Sugano, Y., Okabe, T., Sato, Y.: Inferring human gaze from appearance via adaptive linear regression. In: 2011 IEEE International Conference on Computer Vision (ICCV), pp. 153–160. IEEE (2011)
14. Lu, F., Sugano, Y., Okabe, T., Sato, Y.: Adaptive linear regression for appearance-based gaze estimation. IEEE Trans. Pattern Anal. Mach. Intell. **36**(10), 2033–2046 (2014)
15. Mora, K.A.F., Monay, F., Odobez, J.M.: Eyediap: a database for the development and evaluation of gaze estimation algorithms from rgb and rgb-d cameras. In: Proceedings of the Symposium on Eye Tracking Research and Applications, pp. 255–258. ACM (2014)
16. Ojala, T., Pietikainen, M., Harwood, D.: Performance evaluation of texture measures with classification based on kullback discrimination of distributions. In: Proceedings of the 12th IAPR International Conference on Pattern Recognition, 1994, volume 1-Conference A: Computer Vision & Image Processing, vol. 1, pp. 582–585. IEEE (1994)

17. Rigas, I., Komogortsev, O., Shadmehr, R.: Biometric recognition via eye movements: Saccadic vigor and acceleration cues. ACM Trans. Appl. Percept. (TAP) **13**(2), 6 (2016)
18. Ross, A., Jain, A.: Information fusion in biometrics. Pattern Recogn. Lett. **24**(13), 2115–2125 (2003)
19. Schneider, T., Schauerte, B., Stiefelhagen, R.: Manifold alignment for person independent appearance-based gaze estimation. In: 2014 22nd International Conference on Pattern Recognition (ICPR), pp. 1167–1172. IEEE (2014)
20. Smith, B.A., Yin, Q., Feiner, S.K., Nayar, S.K.: Gaze locking: passive eye contact detection for human-object interaction. In: Proceedings of the 26th Annual ACM Symposium on User Interface Software and Technology, pp. 271–280. ACM (2013)
21. Srivastava, N., Hinton, G., Krizhevsky, A., Sutskever, I., Salakhutdinov, R.: Dropout: a simple way to prevent neural networks from overfitting. J. Mach. Learn. Res. **15**(1), 1929–1958 (2014)
22. Stone, J.: Face recognition: when a nod is better than a wink. Curr. Biol. **11**(16), R663–R664 (2001)
23. Sugano, Y., Matsushita, Y., Sato, Y.: Learning-by-synthesis for appearance-based 3d gaze estimation. In: Proceedings of the IEEE Conference on Computer Vision and Pattern Recognition, pp. 1821–1828 (2014)
24. Vörös, G., Verő, A., Pintér, B., Miksztai-Réthey, B., Toyama, T., Lőrincz, A., Sonntag, D.: Towards a smart wearable tool to enable people with SSPI to communicate by sentence fragments. In: Cipresso, P., Matic, A., Lopez, G. (eds.) MindCare 2014. LNICST, vol. 100, pp. 90–99. Springer, Heidelberg (2014)
25. Xiong, X., Torre, F.: Supervised descent method and its applications to face alignment. In: Proceedings of the IEEE Conference on Computer Vision and Pattern Recognition, pp. 532–539 (2013)
26. Zhang, X., Sugano, Y., Fritz, M., Bulling, A.: Appearance-based gaze estimation in the wild. In: Proceedings of the IEEE Conference on Computer Vision and Pattern Recognition, pp. 4511–4520 (2015)

Sister Conference
Contributions/Extended Abstracts

Exception-Enriched Rule Learning from Knowledge Graphs

Mohamed Gad-Elrab[1], Daria Stepanova[1], Jacopo Urbani[2],
and Gerhard Weikum[1(✉)]

[1] Max Planck Institute of Informatics, Saarbrücken, Germany
{gadelrab,dstepano,weikum}@mpi-inf.mpg.de
[2] Vrije Universiteit Amsterdam, Amsterdam, The Netherlands
jacopo@cs.vu.nl

1 Introduction

Recent developments in information extraction have enabled the construction of huge Knowledge Graphs (KGs), e.g., DBpedia [1] or YAGO [8]. To complete and curate modern KGs, inductive logic programming and data mining methods have been introduced to identify frequent data patterns, e.g., *"Married people live in the same place"*, and cast them as rules like $r1 : livesIn(Y, Z){\leftarrow}isMarriedTo(X, Y), livesIn(X, Z)$. These rules can be used for various purposes: First, since KGs operate under Open World Assumption (OWA – i.e. absent facts are treated as unknown), they can be applied to derive new potentially true facts. Second, rules can be used to eliminate erroneous information from the KG.

Existing learning methods restrict to Horn rules [4] (i.e. rules with only positive body atoms), which are insufficient to capture more complex patterns, for instance like $r2:livesIn(Y, Z){\leftarrow}isMarriedTo(X, Y), livesIn(X, Z), not\ researcher(Y)$, i.e., nonmonotonic rules. While $r1$ generally holds, the additional knowledge that Y is a researcher could explain why few instances of *isMarriedTo* do not live together; this can prevent inferring the missing living place by only relying on the *isMarriedTo* relations.

Thus, for KG completion and curation, understanding exceptions is crucial. While learning non-monotonic rules under Closed World Assumption (CWA – i.e. absent facts are treated as false) is a well-studied problem that lies at the intersection of inductive and abductive logic programming (e.g., [11]), it has not been yet investigated in the context of KGs treated under OWA, despite evident importance of this research direction. To overcome the limitations of prior work on KG rule mining, our goal is to develop methods for learning *non-monotonic rules* from KGs.

We formulate this ambitious task as a version of a theory revision problem [10], where, given a KG and a set of (previously learned) Horn rules, the aim is to update them to nonmonotonic rules, so that their quality is better than

Original paper appeared at the 15th International Semantic Web Conference (ISWC), 2016.

© Springer International Publishing AG 2016
G. Friedrich et al. (Eds.): KI 2016, LNAI 9904, pp. 211–217, 2016.
DOI: 10.1007/978-3-319-46073-4

the Horn rules'. In [9], we made a first step towards tackling this problem by providing an approach of step-wise rule revision, where novel ranking functions are used to quantify the strength of nonmonotonic rules w.r.t the KG. We did not merely estimate the quality of for individual rules in isolation, but considered their cross-talk through a new technique that we call *partial materialization*. We implemented a prototype of our approach and reported on the improvements we obtained both in terms of rules' quality as well as predicted fact quality when performing KG completion. In the remaining of this paper, we summarize the main results from [9] and discuss possible extensions to more general settings.

2 Nonmonotonic Rule Learning from Knowledge Graphs

Problem Statement. On the Web, knowledge graphs (KG) $\mathcal{G}$ are often encoded using the RDF data model, which represents the content of the graph with a set of triples of the form ⟨*subject predicate object*⟩. These triples can be seen as positive unary and binary facts, i.e., the above triple corresponds to *object(subject)* if *predicate* = *isA* and to *predicate(object, subject)* otherwise[1]. KGs are naturally treated under the OWA.

In this work, we focus on non-monotonic rules. A *nonmonotonic logic program* is a set of rules of the form $a_1 \leftarrow b_1, \ldots, b_k \, not \, b_{k+1}, \ldots, b_n$ where each a_i and b_j is a first-order atom and *not* is called negation as failure (NAF) or default negation. The answer set semantics [5] for nonmonotonic logic programs is based on the CWA. Given a ruleset $\mathcal{R}$ and a set of facts $\mathcal{G}$, the models (aka. answers sets) of the program $\mathcal{R} \cup \mathcal{G}$ can be determined following [5]. They reflect the information that can be deduced from $\mathcal{R} \cup \mathcal{G}$ under the answer set semantics.

Let $\mathcal{G}^a$ be a given (possibly incomplete) KG, and let $\mathcal{G}^i$ be the ideal KG that contains nodes from $\mathcal{G}^a$ and all relations between these nodes that hold in the current state of the world. Our ultimate goal is to automatically extract a set of rules $\mathcal{R}$ from $\mathcal{G}^a$, applying which (i.e. computing some answer set of $\mathcal{R} \cup \mathcal{G}^a$) we can obtain the graph $\mathcal{G}^a_{\mathcal{R}}$, which minimally differs from $\mathcal{G}^i$. Our approach is to first learn a set of Horn rules, and then aim at simultaneously revising them by adding negated atoms to the rule bodies. Since normally, the ideal graph $\mathcal{G}^i$ is not available, in order to estimate the quality of a revised ruleset, we devise two generic quality functions q_{rm} and $q_{conflict}$, that take as input a ruleset $\mathcal{R}$ and a KG and output a real value, reflecting the suitability of $\mathcal{R}$ for data prediction. More specifically,

$$q_{rm}(R, \mathcal{G}) = \frac{\sum_{r \in \mathcal{R}} rm(r, \mathcal{G})}{|\mathcal{R}|}, \tag{1}$$

where rm is some standard association rule measure [2]. To measure $q_{conflict}$ for $\mathcal{R}$, we create an extended set of rules $\mathcal{R}^{aux}$, which contains each revised rule in $\mathcal{R}$ together with its auxiliary version. For each rule r in $\mathcal{R}$, its auxiliary version r^{aux} is constructed by: (i) transforming r into a Horn rule by removing *not* from negated body atoms, and (ii) replacing the head predicate a of r with a newly

---

[1] For simplicity in this work we identify a given graph with its factual representation.

introduced predicate *not_a* which intuitively contains instances which are *not* in a. Formally, we define $q_{conflict}$ as follows

$$q_{conflict}(\mathcal{R}_{NM}, \mathcal{G}) = \sum_{p \in pred(\mathcal{R}^{aux})} \frac{|c \,|\, p(c), not\_p(c) \in \mathcal{G}_{\mathcal{R}^{aux}}|}{|c \,|\, not\_p(c) \in \mathcal{G}_{\mathcal{R}^{aux}}|} \quad (2)$$

We are now ready to state our problem: Given a KG $\mathcal{G}$, a set of nonground Horn rules $\mathcal{R}_H$ mined from $\mathcal{G}$, and a quality function rm, our goal is to find a set of rules $\mathcal{R}_{NM}$ obtained by adding negated atoms to $Body(r)$ for some $r \in \mathcal{R}_H$ s.t. (i) $q_{rm}(\mathcal{R}_{NM}, \mathcal{G})$ is maximal, and (ii) $q_{conflict}(\mathcal{R}_{NM}, \mathcal{G})$ is minimal.

Unary Rules. In [9], we focused on rules with unary atoms. To this end, we transformed binary facts in our initial KG to unary ones via propositionalization. Our approach proceeds in four steps.

Step 1. After mining Horn rules using an off-the-shelf algorithm (e.g., FPGrowth [3] or [4], [6] we compute for each rule the *normal* and *abnormal* instance sets, defined as

Definition 1 (r-(ab)normal instance set). *Let $\mathcal{G}$ be a KG and, moreover, let $r : a(X) \leftarrow b_1(X), \ldots, b_k(X)$ be a Horn rule mined from it. Then*

- $NS(r, \mathcal{G}) = \{c \,|\, b_1(c), \ldots c, b_k(c), a(c) \in \mathcal{G}\}$ *is an r-normal instance set;*
- $ABS(r, \mathcal{G}) = \{c \,|\, b_1(c), \ldots, b_k(c) \in \mathcal{A}, a(c) \notin \mathcal{G}\}$ *is an r-abnormal instance set.*

Step 2. Intuitively, if the given data was complete, then the r-normal and r-abnormal instance sets would exactly correspond to instances for which the rule r holds (resp. does not hold) in the real world. Since the KG is potentially incomplete, this is no longer the case and some r-abnormal instances might in fact be classified as such due to data incompleteness. In order to distinguish the "wrongly" and "correctly" classified instances in the r-abnormal set, we construct *exception witness sets (EWS)*, which are defined as follows:

Definition 2. *Let $\mathcal{G}$ be a KG and let r be a Horn rule mined from $\mathcal{G}$. An r-exception witness set $EWS(r, \mathcal{G}) = \{e_1, \ldots, e_l\}$ is a maximal set of predicates, such that*

(i) $e_i(c') \in \mathcal{G}$ for some $c' \in ABS(r, \mathcal{G})$, $1 \leq i \leq l$ and
(ii) $e_1(c), \ldots, e_l(c) \notin \mathcal{A}$ for all $c \in NS(r, \mathcal{G})$.

Steps 3 and 4. After *EWS*s are computed for all rules in $\mathcal{R}_H$, we use them to create potential revisions (Step 3), i.e., from every $e_j \in EWS(r_i, \mathcal{G})$ a revision r_i^j of r_i is constructed by adding a negated atom over e_j to the body of r_i. Finally, we determine a concrete revision for every rule, that will constitute a solution to our problem (Step 4). To find such globally best ruleset revision $\mathcal{R}_{NM}$ many candidate combinations have to be checked, which due to the large size of our $\mathcal{G}$ and *EWS*s might be too expensive. Therefore, instead we incrementally build $\mathcal{R}_{NM}$ by considering every $r_i \in \mathcal{R}_H$ and choosing the locally best revision r_i^j for it.

In order to select r_i^j, we introduce four special ranking functions: a naive one and three more advanced functions, which exploit the novel concept of *partial materialization* (**PM**). Intuitively, the idea behind it is to rank candidate revisions not based on $\mathcal{G}$, but rather on its extension with predictions produced by other (selectively chosen) rules (grouped into a set $\mathcal{R}'$), thus ensuring a cross-talk between the rules. We now describe the ranking functions in more details.

- **Naive** ranker is the most straightforward ranking function. It prefers the revision r_i^j with the highest value of $rm(r_i^j, \mathcal{G})$ among all revisions of r_i.
- **PM** ranking function prefers r_i^j with the highest value of

$$\frac{rm(r_i^j, \mathcal{G}_{\mathcal{G}_{R'}}) + rm(r_i^{j^{aux}}, \mathcal{G}_{\mathcal{R}'})}{2} \tag{3}$$

where $\mathcal{R}'$ is the set of rules r_k', which are rules from $\mathcal{R}_H \backslash r_i$ with all exceptions from $EWS(r_k, \mathcal{G})$ incorporated at once. Informally, $\mathcal{G}'_{\mathcal{R}}$ contains only facts that can be safely predicted by the rules from $\mathcal{R}_H \backslash r_i$, i.e., there is no evident reason (candidate exceptions) to neglect their prediction.
- **OPM** is similar to **PM**, but the selected ruleset $\mathcal{R}'$ contains only those rules whose Horn version appears above the considered rule r_i in the ruleset $\mathcal{R}_H$, ordered (**O**) based on some chosen measure (e.g., the same as rm).
- **OWPM** is the most advanced ranking function. It differs from **OPM** in that the predicted facts in $\mathcal{G}_{\mathcal{R}'} \backslash \mathcal{G}$ inherit weights (**W**) from the rules that produced them, and facts in $\mathcal{G}$ get the highest weight. These weights are taken into account when computing the value of Eq. 3. If the same fact is derived by multiple rules, we store the highest weight. To avoid propagating uncertainty through rule chaining when computing weighted partial materialization of $\mathcal{G}$ we keep predicted facts (i.e., derived by applying rules from $\mathcal{R}'$) separately from the explicit facts (i.e., those in $\mathcal{G}$), and infer new facts using only $\mathcal{G}$.

Extension to Binary Rules. A natural direction for extending the work from [9] is to consider rules involving binary atoms. In this case, there can be a potentially larger number of possible EWS sets to construct and consider. More specifically, if a rule has n distinct variables, then there could be $n + \binom{n}{2}$ candidate EWS sets. Given the large size of KGs, computing all exceptions in every EWS set might be inpractical for scalability reasons. To overcome this issue, the language bias of possible exception candidates should be carefully fixed. Practically, several possibilities for such restriction exist. For instance, one could search only for binary (resp. unary) exceptions, or only consider EWSs w.r.t. to the variables in (a certain position of) the head atom. An in-depth analysis of these possibilities is planned for our future work.

3   Evaluation

We briefly discuss some of experimental results that are reported in more detail in [9].

Step 1. Initially, we considered the Horn rules produced by AMIE [4]. However, they involve unsupported binary predicates and the only unary rules regard the *isA* predicate, which was too limiting for us. Therefore, we used the standard mining algorithm FPGrowth [6] offered by SPMF Library[2] and extracted Horn rules from two well-known KGs: YAGO (general purpose) and IMDB (domain-specific). Before learning Horn rules, we preprocessed a given KG by converting binary facts *predict(subject, object)* into unary ones *predict_object(subject)*, and automatically abstracting the new unary predicates using the type hierarchy of the KG to make them more dense and allow mining expressive data patterns. In order to avoid over-fitting, we applied some restrictions to the rules (e.g. we limited to rules with at most four body atoms, a single head atom, a minimum support of $0.0001 \times$ *#entities*, etc.).

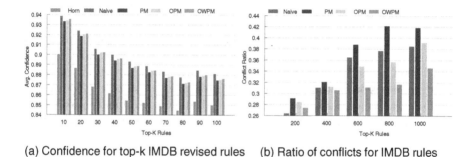

(a) Confidence for top-k IMDB revised rules   (b) Ratio of conflicts for IMDB rules

Fig. 1. Average rules' confidence and number of conflicts on IMDB KG.

Steps 2 and 3. We implemented a simple inductive learning procedure to calculate the *EWS*s. We could find *EWS*s for about 6 K rules mined fromYAGO, and 22 K rules mined from IMDB. On average, the *EWS*s for the YAGO's rules contained 3 exceptions, and 28 exceptions for IMDB.

Step 4. We evaluated the quality of our rule selection procedure in terms of the increase of rules' confidence and the decrease of the number of conflicts introduced by negated atoms. The confidence shows how well the revised rules adhere to the input. The number of conflicts indicates how consistently the revised rules predict the unseen data. Figure 1 reports the obtained average rules' confidence of original Horn rules and rules revised with our ranking functions on the IMDB dataset (YAGO's follows a similar behaviour [9]). Figure 1a reports

---

[2] http://www.philippe-fournier-viger.com/spmf/.

the average confidence of the original Horn rules. For each ranking method, we show the results for the top 10,...,100 % rules ranked by lift.

From Fig. 1a, we make two observations. First, we notice that enriching Horn rules with exceptions increases the average confidence (appr. 3.5 %). Second, as expected, the highest confidence is achieved by the (*Naive*) procedure, as the latter blindly chooses exceptions that maximize confidence, while ignoring the conflict ratio. However, confidence alone is not sufficient to determine the overall rule's quality, and also consistency of the predictions (i.e., $q_{conflict}$ function) should be taken into account.

In order to evaluate $q_{conflict}$, we computed the number of conflicts by executing the revised rules and their corresponding auxiliary versions (r^{aux}) on IMDB KG using the DLV tool [7]. The conflict appears whenever both $p(c)$ and $not\_p(c)$ are derived. Figure 1b reports the ratio between the number of conflicts and negated derived facts. One can observe that *OWPM* and *OPM* produce less conflicts than the *Naive* function in most of the cases. Moreover, the *OWPM* ranking function works generally better than *OPM* and *PM* functions, i.e., taking into account weights of the predicted facts leads to improved revisions. For instance, for IMDB, moving from *OPM* to *OWPM* reduced the number of conflicts from 775 to 685 on a base of about 2000 negated facts.

In another experiment, we counted the number of derivations that our exceptions prevented using the top-1000 YAGO rules. With the original Horn rules, the reasoner inferred about 924K new facts, while the revised rules deduced around 890K facts. In order to assess whether the 34K predictions neglected due to our revision method are actually erroneous, we sampled 259 random facts from the removed set (we selected three facts for each binary predicate to avoid skewness), and manually consulted online resources (mainly Wikipedia) to determine whether they were indeed incorrect. We found that 74.3 % of them were actually faulty predictions. This number provides a first empirical evidence that our method is capable of detecting good exceptions, and hence can improve the general predictive quality of the Horn rules. Unfortunately, since KGs follow OWA, automatic evaluation of predictions is problematic, and human judgment is often required to estimate the validity of exceptions. Cross validation methods could be adapted for our needs and exploited for evaluation purposes to some extent. This is planned for future work. However, since fully complete versions of the real-world KGs (i.e., $\mathcal{G}^i$) are not available, to measure how correct and probable our exceptions actually are, manual assessment might be still required.

4   Discussion and Outlook

We have presented a method for mining nonmonotonic rules from KGs: First learning a set of Horn rules and then revising them by adding negated atoms into their bodies. We evaluated it with various configurations on both general-purpose and domain-specific KGs and observed significant improvements over a baseline Horn rule mining.

Apart from extensions to rules with predicates of higher arity, there are other future directions to explore. First, one can look into extracting evidence for or against exceptions from text and web corpora. Second, our framework can be enhanced by partial completeness assumptions for certain predicates (e.g., all countries are available in the KG) or constants (e.g., knowledge about Barack Obama is complete). We believe these are important research topics that should be studied in the future.

References

1. Auer, S., Bizer, C., Kobilarov, G., Lehmann, J., Cyganiak, R., Ives, Z.: DBpedia: a nucleus for a web of open data. In: Pan, J.Z., Chen, H., Kim, H.-G., Li, J., Wu, Z., Horrocks, I., Mizoguchi, R., Wu, Z. (eds.) JIST 2011. LNCS, vol. 7185, pp. 722–735. Springer, Heidelberg (2007). doi:10.1007/978-3-540-76298-0_52

2. Azevedo, P.J., Jorge, A.M.: Comparing rule measures for predictive association rules. In: Kok, J.N., Koronacki, J., de Mantaras, R.L., Matwin, S., Mladenič, D., Skowron, A. (eds.) ECML 2007. LNCS, vol. 4701, pp. 510–517. Springer, Heidelberg (2007)

3. Chen, Y., Goldberg, S., Wang, D.Z., Johri, S.S.: Ontological pathfinding: mining first-order knowledge from large knowledge bases. In: Proceedings of the SIGMOD (2016, to appear)

4. Galrraga, L., Teflioudi, C., Hose, K., Suchanek, F.M.: Fast rule mining in ontological knowledge bases with AMIE+. VLDB J. (2015)

5. Gelfond, M., Lifschitz, V.: The stable model semantics for logic programming. In: Proceedings of 5th International Conference and Symposium on Logic Programming, ICLP, pp. 1070–1080 (1988)

6. Han, J., Pei, J., Yin, Y., Mao, R.: Mining frequent patterns without candidate generation: a frequent-pattern tree approach. Data Min. Knowl. Discov. **8**(1), 53–87 (2004)

7. Leone, N., Pfeifer, G., Faber, W., Eiter, T., Gottlob, G., Perri, S., Scarcello, F.: The DLV system for knowledge representation and reasoning. ACM Trans. Comput. Logic (TOCL) **7**(3), 499–562 (2006)

8. Mahdisoltani, F., Biega, J., Suchanek, F.M.: YAGO3: a knowledge base from multilingual wikipedias. In: Proceedings of CIDR (2015)

9. Gad-Elrab, M., Stepanova, J.: Exception-enriched rule learning from knowledge graphs. In: Proceedings of the International Semantic Web Conference. TR (2016). http://people.mpi-inf.mpg.de/gadelrab/ExRules_TR.pdf

10. Paes, A., Revoredo, K., Zaverucha, G., Costa, V.S.: Probabilistic first-order theory revision from examples. In: Kramer, S., Pfahringer, B. (eds.) ILP 2005. LNAI, vol. 3625, pp. 295–311. Springer, Heidelberg (2005). doi:10.1007/11536314_18

11. Ray, O.: Nonmonotonic abductive inductive learning. J. Appl. Logic **3**(7), 329–340 (2008)

iRobot: Teaching an Evaluated, Competencies-Based Introductory Artificial Intelligence Class in Highschools

Harald Burgsteiner[1][(✉)], Martin Kandlhofer[2], and Gerald Steinbauer[2]

[1] Institute for eHealth, Graz University of Applied Sciences, Graz, Austria
harald.burgsteiner@fh-joanneum.at
[2] Institute for Software Technology, Graz University of Technology, Graz, Austria
{kandlhofer,steinbauer}@ist.tugraz.at

Abstract. Profound knowledge about at least the fundamentals of Artificial Intelligence (AI) will become increasingly important for careers in science and engineering. Therefore we present an innovative educational project teaching fundamental concepts of artificial intelligence at high school level. We developed a high school AI-course (called *"iRobot"*) dealing with major topics of AI and computer science (automatons, agent systems, data structures, search algorithms, graphs, problem solving by searching, planning, machine learning) according to suggestions in the current literature. The course was divided into seven weekly teaching units of two hours each, comprising both theoretical and hands-on components. We conducted and empirically evaluated a pilot project in a representative Austrian high school. The results of the evaluation show that the participating students have become familiar with the concepts included in the course and the various topics addressed.

1 Introduction

Nearly every day an article is published in a newspaper in which a new gadget or a innovation is being described and labelled with tags like "adaptive", "learning", "smart" or "intelligent". Therefore, it will be important for our civilisation to be able to differentiate between just smart gadgets that contain e.g. an adaptable algorithm to better sort their shopping list and real artificial intelligence (AI) that indeed might eventually become smarter than humans. Many of us know about the existence of services and devices based on AI, but hardly anybody knows about the technology behind them.

But e.g. in Austria currently even basic education about AI is mainly restricted to university programs. One future goal is to include AI topics in the general curriculum of computer science education in schools. Thus, we worked out answers to the following questions (i) what contents are important enough to be fit into e.g. a class of one hour each week? (ii) how could such classes

---

Original paper appeared at the Thirtieth AAAI Conference on Artificial Intelligence (AAAI), 2016.

G. Friedrich et al. (Eds.): KI 2016, LNAI 9904, pp. 218–223, 2016.
DOI: 10.1007/978-3-319-46073-4

be structured? (iii) which suggestions already exist in the literature? (iv) what prior knowledge would be required to understand some foundations of artificial intelligence? (v) what methods or tools could be used during such a class? A prototype of such a class should be taught in one of our partner schools and then be evaluated to acquire valuable feedback from the first students.

In the next section we present the results of the literature research. Based on this we can outline a possible AI class in high schools. Section 3 contains the results of the planning and the outline of the complete course. In the fourth section our experiences and lessons learnt during and after the the conduction of the classes will be described. The last section discusses the whole work and makes implications and outlines for possible future classes about artificial intelligence in high schools.

2   Background and Related Work

Looking at international literature, the teaching of fundamental concepts and techniques of AI independent of any platform or programming language at school level is rare. Many approaches focus on undergraduate/graduate students at university level. [11] describes a research oriented course for undergraduate students in which the IBM Watson was used to teach AI fundamentals. [10] suggests ways to structure lessons and assignments for undergraduates to teach them basic problem solving strategies. In [7] a course for undergraduate and graduate students is presented, where students have to use Java to program suitable agents for certain games. Combinations of programming AI and using LEGO robots can be found in [8] where undergraduate students are encouraged to build an autonomous chess agent. [6] report about the design of a robot lab to be used in introductory AI classes. Some universities also offer training courses for future teachers about how AI can be taught in school (e.g. [4]). Common approaches at school level typically deal with more general areas of AI like its history, the Turing test, chat bots or philosophical questions (e.g. [5]).

2.1   Competencies and Self-directed Learning

A modern approach in education is the use of so called "competencies" the students should acquire during their study instead of traditional facts that they should "know" and be able to reproduce. Typically, competencies can be described with sentences beginning with "I can ...", like "I can evaluate the efficiency of algorithms." Important for us are not only competencies in artificial intelligence, but the connection to important topics of classic computer science like data structures, to be able to explain and possibly program important algorithms (e.g. searching). Resulting from these considerations we defined 17 competencies that the students should acquire until the end of the course. The final competencies are described in detail in [1].

According to [9] learning is more sustainable when the students get eager or curious to know something. Authentic problems lead to gaps in the current knowledge, that require the construction of new knowledge. E.g. students

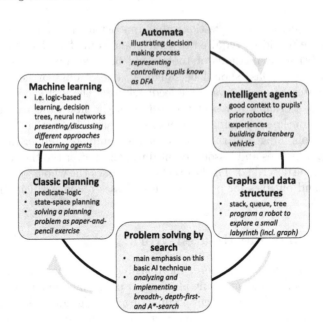

Fig. 1. An illustration from [2] of the various AI topics covered in our introductory course. The topics were spread among the seven classes we held. The assignments are written in italics.

involved in RoboCup can see that it is difficult to let their robot escape from an arbitrary labyrinth. Showing them connections between graphs, searching and labyrinths, the motivated student will probably start to research how such an algorithm works and how it can be implemented. Thus, one premise of our course is to actively involve the students in the learning process. Activities can include e.g. paper-and-pencil or programming exercises, robot construction, discussions, group works etc. depending on given tasks or problems. A course in a school that actively participates e.g. in junior robotics competitions can include assignments on the basis of the existing robots and code and let the students see possible shortcomings or possibilities for enhancements of their current approach.

3   Design of the Classes

Wollowski et al. [12] did a survey of current practice and teaching of AI. This survey asked educators what they are currently teaching in various AI courses and practitioners what techniques they use in practice. According to the educators the primary goal of current AI courses is to teach the basics or main ideas of AI. The views of the practitioners do not differ here. The recommended topics of the educators list "Search" and "Knowledge Representation and Reasoning" (KR&R) in the first places, followed by "Machine Learning". Also the practitioners do say that KR&R is the most wanted topic in AI, followed by

"Machine Learning". These topics will form the basic outline of our course, although machine learning will certainly only be coverable as a sort of overview or outlook, because the variety of different approaches and the necessary mathematical skills demand much more time and background knowledge.

Due to these expected limitations in the students prior knowledge for this course, we can only cover introductory topics of artificial intelligence. We have to include some necessary general topics like data structures (e.g. trees) or fundamental algorithms (like searching) as well. The extent of topics is further limited due to the time restrictions and the planned methods of teaching. The planned final structure and the coarse contents of the seven classes are illustrated in Fig. 1. One can find further details including the planning of the classes as well as the accompanying experiments and assignments in [1].

4   Realization and Evaluation

We partnered with a school that has a focus in natural and computer sciences and is interested in offering some of its students a class in the area of artificial intelligence. The nine students that subscribed to this special course come from the 9th, 10th and 11th year of school attendance (i.e. approximately between 15 and 18 years old, average age 16.5 years). Hence, they also had a very varying previous knowledge in the area of computer science (none of them in AI). But additionally all of them are participating for several years in robotics electives, especially in various leagues in the Robocup. There were 1 female and 8 male students attending. We agreed on seven timeslots on Friday afternoons from 13:20 to 15:20 from May to July 2015. To be able to evaluate a learning success, we apply current methods of learning goal assessments, especially self evaluation and foreign evaluation. For our course we defined 17 core learning goals or competencies. After the course the students were asked to fill out the self-evaluation anonymously. The students stated, that they have fully acquired most of the defined competencies, which coincides the teachers' observations.

The course itself and the teacher were evaluated too. We selected questions that should give us feedback on several measures that can be grouped as (i) the contents, (ii) the presentation and (iii) the dealing with the students. Very positive aspects are, that the students agree to a high degree to the statements that they have learnt something new, that they could actively participate and that they are motivated to deepen their knowledge in the area of AI. The realisation and the presentation of the contents, the material for the course (including the exercises) and especially the explanations have reached very high approval rates, too. More details about the self-evaluation and the course evaluation including all questions, competencies and the feedbacks can again be found in [1].

The final empirical project evaluation was done using reliable quantitative and qualitative empirical research methods []. In terms of quantitative evaluation we applied a paper-and-pencil post-questionnaire (Likert-scale, open-ended questions) comprising a self-assessment of acquired skills as well as feedback on the structure and teaching method of the weekly teaching units. In terms of qualitative evaluation we conducted semi-structured interviews with all 9 participating students using a set of predefined open-ended questions as guideline. The interviews were structured around the topics *background* (technical, prior knowledge), *motivation/reason* for joining the iRobot project, *expectations* (prior and after the project), *memorable AI topics/situations* and *lessons learned*. Further qualitative data was collected by using techniques of participant observation (field notes, discussions, taking pictures) during the weekly teaching units. All collected data were treated confidentially and anonymously.

Summarizing the results of the qualitative evaluation students' main motives for participating in the project were interest in robotics, computers and AI as well as the possibility to prepare for science studies at university. According to students' statements they gained basic knowledge of the principles of AI. They also positively stressed the good balance between theory and hands-on activities, the good atmosphere as well as the technical discussions with university researchers. Finally, students will also benefit from the acquired content in future (e.g. robotics competitions, high school theses, starting university studies).

5   Discussion and Outlook

Like classic literacy which includes writing, reading and mathematics, literacy in AI/computer science will become a major issue in future. Therefore, we presented an educational project teaching fundamental concepts of artificial intelligence and computer science at high school level (grades 9–11). We conducted and empirically evaluated a pilot project in a representative Austrian high school with nine voluntarily participating students in spring 2015. Weekly courses held by university researchers covered major AI topics. The contents were chosen according to current AI education literature and adapted and structured with respect to the students' prior knowledge and educational background. The units focused on the students' experiences and built the new knowledge on the basis of these. Together with a mixture of theory, various work settings (i.e. solitary work, group work, open discussions, learning stations etc.) and hands-on projects we employed a constructionistic learning model as good as it was possible. The course was finally evaluated in three ways. First, the students had to self-evaluate their acquired competencies, second, the course itself was evaluated in terms of content, presentation, methods and dealing with the students and third, by conducting qualitative semi-structured interviews with all participating students.

The first pilot project was successful, nevertheless there were some drawbacks and shortcomings to be dealt with in future realisations of such a course. For a well founded scientific evaluation of the course the sample of the participating students was quite small with only nine attending. Additionally, they had a quite different previous knowledge because they were coming from three different grades. So they formed a very inhomogenous group in terms of prior knowledge. What also should be changed in future courses is the time structure of the course which was not very beneficial. We had too few classes to talk about and discuss all the different foundations of AI that we intended to include. Additionally, the course was quite compact placed at the end of the semester.

Summarizing the results of the evaluations, the project succeeded in teaching high school pupils the foundations of artificial intelligence. The participating students got a well founded understanding of at least the concepts we presented and discussed and the growing importance of artificial intelligence in every day life. We are planning to conduct the project in other high schools in the next few years, pursuing our long-term goal of integrating artificial intelligence topics into the regular science education in high schools and to foster 'AI literacy'.

References

1. Burgsteiner, H.: Design and Evaluation of an Introductory Artificial Intelligence Class in Highschools. Master's thesis, Graz University of Technology (2016)
2. Burgsteiner, H., Kandlhofer, M., Steinbauer, G.: iRobot: Teaching the basics of artificial intelligence in high schools. In: Proceedings of the 6th AAAI Symposium on Educational Advances in AI, pp. 4126–4127. Association for the Advancement of Artificial Intelligence, AAAI Press, Phoenix, USA, February 2016
3. Diekmann, A.: Empirische Sozialforschung. Rowohlt (2007)
4. Dilger, W.: Künstliche Intelligenz in der Schule. TU Chemnitz (2005)
5. Heinze, C., Haase, J., Higgins, H.: An action research report from a multi-year approach to teaching artificial intelligence at the k-6 level. In: 1st Symposium on Educational Advances in Artificial Intelligence (2010)
6. Kumar, D., Meeden, L.: A robot laboratory for teaching artificial intelligence. In: Proceedings of the Twenty-ninth SIGCSE Technical Symposium on Computer Science Education, SIGCSE 1998, pp. 341–344. ACM, New York (1998)
7. McGovern, A., Tidwell, Z., Rushing, D.: Teaching introductory artificial intelligence through java-based games. In: 2nd Symposium on Educational Advances in Artificial Intelligence. Association for the Advancement of Artificial Intelligence, AAAI Press (2011)
8. Selkowitz, R.I., Burhans, D.T.: Shallow blue: Lego-based embodied ai as a platform for cross-curricular project based learning. In: 5th Symposium on Educational Advances in Artificial Intelligence. Association for the Advancement of Artificial Intelligence, AAAI Press (2014)
9. Spohrer, M.: Konzeption und Analyse neuer Maßnahmen in der Fort- und Weiterbildung von Informatiklehrkräften. Ph.D. thesis, TU Munich (2009)
10. Torrey, L.: Teaching problem-solving in algorithms and ai. In: 3rd Symposium on Educational Advances in Artificial Intelligence. Association for the Advancement of Artificial Intelligence, AAAI Press (2012)
11. Wollowski, M.: Teaching with watson. In: 5th Symposium on Educational Advances in AI. Association for the Advancement of AI, AAAI Press (2014)
12. Wollowski, M., Selkowitz, R., Brown, L.E., Goel, A., Luger, G., Marshall, J., Neel, A., Neller, T., Norvig, P.: A survey of current practice and teaching of ai. In: Proceedings of the 6th AAAI Symposium on Educational Advances in AI, pp. 4119–4124. Association for the Advancement of AI, AAAI Press, Phoenix, USA, February 2016

Towards Clause-Learning State Space Search: Learning to Recognize Dead-Ends

Marcel Steinmetz and Jörg Hoffmann[⊠]

Saarland University, Saarbrücken, Germany
{steinmetz,hoffmann}@cs.uni-saarland.de

1 Clause-Learning State Space Search

The ability to learn from conflicts is a key algorithm ingredient in constraint satisfaction (e. g.[2, 6, 8, 20, 22, 24]). For state space search, like goal reachability in classical planning which we consider here, progress in this direction has been elusive, and almost entirely limited to *length-bounded reachability*, where reachability testing reduces to a constraint satisfaction problem, yet requires iterating over different length bounds until some termination criterion applies [5, 16, 19, 28]. But *do we actually need a length bound to be able to do conflict analysis and nogood learning in state space search?*

Arguably, the canonical form of a "conflict" in state space search is a *dead-end* state, from which no solution (of any length) exists. Such conflicts are not as ubiquitous as in constraint satisfaction (including length-bounded reachability), yet they do occur, e. g., in oversubscription planning [26], in planning with limited resources [11], in single-agent puzzles [4, 15], and in explicit-state model checking of safety properties [7] where a dead-end is any state from which the error property cannot be reached.

We introduce a method that learns sound and generalizable knowledge from dead-end states during state space search classical planning. To our knowledge, this is the first of its kind. Prodigy [21] comes closest with its learning of sound action-pruning rules in backward search. Inspired by Prodigy, Bhatnagar and Mostow [3] considered forward-search conflict-based learning, yet their techniques are not sound (do not guarantee that pruned states actually are dead-ends). Kolobov et al's SixthSense technique [17] is sound, yet is placed in probabilistic planning and incorporates classical planning as a sub-procedure. Value function refinement using Bellman updates [1, 18, 25] will eventually learn that a state is a dead-end, yet does not generalize that knowledge.

The key to our technique are *critical-path heuristics* h^C [9, 10], relative to a set C of *atomic conjunctions*. These heuristics incorporate an approximation allowing to break up conjunctive subgoals into the elements of C. We don't give a full definition here, but the central equation should be suitable to get an idea:

$$h^C(s, G) = \begin{cases} 0 & G \subseteq s \\ 1 + \min_{a \in \mathcal{A}[G]} h^C(s, Regress(G, a)) & G \in C \\ \max_{G' \subseteq G, G' \in C} h^C(s, G') & \text{else} \end{cases} \tag{1}$$

Original paper appeared at the Thirtieth AAAI Conference on Artificial Intelligence (AAAI), 2016.

© Springer International Publishing AG 2016
G. Friedrich et al. (Eds.): KI 2016, LNAI 9904, pp. 224–229, 2016.
DOI: 10.1007/978-3-319-46073-4

This equation is easiest understood as a recursive estimation of goal distance. The bottom case in the equation splits up the current subgoal G into its atomic subgoals. The middle case in the equation minimizes over all actions the subgoal can be regressed through. The top case terminates the recursion on subgoals that are true in our state s. The overall distance estimate is obtained through a top-level call (not shown here) on s and the global planning goal specified in the input planning task.

Critical-path heuristics were originally designed for admissible goal distance estimation. Here we are interested only in their ability to *recognize* dead-end states s, returning $h^C(s) = \infty$. This happens if every recursion path in the equation eventually hits an unsupported subgoal. Intuitively, $h^C(s) = \infty$ if s has no solution even when allowing to break up conjunctive subgoals into atomic conjunctions.

It is easy to see that, for sufficiently large C, all dead-ends will be recognized (just let C be the set of *all* conjunctions). But how to find a small yet informative set C useful for search? Our key idea is to *learn C* during search, through *conflict analysis*.

We start from the simple set C that contains only the singleton conjunctions. We augment forward state space search to identify *unrecognized* dead-ends s, where $h^C(s) < \infty$ yet search has already explored all descendants of s and thus proved s to be a dead end. We design h^C-*refinement* methods analyzing the situation at such s, adding new conjunctions into C to obtain $h^C(s) = \infty$, thus learning to recognize s as well as similar dead-ends search may encounter in the future. The refinement step is the most technical part of our work, and we refer to our AAAI'16 paper [27] for details. In a nutshell, the technique assumes as input a component of states s, where all direct successors t of any state s are already pruned (recognized to be dead-ends) by h^C. It then tackles open h^C-paths on the states s, canceling each such path by combining conjunctions canceling corresponding paths on states t. Suitable combined conjunctions necessarily exist, so that the method is constructive, guaranteeing to find the desired new conjunctions to learn, without having to do any search or exploration.

We furthermore learn *clauses* ϕ, in a manner inspired by, and similar to, a nogood certification technique in SixthSense: we minimize the commitments made in a dead-end state s while still preserving that $h^C(s) = \infty$. The clauses are sound in that $s' \not\models \phi$ implies $h^C(s') = \infty$, i.e., we learn sufficient conditions for h^C dead-end detection. While these sufficient conditions constitute a weaker pruning method than h^C itself, they are much faster to evaluate. Doing so prior to computing h^C strongly reduces the runtime overhead, which can otherwise be prohibitive.

Arranging these techniques in a depth-first search, we obtain an algorithm approaching the elegance of clause learning in SAT: When a subtree is fully explored, the h^C-refinement and clause learning (1) learns to refute that subtree, (2) enables backjumping to the shallowest non-refuted ancestor, and (3) generalizes to other similar search branches in the future. Our experiments show that this can be quite powerful. On problems where dead-ends abound, relative

	NoMystery (30 base instances)						Rovers (30 base instances)						TPP (5 base instances)					
		FD-h^{FF}			DFS-CL			FD-h^{FF}			DFS-CL			FD-h^{FF}			DFS-CL	
			M&S						M&S						M&S			
W	Blind	FD-h^{FF}	OA	NM	W/O L	W/ L	Blind	FD-h^{FF}	OA	NM	W/O L	W/ L	Blind	FD-h^{FF}	OA	NM	W/O L	W/ L
0.5	19	25	**30**	**30**	25	**30**	2	5	**30**	29	5	**30**	4	4	**5**	**5**	**5**	**5**
0.6	10	16	**30**	**30**	16	**30**	1	2	29	25	2	**30**	1	1	**5**	**5**	2	4
0.7	0	11	**30**	29	11	29	0	0	29	23	0	**30**	0	0	**5**	3	0	3
0.8	0	0	**30**	26	0	24	0	0	24	21	0	**24**	0	0	**1**	**1**	0	0
0.9	0	0	**29**	24	0	16	0	0	16	13	0	**22**	0	0	0	0	0	0
1.0	0	6	**26**	20	0	12	0	1	10	6	0	**21**	0	1	0	**2**	0	0
1.1	0	10	**24**	21	0	11	0	0	5	3	6	**14**	0	3	0	**4**	0	2
1.2	0	16	19	**22**	0	13	0	1	3	1	1	**14**	0	3	0	3	3	3
1.3	0	20	18	**24**	0	8	0	2	1	2	1	**12**	0	4	0	**4**	3	3
1.4	0	25	15	**27**	0	11	0	2	0	3	3	**12**	0	4	0	**4**	4	**5**
Σ	29	129	251	**253**	52	184	3	13	147	126	12	**208**	5	20	16	**31**	17	25

Fig. 1. Coverage results. Best per-domain results highlighted in **boldface**. DFS-CL is our approach, "W/O L" without learning, "W/L" with learning. Other abbreviations see text. For each base instance and value of W, the resource budget is set according to W.

to the same search but without learning, our technique often reduces the search space by several orders of magnitude.

2   Empirical Results

Our implementation is in FD [12]. Our current experiments focus on *resource-constrained* planning, where the goal must be achieved subject to a fixed resource budget. We use the benchmarks by Nakhost et al. [23], which are *controlled* in that the minimum required budget b_{min} is known, and the actual budget is set to $W * b_{min}$. The parameter W allows to control the frequency of dead-ends; values of W close to 1.0 are notoriously difficult. In difference to Nakhost et al., we also consider values $W < 1$ where the tasks are unsolvable.[1]

We use a cluster of Intel E5-2660 machines running at 2.20 GHz, with runtime (memory) limits of 30 min (4 GB). Our technique runs a forward depth-first search; in selecting the next children node to expand, it prefers children with smaller h^{FF} [14] value. We compare to blind search, and to FD's greedy best-first dual-queue search with h^{FF} and preferred operators (denoted "FD-h^{FF}"), as baselines. We compare to Hoffmann et al.'s [13] two most competitive configurations of merge-and-shrink (M&S) heuristics for proving unsolvability (denoted here "OA" and "NM"). We run the latter as dead-end detectors in FD-h^{FF} to obtain variants competitive also for satisficing planning.

Figure 1 gives coverage data. Our approach easily outperforms the standard planner FD-h^{FF}. It is vastly superior in Rovers, and generally for budgets close

---

[1] Not all actions consume resources, so that the fixed budget does not per se entail an upper bound on plan length. The more important role of the fixed budget for our technique, to our current understanding, is that search paths will tend to be short, i.e., a depth-first forward search will quickly run into dead-ends from which we are then able to learn.

to, or below, the minimum needed. The stronger planners using FD-h^{FF} with M&S dead-end detection are better than DFS-CL in NoMystery, worse in Rovers, and about on par in TPP.

For the exciting news, consider the comparison between with vs. without learning. The former outperforms the latter dramatically. The *only* reason for this is generalization, i.e., refinements of h^C on states s leading to pruning on states other than s. Without generalization, the search spaces would be *identical*, including tie breaking. So generalization occurs at *massive* scale. It lifts a hopeless planner (DFS with singleton-conjunction, aka h^1, dead-end detection) to a planner competitive with the state of the art in resource-constrained planning.

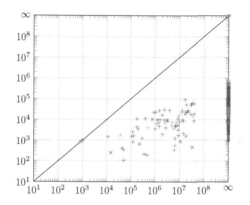

Fig. 2. Search space size for DFS-CL with learning (y-axis) vs. without learning (x-axis). "+" (red) NoMystery, "×" (blue) Rovers, "⋆" (orange) TPP, "∞": out of time or memory.

Figure 2 compares the search space sizes directly. On instances solved by both, the reduction factor min/geometric mean/maximum is: NoMystery 7.5/412.0/18117.9; Rovers 58.9/681.3/70401.5; TPP 1/34.4/1584.3.

3   Conclusion

Our work pioneers conflict-directed learning, of sound generalizable knowledge, from dead-end states in forward state-space search. This is made possible by the progress in modern classical-planning heuristic functions, specifically h^C, and our key technical contribution in that context is a method for refining h^C's dead-end detection capabilities during search. The resulting technique is, in our humble opinion, quite elegant, and suggests that the learning from "true" conflicts in state space search, not necessitating a solution length bound, is worth the community's attention.

Beauty contests aside, from a pragmatical point of view the technique certainly does, as it stands, not deliver an empirical breakthrough. It vastly improves over using the same technique without learning, and it appears to have strengths in (certain) resource-constrained situations. As ours is merely a first foray into this kind of technique, and lots more remains to be explored – combinations with alternate search techniques, refinement of different dead-end detection machineries, reasoning over knowledge learned from different sources, etc. – we expect this to be the beginning of the story, not its end.

One thing we would particularly like to see is the export of this (kind of) technique, from classical planning where it is presently placed, to game-playing and model checking. For h^C refinement, this works "out of the box" modulo the applicability of Eq. 1, i.e., the definition of critical-path heuristics. As is, this requires conjunctive subgoaling behavior. But more general logics (e.g. minimization to handle disjunctions) should be manageable.

Acknowledgments. This work was partially supported by the German Research Foundation (DFG), under grant HO 2169/5-1 "Critically Constrained Planning via Partial Delete Relaxation".

References

1. Barto, A.G., Bradtke, S.J., Singh, S.P.: Learning to act using real-time dynamic programming. Artif. Intell. **72**(1–2), 81–138 (1995)
2. Beame, P., Kautz, H.A., Sabharwal, A.: Towards understanding and harnessing the potential of clause learning. J. Artif. Intell. Res. **22**, 319–351 (2004)
3. Bhatnagar, N., Mostow, J.: On-line learning from search failures. Mach. Learn. **15**(1), 69–117 (1994)
4. Bjarnason, R., Tadepalli, P., Fern, A.: Searching solitaire in real time. J. Int. Comput. Games Assoc. **30**(3), 131–142 (2007)
5. Blum, A.L., Furst, M.L.: Fast planning through planning graph analysis. Artif. Intell. **90**(1–2), 279–298 (1997)
6. Dechter, R.: Enhancement schemes for constraint processing: backjumping, learning, and cutset decomposition. Artif. Intell. **41**(3), 273–312 (1990)
7. Edelkamp, S., Lluch-Lafuente, A., Leue, S.: Directed explicit-state model checking in the validation of communication protocols. Int. J. Softw. Tools Technol. Transfer **5**(2–3), 247–267 (2004)
8. Eén, N., Sörensson, N.: An extensible sat-solver. In: Giunchiglia, E., Tacchella, A. (eds.) SAT 2003. LNCS, vol. 2919, pp. 502–518. Springer, Heidelberg (2004)
9. Fickert, M., Hoffmann, J., Steinmetz, M.: Combining the delete relaxation with critical-path heuristics: a direct characterization. J. Artif. Intell. Res. **56**(1), 269–327 (2016)
10. Haslum, P., Geffner, H.: Admissible heuristics for optimal planning. In: Chien, S., Kambhampati, R., Knoblock, C. (eds.) Proceedings of the 5th International Conference on Artificial Intelligence Planning Systems (AIPS 20000), Breckenridge, CO, 2000, pp. 140–149. AAAI Press, Menlo Park
11. Haslum, P., Geffner, H.: Heuristic planning with time and resources. In: Cesta, A., Borrajo, D. (eds.) Proceedings of the 6th European Conference on Planning (ECP 2001), pp. 121–132. Springer-Verlag (2001)
12. Helmert, M.: The fast downward planning system. J. Artif. Intell. Res. **26**, 191–246 (2006)

13. Hoffmann,J., Kissmann, P., Torralba, Á.: "Distance"? Who Cares? Tailoring merge-and-shrink heuristics to detect unsolvability. In: Schaub, T. (ed.) Proceedings of the 21st European Conference on Artificial Intelligence (ECAI 2014), Prague, Czech Republic, August 2014. IOS Press (2014)

14. Hoffmann, J., Nebel, B.: The FF planning system: fast plan generation through heuristic search. J. Artif. Intell. Res. **14**, 253–302 (2001)

15. Junghanns, A., Schaeffer, J.: Sokoban: evaluating standard single-agent search techniques in the presence of deadlock. In: Mercer, R.E., Neufeld, E. (eds.) AI 1998. LNCS, vol. 1418, pp. 1–15. Springer, Heidelberg (1998)

16. Kambhampati, S.: Planning graph as a (dynamic) CSP: Exploiting EBL, DDB and other CSP search techniques in graphplan. J. Artif. Intell. Res. **12**, 1–34 (2000)

17. Kolobov, A., Mausam, Weld, D.S.: Discovering hidden structure in factored MDPs. Artif. Intell. **189**, 19–47 (2012)

18. Korf, R.E.: Real-time heuristic search. Artif. Intell. **42**(2–3), 189–211 (1990)

19. Long, D., Fox, M.: Efficient implementation of the plan graph in stan. J. Artif. Intell. Res. **10**, 87–115 (1999)

20. Marques-Silva, J., Sakallah, K.: GRASP: a search algorithm for propositional satisfiability. IEEE Trans. Comput. **48**(5), 506–521 (1999)

21. Minton, S., Carbonell, J.G., Knoblock, C.A., Kuokka, D., Etzioni, O., Gil, Y.: Explanation-based learning: a problem solving perspective. Artif. Intell. **40**(1–3), 63–118 (1989)

22. Moskewicz, M., Madigan, C., Zhao, Y., Zhang, L., Malik, S.: Chaff: engineering an efficient SAT solver. In: Proceedings of the 38th Conference on Design Automation (DAC-01), Las Vegas, Nevada, USA, 2001. IEEE Computer Society (2001)

23. Nakhost, H., Hoffmann, J., Müller, M.: Resource-constrained planning: a monte carlo random walk approach. In: Bonet, B., McCluskey, L., Silva, J.R., Williams, B. (eds.) Proceedings of the 22nd International Conference on Automated Planning and Scheduling (ICAPS 2012), pp. 181–189. AAAI Press, (2012)

24. Prosser, P.: Hybrid algorithms for the constraint satisfaction problem. Comput. Intell. **9**, 268–299 (1993)

25. Reinefeld, A., Marsland, T.A.: Enhanced iterative-deepening search. IEEE Trans. Pattern Anal. Mach. Intell. **16**(7), 701–710 (1994)

26. Smith, D.E.: Choosing objectives in over-subscription planning. In: Koenig, S., Zilberstein, S., Koehler, J. (eds.) Proceedings of the 14th International Conference on Automated Planning and Scheduling (ICAPS 2004), Whistler, Canada, 2004, pp. 393–401. Morgan Kaufmann (2004)

27. Steinmetz, M., Hoffmann, J.: Towards clause-learning state space search: learning to recognize dead-ends. In: Schuurmans, D., Wellman, M. (eds.) Proceedings of the 30th AAAI Conference on Artificial Intelligence (AAAI 2016). AAAI Press, February 2016

28. Suda, M.: Property directed reachability for automated planning. J. Artif. Intell. Res. **50**, 265–319 (2014)

VLog: A Column-Oriented Datalog Reasoner

Jacopo Urbani[1], Ceriel Jacobs[1], and Markus Krötzsch[2(⊠)]

[1] Department of Computer Science, VU University Amsterdam,
Amsterdam, The Netherlands
[2] Center for Advancing Electronics Dresden (cfaed), TU Dresden,
Dresden, Germany
markus.krotzsch@tu-dresden.de

1 Introduction

Knowledge representation and reasoning is a central concern of modern AI. Its importance has grown with the availability of large structured data collections, which are published, shared, and integrated in many applications today. Graph-based data representations, so called *knowledge graphs* (KGs), have become popular in industry and academia, and occur in many formats. RDF [8] is most popular for exchanging such data on the Web, and examples of large KGs in this format include Bio2RDF [7], DBpedia [6], Wikidata [20], and YAGO [9]. Nevertheless, KGs are not always stored in their native graph format, and many reside in relational databases as well.

The great potential of the conceptual view offered by KGs is the ability to connect heterogeneous and often incomplete data sources. Inferring implicit information from KGs is therefore essential in many applications, such as onto-logical reasoning, data integration, and information extraction. A common foundation for specifying such inferences is the rule-based language Datalog [3]. While Datalog rules are rather simple types of *if-then* rules, their recursive nature is making them powerful. Many inference tasks can be captured in this framework, including many types of ontological reasoning commonly used with RDF. In particular, Datalog can be used to perform reasoning in all of the three lightweight profiles of the OWL Web Ontology Language, as shown by Krötzsch [12, 13] and (implicitly by translation to path queries) Bischoff et al. [4]. Datalog thus provides an excellent basis for exploiting KGs to the full, and a foundation for more advanced inferencing mechanisms and more expressive features.

Unfortunately, the implementation of Datalog inferencing on large KGs remains very challenging. The task is worst-case time-polynomial in the size of the KG, and hence tractable in principle, but huge KGs are difficult to manage. A preferred approach is therefore to *materialize* (i.e., pre-compute) inferences. Modern DBMS such as Oracle 11g and OWLIM materialize KGs of 100M–1B edges in times ranging from half an hour to several days [5, 11]. Research prototypes such as Marvin [15], C/MPI [21], WebPIE [18], and DynamiTE [19] achieve

---

Original paper appeared at the Thirtieth AAAI Conference on Artificial Intelligence (AAAI), 2016.

G. Friedrich et al. (Eds.): KI 2016, LNAI 9904, pp. 230–236, 2016.
DOI: 10.1007/978-3-319-46073-4

scalability by using parallel or distributed computing, but often require significant hardware resources. Urbani et al., e.g., used up to 64 high-end machines to materialize a KG with 100B edges in 14 hours [18]. In addition, all of the above systems only support (fragments of) the OWL RL ontology language, which is subsumed by Datalog but significantly simpler.

In our recent work, we have therefore presented a new approach of in-memory Datalog materialization [17]. Performing recursive reasoning tasks in main memory can lead to significant performance gains; recent works by Motik et al. have been the first to adapt this insight to large-scale Datalog materialization [14]. However, a challenge for this approach is that KGs (and the inferences one may draw from them) may require large amounts of memory, so that powerful high-end machines are necessary. The primary goal of our work therefore has been to reduce memory consumption to enable even larger KGs to be processed on even simpler computers.

To this end, we have proposed to maintain inferences in a customised *column-based* storage layout. In contrast to traditional row-based layouts, where a data table is represented as a list of tuples (rows), column-based approaches use a tuple of columns (value lists) instead. This enables more efficient joins [10] and effective, yet simple data compression schemes [1]. However, these advantages are set off by the comparatively high cost of updating column-based data structures [2]. This is a key challenge for using this technology during Datalog materialization, where frequent insertions of large numbers of newly derived inferences need to be processed.

We have shown that our approach can overcome this challenge, and we have presented a working implementation, *VLog* (for *Vertical Datalog*), which exhibits significant memory savings while remaining competitive in terms of performance. More recently, we have further extended VLog to support both RDF and relational database management systems to store the KGs upon which reasoning is performed.

In this extended abstract, we summarize the main contributions in our recent work and give a short report on recent improvements, including some new evaluation results.

2   A Short Introduction to Datalog

To illustrate the basic principles of Datalog reasoning, we give a short example. Readers looking for a more detailed introduction may wish to consult the full paper [17]. The following rules use a ternary predicate triple to represent RDF triples (edges in directed, labelled graphs):

$$\mathsf{T}(x, v, y) \leftarrow \mathsf{triple}(x, v, y) \tag{1}$$

$$\mathsf{Inverse}(v, w) \leftarrow \mathsf{T}(v, \mathsf{owl:inverseOf}, w) \tag{2}$$

$$\mathsf{T}(y, w, x) \leftarrow \mathsf{Inverse}(v, w), \mathsf{T}(x, v, y) \tag{3}$$

$$\mathsf{T}(y, v, x) \leftarrow \mathsf{Inverse}(v, w), \mathsf{T}(x, w, y) \tag{4}$$

$$\mathsf{T}(x, \mathsf{hasPart}, z) \leftarrow \mathsf{T}(x, \mathsf{hasPart}, y), \mathsf{T}(y, \mathsf{hasPart}, z) \tag{5}$$

The first rule (1) simply copies RDF data from triple to T. Rule (2) "extracts" an RDF-encoded OWL statement that declares a property to be the inverse of another. Rules (3) and (4) apply this information to derive inverted triples. Finally, rule (5) is a typical transitivity rule for the RDF property hasPart.

We follow the common practice in Datalog to distinguish *extentional (EDB) predicates*, which store the fixed input data, from *intentional (IDB) predicates*, which store the inferred information. This is useful in our setting, since we want to keep KGs (EDB) in their native databases and represent inferences (IDB) in memory. In the previous example, the inferred prediates T and Inverse are IDB, while triple is EDB.

The semantics of Datalog can be defined as the least fixed point of an iterative bottom-up application of rules, which starts from an input database $\mathcal{I} = \mathbb{P}^0(\mathcal{I})$ and proceeds to compute increasing sets of inferences $\mathbb{P}^1(\mathcal{I})$, $\mathbb{P}^2(\mathcal{I})$, ... until no further derivations follow. For the above example, consider an input database $\mathcal{I} = \{\mathsf{triple}(\mathsf{a}, \mathsf{hasPart}, \mathsf{b}), \mathsf{triple}(\mathsf{b}, \mathsf{hasPart}, \mathsf{c}), \mathsf{triple}(\mathsf{hasPart}, \mathsf{owl:inverseOf}, \mathsf{partOf})\}$. Iteratively applying rules (1)–(5) to $\mathcal{I}$, we obtain the following new derivations in each step, where superscripts indicate the rule used to produce each fact:

$\mathbb{P}^1(\mathcal{I})$: $\mathsf{T}(\mathsf{hasPart}, \mathsf{owl:inverseOf}, \mathsf{partOf})^{(1)}$ $\mathsf{T}(\mathsf{a}, \mathsf{hasPart}, \mathsf{b})^{(1)}$ $\mathsf{T}(\mathsf{b}, \mathsf{hasPart}, \mathsf{c})^{(1)}$

$\mathbb{P}^2(\mathcal{I})$: $\mathsf{Inverse}(\mathsf{hasPart}, \mathsf{partOf})^{(2)}$ $\mathsf{T}(\mathsf{a}, \mathsf{hasPart}, \mathsf{c})^{(5)}$

$\mathbb{P}^3(\mathcal{I})$: $\mathsf{T}(\mathsf{b}, \mathsf{partOf}, \mathsf{a})^{(3)}$ $\mathsf{T}(\mathsf{c}, \mathsf{partOf}, \mathsf{b})^{(3)}$ $\mathsf{T}(\mathsf{c}, \mathsf{partOf}, \mathsf{a})^{(3)}$

No further facts can be inferred after this. For example, applying rule (4) to $\mathbb{P}^3(\mathcal{I})$ only yields duplicates of previous inferences.

A naive application of rules as in the example is not practical, and our approach therefore adopts a slightly modified version of the more efficient *semi-naive evaluation* [17]. The key idea is to restrict recursive rule applications to cases that rely on inferences made in the previous step. To this end, one uses more fine-grained data structures that store the newly derived facts in each step. We use Δ_p^i to denote the set of new facts with predicate p derived in step i.

3   VLog: Vertical Datalog

We have implemented our approach to Datalog materialization in our system VLog, which can evaluate arbitrary (positive) Datalog programs over a range of databases. VLog was designed to be easy to use, and offers a command line and a Web interface. The main features of the system include:

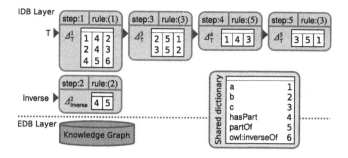

Fig. 1. Column-Based Storage Layout in VLog

1. Support for a variety of database systems that can be the source for the (EDB) data on which the recursive computation is evaluated.
2. Space-efficient in-memory storage of derivations using column-store technology
3. Dynamic optimization techniques for more efficient processing at runtime
4. Combinations of bottom-up and top-down computation strategies
5. Free and open source C++ code available at https://github.com/jrbn/vlog

VLog completely isolates the IDB layer, which is a column-based in-memory store, from the EDB layer, which can be any database. In addition to an RDF backend[1], VLog also natively supports popular relational databases (MySQL, MonetDB) and a generic ODBC interface. Datalog rules are specified in a simple text format.

The heart of VLog is its columnar storage layout for IDB relations. Figure 1 illustrates our approach using the previous example. Each of the IDB tables in the upper part of the figure is stored column-by-column instead of row-by-row. A dictionary is used to translate constant names into numeric identifiers. To avoid costly updates, VLog never inserts new tuples into existing tables, but creates new tables instead. The figure therefore contains four tables for derivations of T. This approach is efficient when processing data *set-at-a-time*, with many new facts derived and stored in one step. Column-based layouts can safe memory through simple yet effective data compression, such as run-length-encoding [1], and by sharing whole columns between multiple tables.

A downside of our approach is that single IDB relations may be stored in many tables, which adds processing overhead to rule applications. We counter this effect by several dynamic optimizations that enable us to disregard, at runtime, the contents of some IDB tables. This can avoid expensive unions and save significant computation.

The aforementioned techniques are the basis for VLog's bottom-up materialization. In addition, VLog uses top-down reasoning algorithms to pre-compute ("memoize") some IDB relations before bottom-up reasoning. We use a heuristics: if an IDB relation can be pre-computed top down within a short time-out,

---

[1] *Trident*, the in-house RDF triple store used in our earlier work.

we memoize it; otherwise we leave it for semi-naive bottom-up reasoning. Memoization can simply rule applications significantly, since memoized predicates can be treated like EDB predicates.

4 Experiments

We present some experimental results that illustrate the performance of VLog on a laptop.[2] Further experiments and methodological details can be found in our full paper.

Runtime and Memory Usage. In a first experiment, we have compared performance to RDFox [14]. For better comparability with VLog (which does not support parallel processing yet), we have used the sequential version of RDFox. Note that RDFox may achieve almost linear speed-ups in multi-processor settings, but memory usage is hardly affected by this. We have used several datasets here: DBpedia (112M triples), LUBM-1K (133M triples), LUBM-5K (691M triples), Claros (19M triples), and Claros-S (0.5M triples). Datalog rules were derived from OWL ontologies, leading to rule sets with a varied number of rules: from 170 (LUBM L) and 202 (LUBM U) over 2,689 (Claros L) and 2,749 (Claros LE) up to 9,396 (DBpedia). Table 1 (left) shows the results measured for these inputs, and the number of IDB facts derived in VLog in each case. As we can see, VLog shows the hoped-for memory savings while maintaining competitive performance, even when anticipating some speed-up for RDFox on multi-CPU systems.

Performance on Different Backends. To investigate the performance of VLog on various types of database backends, we have used a smaller version of LUBM (17M triples) with a reduced set of 66 rules. Table 1 (top right) shows the

Table 1. Evaluation results: time [sec] and memory [MB] vs. RDFox (left); time depending on backend (top right); time vs. SocialLite (bottom right)

Data/Rules	RDFox (seq)		VLog/Trident			VLog/ Trident	VLog/ MySQL	VLog/ MonetDB	VLog/ ODBC
	time	mem	time	mem	IDBs				
LUBM1K/L	82	11,884	38	2,198	172M	16sec	459sec	209sec	232sec
LUBM1K/U	148	14,593	80	2,418	197M				
LUBM5K/L	oom	oom	196	8,280	815M			VLog/	
LUBM5K/U	oom	oom	434	7,997	994M	Task		MonetDB	SociaLite
DBpedia	177	7,917	91	532	33M	Google		1,768sec	>12h
Claros/L	2,418	5,696	644	2,406	89M	Google (sample1)		271sec	16,566sec
Claros/LE	oom	oom	tout	tout	—	Google (sample2)		35sec	505sec
Claros-S/LE	8.5	271	2.5	127	3.7M	Twitter Soc. Net.		66sec	277sec

[2] Macbook Pro; 2.2GHz Intel Core i7; 512GB SDD; 16GB RAM; MacOS Yosemite OS.

runtimes for several backends. Trident is our own RDF store, MonetDB (column-based) and MySQL (row-based) are popular RDBMS for which VLog has custom bindings, and "ODBC" refers to the use of MonetDB through VLog's generic ODBC driver. Trident enjoys performance advantages due to tighter integration and specialization towards KGs.

Social Network Analysis with Datalog. Finally, we have compared VLog's performance to SocialLite, a Datalog-based tool to analyse networks [16]. Here we used networks from the popular SNAP repository: the Google WebGraph (875K nodes, 5M edges) and a Twitter Network graph (80K nodes, 1.75M edges). For Google WebGraph we created two smaller samples (sample1: 2M edges; sample2: 1M edges). We used simple Datalog rule sets for two tasks: reachability within four hops (5 rules) and triangle matching (2 rules). The results for these tasks are shown in Table 1 (top left). VLog performs significantly faster than SocialLite even with MonetDB as a backend.

5 Outlook

VLog is still a prototype, but it can already be used productively in applications that require rule-based reasoning. Our evaluation indicates that it is a viable alternative to existing Datalog engines, with competitive runtimes at a significantly reduced memory consumption. At the same time, our experiments show that some tasks are still difficult for current systems, which motivates further research in this field. Current development of VLog is focussed on further runtime optimizations, the effective use of parallel processing, the expansion of existing interfaces and general usability improvements.

Acknowledgments. This work was partially funded by COMMIT, the NWO VENI project 639.021.335, and the DFG in grant KR 4381/1-1 and CRC 912 *HAEC*.

References

1. Abadi, D., Madden, S., Ferreira, M.: Integrating compression and execution in column-oriented database systems. In: Proceedings of SIGMOD, pp. 671–682 (2006)
2. Abadi, D.J., Marcus, A., Madden, S., Hollenbach, K.: SW-Store: a vertically partitioned DBMS for semantic web data management. VLDB J. **18**(2), 385–406 (2009)
3. Abiteboul, S., Hull, R., Vianu, V.: Foundations of Databases. Addison Wesley (1995)
4. Bischof, S., Krötzsch, M., Polleres, A., Rudolph, S.: Schema-agnostic query rewriting in SPARQL 1.1. In: Mika, P., Tudorache, T., Bernstein, A., Welty, C., Knoblock, C., Vrandečić, D., Groth, P., Noy, N., Janowicz, K., Goble, C. (eds.) ISWC 2014. LNCS, vol. 8796, pp. 584–600. Springer, Heidelberg (2014). doi:10.1007/978-3-319-11964-9_37
5. Bishop, B., Kiryakov, A., Ognyanoff, D., Peikov, I., Tashev, Z., Velkov, R.: OWLIM: a family of scalable semantic repositories. Semant. Web J. **2**(1), 33–42 (2011)

6. Bizer, C., Lehmann, J., Kobilarov, G., Auer, S., Becker, C., Cyganiak, R., Hellmann, S.: DBpedia - a crystallization point for the web of data. J. Web Semant. **7**(3), 154–165 (2009)

7. Callahan, A., Cruz-Toledo, J., Dumontier, M.: Ontology-based querying with Bio2RDF's linked open data. J. Biomed. Semant. 4(S-1) (2013)

8. Cyganiak, R., Wood, D., Lanthaler, M. (eds.): RDF 1.1 Concepts and Abstract Syntax. W3C Recommendation (2014). http://www.w3.org/TR/rdf11-concepts/

9. Hoffart, J., Suchanek, F.M., Berberich, K., Weikum, G.: YAGO2: a spatially and temporally enhanced knowledge base from Wikipedia. Artif. Intell., Special Issue Artif. Intell. Wikipedia and Semi-Structured Resour. **194**, 28–61 (2013)

10. Idreos, S., Groffen, F., Nes, N., Manegold, S., Mullender, K.S., Kersten, M.L.: MonetDB: two decades of research in column-oriented database architectures. IEEE Data Eng. Bull. **35**(1), 40–45 (2012)

11. Kolovski, V., Wu, Z., Eadon, G.: Optimizing enterprise-scale OWL 2 RL reasoning in a relational database system. In: Patel-Schneider, P.F., Pan, Y., Hitzler, P., Mika, P., Zhang, L., Pan, J.Z., Horrocks, I., Glimm, B. (eds.) ISWC 2010. LNCS, vol. 6496, pp. 436–452. Springer, Heidelberg (2010). doi:10.1007/978-3-642-17746-0_28

12. Krötzsch, M.: Efficient rule-based inferencing for OWL EL. In: Walsh, T. (ed.) Proceedings of the 22nd International Joint Conference on Artificial Intelligence (IJCAI 2011), pp. 2668–2673. AAAI Press/IJCAI (2011)

13. Krötzsch, M.: The not-so-easy task of computing class subsumptions in OWL RL. In: Cudré-Mauroux, P., Heflin, J., Sirin, E., Tudorache, T., Euzenat, J., Hauswirth, M., Parreira, J.X., Hendler, J., Schreiber, G., Bernstein, A., Blomqvist, E. (eds.) ISWC 2012. LNCS, vol. 7649, pp. 279–294. Springer, Heidelberg (2012). doi:10.1007/978-3-642-35176-1_18

14. Motik, B., Nenov, Y., Piro, R., Horrocks, I., Olteanu, D.: Parallel materialisation of datalog programs in centralised, main-memory RDF systems. In: Proceedings of the 28th AAAI Conference on Artificial Intelligence (AAAI 2014), pp. 129–137. AAAI Press (2014)

15. Oren, E., Kotoulas, S., Anadiotis, G., Siebes, R., ten Teije, A., van Harmelen, F.: Marvin: distributed reasoning over large-scale semantic web data. J. Web Semant. **7**(4), 305–316 (2009)

16. Seo, J., Guo, S., Lam, M.: SociaLite: datalog extensions for efficient social network analysis. In: Proceedings ot the ICDE, pp. 278–289 (2013)

17. Urbani, J., Jacobs, C., Krötzsch, M.: Column-oriented datalog materialization for large knowledge graphs. In: Schuurmans, D., Wellman, M.P. (eds.) Proceedings of the 30th AAAI Conference on Artificial Intelligence (AAAI 2016), pp. 258–264. AAAI Press (2016)

18. Urbani, J., Kotoulas, S., Maassen, J., van Harmelen, F., Bal, H.: WebPIE: a Web-scale parallel inference engine using MapReduce. J. Web Semant. **10**, 59–75 (2012)

19. Urbani, J., Margara, A., Jacobs, C., van Harmelen, F., Bal, H.: Dynamite: parallel materialization of dynamic RDF data. In: The Semantic Web-ISWC 2013, pp. 657–672. Springer (2013)

20. Vrandečić, D., Krötzsch, M.: Wikidata: a free collaborative knowledge base. Commun. ACM **57**(10) (2014)

21. Weaver, J., Hendler, J.A.: Parallel materialization of the finite RDFS closure for hundreds of millions of triples. In: Bernstein, A., Karger, D.R., Heath, T., Feigenbaum, L., Maynard, D., Motta, E., Thirunarayan, K. (eds.) ISWC 2009. LNCS, vol. 5823, pp. 682–697. Springer, Heidelberg (2009). doi:10.1007/978-3-642-04930-9_43

Driver Frustration Detection from Audio and Video in the Wild

Irman Abdić[1,2]([⊠]), Lex Fridman[1], Daniel McDuff[1], Erik Marchi[2],
Bryan Reimer[1], and Björn Schuller[3]

[1] Massachusetts Institute of Technology (MIT), Cambridge, USA
abdic@mit.edu
[2] Technische Universität München (TUM), Munich, Germany
[3] Imperial College London (ICL), London, UK

Abstract. We present a method for detecting driver frustration from both video (driver's face) and audio (driver's voice) streams captured during the driver's interaction with an in-vehicle voice-based navigation system. We analyze a dataset of 20 drivers that contains 596 audio epochs (audio clips, with duration from 1 sec to 15 sec) and 615 video epochs (video clips, with duration from 1 sec to 45 sec). The dataset is balanced across 2 age groups, 2 vehicle systems, and both genders. The model was subject-independently trained and tested using 4-fold cross-validation. We achieve an accuracy of 77.4 % for detecting frustration from a single audio epoch and 81.2 % for detecting frustration from a single video epoch. We then treat the video and audio epochs as a sequence of interactions and use decision fusion to characterize the trade-off between decision time and classification accuracy, which improved the prediction accuracy to 88.5 % after 9 epochs.

Keywords: Frustration detection · Affective computing · Voice control · Voice navigation system · HCI · SVMs

1 Introduction

The question of how to design an interface in order to maximize driver safety has been extensively studied over the past two decades [13]. Numerous publications seek to aid designers in the creation of in-vehicle interfaces that limit demands placed upon the driver [10]. As such, these efforts aim to improve the likelihood of driver's to multi-task safely. Evaluation questions usually take the form of "Is HCI system A better than HCI system B, and why?". Rarely do applied evaluations of vehicle systems consider the emotional state of the driver as a component of demand that is quantified during system prove out, despite of numerous studies that show the importance of affect and emotions in hedonics and aestetics to improve user experience [8]. The work in this paper is motivated by a vision for

Original paper appeared at the 25th International Joint Conference on Artificial Intelligence (IJCAI), 2016.

© Springer International Publishing AG 2016
G. Friedrich et al. (Eds.): KI 2016, LNAI 9904, pp. 237–243, 2016.
DOI: 10.1007/978-3-319-46073-4

(a) Class 1: Satisfied with Voice-Based In-   (b) Class 2: Frustrated with Voice-Based
teraction   Interaction

Fig. 1. Representative video snapshots from voice navigation interface interaction for two subjects. The subject (a) self-reported as not frustrated (satisfied) with the interaction and the (b) subject self-reported as frustrated (frustrated).

an adaptive system that is able to detect the emotional response of the driver and adapt, in order to aid driving performance. The critical component of this vision is the detection of emotion in the interaction of the human driver with the driver vehicle interface (DVI) system. We consider the binary classification problem of a "frustrated" driver versus a "satisfied" driver annotated based on a self-reported answer to the following question: "To what extent did you feel frustrated using the car voice navigation interface?" The answers were on a scale of 1 to 10 and naturally clustered into two partitions as discussed in Sect. 2. As presented in Fig. 1, the "satisfied" interaction is relatively emotionless, and the "frustrated" interaction is full of affective facial actions.

The task of detecting drivers' frustration has been researched in the past [1]. Boril *et al.* exploited the audio stream of the drivers' speech and discriminated "neutral" and "negative" emotions with 81.3 % accuracy (measured in Equal Accuracy Rate – EAR) across 68 subjects. This work used SVMs to discriminate between classes. The ground truth came from one annotation sequence. A "humored" state was presented as one of the 5 "neutral" (non-negative) emotions. This partitioning of emotion contradicts our findings that smiling and humor are often part of the response by frustrated subject.

Contributions. We extend this prior work by (a) leveraging audiovisual data collected under real driving conditions, (b) using self-reported rating of the frustration for data annotation, (c) fusing audio and video as complimentary data sources, and (d) fusing audio and video streams across time in order to characterize the trade-off between decision time and classification accuracy. We believe that this work is the first to address the task of detecting self-reported frustration under real driving conditions.

2   Dataset for Detecting Frustration

The dataset used for frustration detection was collected as part of a study for multi-modal assessment of on-road demand of voice and manual phone calling and voice navigation entry across two embedded vehicle systems [9]. Participants drove one of two standard production vehicles, a 2013 Chevrolet Equinox (Chevy) equipped with the MyLink system and a 2013 Volvo XC60 (Volvo) equipped with the Sensus system.

For the frustration detection task we selected 20 subjects from the initial dataset of 80 such that our selection spanned both vehicles, gender (male, female) and four age groups (18–24, 25–39, 40–54, 55 and older). This pruning step was made for two reasons. First, a significant amount of videos had poor lighting conditions where extraction of facial expressions was not possible or was very difficult. To address this issue, we discarded subjects where less than 80 % of video frames contained a successfully detected face. We applied the face detector described in [4] that uses a Histogram of Oriented Gradients (HOG) combined with a linear SVM classifier, an image pyramid, and a sliding window detection scheme. Second, a substantially higher proportion of subjects self-reported low frustration level (class "satisfied"), thus we had to select our subjects viligantly to keep the dataset balanced and have both classes represented equally.

It is important to note that all subjects drove the same route and all tasks were performed while driving. For this paper, we focused in on the navigation task. After each task, subjects completed a short written survey in which they self-reported the workload and rated an accomplished task, including their frustration level on a scale from 1 to 10, with 1 being "not at all" and 10 "very". The question that the subjects were asked to answer is as follows: "To what extent did you feel frustrated using the car voice navigation system?". We found that the navigation system task had a clustering of responses for self-reported frustration that naturally fell into two obvious classes, after removing the minority of "neutral" responses with self-reported frustration level from 4 to 6. The "frustrated" class contained all subjects with self-reported frustration level between 7 and 9, and "satisfied" class contained all subjects with self-reported frustration level from 1 to 3. There are two different types of epochs: (1) audio epochs, where subjects are dictating commands to the machine, and (2) video epochs, where subjects are listening to a response from the machine and signaling frustration through various facial movements.

3 Methods

3.1 Audio Features

In contrast to large scale brute-force feature sets [11], a smaller, expert-knowledge based feature set has been applied. In fact, a minimalistic standard parameter set reduces the risk of over-fitting in the training phase as compared to brute-forced large features sets, which in our task is of great interest. Recently, a recommended minimalistic standard parameter set for the acoustic analysis of speaker states and traits has been proposed in [2]. The proposed feature set is the so-called Geneva Minimalistic Acoustic Parameter Set (GeMAPS). Features were mainly selected based on their potential to index affective physiological changes in voice production, for their proven value in former studies, and for their theoretical definition. Acoustic low-level descriptors (LLD) were automatically extracted from the speech waveform on a per-chunk level by using the open-source openSMILE feature extractor in its 2.1 release [3].

3.2   Video Features

We used automated facial coding software to extract features from the videos. The software (Affdex - Affectiva, Inc.) has three main components. First, the face is detected using the Viola-Jones method [14] (OpenCV implementation). Thirty-four facial landmarks are then detected using a supervised descent based landmark detector and an image region of interest (ROI) is segmented. The ROI includes the eyes, eyebrows, nose and mouth. The region of interest is normalized using rotation and scaling to 96×96 pixels. Second, histogram of oriented gradient (HOG) features are extracted from the ROI within each frame. Third, support vector machine classifiers are used to detect the presence of each facial action. Details of how the classifiers were trained and validated can be found in [12]. The facial action classifiers return a confidence score from 0 to 100. The software provided scores for 14 facial actions. In addition to facial actions we used the three axes of head pose and position of the face (left and right eye corners and center of top lip) as observations from which to extract features. For each epoch the mean, standard deviation, minimum and maximum values for each action, head pose and position metric were calculated to give 60 video features ((14 actions + 3 head pose angles + 3 landmark positions)*4).

3.3   Classifier

We used a Weka 3 implementation of Support Vector Machines (SVMs) with the Sequential Minimal Optimization (SMO), and audio and video features described in Sect. 3 [5]. We describe a set of SMO complexity parameters as:

$$C \in \{10^{-4}, 5 \times 10^{-4}, 10^{-3}, 5 \times 10^{-3}, ..., 1\}. \qquad (1)$$

For each SMO complexity parameter C from (1) we upsampled the feature vectors (one per epoch) from the original datasets to balance the number of epochs per class by calculating the upsampling factors. An average upsampling factor across four folds is 1.03 for the "frustrated" class and 1.24 for the "satisfied" class. We kept the original datasets, and produced an additional upsampled dataset for further experiments. We then (a) normalized and (b) standardized both upsampled and original datasets for each SMO complexity parameter C, and obtained 36 different configurations per fold. We carried out 144 experiments across four folds, computed accuracy, and selected the configuration that gave us the best average result. The term "accuracy" stands for Unweighted Average Recall (UAR).

4   Results

We used features and a classifier as described in Sect. 3 and achieved an accuracy of 77.4 % for "audio" epochs and 81.2 % for "video" epochs as presented in Table 1. The *epoch type* column indicates whether the human or the machine are speaking and *data source* indicates the source of the signal which is being used for extracting features. The presented results are the average accuracy for the subject-independent cross-validation over four folds.

Table 1. Results for predicting frustration from a single epoch of audio and video.

Epoch type	Data source	C	Acc. (%)
Machine speaking	Video	$1e^{-3}$	81.2
Human speaking	Audio	$5e^{-3}$	77.4

In order to characterize the tradeoff between classification accuracy and the duration of the interaction, we fused the predictions from consecutive epochs for both video and audio using a majority vote fusion rule [7]. The interaction of the driver with the voice-based system is a sequence of mostly-alternating epochs of face video data and voice data. In presenting the results, we consider two measures of duration: (1) d_e is the duration in the number epochs and (2) d_s is the duration in the number of seconds. Both measures are important for the evaluation of systems performance, since classifier decisions are made once per epoch (as measured by d_e) but the driver experiences the interaction in real-time (as measured by d_s). The fused results for up to 17 epochs are presented in Fig. 2 where duration d_e is used. The average accuracy is shown with the red line and the accuracy for each of the four folds is shown with the gray line. The average accuracy does not monotonically increase with the number of predictions fused. Instead, it slightly fluctuates due to a broad variation in complexity of the underlying subtasks. An average accuracy of 88.5 % is achieved for an interaction that lasts approximately 1 min but a lower average accuracy of 82.8 % is achieved for an interaction that lasts approximately 2 minutes. Evaluation over one of the folds in Fig. 2 achieves 100 % accuracy after 9 epochs. This is possible due to the fact that the number of epochs for total interaction varies between subjects, and the reported accuracy for a specific duration d_e is averaged over only the interactions that last at least that long. It follows that with the longer durations d_e (x-axis), the number of subjects over which the accuracy is averaged decreases and the variance of the accuracy increases.

We used a Weka implementation of the Information Gain (IG) feature evaluation to rank video features [6]. Then, we grouped features into the feature categories by summing corresponding category IG ranking values for mean, maximum, minimum and standard deviation. Each feature category represents one action, *i. e.*, inner brow rise, nose wrinkle or lip depressor. The 5 best discriminating feature categories are: (1) horizontal location of the left eye corner,

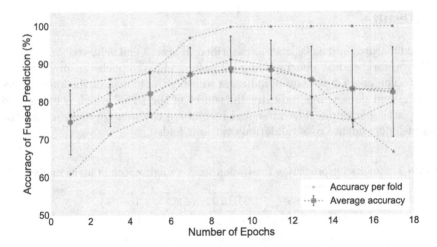

Fig. 2. Trade-off between fused prediction accuracy and the number of epochs per interaction (d_e).

(2) horizontal location of the top of the mouth, (3) horizontal location of the right eye corner, (4) the angle of head tilt (i.e. rotation of the head about an axis that passes from the back of the head to the front of the head), and (5) smile confidence (on a scale of 0–100). We ranked only video features to select the most interesting epochs for our presentation video: http://lexfridman.com/driverfrustration.

5   Conclusion

We presented a method for detecting driver frustration from 615 video epochs and 596 audio epochs captured during the driver's interaction with an in-vehicle voice-based navigation system. The data was captured in a natural driving context. Our method has been evaluated across 20 subjects that span over different demographic parameters and both cars that were used in our study. This method resulted in an accuracy of 81.2 % for detecting driver frustration from the video stream and 77.4 % from the audio stream. We then treated the video and audio streams as a sequence of interactions and achieved 88.5 % accuracy after 9 epochs by using decision fusion. Future work will include additional data streams (i. e., heart rate, skin conductance) and affective annotation methods to augment the self-reported frustration measure.

Acknowledgments. Support for this work was provided by the New England University Transportation Center, and the Toyota Class Action Settlement Safety Research and Education Program. The views and conclusions being expressed are those of the authors, and have not been sponsored, approved, or endorsed by Toyota or plaintiffs class counsel. Data was drawn from studies supported by the Insurance Institute for Highway Safety (IIHS) and Affectiva.

References

1. Boril, H., Sadjadi, S.O., Kleinschmidt, T., Hansen, J.H.L.: Analysis and detection of cognitive load and frustration in drivers' speech. In: Proceedings of INTER-SPEECH 2010, pp. 502–505 (2010)
2. Eyben, F., Scherer, K., Schuller, B., Sundberg, J., André, E., Busso, C., Devillers, L., Epps, J., Laukka, P., Narayanan, S., Truong, K.: The geneva minimalistic acoustic parameter set (GeMAPS) for voice research and affective computing. IEEE Trans. Affect. Comput. (2015)
3. Eyben, F., Weninger, F., Groß, F., Schuller, B.: Recent developments in openSMILE, the munich open-source multimedia feature extractor. In: Proceedings of the 21st ACM International Conference on Multimedia, MM 2013, Barcelona, Spain, October 2013, pp. 835–838. ACM
4. Fridman, L., Lee, J., Reimer, B., Victor, T.: Owl and lizard: patterns of head pose and eye pose in driver gaze classification. IET Comput. Vis. (2016, in Press)
5. Hall, M., Frank, E., Holmes, G., Pfahringer, B., Reutemann, P., Witten, I.H.: The weka data mining software: an update. ACM SIGKDD Explor. Newsl. **11**(1), 10–18 (2009)
6. Karegowda, A.G., Manjunath, A.S., Jayaram, M.A.: Comparative study of attribute selection using gain ratio, correlation based feature selection. Int. J. Inf. Technol. Knowl. Manage. **2**(2), 271–277 (2010)
7. Kuncheva, L.I.: A theoretical study on six classifier fusion strategies. IEEE Trans. Pattern Anal. Mach. Intell. **2**, 281–286 (2002)
8. Mahlke, S.: Understanding users' experience of interaction. In: Proceedings of the 2005 Annual Conference on European Association of Cognitive Ergonomics, pp. 251–254. University of Athens (2005)
9. Mehler, B., Kidd, D., Reimer, B., Reagan, I., Dobres, J., McCartt, A.: Multi-modal assessment of on-road demand of voice and manual phone calling and voice navigation entry across two embedded vehicle systems. Ergonomics, pp. 1–24 (2015). PMID: 26269281
10. NHTSA: Visual-manual nhtsa driver distraction guidelines for in-vehicle electronic devices (docket no. nhtsa-2010-0053). Washington, DC: US Department of Transportation National Highway Traffic Safety Administration (NHTSA) (2013)
11. Schuller, B., Steidl, S., Batliner, A., Vinciarelli, A., Scherer, K., Ringeval, F., Chetouani, M., Weninger, F., Eyben, F., Marchi, E., Mortillaro, M., Salamin, H., Polychroniou, A., Valente, F., Kim, S.: The INTERSPEECH 2013 Computational Paralinguistics Challenge: Social Signals, Conflict, Emotion, Autism. In: Proceedings INTERSPEECH 2013, 14th Annual Conference of the International Speech Communication Association, Lyon, France, August 2013. ISCA (2013) 5 pages
12. Senechal, T., McDuff, D., Kaliouby, R.: Facial action unit detection using active learning and an efficient non-linear kernel approximation. In: Proceedings of the IEEE International Conference on Computer Vision Workshops, pp. 10–18 (2015)
13. Stevens, A., Quimby, A., Board, A., Kersloot, T., Burns, P.: Design guidelines for safety of in-vehicle information systems. TRL Limited (2002)
14. Viola, P., Jones, M.J.: Robust real-time face detection. Int. J. Comput. Vis. **57**(2), 137–154 (2004)

An Object-Logic Explanation for the Inconsistency in Gödel's Ontological Theory

Christoph Benzmüller[1](✉) and Bruno Woltzenlogel Paleo[2]

[1] Freie Universität Berlin, Berlin, Germany
c.benzmueller@fu-berlin.de
[2] Australian National University, Canberra, Australia
bruno.wp@gmail.com

Abstract. This paper discusses the inconsistency in Gödel's ontological argument. Despite the popularity of Gödel's argument, this inconsistency remained unnoticed until 2013, when it was detected automatically by the higher-order theorem prover LEO-II. Complementing the meta-logic explanation for the inconsistency available in our IJCAI 2016 paper [6], we present here a new purely object-logic explanation that does not rely on semantic argumentation.

1 Introduction

Kurt Gödel's ontological argument for the existence of God [9, 14] is amongst the most discussed formal proofs in modern literature. A rich body of publications – including very recent ones – present, discuss, assess, criticize, modify and improve Gödel's original work (see e.g. Sobel [15] and Oppy [12] and the references therein).

Scott's version of Gödel's argument was automatically reconstructed by higher-order automated theorem provers [4] and its correctness was verified step-by-step in the CoQ proof assistant [5]. To bridge the gap between higher-order logics (HOL; cf. [1] and the references therein), as used by these systems, and higher-order *modal* logics (HOML; cf. [10] and the references therein), on which the ontological argument is based, the logic embedding approach [2, 4] was used.

However, Gödel's original axioms, as used in his manuscript [9], are inconsistent. This fact has remained unnoticed to philosophers until 2013, when LEO-II [3] found a surprising refutation of the axioms. In [6] we extracted from Leo-II's machine-oriented refutation an informal and human-oriented intuitive explanation for the inconsistency, and we reconstructed and verified it in the ISABELLE proof assistant. But that explanation relied on reasoning at the *meta-logic* (HOL) level, which was only possible because of the embedding. Here we complement

C. Benzmüller—This work was supported by the German Research Foundation DFG grant BE2501/9-1,2

Original paper appeared at the 25th International Joint Conference on Artificial Intelligence (IJCAI), 2016.

G. Friedrich et al. (Eds.): KI 2016, LNAI 9904, pp. 244–250, 2016.
DOI: 10.1007/978-3-319-46073-4

that work with a purely *object-logic* (HOML) explanation, and we compare and formalize both explanations in the CoQ proof assistant.

Applications of (first-order) theorem proving technology in metaphysics were first reported by Fitelson, Oppenheimer and Zalta [8, 11]. Later on, Rushby [13] used the PVS proof assistant. Common to both works is a significant amount of proof-hand-coding work as well as their focus on a non-modal formalization of St. Anselm's simpler and older ontological argument.

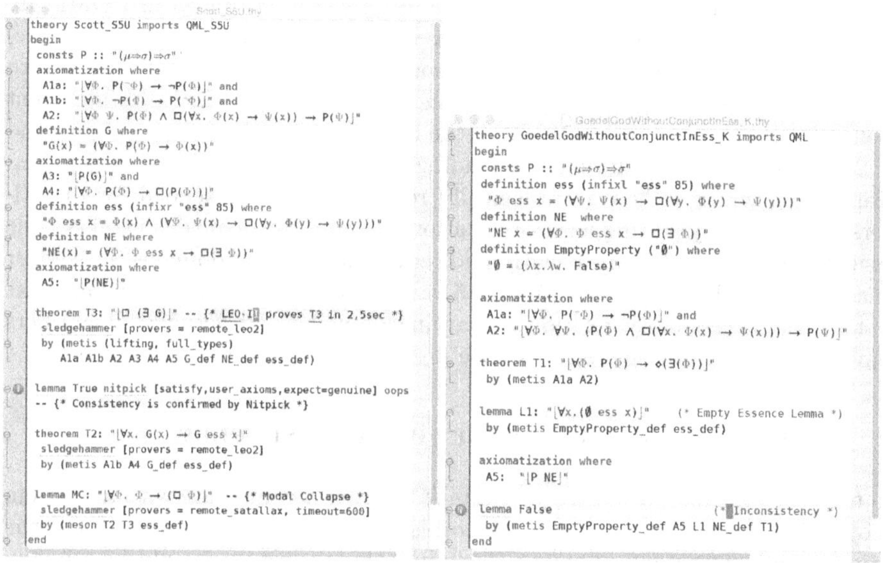

Fig. 1. Scott's consistent axioms (left) and proof of the inconsistency of (a subset of) Gödel's original axioms (right)

2   An Essential Difference in the Definitions of Essence

Gödel's manuscript can be considered a translation of Leibniz's ideas on the argument into modern modal logic. Gödel discussed his manuscript with Scott, who shared a slightly different version with a larger public. Scott's version of the axioms and definitions, formalized in ISABELLE, is shown in Fig. 1. The main difference to Gödel's version is an extra conjunct in the definition of *essence* (*ess*). For Scott, an essential property of an individual must be possessed by him/her. For Gödel, this is not required.

Gödel's omission has been considered inessential and merely an oversight by many. For more than four decades, its serious consequences remained unnoticed, despite numerous analyses and criticisms of the argument. However, as explained here, the extra conjunct is in fact crucial. Without it, Gödel's original axioms are inconsistent. With it, Scott's axioms are consistent (cf. Fig. 1, where the model finder NITPICK [7] confirms consistency). In personal communication, Dana Scott confirmed that he was unaware that Gödel's original axioms were inconsistent.

3   Automating HOML in HOL

In our experiments in this branch of metaphysics we utilize an embedding of HOMLs, such as **K**, **KB** and **S5** with various domain conditions (possibilist and actualist quantification), in HOL. More precisely, formulas in HOML are *lifted*, i.e., converted into predicates over worlds, which are themselves explicitly represented as terms. The logical constants of HOML are translated to HOL terms in such a way that, for instance, $\Box\varphi$ and $\Diamond\varphi$ (relative to a current world w_0) are mapped, respectively, to the HOL formulas $\forall w.(rw_0w)\rightarrow(\varphi w)$ and $\exists w.(rw_0w)\wedge(\varphi w)$. This form of embedding is precisely the well-known standard translation, which is here intra-logically realized — and extended for quantifiers — in HOL by stating a set of equations defining the logical constants. The resulting logic is the HOML **K** with rigid terms and constant domains (possibilist quantifiers). Other logics (e.g. **KB**, **S5**) are embedded by adding axioms that restrict the accessibility relation r. Varying domains and actualist quantifiers can be simulated by using an existence predicate to guard the quantifiers.

4   Intuitive Explanations for the Inconsistency

In the typical workflow during an attempt to prove a conjecture with a theorem prover, it is customary to check the consistency of the axioms first. For if the axioms are inconsistent, anything (including the conjecture) would be trivially derivable in classical logic (*ex falso quodlibet*). Surprisingly, when this routine check was performed on Gödel's axioms [4], the LEO-II prover claimed that the axioms were inconsistent. Unfortunately, the refutation generated by LEO-II was barely human-readable. The refutation was based on machine-oriented inference rules (a higher-order resolution calculus [3]), and the text file had 153 lines (with an average of 184 characters per line) and used a machine-oriented syntax (TPTP THF [16]).

Although LEO-II's resolution refutation is not easy to read for humans, it did contain relevant hints to the importance of the empty property[1] $\lambda x.\bot$ (also denoted $\emptyset$, as in HOL it is customary to think of unary predicates as sets)[2]. Based on this hint, we conceived the following informal explanation for the inconsistency of Gödel's axioms (reproduced without change from [6]):

---

[1] Note that the terms for the empty property ($\lambda x.\bot$) and for the property of self-difference ($\lambda x.x \neq x$) have identical denotations in the logic setting with functional and Boolean extensionality assumed here. For the proof to go through, it is irrelevant which property is used.

[2] An additional lambda abstraction occurs in the empty property in LEO-II's proof (and in the reconstruction in ISABELLE) because the embedding approach lifts the boolean type o to $\iota\rightarrow o$.

1. From Gödel's definition of essence (ϕ *ess* $x \leftrightarrow \forall\psi(\psi(x)\rightarrow\Box\forall y(\phi(y)\rightarrow\psi(y)))$) it follows that the empty property (or self-difference) is an essence of every individual
   (Empty Essence Lemma): $\forall x\ (\emptyset\ ess\ x)$
2. From axiom A5 ('necessary existence' is a positive property: $P(NE)$) and theorem T1 (*Positive properties are possibly exemplified*: $\forall\phi[P(\phi)\rightarrow\Diamond\exists x\phi(x)]$), it follows that NE is possibly exemplified: $\Diamond\exists x[NE(x)]$
3. Expanding the definition of 'necessary existence' ($NE(x) \equiv \forall\phi[\phi\ ess\ x\rightarrow\Box\exists y\phi(y)]$), the following is obtained: $\Diamond\exists x[\forall\varphi[\varphi\ ess\ x\rightarrow\Box\exists y[\varphi(y)]]]$
4. The sentence above holds for all φ and thus, in particular, for the empty property (or self-difference): $\Diamond\exists x[\emptyset\ ess\ x\rightarrow\Box\exists y[\emptyset(y)]]$
5. By the Empty Essence Lemma, the antecedent of the implication above is valid. Therefore, the sentence above entails: $\Diamond\exists x[\Box\exists y[\emptyset(y)]]$
6. By definition of $\emptyset$: $\Diamond\exists x[\Box\bot]$
7. As the existential quantifier is binding no variable within its scope, the sentence is equi-valid with: $\Diamond\Box\bot$
8. To see that the sentence above is contradictory, we may reason semantically, thinking of possible worlds. If w_0 is the arbitrary current world, the $\Diamond$ operator forces the existence of a world w accessible from w_0 such that $\Box\bot$ is true in w. But $\Box\bot$ can only be true in w, if there is no world w' accessible from w. In logics[3] with a reflexive or symmetric accessibility relation (e.g. **KB**), it is easy to see that there must be a world w' accessible from w: either w' itself, in case of a reflexive relation, or w_0, in case of a symmetric relation. In fact, even in **K**, with no accessibility condition, there must be a world w' accessible from w. The reason is that $\Diamond\Box\bot$ should be *valid* (true in all worlds). Therefore, it is true in w as well, where the existence of an accessible world w' is forced by the $\Diamond$ operator. As a model for $\Diamond\Box\bot$ (which is a consequence of Gödel's axioms) cannot be built, Gödel's axioms are inconsistent.

If we were to convert the informal proof above to a formal proof, the semantic reasoning in step 8 would require a leap to the meta-logic (HOL), in order to expand the definitions of modal operators and reason directly about possible worlds. The alternative proof below avoids this leap and remains purely within the object logic (HOML **K**):

8*. We must derive $\bot$ from $\Diamond\Box\bot$. In order to derive $\bot$, it suffices to show that there exists a derivable proposition such that its negation is also derivable. We choose $\Diamond\Diamond\bot$ as the candidate proposition, and hence we must show that:

---

[3] Interestingly, the refutation automatically generated by LEO-II uses a symmetric accessibility relation, and thus requires the modal logic **KB**. The informal, human-constructed refutations described here, on the other hand, requires only the weaker modal logic **K**. In our experiments LEO-II (like all other HOL provers) was still too weak to automatically prove the inconsistency already in logic **K**. Hence, this remains an open problem for automated theorem provers.

(a) $\neg\Diamond\Diamond\bot$ *is derivable:* this proposition is equi-valid to $\Box\Box\top$, which is trivially derivable from $\top$ by two applications of the necessitation inference rule.

(b) $\Diamond\Diamond\bot$ *is derivable:* and indeed, it can be derived (using a recently developed natural deduction calculus for modal logic **K** [5]) as follows:

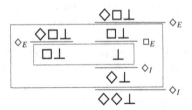

An interesting and unusual feature of the derivation shown above is that the leftmost $\Diamond_E$ (diamond elimination) inference derives a formula ($\Box\bot$) that is never used as a premise. This is necessary because of the *eigen-box* condition, which requires that every box must be accessed by exactly one *strong* modal rule. The purpose of the *strong* $\Diamond_E$ inference is merely to create and access the innermost box that is needed by the *weak* $\Box_E$ and $\Diamond_I$ inferences inside the outermost box.

The proofs above have been formalized and verified step-by-step in CoQ. The complete proofs can be found in https://github.com/FormalTheology/GoedelGod. The following CoQ script shows the formalization of step 8 of the meta-logic proof.

```
Lemma dia_box_false_to_false_meta: [(dia (box mFalse))] -> [mFalse].
Proof. intro H. intro w.
destruct (H w) as [w0 [R0 H0]]. destruct (H w0) as [w1 [R1 H1]].
box_elim H0 w1 HF. unfold mFalse in HF. destruct HF as [p [HF1 HF2]].
contradiction. Qed.
```

The other CoQ scripts below show the formalization of step 8[*] of the object-logic proof.

```
Lemma mimplies_to_mnot: [mforall p:o, (p m-> mFalse) m-> (m~ p)].
Proof. mv. intro p. intro H. intro H0.
destruct (H H0) as [p0 [H1 H2]]. apply H2. exact H1. Qed.

Lemma dia_not_not_box: [ mforall p, (dia (m~ p)) m-> (m~ (box p)) ].
Proof. mv. intro p. intro H1. intro H2.
dia_e H1. apply H. box_e H2 H3. exact H3. Qed.

Lemma dia_box_false_to_false_object: [(dia (box mFalse))] -> [mFalse].
Proof. intro H. intro w. exists (dia (dia mFalse)).
split.
  dia_e (H w). dia_e (H w0). dia_i w0. dia_i w1. box_e H0 H3. exact H3.

apply box_not_not_dia. box_i. apply box_not_not_dia. box_i.
apply mimplies_to_mnot. intro H4. exact H4. Qed.
```

Due to a deliberate and disciplined use of only the simplest (and non-automatic) CoQ tactics, there is a straightforward correspondence between the tactics used in the scripts above and the inference rules of the modal natural deduction calculus [5]. Therefore, the lengths of the proof scripts (in number of tactic applications) can serve as estimations for the lengths of the corresponding natural deduction proof. It is noticeable that the meta-logic proof is significantly shorter than the pure object-logic proof. An in-depth analysis reveals that the reasoning about the possible worlds semantics in the meta-logic proof acts as a short-cut: when it becomes impossible (in step 8) to build the third world w' (because $\perp$ would have to hold in it, and thus w' would be contradictory), a contradiction at the HOL level can be immediately derived, completing the proof. In the object-level proof, on the other hand, such a contradiction has to be found in the arbitrary initial world w. This requires not only additional tedious logical inferences (cf. the proofs of the lemmas mimplies_to_mnot and dia_not_not_box), but also a non-trivial guessing of the contradictory proposition $\diamond\diamond\perp$, whose purpose is precisely to carry over the contradiction from w' back to w.

5   Conclusion

The axioms and definitions in Gödel's manuscript are inconsistent (even in the weakest modal logic **K**); this was detected automatically by the prover LEO-II. In our previous work [6], we presented a human-readable and intuitive meta-logic explanation for the inconsistency, and we formalized and semi-automatically reconstructed it in the ISABELLE proof assistant. Here this work was extended with an object-level explanation, and both explanations were formalized step-by-step in COQ proof assistant. A comparison of the formal COQ proofs of both explanations revealed that the meta-logic reasoning is more powerful, because it enables shortcuts and, therefore, requires fewer inferences and guesses. We conjecture that this is not accidental, but rather a fundamental reason why the embedding approach is effective in practice.

It is kind of entertaining that our work reveals a mistake in Gödel's manuscript and at same time further substantiates Gödel's belief that "there is a scientific (exact) philosophy and theology, which deals with concepts of the highest abstractness; and this is also most highly fruitful for science." [17, p. 316]. Indeed, through the investigation of Gödel's mistake, we have been led to an interesting little conjecture in automated reasoning and proof theory (the global axiom $\diamond\Box\perp$ is inconsistent).

References

1. Andrews, P.B.: Church's type theory. In: Zalta, E.N. (ed.) The Stanford Encyclopedia of Philosophy. Spring 2014th edn. (2014)
2. Benzmüller, C., Paulson, L.C.: Quantified multimodal logics in simple type theory. Log. Univers. **7**(1), 7–20 (2013)
3. Benzmüller, C., Paulson, L.C., Sultana, N., Theiß, F.: The higher-order prover LEO-II. J. Autom. Reasoning **55**(4), 389–404 (2015)

4. Benzmüller, C., Woltzenlogel-Paleo, B.: Automating Gödel's ontological proof of God's existence with higher-order automated theorem provers. In: Schaub, T., Friedrich, G., O'Sullivan, B. (eds.) ECAI 2014, vol. 263 of Frontiers in Artificial Intelligence and Applications, pp. 93–98. IOS Press (2014)

5. Benzmüller, C., Woltzenlogel Paleo, B.: Interacting with modal logics in the coq proof assistant. In: Beklemishev, L.D., Musatov, D.V. (eds.) CSR 2015. LNCS, vol. 9139, pp. 398–411. Springer, Heidelberg (2015). doi:10.1007/978-3-319-20297-6_25

6. Benzmüller, C., Woltzenlogel Paleo, B.: The inconsistency in Gödel's ontological argument: a successstory for AI in metaphysics. In: IJCAI 2016 (2016)

7. Blanchette, J.C., Nipkow, T.: Nitpick: a counterexample generator for higher-order logic based on a relational model finder. In: Kaufmann, M., Paulson, L.C. (eds.) ITP 2010. LNCS, vol. 6172, pp. 131–146. Springer, Heidelberg (2010)

8. Fitelson, B., Zalta, E.N.: Steps toward a computational metaphysics. J. Philos. Logic **36**(2), 227–247 (2007)

9. Gödel, K.: Appx. A: Notes in kurt Gödel's hand. In: Sobel [15], pp. 144–145 (1970)

10. Muskens, R.: Higher order modal logic. In: Blackburn, P., et al. (eds.) Handbook of Modal Logic. Studies in Logic and Practical Reasoning, pp. 621–653. Elsevier, Dordrecht (2006)

11. Oppenheimer, P.E., Zalta, E.N.: A computationally-discovered simplification of the ontological argument. Australas. J. Philos. **89**(2), 333–349 (2011)

12. Oppy, G.: Ontological arguments. In: Zalta, E.N. (ed.) The Stanford Encyclopedia of Philosophy, Spring 2015th edn. (2015)

13. Rushby, J.: The ontological argument in PVS. In: Proceedings of CAV Workshop "Fun With Formal Methods", St. Petersburg, Russia (2013)

14. Scott, D.: Appx. B: Notes in Dana Scott's Hand. In: Sobel [15], pp. 145–146 (1972)

15. Sobel, J.H.: Logic and Theism: Arguments for and Against Beliefs in God. Cambridge University Press (2004)

16. Sutcliffe, G., Benzmüller, C.: Automated reasoning in higher-order logic using the TPTP THF infrastructure. J. Formalized Reasoning **3**(1), 1–27 (2010)

17. Wang, H., Logical Journey, A.: From Gödel to Philosophy. MIT Press (1996)

A New Tableau-Based Satisfiability Checker for Linear Temporal Logic

Matteo Bertello[1], Nicola Gigante[1], Angelo Montanari[1(✉)], and Mark Reynolds[2]

[1] University of Udine, Udine, Italy
{bertello.matteo,gigante.nicola}@spes.uniud.it,
angelo.montanari@uniud.it
[2] University of Western Australia, Perth, Australia
mark.reynolds@uwa.edu.au

Abstract. Tableaux-based methods were among the first techniques proposed for Linear Temporal Logic satisfiability checking. The earliest tableau for LTL by [21] worked by constructing a graph whose path represented possible models for the formula, and then searching for an actual model among those paths. Subsequent developments led to the tree-like tableau by [17], which works by building a structure similar to an actual search tree, which however still has back-edges and needs multiple passes to assess the existence of a model. This paper summarizes the work done on a new tool for LTL satisfiability checking based on a novel tableau method. The new tableau construction, which is very simple and easy to explain, builds an actually tree-shaped structure and it only requires a single pass to decide whether to accept a given branch or not. The implementation has been compared in terms of speed and memory consumption with tools implementing both existing tableau methods and different satisfiability techniques, showing good results despite the simplicity of the underlying algorithm.

1 Introduction

Linear Temporal Logic (LTL) is a modal logic useful to reason about propositions whose truth value depends on a linear and discrete flow of time. Initially introduced in the field of formal methods for the verification of properties of programs and circuit designs [13], it has found applications also in AI, *e.g.,* as a specification language for temporally extended goals in planning problems [3].

The most studied problem regarding LTL is probably *model checking, i.e.,* the problem of establishing whether a given temporal structure satisfies an LTL formula. However, *satisfiability checking*, that is, the problem of deciding whether a formula has a satisfying model in the first place, has also received a lot of attention. After being proved to be PSPACE-complete [18], the satisfiability problem for LTL was solved by a number of different methods developed over the years.

Original paper appeared at the 25th International Joint Conference on Artificial Intelligence (IJCAI), 2016.

G. Friedrich et al. (Eds.): KI 2016, LNAI 9904, pp. 251–256, 2016.
DOI: 10.1007/978-3-319-46073-4

First of all, LTL satisfiability can be easily reduced to the model checking problem, for which a number of successful techniques exist [5]. Substantial work has also been devoted to methods based on *temporal resolution*, first pioneered by Cavalli and Fariñas del Cerro, and later refined by [8] in [7, 8]. Temporal resolution is also at the core of the more recent *labeled superposition* method [19], which proved to be very fast in practice. See [15, 16, 20] for comprehensive experimental comparisons among the tools implementing these techniques.

This paper focuses on tableau-based decision procedures for LTL, which were among the first satisfiability checking methods proposed for it. The first tableau-based method for LTL has been proposed by [21]. His tableau works by first building a graph-shaped structure, and then performing a number of operations on this graph. Thus, it can be classified as a *graph-shaped* and *multiple-pass* tableau method. An incremental version, which does not require to build the whole graph, was later proposed in [10]. In a subsequent development by [17], a tree-like tableau was proposed which, according to experimental comparisons [9], outperformed the graph-shaped one. The major breakthrough of this new tableau was that of being *single-pass*. While the shape of [17]'s tableau is arguably similar to a tree, it is actually still a graph since a number of back-edges have to be maintained. Moreover, the extraction of an actual model from the built tableau is possible, but it requires some work.

Here, we describe an original tool to check LTL satisfiability based on the tree-shaped tableau proposed in [14]. A detailed account of the tool and of relevant experiments can be found in [4]. In contrast to the tableau by [17], an actual tree is built, and a successful branch directly provides the corresponding satisfying model. Moreover, the tableau rules are very easy to explain and to reason about, but, despite this simplicity, an efficient implementation has shown to offer good average performance on a number of standard benchmarks.

The next sections are organized as follows. Section 2 introduces LTL syntax and semantics, and it quickly describes how previous tableau-based methods behave. Section 3 gives a short account of the new one-pass tree-shaped tableau, and it summarizes the result of experimental comparisons that were reported in [4]. Section 4 outlines possible future developments of the work.

2   Tableau-Based Methods for LTL

Before illustrating tableau-based decision procedures for LTL, we briefly recap syntax and semantics of the logic. An LTL formula is obtained from a set Σ of proposition letters by possibly applying the usual Boolean connectives and the two temporal operators X (*tomorrow*) and $\mathcal{U}$ (*until*). Formally, LTL formulae ϕ are generated by the following syntax:

$$\phi := p \mid \neg\phi_1 \mid \phi_1 \vee \phi_2 \mid \mathsf{X}\phi_1 \mid \phi_1 \, \mathcal{U} \, \phi_2, \tag{1}$$

where ϕ_1 and ϕ_2 are LTL formulae and $p \in \Sigma$. Standard derived Boolean connectives can also be used, together with logical constants $\bot \equiv p \wedge \neg p$, for $p \in \Sigma$, and $\top \equiv \neg\bot$. Moreover, two derived temporal operators $F\phi \equiv \top \mathcal{U} \phi$ (*eventually*) and $G\phi \equiv \neg F\neg\phi$ (*always*) are defined.

LTL formulae are interpreted over temporal structures. A *temporal structure* is a triple $M = (S, R, g)$, where S is a finite set of states, $R \subseteq S \times S$ is a binary relation, and, for each $s \in S$, $g(s) \subseteq \Sigma$. R is the transition relation, which is assumed to be total, and g is a labeling function, that tells us which proposition letters are true at each state. Given a structure M, we say that an ω-sequence of states $\langle s_0, s_1, s_2, \ldots \rangle$ from S is a *full-path* if and only if, for all $i \geq 0$, $(s_i, s_{i+1}) \in R$. If $\sigma = \langle s_0, s_1, s_2, \ldots \rangle$ is a full-path, then we write σ_i for s_i and $\sigma_{\geq i}$ for the infinite suffix $\langle s_i, s_{i+1}, \ldots \rangle$ (also a full-path). We write $M, \sigma \models \varphi$ if and only if the LTL formula φ is true on the full-path σ in the structure M, which is defined by induction on the structural complexity of the formula:

- $M, \sigma \models p$ iff $p \in g(\sigma_0)$, for $p \in \Sigma$,
- $M, \sigma \models \neg\varphi$ iff $M, \sigma \not\models \varphi$
- $M, \sigma \models \varphi_1 \vee \varphi_2$ iff $M, \sigma \models \varphi_1$ or $M, \sigma \models \varphi_2$
- $M, \sigma \models X\varphi$ iff $M, \sigma_{\geq 1} \models \varphi$
- $M, \sigma \models \varphi_1 \mathcal{U} \varphi_2$ iff there is some $i \geq 0$ such that $M, \sigma_{\geq i} \models \varphi_2$ and for all j, with $0 \leq j < i$, it holds that $M, \sigma_{\geq j} \models \varphi_1$

Most existing tableau methods for LTL, including the one described in this paper, make use of the observation that any LTL formula can be rewritten by splitting it into two parts, one prescribing something about the current state, and one talking about the next state. In particular, this is true for formulae whose outermost operator is a temporal one:

$$\alpha \mathcal{U} \beta \equiv \beta \vee (\alpha \wedge X(\alpha \mathcal{U} \beta)); \quad F\beta \equiv \beta \vee XF\beta; \quad G\alpha \equiv \alpha \wedge XG\alpha \qquad (2)$$

Here, the formulae $X(\alpha \mathcal{U} \beta)$ and $XF\beta$ are called X-*eventualities*, *i.e.*, pending requests that has to be eventually fulfilled somewhere in the future, but that can for the moment be postponed. Note that $G\alpha$ does not lead to an eventuality, since it has to be fulfilled immediately in any case.

The first tableau by [21] starts by building a graph where each node is labeled by a set of *locally consistent* formulae belonging to the *closure* of ϕ. Each node collects the relevant formulae that are true at a specific state. Nodes u and v are connected by an edge if v can be a successor state of u according to the semantics of the logic. The equivalences shown above are useful in determining these edges. Paths in the graph represent potential models, which are consistent when we look at the single transitions. Finding an actual model then consists of searching for a path that fulfills all the pending *eventualities*. This approach requires the construction of the entire graph before the actual search, which means that an exponential amount of memory was required, which is not optimal with regards to the complexity of the problem, which is PSPACE-complete. An incremental version of this tableau, which does not require to build the whole graph beforehand, thus achieving the polynomial space lower bound, was introduced by [10]. Later, a tableau *à la* Wolper was provided by Lichtenstein and Pnueli [12] to also handle *past* temporal operators.

Marking a significant development, a new *one-pass* tableau for LTL was introduced by [17]. His tableau method works by building a tree-like structure, more similar to a search tree. Since the fulfillment of the eventualities in a branch are checked during the construction, subsequent passes are not needed. While the tableau structure resembles a tree, it is actually still a sort of cyclic graph (called *loop tree* in the original presentation), and the searches performed on separate branches are not completely independent. Although the complexity of the decision procedure based on [17]'s tableau is worse than the one by [21], since it requires *doubly* exponential time in the worst case, experimental comparisons [9] have shown that in practice this method outperforms previous tableaux, in some cases by large margins.

3   A New One-Pass and Tree-Shaped Tableau for LTL

A new *one-pass* and *tree-shaped* tableau for LTL was proposed in [14]. A satisfiability checker based on it[1], written in C++, and a detailed comparison with previous tableaux as well as with tools implementing different satisfiability checking techniques are given in [4].

In contrast to [17]'s one, the new tableau works by building an actual tree. In the tableau tree for a formula ϕ, each node is labeled by a set Γ of *formulae*. For each $\psi \in \Gamma$, ψ is a subformula of ϕ or is a formula of the form $X\psi'$, where ψ' is a subformula of ϕ. The tree construction starts from the root being labeled by $\{\phi\}$. The tree is then built by applying a sequence of *rules* which, for what concerns Boolean connectives, resembles the classical tableau for propositional logic, with disjunctions causing a node to fork into different *branches*. Temporal formulae are instead expanded using the already mentioned equivalences from Sect. 2. A node where no further expansion is possible is said to have a *poised* label, and it represents what is true at the current state in the resulting model. In a poised label, only literals or *tomorrow* temporal operators are present at top level. A STEP rule is then used to advance the branch to the next temporal state, by creating a new node whose label includes a formula α for each formula of the form $X\alpha$ found in the previous node. If contradictory literals are ever introduced into a label, the branch is rejected (✗), while if a STEP rule results into an empty label, the branch is accepted (✓), and a model can be extracted from all the nodes preceding the application of the STEP rule from there to the root of the tree.

These rules alone, however, are insufficient to handle formulae satisfiable by infinite models only as well as formulae that are unsatisfiable not because of propositional contradictions but because of unsatisfiable eventualities. To handle these cases, the following two rules are applied before the STEP one. The first, the LOOP rule, accepts a branch each time we find ourselves on a label that have already been expanded before, and all the eventualities have been fulfilled in between, meaning that the node needs not to be further expanded because the repeating part of an ultimately periodic model has been found. The second, the

---

[1] http://www.github.com/corralx/leviathan.

Prune rule, handles unsatisfiable formulae like, for instance, $G\neg p \wedge q\,\mathcal{U}\,p$, by ensuring that the tableau expansion does not hang into the infinite expansion of a branch that would not be able to fulfill the remaining pending eventualities. The latter is definitely the most sophisticated rule of the tableau system. One of its distinctive features is that it needs to go through three different nodes with the same label before crossing the branch.

A complete description of the rules can be found in [14], but it can already be noted how simple the whole construction is. The space and running time worst cases are the same as those of the tableau system by [17], but the rules and the bookkeeping required to apply them is simpler and can be implemented in an efficient way. The result is an implementation that, despite its simplicity, has good performance on average both in terms of speed and memory consumption on a number of standard benchmarks [4].

4   Conclusions and Future Work

In this extended abstract, we described a new one-pass and tree-shaped tableau for LTL which is very simple to state and to reason about and can be implemented in an efficient way, showing good performance when compared with previous tableau-based systems. Simplicity may be regarded as its major advantage, that we plan to exploit in future developments. For example, we expect that its simple search procedure can be augmented with advanced search heuristics like clause-learning techniques used in propositional SAT solvers. SAT and SMT technologies can also be exploited in order to improve performance when dealing with temporal formulae that sport large propositional parts.

Such a simple tableau can also be viewed as a useful tool to reason about theoretical properties of LTL and its extensions. For instance, extending its rules to support a parametric X^n operator, with n represented succinctly, appears to be straightforward, and immediately results into an optimal decision procedure for this simple EXPSPACE extension of LTL. In a similar way, we plan to investigate the possibility of implementing other LTL extensions on top of this framework, such as logics that feature metric variants of the *until* operator [1], past operators with forgettable past [11], freeze quantifiers [2], finite models [6], and others.

References

1. Alur, R., Henzinger, T.A.: Real-time logics: complexity and expressiveness. Inf. Comput. **104**, 35–77 (1993)
2. Alur, R., Henzinger, T.A.: A really temporal logic. J. ACM **41**(1), 181–204 (1994)
3. Bacchus, F., Kabanza, F.: Planning for temporally extended goals. Ann. Math. Artif. Intell. **22**, 5–27 (1998)
4. Bertello, M., Gigante, N., Montanari, A., Reynolds, M.: Leviathan: a new LTL satisfiability checking tool based on a one-pass tree-shaped tableau. In: Proceedings of the 25th International Joint Conference on Artificial Intelligence (2016)
5. Clarke, E.M., Grumberg, O., Peled, D.A.: Model Checking. The MIT Press (1999)

6. De Giacomo, G., Vardi, M.Y.: Linear temporal logic and linear dynamic logic on finite traces. In: Proceedings of the 23rd International Joint Conference on Artificial Intelligence (2013)

7. Fisher, M.: A normal form for temporal logics and its applications in theorem-proving and execution. J. Logic Comput. **7**(4), 429–456 (1997)

8. Fisher, M., Dixon, C., Peim, M.: Clausal temporal resolution. ACM Trans. Comput. Logic **2**(1), 12–56 (2001)

9. Goranko, V., Kyrilov, A., Shkatov, D.: Tableau tool for testing satisfiability in LTL: implementation and experimental analysis. Electron. Notes Theor. Comput. Sci. **262**, 113–125 (2010)

10. Kesten, Y., Manna, Z., McGuire, H., Pnueli, A.: A decision algorithm for full propositional temporal logic. In: Courcoubetis, C. (ed.) CAV 1993. LNCS, vol. 697, pp. 97–109. Springer, Heidelberg (1993). doi:10.1007/3-540-56922-7

11. Laroussinie, F., Markey, N., Schnoebelen, P.: Temporal logic with forgettable past. In: Proceedings of the 17th IEEE Symposium on Logic in Computer Science, pp. 383–392 (2002)

12. Lichtenstein, O., Pnueli, A.: Propositional temporal logics: decidability and completeness. Logic J. IGPL **8**(1), 55–85 (2000)

13. Pnueli, A.: The temporal logic of programs. In: Proceedings of the 18th Annual Symposium on Foundations of Computer Science, pp. 46–57 (1977)

14. Reynolds, M.: A new rule for LTL tableaux. In: Proceedings of the 7th International Symposium on Games, Automata, Logics and Formal Verification (2016)

15. Rozier, K.Y., Vardi, M.Y.: LTL satisfiability checking. Int. J. Softw. Tools Technol. Transfer **12**(2), 123–137 (2010)

16. Schuppan, V., Darmawan, L.: Evaluating LTL satisfiability solvers. In: Bultan, T., Hsiung, P.-A. (eds.) ATVA 2011. LNCS, vol. 6996, pp. 397–413. Springer, Heidelberg (2011). doi:10.1007/978-3-642-24372-1

17. Schwendimann, S.: A new one-pass tableau calculus for PLTL. In: de Swart, H. (ed.) TABLEAUX 1998. LNCS (LNAI), vol. 1397, pp. 277–292. Springer, Heidelberg (1998). doi:10.1007/3-540-69778-0

18. Sistla, A.P., Clarke, E.M.: The complexity of propositional linear temporal logics. J. ACM **32**(3), 733–749 (1985)

19. Suda, M., Weidenbach, C.: A PLTL-prover based on labelled superposition with partial model guidance. In: Gramlich, B., Miller, D., Sattler, U. (eds.) IJCAR 2012. LNCS (LNAI), vol. 7364, pp. 537–543. Springer, Heidelberg (2012). doi:10.1007/978-3-642-31365-3

20. Vardi, M.Y., Li, J., Zhang, L., Pu, G., He, J.: LTL satisfiability checking revisited. In: Proceedings of the 20th International Symposium on Temporal Representation and Reasoning, pp. 91–98 (2013)

21. Wolper, P.: The tableau method for temporal logic: an overview. Logique et Analyse **28** (1985)

ASP for Anytime Dynamic Programming on Tree Decompositions

Bernhard Bliem[1]([✉]), Benjamin Kaufmann[2], Torsten Schaub[2,3],
and Stefan Woltran[1]

[1] TU Wien, Vienna, Austria
bliem@dbai.tuwien.ac.at
[2] University of Potsdam, Potsdam, Germany
[3] INRIA Rennes, Rennes, France

Abstract. Answer Set Programming (ASP) has recently been employed
to specify and run dynamic programming (DP) algorithms on tree
decompositions, a central approach in the field of parameterized complexity, which aims at solving hard problems efficiently for instances of
certain structure. This ASP-based method followed the standard DP
approach where tables are computed in a bottom-up fashion, yielding
good results for several counting or enumeration problems. However,
for optimization problems this approach lacks the possibility to report
solutions before the optimum is found, and for search problems it often
computes a lot of unnecessary rows. In this paper, we present a novel
ASP-based system allowing for "lazy" DP, which utilizes recent multi-
shot ASP technology. Preliminary experimental results show that this
approach not only yields better performance for search problems, but
also outperforms some state-of-the-art ASP encodings for optimization
problems in terms of anytime computation, i.e., measuring the quality
of the best solution after a certain timeout.

1 Introduction

Answer Set Programming (ASP) [1] is a vibrant area of AI providing a declarative formalism for solving hard computational problems. Thanks to the power
of modern ASP technology [2], ASP was successfully used in many application
areas, including product configuration [3], bio-informatics [4], and many more.

Recently, ASP has been proposed as a vehicle to specify and execute dynamic
programming (DP) algorithms on tree decompositions (TDs). TDs [5] are a
central method in the field of parameterized complexity [6], offering a natural
parameter (called treewidth) in order to identify instances that can be solved
efficiently due to inherent structural features. Indeed, many real-world networks
enjoy small treewidth; problems like STEINER TREE can then be solved in linear

---

Original paper appeared at the 25th International Joint Conference on Artificial
Intelligence (IJCAI), 2016.

G. Friedrich et al. (Eds.): KI 2016, LNAI 9904, pp. 257–263, 2016.
DOI: 10.1007/978-3-319-46073-4

time in the size of the network (see, e.g., [7]). Such efficient algorithms process a TD in a bottom-up manner, storing in each node of the TD a table containing partial solutions; see, e.g., [8, 9]. The size of these tables is bounded by the treewidth, which, roughly speaking, guarantees the aforementioned running times. Abseher et al. [10] proposed a system that calls an ASP solver in each node of the TD on a user-provided specification (in terms of an ASP program) of the DP algorithm, such that the answer sets characterize the current table. Its contents are then handed over to the next call which materializes the table of the parent node and so on.

Albeit this method proved useful for rapid prototyping of DP algorithms and performed well on certain instances, there is one major drawback: A table is always computed in its entirety before the next table is processed. Hence, the system cannot report anything before it has finished the table of the TD's root node (and thus computed all tables entirely). Moreover, this final table implicitly contains information on all solutions. This leads to situations where unnecessarily many rows are computed, in particular if we only need one solution. Even worse, in optimization problems the system cannot give any solution until all solutions have been obtained.

In this paper, we present an alternative approach to using ASP for DP on TDs that overcomes these shortcomings. Our method is based on a "lazy" table computation scheme. In particular, for optimization problems this allows us to interrupt the run and deliver the best solution found so far.

We first describe our general framework independently of ASP. Then we show how we use ASP in the core of our algorithm for computing the DP tables. In contrast to the standard approach from [10], we now require multiple coexisting ASP solvers that communicate with each other. Achieving this in an efficient way poses a challenge, however: A naive way would be to restart a solver every time new information comes in. Alternatively, the recent *multi-shot ASP solving* approach [11] might be useful, as it allows us to add information to a solver while it is running.

We implemented both alternatives and performed an experimental evaluation, which we omitted from this extended abstract. The multi-shot approach turns out to have clear advantages and the performance of our new "lazy" algorithm is typically superior to the traditional "eager" approach. Finally, on some problems our system performs better in an anytime setting than the state-of-the-art ASP system clingo [11].

This extended abstract is based on a longer conference paper [12]. That work contains pseudocode, a detailed description of our algorithm and experiments, which we omitted.

Related Work. Anytime algorithms for certain ASP problem have been investigated in the literature. Alviano et al. [13] presented such an algorithm for computing atoms that occur in all answer sets. Nieuwenborgh et al. [14] proposed an approximation theory for standard answer sets. Also related to our approach, Gebser et al. [15] propose a method for improving the quality of solutions for optimization problems within a certain time bound. They customize the heuristics to find the first solutions faster, with the drawback that checking for optimality becomes more expensive. In contrast to that, our lazy evaluation method does not have such undesirable side-effects compared to the eager approach.

2   Background

Answer Set Programming. ASP [1] is a popular tool for declarative problem solving due to its attractive combination of a high-level modeling language with high-performance search engines. In ASP, problems are described as logic programs, which are sets of rules of the form $a_0 \leftarrow a_1, \ldots, a_m, \mathbf{not}\ a_{m+1}, \ldots, \mathbf{not}\ a_n$ where each a_i is a propositional atom and **not** stands for *default negation*. We call a rule a *fact* if $n = 0$, and an *integrity constraint* if we omit a_0. Semantically, a logic program induces a collection of so-called *answer sets*, which are distinguished models of the program determined by answer sets semantics; see [16] for details.

To facilitate the use of ASP in practice, several extensions have been developed. For instance, rules with variables are viewed as shorthand for the set of their ground instances. Further language constructs include *conditional literals* and *cardinality constraints* [17].

Tree Decompositions. Tree decompositions (TDs), originally introduced in [5], are tree-shaped representations of (potentially cyclic) graphs. The intuition is that multiple vertices of a graph are subsumed under one TD node, thus isolating the parts responsible for cyclicity.

A tree decomposition of a graph $G = (V, E)$ is a pair $\mathcal{T} = (T, \chi)$ where $T = (N, E')$ is a (rooted) tree and $\chi : N \to 2^V$ assigns to each node a set of vertices (called the node's *bag*) as follows: (1) For each vertex $v \in V$, there is a node $n \in N$ such that $v \in \chi(n)$. (2) For each edge $e \in E$, there is a node $n \in N$ such that $e \subseteq \chi(n)$. (3) For each $v \in V$, the subtree of T induced by $\{n \in N \mid v \in \chi(n)\}$ is connected. We call $\max_{n \in N} |\chi(n)| - 1$ the *width* of $\mathcal{T}$. We call a node $n \in N$ a *join node* if it has two children with equal bags, and we call $\mathcal{T}$ *semi-normalized* if all nodes with more than one child are join nodes.

In general, constructing a minimum-width TD is intractable [18]. However, there are heuristics that give "good" TDs in polynomial time [19–21], and anytime algorithms that allow for a trade-off between time and width [22]. We can transform any TD into a semi-normalized one in linear time without increasing the width [23].

Many computationally hard problems become tractable if the instances admit TDs whose width can be bounded by a constant. This is commonly achieved by DP algorithms that traverse a TD in post-order (cf. [8]). We use the following framework for such computations: At each TD node n, partial solutions for the subgraph induced by the vertices encountered so far are computed and stored in a *table* T_n. When clear from the context, we equate nodes with their tables (e.g., "child tables" are tables at child nodes). Each table is a set of *rows* r consisting of (a) a set items(r) that stores problem-specific data to be handled by the DP algorithm, (b) a nonempty set extend(r) of tuples $(e_1, \ldots, e_k)$, where k is the number of child tables and e_i is a row in the i-th child table, and (c) cost(r) whose intended purpose is to indicate the cost of each (partial) solution obtainable by recursively combining predecessor rows from extend(r). If the root table is nonempty in the end, we can obtain complete solutions by recursively combining rows with their predecessors. To achieve tractability if the width w is bounded, the size of each table should be bounded by some function $f(w)$.

Traditional TD-based DP algorithms follow an "eager evaluation" approach: At each decomposition node, they compute a table in its entirety based on the (entire) child tables. While this is theoretically efficient in many cases (as long as the width is bounded), it has the property that we cannot give any solution until all tables are computed and we can construct an optimal solution. In many practical applications, though, we would like to report the best solution found after a certain amount of time even if this solution is not optimal. Traditional DP on TDs lacks such an anytime feature.

3   ASP for Anytime Dynamic Programming on TDs

We present an algorithm that performs DP on TDs via "lazy evaluation" in contrast to the traditional "eager" approach. The basic idea is that whenever a new row r is inserted into a table T, we try to extend r to a new row in the parent table, and we only compute a new row at T if all attempts of extending r have failed. In the best case, we thus only need to compute a single row at each table to reach a solution, whereas the eager approach would compute potentially huge tables. In the worst case, we compute as many rows as the eager approach, with some additional overhead due to the constant "jumping around" between tables.

For each table T we start an instance of an external solver, denoted by solver$_T$, which for now we consider as a black box responsible for computing rows at T when given a combination of child rows. When we compute a row at table T, there is exactly one row in each child table T' that has been marked as the *active row* of T' (denoted by active$_{T'}$). The meaning of active rows is the following: At any point of the execution, the tuple (active$_{T_1}, \ldots,$ active$_{T_n}$) indicates the combination of child rows that we are currently trying to extend to a new row at T. Whenever solver$_T$ is invoked, it uses this tuple to construct row candidates that extend the active rows.

We implemented two further optimizations. First of all, especially TD nodes with more than one child incur a big computational effort. For this reason, in addition to our general algorithm that works on every TD, we implemented a special treatment for semi-normalized TDs that does not call an external solver at join nodes. Rather, it uses the fact that many DP algorithms produce a row at a join node if and only if there is a combination of child rows that "fits together", which means that they all contain the same "join-relevant" items. Which items are "join-relevant" depends on the problem. In our implementation, the user can mark the desired items with a special flag.

This join behavior allows us to greatly restrict the active row combinations that must be considered. In fact, we can ignore all combinations where some active$_i$ and active$_j$ differ on their "join-relevant" items. Whenever a new row r is added to a child table, we can quickly identify which rows from the other child tables can be combined with r. To find such matches, we keep tables sorted and use binary search.

The second optimization regards the cost bound that is used to discard rows that are too expensive. A naive algorithm eliminates rows whose cost exceeds the cost of the best solution found so far. However, we can do better if the DP algorithm exhibits "monotone costs" (i.e., the cost of a row is at least the sum of the costs of its origins): Suppose, for example, that T is a table with children T_1, T_2, and that T_1 is exhausted, which means that all tables below it are exhausted, too. Then, in a way, we "know everything" about the subgraph G' induced by the vertices that occur somewhere below T_1 but have been forgotten. In particular, we know that G' contributes *at least* a certain amount c to the cost of every solution, since each solution in part originates from some row in T_1. If the currently best solution has cost k and we now try to compute a new row at T_2, we can restrict ourselves to rows whose cost is below $k - c$: If a row r at T_2 had $\mathsf{cost}(r) \geq k - c$, any row in T that originates from r would have a cost of at least k (due to monotonicity) and would thus not lead to a better solution. This argument can easily be extended to the case where not T_1 but some table below T_1 is exhausted, and to the case of more than two child tables. In this way, our implementation can tighten the cost bound for new rows in many cases, which often results in significantly fewer rows being computed.

We implemented our algorithm by modifying the publicly available *D-FLAT* system [10]. This system so far only allowed for an eager evaluation technique that works as follows. The user provides an ASP specification Π of a DP algorithm for her problem. At each TD node, D-FLAT runs the ASP system *clingo* on Π. From each answer set D-FLAT then extracts a table row. This is done until the table is complete.

Our lazy evaluation algorithm on the other hand also calls clingo on Π with the relevant bags and part of the instance as input, but this time we do not provide the entire child tables. Instead, we only supply the currently *active* child rows. Note that we perform grounding only in an initialization step and use the resulting propositional program for all of the remaining execution. For each item that may occur in a row from a child table, we declare a corresponding atom as *external*. This causes the grounder not to assume these atoms to be false even though no rule can derive them. Assumption-based solving allows us to temporarily freeze the truth value of these atoms according to the currently *active rows*, compute answer sets, then possibly change the active rows and repeat the process. Our experiments showed that this technique is far more efficient than the naive approach of re-grounding the program for each active row combination.

4   Conclusion

We presented a generic algorithm for performing DP on TDs via lazy evaluation, and we implemented a system that allows the user to specify the DP steps for a particular problem in a declarative language. In contrast to existing solutions like [10], this allows us to print solutions before the optimum is found. Experiments showed that this is typically more efficient, also for search problems without optimization, and on some problems it outperforms state-of-the-art ASP systems. We verified that assumption-based solving, a recent advance in ASP solving technology, is indispensable for good performance.

In the future, we intend to improve efficiency by integrating the ASP solver tighter and tuning its parameters. Alternatively, it might be interesting to incorporate different formalisms instead of ASP. Moreover, for deciding at which table we should compute a new row, we proposed a round-robin strategy, and we plan to investigate different strategies. We implemented a branch-and-bound technique by discarding table rows that are more expensive than the best known (global) solution so far. Currently, we just ignore models that would induce such rows. We plan to compare this to a version that adds constraints in ASP instead. Finally, our experiments indicate that the actual shape of the TD has a high impact on running times, so techniques from [24] could help.

Acknowledgments. This work was funded by DFG grant SCHA 550/9 and by the Austrian Science Fund (FWF): Y698, P25607.

References

1. Brewka, G., Eiter, T., Truszczyński, M.: Answer set programming at a glance. Commun. ACM **54**(12), 92–103 (2011)
2. Gebser, M., Kaminski, R., Kaufmann, B., Schaub, T.: Answer set solving in practice. In: Synthesis Lectures on Artificial Intelligence and Machine Learning. Morgan & Claypool Publishers (2012)
3. Soininen, T., Niemelä, I.: Developing a declarative rule language for applications in product configuration. In: Gupta, G. (ed.) PADL 1999. LNCS, vol. 1551, pp. 305–319. Springer, Heidelberg (1998). doi:10.1007/3-540-49201-1
4. Guziolowski, C., Videla, S., Eduati, F., Thiele, S., Cokelaer, T., Siegel, A., Saez-Rodriguez, J.: Exhaustively characterizing feasible logic models of a signaling network using answer set programming. Bioinformatics **29**(18), 2320–2326 (2013). Erratum see Bioinformatics **30**, 13 (1942)
5. Robertson, N., Seymour, P.D.: Graph minors. III. Planar tree-width. J. Comb. Theory, Ser. B **36**(1), 49–64 (1984)
6. Downey, R.G., Fellows, M.R.: Parameterized Complexity. Monographs in Computer Science. Springer (1999)
7. Chimani, M., Mutzel, P., Zey, B.: Improved Steiner tree algorithms for bounded treewidth. J. Discrete Algorithms **16**, 67–78 (2012)
8. Niedermeier, R.: Invitation to Fixed-Parameter Algorithms. Oxford Lecture Series in Mathematics and its Applications, OUP (2006)
9. Bodlaender, H.L.: A tourist guide through treewidth. Acta Cybern. **11**(1–2), 1–22 (1993)
10. Abseher, M., Bliem, B., Charwat, G., Dusberger, F., Hecher, M., Woltran, S.: The D-FLAT system for dynamic programming on tree decompositions. In: Fermé, E., Leite, J. (eds.) JELIA 2014. LNCS (LNAI), vol. 8761, pp. 558–572. Springer, Heidelberg (2014). doi:10.1007/978-3-319-11558-0

11. Gebser, M., Kaminski, R., Kaufmann, B., Schaub, T.: Clingo = ASP + control: Preliminary report. CoRR abs/1405.3694 (2014)
12. Bliem, B., Kaufmann, B., Schaub, T., Woltran, S.: ASP for anytime dynamic programming on tree decompositions. Accepted for publication at IJCAI 2016
13. Alviano, M., Dodaro, C., Ricca, F.: Anytime computation of cautious consequences in answer set programming. TPLP 14(4–5), 755–770 (2014)
14. Nieuwenborgh, D.V., Heymans, S., Vermeir, D.: Approximating extended answer sets. In: Proceedings of the ECAI, pp. 462–466 (2006)
15. Gebser, M., Kaminski, R., Kaufmann, B., Romero, J., Schaub, T.: Progress in clasp series 3. In: Calimeri, F., Ianni, G., Truszczynski, M. (eds.) LPNMR 2015. LNCS (LNAI), vol. 9345, pp. 368–383. Springer, Heidelberg (2015)
16. Gelfond, M., Lifschitz, V.: Classical negation in logic programs and disjunctive databases. New Gener. Comput. 9(3/4), 365–386 (1991)
17. Simons, P., Niemelä, I., Soininen, T.: Extending and implementing the stable model semantics. Artif. Intell. 138(1–2), 181–234 (2002)
18. Arnborg, S., Corneil, D.G., Proskurowski, A.: Complexity of finding embeddings in a k-tree. SIAM J. Algebraic Discrete Meth. 8(2), 277–284 (1987)
19. Dechter, R.: Constraint Processing. Morgan Kaufmann (2003)
20. Dermaku, A., Ganzow, T., Gottlob, G., McMahan, B.J., Musliu, N., Samer, M.: Heuristic methods for hypertree decomposition. In: Gelbukh, A., Morales, E.F. (eds.) MICAI 2008. LNCS (LNAI), vol. 5317, pp. 1–11. Springer, Heidelberg (2008). doi:10.1007/978-3-540-88636-5
21. Bodlaender, H.L., Koster, A.M.C.A.: Treewidth computations I. Upper bounds. Inf. Comput. 208(3), 259–275 (2010)
22. Gogate, V., Dechter, R.: A complete anytime algorithm for treewidth. In: Chickering, D.M., Halpern, J.Y. (eds.) Proceedings of the UAI 2004, pp. 201–208. AUAI Press (2004)
23. Kloks, T.: In: Kloks, T. (ed.) Treewidth: Computations and Approximations. LNCS, vol. 842. Springer, Heidelberg (1994). doi:10.1007/BFb0045375
24. Abseher, M., Dusberger, F., Musliu, N., Woltran, S.: Improving the efficiency of dynamic programming on tree decompositions via machine learning. In: Proceedings of the IJCAI, pp. 275–282 (2015)

Preferential Query Answering in the Semantic Web with Possibilistic Networks

Stefan Borgwardt[1]([✉]), Bettina Fazzinga[2], Thomas Lukasiewicz[3],
Akanksha Shrivastava[3], and Oana Tifrea-Marciuska[3]

[1] Faculty of Computer Science, Technische Universität Dresden,
Dresden, Germany
stefan.borgwardt@tu-dresden.de
[2] ICAR, National Research Council (CNR), Rome, Italy
fazzinga@icar.cnr.it
[3] Department of Computer Science, University of Oxford, Oxford, UK
akanksha.shrivstv@gmail.com
{thomas.lukasiewicz,oana.tifrea}@cs.ox.ac.uk

Abstract. In this paper, we explore how ontological knowledge expressed via existential rules can be combined with possibilistic networks (i) to represent qualitative preferences along with domain knowledge, and (ii) to realize preference-based answering of conjunctive queries (CQs). We call these combinations ontological possibilistic networks (OP-nets). We define skyline and k-rank answers to CQs under preferences and provide complexity (including data tractability) results for deciding consistency and CQ skyline membership for OP-nets. We show that our formalism has a lower complexity than a similar existing formalism.

1 Introduction

The abundance of information on the Web requires new personalized filtering techniques to retrieve resources that best fit users' interests and preferences. Moreover, the Web is evolving at an increasing pace towards the so-called Social Semantic Web (or Web 3.0), where classical linked information lives together with ontological knowledge and social interactions of users. While the former may allow for more precise and rich results in search and query answering tasks, the latter can be used to enrich the user profile, and it paves the way to more sophisticated personalized access to information. This requires new techniques for ranking search results, fully exploiting ontological and user-centered data, i.e., user preferences.

Conditional preferences are statements of the form "in the context of c, a is preferred over b", denoted $c: a \succ b$ [1, 7, 13]. Two preference formalisms that can represent such preferences are *possibilistic networks* and *CP-nets*.

Original paper appeared at the 25th International Joint Conference on Artificial Intelligence (IJCAI), 2016.

G. Friedrich et al. (Eds.): KI 2016, LNAI 9904, pp. 264–270, 2016.
DOI: 10.1007/978-3-319-46073-4

id	color	feature	type
t_1	s_1	b	f_1	o
t_2	s_2	c	f_2	n
t_3	s_3	c	f_2	o

specs

id	name
t_7	f_1	ac
t_8	f_2	map
t_9	f_3	cd

feature

vendor	price	specs
t_4	v_1	30	s_1
t_5	v_1	40	s_2
t_6	v_2	50	s_3

offer

id	review
t_{10}	v_1	p
t_{11}	v_2	n

vendor

Fig. 1. Database D

Example 1. Bob wants to rent a car and (i) he prefers a new car over an old one, (ii) given he has a new car, he prefers it to be black over not black, and (iii) if he has an old car, he prefers it to be colorful over being black. We have two variables for car type (new (n) or old (o)) and car color (black (b) or colorful (c)), T and C, respectively, such that $Dom(T) = \{n, o\}$ and $Dom(C) = \{b, c\}$. Bob's preferences can be encoded as $\top: n \succ o$, $n: b \succ c$, and $o: c \succ b$. In CP-nets [7], we have the following ordering of outcomes: $nb \succ nc \succ oc \succ ob$. That is, a new and colorful car is preferred over an old and colorful one, which is not a realistic representation of the given preferences. A more desirable order of outcomes for Bob would be $nb \succ oc \succ nc \succ ob$, which can be induced in possibilistic networks with an appropriate preference weighting in the possibility distribution.   □

We propose a novel language for expressing preferences over the Web 3.0 using possibilistic networks. It has lower complexity compared to a similar existing formalism called OCP-theories [9], which are an integration of Datalog+/− with CP-theories [13]. This is because deciding dominance in possibilistic networks can be done in polynomial time, while it is PSPACE-complete in CP-theories. Every possibilistic network encodes a unique (numerical) ranking on the outcomes, while CP-theories encode a set of (qualitative) total orders on the outcomes. Our framework also allows to specify the relative importance of preferences [1]. Possibilistic networks are also a simple and natural way of representing conditional preferences and obtaining rankings on outcomes, and can be easily learned from data [5]. We choose existential rules in Datalog+/− as ontology language for their intuitive nature, expressive power for rule-based knowledge bases, and the capability of performing query answering.

All details can be found in the full paper [6].

2   Ontological Possibilistic Networks (OP-nets)

See [3, 8] for the basic notions regarding possibilistic networks and Datalog+/−. Let $O = (D, \Sigma)$ be a Datalog+/− *ontology*, where D is a database and Σ a finite set of *tuple-generating dependencies (TGDs)* and *negative constraints (NCs)*.

Example 2. Consider the database D in Fig. 1, modeling the domain of an online car booking system. Moreover, the dependencies

$$\Sigma = \{ offer(V, P, S) \rightarrow \exists C, F, T \; specs(S, C, F, T),$$

$$offer(V, P, S) \rightarrow \exists R \; vendor(V, R),$$
$$specs(S, C, F, T) \rightarrow color(C) \wedge type(T),$$
$$specs(S, C, F, T) \rightarrow \exists N \; feature(F, N),$$
$$offer(V, P1, S) \wedge offer(V, P2, S) \rightarrow P1 = P2 \; \}$$

say that every offer must have a specification and a vendor and that there cannot be two equivalent offers from the same company with different prices. We denote by $\mathbf{t}_1$ the term $specs(s_1, b, f_1, o)$ and by t_1 the tuple (s_1, b, f_1, o). □

Let now $\mathcal{X}_O$ be a finite set of variables, where each $X \in \mathcal{X}_O$ corresponds to a predicate from O, denoted $pred(X)$. The *domain* $Dom(X)$ consists of at least two ground atoms $p(c_1, \dots c_k)$ with $p = pred(X)$. An *outcome* $o \in Dom(\mathcal{X}_O)$ assigns to each variable an element of its domain, and can be seen as a conjunction of ground atoms. An *OP-net* is of the form (O, Γ), where Γ is a possibilistic network over $\mathcal{X}_O$, i.e., a collection of conditional possibility distributions $\pi(X_i | pa(X_i))$, where $pa(X_i)$ are the *parents* of X_i. Taken altogether, they define a joint possibility distribution over $Dom(\mathcal{X}_O)$. An outcome o *dominates* another outcome o' (written $o \succ o'$) if $\pi(o) > \pi(o')$. This relation can be decided in polynomial time.

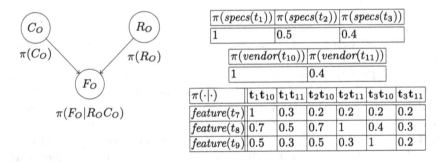

Fig. 2. Graph and possibility distribution for Example 3.

Example 3. Consider the OP-net (O, Γ) given by the ontology O of Example 2 and the dependency graph and the conditional possibility distribution in Fig. 2. Here, we have $\mathcal{X}_O = \{C_O, R_O, F_O\}$ with the domains

$$Dom(C_O) = \{specs(t_1), specs(t_2), specs(t_3)\},$$
$$Dom(F_O) = \{feature(t_7), feature(t_8), feature(t_9)\},$$
$$Dom(R_O) = \{vendor(t_{10}), vendor(t_{11})\}.$$

The parents of F_O are $\{C_O, R_O\}$, which in turn do not depend on other variables. The distribution could either be learned or derived from explicit preferences; see Example 4 below. The possibilities of outcomes are then computed as

$$\pi(C_O R_O F_O) = \pi(F_O | C_O R_O) \otimes \pi(C_O) \otimes \pi(R_O).$$

The outcome o with $o(C_O) = specs(t_1), o(R_O) = vendor(t_{10}), o(F_O) = feature(t_7)$ represents the conjunction $\mathbf{t}_1 \wedge \mathbf{t}_{10} \wedge \mathbf{t}_7$ and has the possibility 1.   □

Since outcomes are conjunctions of ground atoms, they may be inconsistent or equivalent w.r.t. Σ. An outcome o of (O, Γ) is *consistent* if the ontology $O_o = O \cup \{o(X) \mid X \in \mathcal{X}_O\}$ is consistent. Two outcomes o and o' are *equivalent*, denoted $o \sim o'$, if O_o and $O_{o'}$ have the same models. An *interpretation* $\mathcal{I}$ for (O, Γ) is a total preorder over the consistent outcomes in $Dom(\mathcal{X}_O)$. It *satisfies* (or is a *model* of) (O, Γ) if it is compatible with the dominance and equivalence relations, i.e., for all consistent outcomes o and o', (i) if $o \prec o'$, then $(o, o') \in \mathcal{I}$ and $(o', o) \notin \mathcal{I}$, and (ii) if $o \sim o'$, then $(o, o'), (o', o) \in \mathcal{I}$. An OP-net is *consistent* if it has at least one consistent outcome and it has a model.

3 Encoding Preferences with OP-Nets

In [9], conditional preferences were generalized to Datalog+/− as follows. Let $Dom^+(X)$ be the set of all (possibly non-ground) atoms $p(t_1, \ldots, t_k)$ with $p = pred(X)$. An *ontological conditional preference* φ is of the form $v : \xi \succ \xi'$, where

- $v \in Dom^+(U_\varphi)$ for some $U_\varphi \subseteq \mathcal{X}_O$ is the context, and
- $\xi, \xi' \in Dom^+(X_\varphi)$ for some $X_\varphi \in \mathcal{X}_O - U_\varphi$.

A *ground instance* $v\theta : \xi\theta \succ \xi'\theta$ of φ is obtained via a substitution θ such that $v\theta \in Dom(U_\varphi)$ and $\xi\theta, \xi'\theta \in Dom(X_\varphi)$. Under suitable acyclicity conditions, one can construct an OP-net (O, Γ) that respects all ground instances of some given ontological conditional preferences.

Example 4. Consider the ontological conditional preference $specs(I, C, F, o)$: $vendor(V_1, p) \succ vendor(V_2, n)$, i.e., for an old car, it is preferable to have a vendor with positive feedback. One ground instance for this preference is $specs(t_1)$: $vendor(t_{10}) \succ vendor(t_{11})$. We could choose $\pi(vendor(t_{10}) | specs(t_1)) = 1$ and $\pi(vendor(t_{11}) | specs(t_1)) = \alpha < 1$ to encode this in an OP-net   □

Although possibilistic networks are less expressive than conditional preference theories (CP-theories) [3, 13], they allow for a more compact encoding of conditional preferences over ground atoms and have lower complexity.

4 Query Answering Under OP-Nets

The notions of skyline and k-rank answers are defined in the same way as for OCP-theories [9]. In a conjunctive query (CQ), a variable X of the OP-net may be used to annotate an atom over the predicate $pred(X)$. Hence, an *answer (tuple)* $\mathbf{a}$ to a CQ q w.r.t. an outcome o is an assignment of the distinguished variables that can be used to satisfy q in such a way that the marked atoms of q evaluate to the ones given by o. A *skyline answer* is an answer w.r.t. an undominated outcome of the OP-net. *CQ skyline membership* is the problem of deciding whether a given tuple is a skyline answer. Similarly, one can define k-*rank* answers as the k "most preferred" answers, i.e., those resulting from the outcomes with the highest possibilities.

Example 5. Consider the consistent OP-net (O, Γ) of Example 3 and the CQ $q(C, F, T, N) = \exists I \; specs(I, C, F, T) \wedge feature(F, N)$. Then, $\langle b, f_1, o, ac \rangle$ is the skyline answer under the consistent outcome $t_1 \wedge t_{10} \wedge t_7$. The skyline answer for $q'(C, T) = \exists N \; q(C, f_2, T, N)$ is $\langle c, n \rangle$ with possibility $\pi(t_2 t_{10} t_8) = 0.5 \cdot 1 \cdot 0.7 = 0.35$, while the 2-rank answer is $\langle \langle c, n \rangle, \langle c, o \rangle \rangle$. Hence, if feature f_2 is mandatory, the offered new and colorful car is preferred over the old and colorful one, mainly due to positive feedback about vendor v_1.   □

5   Computational Complexity

We now analyze the computational complexity of the consistency and CQ skyline membership problems for OP-nets. We assume familiarity with the complexity classes AC^0, P, NP, CO-NP, Δ_2^P, Σ_2^P, Π_2^P, Δ_3^P, PSPACE, EXP, and 2EXP. The class $D^P = NP \wedge CO\text{-}NP$ (resp., $D_2^P = \Sigma_2^P \wedge \Pi_2^P$) is the class of all problems that are the intersection of a problem in NP (resp., Σ_2^P) and a problem in CO-NP (resp., Π_2^P).

Following Vardi's taxonomy [12], the *combined complexity* is calculated by considering all the components, i.e., the database, the set of dependencies, and the query, as part of the input. The *bounded-arity combined (ba-combined) complexity* assumes that the arity of the underlying schema is bounded by a constant. For example, in description logics (DLs) [4], the arity is always bounded by 2. The *fixed-program combined (fp-combined) complexity* is calculated by considering the set of TGDs and NCs as fixed. Finally, for *data complexity*, we take only the size of the database into account.

Although CQ answering in Datalog+/− is undecidable in general, there exist many syntactic conditions that guarantee decidability. We refer the reader to [6] for a short overview of the classes of acyclic (A), guarded (G), and sticky (S) sets of TGDs, their "weak" counterparts WA, WG, and WS, linear TGDs (L), full TGDs (F), and the combinations AF, GF, SF, and LF.

Our complexity results for the consistency and the CQ skyline membership problems for OP-nets are compactly summarized in Tables 1 and 2, respectively. Compared to OCP-theories [9], we obtain lower complexities for L, LF, AF, G, S, F, GF, SF, WS, and WA in the fp-combined complexity (completeness for D^P and Δ_2^P, respectively, rather than PSPACE), and for L, LF, AF, S, F, GF, and SF in the ba-complexity (completeness for D_2^P and Δ_3^P, respectively, rather than PSPACE).

Theorem 6. Let $\mathcal{T}$ be a class of OP-nets (O, Γ). If checking non-emptiness of the answer set of a CQ w.r.t. O is in a complexity class $\mathcal{C}$, then consistency in $\mathcal{T}$ is in $NP^{\mathcal{C}} \wedge CO\text{-}NP^{\mathcal{C}}$ and CQ skyline membership in $\mathcal{T}$ is in $P^{NP^{\mathcal{C}}}$. If $\mathcal{C} = NP$ and we consider the fp-combined complexity, then consistency in $\mathcal{T}$ is in D^P and CQ skyline membership in $\mathcal{T}$ is in Δ_2^P.

In particular, for $\mathcal{C} = $ PSPACE, we obtain inclusion in PSPACE for both problems, and the same for any deterministic complexity class above PSPACE. For $\mathcal{C} = NP$, we get the classes D_2^P and Δ_3^P. The lower bounds PSPACE and above follow from consistency and equivalence of outcomes being as powerful as checking entailment of arbitrary ground CQs. The remaining lower bounds for the

Table 1. Complexity of deciding consistency of OP-nets

Class	Comb	ba-comb	fp-comb	Data
L, LF, AF	PSPACE	D_2^P	D^P	in AC^0
G	2EXP	EXP	D^P	P
WG	2EXP	EXP	EXP	EXP
S, SF	EXP	D_2^P	D^P	in AC^0
F, GF	EXP	D_2^P	D^P	P
WS, WA	2EXP	2EXP	D^P	P

Table 2. Complexity of deciding CQ skyline membership for OP-nets

Class	Comb.	ba-comb.	fp-comb.	Data
L, LF, AF	PSPACE	Δ_3^P	Δ_2^P	in AC^0
G	2EXP	EXP	Δ_2^P	P
WG	2EXP	EXP	EXP	EXP
S, SF	EXP	Δ_3^P	Δ_2^P	in AC^0
F, GF	EXP	Δ_3^P	Δ_2^P	P
WS, WA	2EXP	2EXP	Δ_2^P	P

(fp-/ba-)combined complexity hold already if only NCs are allowed, and are shown by reductions from variants of the validity problem for QBFs. For example, the problem of deciding, given a valid formula $\exists \mathbf{X} \forall \mathbf{Y} \varphi(\mathbf{X}, \mathbf{Y})$ where $\varphi(\mathbf{X}, \mathbf{Y})$ is a propositional 3-DNF formula, whether the lexicographically maximal satisfying truth assignment for $\mathbf{X} = \{x_1, \ldots, x_n\}$ maps x_n to *true* is Δ_3^P-complete [11].

Finally, we can show that tractability in data complexity for deciding consistency and CQ skyline membership for OP-nets carries over from classical CQ answering. Here, data complexity means that Σ and the variables and possibility distributions of Γ are both fixed, while D is part of the input.

Theorem 7. Let $\mathcal{T}$ be a class of OP-nets (O, Γ) for which CQ answering in O is possible in polynomial time (resp., in AC^0) in the data complexity. Then, deciding consistency and CQ skyline membership in $\mathcal{T}$ is possible in polynomial time (resp., in AC^0) in the data complexity.

The listed P-hardness results hold due to a standard reduction of propositional logic programming to guarded full TGDs. These results do not apply to WG, where CQ answering is data complete for EXP, and data hardness holds even for ground atomic CQs; however, data completeness for EXP can be proved similarly to the results for combined complexity above.

We want to emphasize that our complexity results are generic, applying also to Datalog+/− languages beyond the ones listed. Even more, they are valid for arbitrary preference formalisms for which dominance between two outcomes can be decided in polynomial time, e.g., combinations of Datalog+/− with rankings computed by information retrieval methods [10].

Interesting topics of ongoing and future research include the implementation and experimental evaluation of the presented approach, as well as a generalization based on possibilistic logic [3] to gain more expressivity and some new features towards non-monotonic reasoning [1]; moreover, an apparent relation between possibilistic logic and quantitative choice logic [2] may be exploited.

Acknowledgments. This work was supported by a Google European Doctoral Fellowship, by the UK EPSRC grants EP/J008346/1, EP/L012138/1, and EP/M025268/1, and by the grant PON02_00563_3470993 ("VINCENTE").

References

1. Ben Amor, N., Dubois, D., Gouider, H., Prade, H.: Possibilistic networks: a new setting for modeling preferences. In: Straccia, U., Calì, A. (eds.) SUM 2014. Lecture Notes in Artificial Intelligence (LNAI), vol. 8720, pp. 1–7. Springer, Heidelberg (2014). doi:10.1007/978-3-319-11508-5_1
2. Benferhat, S., Brewka, G., Le Berre, D.: On the relationship between qualitative choice logic and possibilistic logic. In: Proceedings of the IPMU, pp. 951–957 (2004)
3. Benferhat, S., Dubois, D., Garcia, L., Prade, H.: On the transformation between possibilistic logic bases and possibilistic causal networks. Int. J. Approx. Reas. **29**(2), 135–173 (2002)
4. Bienvenu, M., Ortiz, M.: Ontology-mediated query answering with data-tractable description logics. In: Faber, W., Paschke, A. (eds.) Reasoning Web 2015. LNCS, vol. 9203, pp. 218–307. Springer, Heidelberg (2015). doi:10.1007/978-3-319-21768-0_9
5. Borgelt, C., Kruse, R.: Operations and evaluation measures for learning possibilistic graphical models. Artif. Intell. **148**, 385–418 (2003)
6. Borgwardt, S., Fazzinga, B., Lukasiewicz, T., Shrivastava, A., Tifrea-Marciuska, O.: Preferential query answering in the Semantic Web with possibilistic networks. In: Proceedings of the IJCAI. AAAI Press (2016, to appear). https://db.tt/GNqy1xDC
7. Boutilier, C., Brafman, R.I., Domshlak, C., Hoos, H.H., Poole, D.: CP-nets: a tool for representing and reasoning with conditional ceteris paribus preference statements. J. Artif. Intell. Res. **21**, 135–191 (2004)
8. Calì, A., Gottlob, G., Lukasiewicz, T.: A general datalog-based framework for tractable query answering over ontologies. J. Web Semant. **14**, 57–83 (2012)
9. Di Noia, T., Lukasiewicz, T., Martinez, M.V., Simari, G.I., Tifrea-Marciuska, O.: Combining existential rules with the power of CP-theories. In: Proceedings of the IJCAI. AAAI Press (2015)
10. Joachims, T.: Optimizing search engines using clickthrough data. In: Proceedings of the SIGKDD, pp. 133–142 (2002)
11. Krentel, M.W.: Generalizations of Opt P to the polynomial hierarchy. Theor. Comput. Sci. **97**, 183–198 (1992)
12. Vardi, M.Y.: The complexity of relational query languages. In: Proceedings of the STOC, pp. 137–146. ACM (1982)
13. Wilson, N.: Extending CP-nets with stronger conditional preference statements. In: Proceedings of the AAAI, pp. 735–741. AAAI Press (2004)

Investigating the Relationship between Argumentation Semantics via Signatures

Paul E. Dunne[1], Thomas Linsbichler[2], Christof Spanring[1,2],
and Stefan Woltran[2(✉)]

[1] Department of Computer Science, University of Liverpool, Liverpool, UK
[2] Institute of Information Systems, TU Wien, Vienna, Austria
woltran@dbai.tuwien.ac.at

Abstract. Understanding the relation between different semantics in abstract argumentation is an important issue, not least since such semantics capture the basic ingredients of different approaches to non-monotonic reasoning. The question we are interested in relates two semantics as follows: What are the necessary and sufficient conditions, such that we can decide, for any two sets of extensions, whether there exists an argumentation framework which has exactly the first extension set under one semantics, and the second extension set under the other semantics. We investigate in total nine argumentation semantics and give a nearly complete landscape of exact characterizations. As we shall argue, such results not only give an account on the independency between semantics, but might also prove useful in argumentation systems by providing guidelines for how to prune the search space.

1 Introduction

Within Artificial Intelligence argumentation has become one of the major fields over the last two decades [3]. In particular, abstract argumentation frameworks (AFs) introduced by Dung [6] are a simple, yet powerful formalism for modeling and deciding argumentation problems that are integral to many advanced argumentation systems. Evaluating AFs is done via semantics (cf. [1] for an overview) that deliver subsets of jointly acceptable arguments.

Over the years, several semantics have been introduced [4–6, 15], and relations between them have been thoroughly studied. For instance, it is known that for any AF, its set of stable extensions is a subset of its set of preferred extensions (already proven by Dung [6]). Moreover, for any AF F, its set of stable extensions (if not empty) can be realized via preferred semantics (i.e. there exists an AF F' such that the preferred extensions of F' equal the stable extensions of F). However, there is one aspect which has not been addressed yet. In fact, in this paper we are interested in questions of the following kind: Given sets

Original paper appeared at the 25th International Joint Conference on Artificial Intelligence (IJCAI), 2016.

This research has been supported by FWF through projects I1102 and P25521.

G. Friedrich et al. (Eds.): KI 2016, LNAI 9904, pp. 271–277, 2016.
DOI: 10.1007/978-3-319-46073-4

$\mathbb{S}, \mathbb{T}$ of extensions, does there exist an AF F such that its stable extensions are given by $\mathbb{S}$ and its preferred extensions are given by $\mathbb{T}$. More formally, we are interested in characterizing the following concepts for semantics σ, τ, which we call two-dimensional signatures:

$$\Sigma_{\sigma,\tau} = \{\langle \sigma(F), \tau(F) \rangle \mid F \text{ is an AF} \}.$$

Such signatures help to determine the amount of independence between semantics. Let us again consider stable (sb) and preferred (pr) extensions and suppose we have two AFs F, F' with $sb(F) \subseteq pr(F')$. Is there also an AF F'' with $sb(F'') = sb(F)$ and $pr(F'') = pr(F')$? This might not always be possible since there are certain dependencies between the two semantics which can make the existence of such an F'' impossible, and – as we will show – this is indeed the case for this particular pair of semantics, i.e.

$$\Sigma_{sb,pr} \neq \{ \langle sb(F), pr(F') \rangle \mid sb(F) \subseteq pr(F'); F, F' \text{ AFs} \}. \tag{1}$$

However, for certain other pairs of semantics such a strong form of independence holds; for instance, for naive (na) semantics, it is known that $sb(F) \subseteq na(F)$, and we will show that this is sufficient for the corresponding two-dimensional signature:

$$\Sigma_{sb,na} = \{ \langle sb(F), na(F') \rangle \mid sb(F) \subseteq na(F'); F, F' \text{ AFs} \}$$

Another application of two-dimensional signatures is pruning the search space for systems designed to enumerate all extensions of a given semantics τ. This is of particular interest when the complexity for some other semantics σ is milder than the one for τ. Again consider stable and preferred semantics, the latter being more complex [7]. Results like (1) indicate that for enumerating all preferred extensions, starting with the computation of all stable extensions not only yields a subset of the desired preferred extensions but ultimately rules out certain candidates to become preferred extensions.

Main Contributions. The paper gives exact characterizations for 32 two-dimensional signatures.

Related Work. There has been thorough research on translations [10, 11] where mappings θ are studied such that, for any AF F, $\sigma(\theta(F))$ is in a certain relation to $\tau(F)$. Naturally, these results are concerned with two different AFs; we on the other hand explore the range of pairs of extensions a single AF is able to express via two types of semantics. The work by Dunne et al. [8] has initiated this kind of research but treated semantics separately.

2   Background

We first recall basic notions of Dung's abstract frameworks (the reader is referred to [1, 6] for further background). An *Argumentation Framework* (AF) is a pair $F = (A, R)$, where $A \subset \mathfrak{A}$ is a finite set of *arguments* for $\mathfrak{A}$ being the (countably infinite) universe of all arguments available, and $R \subseteq A \times A$ is its *attack* relation. The collection of all AFs is given by $AF_{\mathfrak{A}}$. For $(a, b) \in R$ we say that a attacks b (in F), accordingly a set $S \subseteq A$ attacks an argument $a \in A$ (in F) if $\exists b \in S : (b, a) \in R$. The *range* in F of a set of arguments $S \subseteq A$ is given as $S_F^+ = S \cup \{a \in A \mid S \text{ attacks } a\}$. Subscript F may be dropped if clear from the context. A set $S \subseteq A$ *defends* argument $a \in A$ (in F) if S attacks all attackers of a.

A *semantics* σ is a mapping from AFs to sets of arguments. For a given AF $F = (A, R)$ the members of $\sigma(F)$ are called $(\sigma\text{-})extensions$. A set $S \subseteq A$ is *conflict-free* in F ($S \in cf(F)$) if it does not contain any attacks, i.e. $(S \times S) \cap R = \emptyset$; $S \in cf(F)$ is *admissible* in F ($S \in ad(F)$) if each $a \in S$ is defended by S; $S \in ad(F)$ is *complete* ($S \in co(F)$) if S contains all $a \in A$ it defends. We define the *naive, stable, preferred* and *semi-stable* extensions as follows:

- $S \in na(F)$, if $S \in cf(F)$ and $\nexists T \in cf(F)$ s.t. $S \subset T$;
- $S \in sb(F)$, if $S \in cf(F)$ and $S_F^+ = A$;
- $S \in pr(F)$, if $S \in ad(F)$ and $\nexists T \in ad(F)$ s.t. $S \subset T$;
- $S \in sm(F)$, if $S \in ad(F)$ and $\nexists T \in ad(F)$ s.t. $S_F^+ \subset T_F^+$.

Finally, for semantics σ, τ we define the *ideal reasoning* semantics (see e.g. [4]) for σ under τ $(id_{\sigma,\tau})$ as sets $S \in \sigma(F)$ being $\subseteq$-maximal in satisfying $S \subseteq T$ for each $T \in \tau(F)$. In this paper, we use the *grounded* $(gr(F) = id_{ad,}(F))$, *ideal* $(id(F) = id_{ad,pr}(F))$ and *eager* $(eg(F) = id_{ad,sm}(F))$ semantics. Recall that gr, id and eg always provide exactly one extension.

Towards the characterization of signatures, we require a few more concepts, mostly taken from [2, 8] (however, written in a slightly different way). A set of sets of arguments $\mathbb{S} \subseteq 2^{\mathfrak{A}}$ is called *extension-set* if $\bigcup \mathbb{S}$ is finite. Given an extension-set $\mathbb{S}$, we denote the $\subseteq$-maximal elements of $\mathbb{S}$ by $max(\mathbb{S})$. Moreover, we define the *conflicts* in $\mathbb{S}$ ($Confs_{\mathbb{S}}$) and the *borders* of $\mathbb{S}$ ($bd(\mathbb{S})$) as

$$Confs_{\mathbb{S}} = \{(a, b) \in \bigcup \mathbb{S} \times \bigcup \mathbb{S} \mid \nexists S \in \mathbb{S} : a, b \in S\}, \text{ and}$$

$$bd(\mathbb{S}) = \{T \subseteq \bigcup \mathbb{S} \mid b \in \bigcup \mathbb{S} \setminus T \text{ iff } \exists a \in T : (a, b) \in Confs_{\mathbb{S}}\}.$$

Finally, given $\mathbb{S}, \mathbb{T} \subseteq 2^{\mathfrak{A}}$, $\mathbb{S}$ is called *conflict-sensitive* wrt. $\mathbb{T}$ ($\mathbb{S} \bowtie \mathbb{T}$) if for all $A, B \in \mathbb{S}$ such that $A \cup B \notin \mathbb{S}$ there are $a \in A$, $b \in B$ with $(a, b) \in Confs_{\mathbb{T}}$.

Example 1. Let $\mathbb{S} = \{\{a, b\}, \{a, c, e\}, \{b, d, e\}\}$. We have $max(\mathbb{S}) = \mathbb{S}$, $Confs_{\mathbb{S}} = \{(a, d), (d, a), (b, c), (c, b), (c, d), (d, c)\}$, and $bd(\mathbb{S}) = \{\{a, b, e\}, \{a, c, e\}, \{b, d, e\}\}$. Finally, $\mathbb{S} \bowtie \mathbb{S}$ as, for instance, $(b, c) \in Confs_{\mathbb{S}}$ for $\{a, b\}$ and $\{a, c, e\}$.

3   Characterizations of Two-Dimensional Signatures

We first recall the results from [8] (similar in style of presentation to [2]) on signatures and then generalize this concept to multiple semantics.

Definition 1. *Given a semantics σ, a set $\mathbb{S} \subseteq 2^{\mathfrak{A}}$ is realizable under σ if there is an AF F with $\sigma(F) = \mathbb{S}$ (F realizes $\mathbb{S}$ under σ). The signature of σ is defined as $\Sigma_{\sigma} = \{\sigma(F) \mid F \in AF_{\mathfrak{A}}\}$.*

Proposition 1. *The following collections of extension-sets* $\mathbb{S}$ *yield the signatures of the semantics under consideration.*

- $\Sigma_{gr} = \Sigma_{id} = \Sigma_{eg} = \{\mathbb{S} \mid |\mathbb{S}| = 1\};$
- $\Sigma_{cf} = \{\mathbb{S} \neq \emptyset \mid max(\mathbb{S}) = bd(\mathbb{S}), \forall S \in \mathbb{S} \forall S' \subseteq S : S' \in \mathbb{S}\};$
- $\Sigma_{na} = \{\mathbb{S} \neq \emptyset \mid \mathbb{S} = bd(\mathbb{S})\};$
- $\Sigma_{sb} = \{\mathbb{S} \mid \mathbb{S} \subseteq bd(\mathbb{S})\};$
- $\Sigma_{ad} = \{\mathbb{S} \neq \emptyset \mid \emptyset \in \mathbb{S}, \mathbb{S} \bowtie \mathbb{S}\};$
- $\Sigma_{pr} = \Sigma_{sm} = \{\mathbb{S} \neq \emptyset \mid \mathbb{S} = max(\mathbb{S}), \mathbb{S} \bowtie \mathbb{S}\}.$

The natural generalization of signatures is now defined as follows. It captures the capabilities of AFs with respect to different sets of semantics.

Definition 2. *Given semantics* $\sigma_1, \ldots, \sigma_n$, *their* (n-dimensional) *signature is defined as* $\Sigma_{\sigma_1, \ldots, \sigma_n} = \{\langle \sigma_1(F), \ldots, \sigma_n(F) \rangle \mid F \in AF_{\mathfrak{A}}\}$. *We say that AF F realizes* $\langle \mathbb{S}_1, \ldots, \mathbb{S}_n \rangle$ *under* $(\sigma_1, \ldots, \sigma_n)$ *if* $\sigma_i(F) = \mathbb{S}_i$ *for all* $i \in \{1, \ldots, n\}$.

In this paper, we will restrict to two-dimensional signatures. The following observation is crucial. Given arbitrary semantics σ and τ it always holds for members $\langle \mathbb{S}, \mathbb{T} \rangle$ of $\Sigma_{\sigma, \tau}$ that $\mathbb{S} \in \Sigma_\sigma$ and $\mathbb{T} \in \Sigma_\tau$. When characterizing the two-dimensional signatures we will omit this necessary condition by using the following abbreviation: $\langle \mathbb{S}, \mathbb{T} \rangle_{\sigma, \tau} := \langle \mathbb{S}, \mathbb{T} \rangle \in \Sigma_\sigma \times \Sigma_\tau$.

We now give characterizations for the nine semantics we consider in this paper. Exploiting the obvious symmetry $\Sigma_{\sigma, \tau} = \{\langle \mathbb{S}, \mathbb{T} \rangle \mid \langle \mathbb{T}, \mathbb{S} \rangle \in \Sigma_{\tau, \sigma}\}$, characterizing in total 36 signatures is still required.

Showing the exact characterization of a signature $\Sigma_{\sigma, \tau}$ usually consists of two parts. First, one has to show that for each AF, the σ- and τ-extensions fulfill the conditions given by the characterization. Second, one has to provide a canonical construction for an AF $F_{\sigma, \tau}$ such that, given an arbitrary pair of extension-sets $\langle \mathbb{S}, \mathbb{T} \rangle$ fulfilling the conditions, it holds that $\sigma(F_{\sigma, \tau}(\mathbb{S}, \mathbb{T})) = \mathbb{S}$ and $\tau(F_{\sigma, \tau}(\mathbb{S}, \mathbb{T})) = \mathbb{T}$. The concrete constructions can be found in [9].

Our results can be summarized as follows.

Theorem 1. *For* $(\sigma_0, \tau_0) \in \{(gr, id), (gr, eg), (id, eg)\}$, $(\sigma_1, \tau_1) \in \{(id, sm), (gr, sm), (gr, pr)\}$, $\sigma_2 \in \{id, gr\}$, $(\sigma_3, \tau_3) \in \{(eg, sm), (id, pr)\}$, $\sigma_4 \in \{sm, pr\}$, $\sigma_5 \in \{gr, id, eg\}$, $\tau_6 \in \{ad, sm, pr\}$ *it holds that*

$$\Sigma_{\sigma_0, \tau_0} = \{\langle \{S\}, \{T\} \rangle_{\sigma_0, \tau_0} \mid S \subseteq T \subseteq \mathfrak{A}\}$$

$$\Sigma_{\sigma_1, \tau_1} = \{\langle \{S\}, \mathbb{T} \rangle_{\sigma_1, \tau_1} \mid S \subseteq \bigcap \mathbb{T}\}$$

$$\Sigma_{\sigma_2, sb} = \{\langle \{S\}, \mathbb{T} \rangle_{\sigma_2, sb} \mid \mathbb{T} \neq \emptyset, S \subseteq \bigcap \mathbb{T}\} \cup \{\langle \{S\}, \emptyset \rangle_{\sigma_2, sb}\}$$

$$\Sigma_{\sigma_3, \tau_3} = \{\langle \{S\}, \mathbb{T} \rangle_{\sigma_3, \tau_3} \mid |\mathbb{T}| > 1, S \subseteq \bigcap \mathbb{T}\} \cup \{\langle \{S\}, \{S\} \rangle_{\sigma_3, \tau_3}\}$$

$$\Sigma_{eg, sb} = \{\langle \{S\}, \mathbb{T} \rangle_{eg, sb} \mid |\mathbb{T}| > 1, S \subseteq \bigcap \mathbb{T}\} \cup \{\langle \{S\}, \{S\} \rangle_{eg, sb}, \langle \{S\}, \emptyset \rangle_{eg, sb}\}$$

$$\Sigma_{na,sb} =\{\langle \mathbb{S}, \mathbb{T}\rangle_{na,sb} \mid \mathbb{T}\subseteq \mathbb{S}\}$$

$$\Sigma_{na,\sigma_4} =\{\langle \mathbb{S}, \mathbb{T}\rangle_{na,\sigma_4} \mid \forall T\in \mathbb{T}\exists S\in \mathbb{S}: T\subseteq S, \mathbb{T}\bowtie \mathbb{S}\}$$

$$\Sigma_{sb,sm} =\{\langle \mathbb{T}, \mathbb{T}\rangle_{sb,sm}\} \cup \{\langle \emptyset, \mathbb{T}\rangle_{sb,sm}\}$$

$$\Sigma_{sb,pr} =\{\langle \mathbb{S}, \mathbb{T}\rangle_{sb,pr} \mid \mathbb{S}\subseteq \mathbb{T}\cap bd(\mathbb{T})\}$$

$$\Sigma_{\sigma_5,cf} =\{\langle \{S\}, \mathbb{T}\rangle_{\sigma_5,cf} \mid S\in \mathbb{T}\}$$

$$\Sigma_{cf,sb} =\{\langle \mathbb{S}, \mathbb{T}\rangle_{cf,sb} \mid \mathbb{T}\subseteq max(\mathbb{S})\};$$

$$\Sigma_{cf,\tau_6} =\{\langle \mathbb{S}, \mathbb{T}\rangle_{cf,\tau_6} \mid \mathbb{T}\subseteq \mathbb{S}, \mathbb{T}\bowtie \mathbb{S}\}$$

$$\Sigma_{id,ad} =\{\langle \{S\}, \mathbb{T}\rangle_{id,ad} \mid \{S\} = max(\{T\in \mathbb{T}\mid T\subseteq \bigcap max(\mathbb{T})\})\}$$

$$\Sigma_{na,ad} =\{\langle \mathbb{S}, \mathbb{T}\rangle_{na,ad} \mid \forall T\in \mathbb{T}\exists S\in \mathbb{S}: T\subseteq S, \mathbb{T}\bowtie \mathbb{S}\}$$

$$\Sigma_{sb,ad} =\{\langle \mathbb{S}, \mathbb{T}\rangle_{sb,ad} \mid \mathbb{S}\subseteq \mathbb{T}\cap bd(\mathbb{T})\}$$

$$\Sigma_{gr,ad} =\{\langle \{S\}, \mathbb{T}\rangle_{gr,ad} \mid \exists\, strict\ total\ order <\ on\ S\ s.t.$$

$$\forall s\in S: \{s\}\cup \{s'\in S\mid s'<s\}\in \mathbb{T}, S\subseteq \bigcap max(\mathbb{T})\}.$$

We briefly discuss the two-dimensional signature of stable and preferred semantics that was already mentioned in the introduction. First observe that for any pair $\langle \mathbb{S}, \mathbb{T}\rangle \in \Sigma_{sb,pr}$ it holds that $\mathbb{S}\subseteq \mathbb{T}$. However, already the fact that $\Sigma_{sb}\subset \Sigma_{pr}$ [8] implies that this condition cannot be sufficient as not all pairs with $\mathbb{S} = \mathbb{T}$ are realizable under (sb, pr). The following example illustrates that stable extensions may only be certain subsets of the preferred extensions. In [9] we show that also $\mathbb{S}\subseteq bd(\mathbb{T})$ must hold in order to have $\langle \mathbb{S}, \mathbb{T}\rangle \in \Sigma_{sb,pr}$.

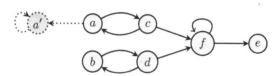

Fig. 1. AFs F and F' discussed in Example 2.

Example 2. Consider the extension-sets $\mathbb{S} = \{\{a, d, e\}, \{b, c, e\}, \{c, d, e\}\}$ and $\mathbb{T} = \mathbb{S}\cup \{\{a, b\}\}$. The pair $\langle \mathbb{S}, \mathbb{T}\rangle$ is realized under (sb, pr) by the AF F depicted in Fig. 1 (without the dotted part). However, observe that $\mathbb{T}\not\subseteq bd(\mathbb{T})$ (since $\{a, b, e\}\in bd(\mathbb{T})$) and therefore $\langle \mathbb{T}, \mathbb{T}\rangle$ is not realizable under (sb, pr). In fact, no AF with $\mathbb{T}$ as preferred extensions can contain $\{a, b\}$ as stable extension since $\{a, b\}\notin bd(\mathbb{T})$ cannot achieve full range in such an AF. We can get an arbitrary subset of $\mathbb{S}$ under sb though: take AF F' in Fig. 1 including the dotted part. Then, $pr(F') = \mathbb{T}$ and $sb(F') = \{\{a, d, e\}\}$.

What has to be left open are the characterizations of $\Sigma_{\sigma,\tau}$ for $\sigma \in \{sm, eg\}$ and $\tau \in \{ad, pr\}$. A detailed discussion on the difficulties involved is given in [9]. As it turns out, particular realizations of pairs under these semantics must make use of implicit conflicts [13].

4 Discussion

In this paper, we have given a full characterization of all but four two-dimensional signatures for the semantics of conflict-free, admissible, naive, stable, preferred, semi-stable, grounded, ideal, and eager extensions. Two-dimensional signatures give further insights about the relationship between semantics, but also yield practical implications. For example, when enumerating preferred extensions, we may start with computing the less complex stable semantics. Assume we have found $\{a, b\}$ and some $S \cup \{a\}$ as stable (and therefore preferred) extensions. By our insights we can now, for instance, exclude any $S' \cup \{b\}$ with $S \cap S' \neq \emptyset$ from the search-space, even if it could still be compatible with Σ_{pr}. The research on multi-dimensional signatures is not limited to argumentation. We plan to apply our method also to logic programming in order to compare stable, well-founded, and supported semantics [12, 14] in a similar vein.

References

1. Baroni, P., Caminada, M., Giacomin, M.: An introduction to argumentation semantics. Knowl. Eng. Rev. **26**(4), 365–410 (2011)
2. Baumann, R., Dvořák, W., Linsbichler, T., Strass, H., Woltran, S.: Compact argumentation frameworks. In: Proceedings of the ECAI, pp. 69–74 (2014)
3. Bench-Capon, T.J.M., Dunne, P.E.: Argumentation in artificial intelligence. Artif. Intell. **171**(10–15), 619–641 (2007)
4. Caminada, M.: Comparing two unique extension semantics for formal argumentation: Ideal and eager. In: Proceedings of the BNAIC, pp. 81–87 (2007)
5. Caminada, M., Carnielli, W.A., Dunne, P.E.: Semi-stable semantics. JLC **22**(5), 1207–1254 (2012)
6. Dung, P.M.: On the acceptability of arguments and its fundamental role in non-monotonic reasoning, logic programming and n-person games. Artif. Intell. **77**(2), 321–357 (1995)
7. Dunne, P.E., Bench-Capon, T.J.M.: Coherence in finite argument systems. Artif. Intell. **141**(1/2), 187–203 (2002)
8. Dunne, P.E., Dvořák, W., Linsbichler, T., Woltran, S.: Characteristics of multiple viewpoints in abstract argumentation. Artif. Intell. **228**, 153–178 (2015)
9. Dunne, P.E., Linsbichler, T., Spanring, C., Woltran, S.: Investigating the relationship between argumentation semantics via signatures. In: Proceedings of the IJCAI (2016)
10. Dvořák, W., Spanring, C.: Comparing the expressiveness of argumentation semantics. In: Proceedings of the COMMA, pp. 261–272 (2012)
11. Dvořák, W., Woltran, S.: On the intertranslatability of argumentation semantics. J. Artif. Intell. Res. (JAIR) **41**, 445–475 (2011)
12. Gelfond, M., Lifschitz, V.: The stable model semantics for logic programming. In: Logic Programming: Proceedings of the 5th International Conference, pp. 1070–1080 (1988)
13. Linsbichler, T., Spanring, C., Woltran, S.: The hidden power of abstract argumentation semantics. In: Black, E., Modgil, S., Oren, N. (eds.) TAFA 2015. Lecture Notes in Artificial Intelligence (LNAI), vol. 9524, pp. 146–162. Springer, Heidelberg (2015). doi:10.1007/978-3-319-28460-6_9

14. Van Gelder, A., Ross, K.A., Schlipf, J.S.: Unfounded sets and well-founded semantics for general logic programs. In: Proceedings of the ACM SIGACT-SIGMOD-SIGART Symposium on Principles of Database Systems, pp. 221–230 (1988)
15. Verheij, B.: Two approaches to dialectical argumentation: admissible sets and argumentation stages. In: Proceedings of the NAIC, pp. 357–368 (1996)

Decoupled Strong Stubborn Sets

Daniel Gnad[1]([✉]), Martin Wehrle[2], and Jörg Hoffmann[1]

[1] Saarland University, Saarbrücken, Germany
{gnad,hoffmann}@cs.uni-saarland.de
[2] University of Basel, Basel, Switzerland
martin.wehrle@unibas.ch

1 Star-Topology Decoupled State Space Search

State space search is a canonical approach to testing reachability in large transition systems, like goal reachability in classical planning which is where this work is placed. Decomposition techniques for state space search have a long tradition, most notably in the form of *Petri net unfolding* [7, 14, 20] decomposing the search over concurrent transition paths, and *factored planning* [2, 4, 8, 19] decomposing the search into local vs. global planning over separate components of state variables.

Recent work by part of the authors [9, 10] has devised *star-topology decoupling*, which can be viewed as a hybrid between Petri net unfolding and factored planning, geared at star topologies. The state variables are factored into components whose cross-component interactions form a star topology. The search is akin to a Petri net unfolding whose atomic elements are component states, exploring concurrent paths of leaf components in the star independently. Relative to both Petri net unfolding and traditional factored planning, the key advantage lies in exploiting the star topology, which gets rid of major sources of complexity: the need to reason about conflicts and reachable markings, respectively the need to resolve arbitrary cross-component interactions.

The best way to understand the star topology impact is in terms of a particular form of "conditional independence": *given a fixed path of transitions by the center component in the star, the possible center-compliant paths are independent across the leaf components.* For example, say the center is a single truck-position variable t, and each leaf is a single package-position variable p_i. Given a fixed state-transition path π^C for t, the compliant state-transition paths for any p_i, alongside π^C, are those which load/unload p_i at suitable points along π^C. Any such load/unload sequence – any π^C-*compliant path* – can be committed to for p_i, independently of what any other p_j is committed to. Star-topology decoupled search exploits this by searching over center paths π^C only. Alongside each π^C, it maintains, for each leaf separately, the leaf states reachable on π^C-compliant paths. This avoids the enumeration of combined states across leaves. In imprecise analogy to conditional independence in graphical models, star-topology decoupling "instantiates" the center to break the dependencies between the leaves.

Original paper appeared at the 25th International Joint Conference on Artificial Intelligence (IJCAI), 2016.

G. Friedrich et al. (Eds.): KI 2016, LNAI 9904, pp. 278–284, 2016.
DOI: 10.1007/978-3-319-46073-4

Table 1. State space size data. Best results highlighted in **boldface**. "Success": reachable state space fully explored. "X": X-shape factoring identified. "Std": standard state space. Other notations see text. All planning competition benchmark domains were run. Domains on which no X-shape was identified anywhere, and domains where no approach could build any state space, are not included in the table. Multiple test suites of the same domain are accumulated into the same table row. Runtime limit 30 minutes, memory limit 4 GB.

Domain	# Instances	Reachable state space. Right: average over instances commonly built											
		Success								Representation size (in thousands)			
		All	X	Std	POR	Punf	Cunf	OPT	COM	Std	POR	OPT	COM
Solvable benchmarks: from the International Planning Competition (IPC)													
Depots	22	22	4	4	2	2	3	**5**	30,954.8	30,954.8	35,113.1	**3,970.0**	
Driverlog	20	20	5	5	3	3	8	**10**	35,632.4	35,632.4	706.1	**127.2**	
Elevators	100	100	21	17	1	3	8	**41**	22,652.1	22,651.1	21,046.2	**186.7**	
Floortile	80	80	**2**	**2**	0	0	0	**2**					
Logistics	63	63	12	12	7	11	23	**27**	3,793.8	3,793.8	85.5	**8.2**	
Miconic	150	145	50	45	25	30	45	**145**	52,728.9	52,673.1	218.8	**2.4**	
NoMystery	40	40	11	11	5	7	**40**	40	29,459.3	25,581.5	11.5	**10.0**	
Pathways	30	30	4	**4**	3	3	4	4	54,635.5	**1,229.0**	11,211.9	11,211.9	
PSR	50	3	3	3	3	3	3	3	39.4	33.9	**11.1**	11.1	
Rovers	40	40	5	**6**	4	4	5	5	98,051.6	6,534.4	4,045.9	**4,032.9**	
Satellite	36	36	**5**	5	**5**	**5**	4	4	2,864.2	582.5	2,219.1	**352.7**	
TPP	30	29	5	5	4	4	**11**	**11**	340,961.5	326,124.8	.9	.8	
Transport	140	140	28	23	11	11	18	**34**	4,958.6	4,958.5	12,486.4	**173.3**	
Woodworking	100	87	11	20	16	**22**	16	16	438,638.5	**226.8**	16,624.1	9,688.9	
Zenotravel	20	20	**7**	**7**	2	4	**7**	**7**	17,468.0	17,467.5	1,028.5	**99.4**	
Unsolvable benchmarks: extended from [15]													
NoMystery	40	40	9	8	2	4	**40**	40	85,254.2	65,878.2	3.9	**3.8**	
Rovers	40	40	**4**	**4**	0	0	**4**	4	697,778.9	302,608.9	22,001.8	**20,924.4**	
Σ	1001	935	186	181	93	116	239	**398**					

Star-topology decoupling is exponentially separated from all previous search reduction techniques, i.e., there are example families which it handles exponentially more effectively than Petri-net unfolding, factored planning, partial-order reduction [23, 24], symmetry reduction [6, 22], etc. While this is merely a theoretical result pointing out that star-topology decoupling is, in principle, complementary to previous methods, the potential advantage of star-topology decoupling is also very much manifested in practice. On planning problems with a pronounced star topology, the empirical impact of star-topology decoupling is dramatic. Taking the effort required to build and represent the entire state space as the most basic measure of reduction power, Table 1 gives data comparing star-topology decoupling to its closest relatives.

The "OPT" variant of our technique keeps track of leaf-state costs and preserves optimality, the "COM" variant keeps track of leaf-state reachability and preserves completeness only. We compare to Petri-net unfolding using "Punf" [18], as well as contextual Petri net unfolding using "Cunf" [21] which directly supports non-consumed (prevail) preconditions. We compare to standard state space search with *strong stubborn set* pruning [24], as star-topology decoupling can also be viewed (like Petri net unfolding) as a form of partial-order reduction. We do not compare here to factored planning because, while conceptually the use of separate components is a commonality, the concrete algorithms end up being completely different when considering arbitrary cross-component interactions (as all previous method do), vs. exploiting a star topology. Representation size is the number of integer variables in our C++ implementation based on FD [12]. We do not include representation size data for Petri net unfolding as these lag far behind in terms of the number of state spaces built.

The data clearly attest to the power of our approach. There are some domains where previous techniques are stronger, but overall the picture is very clearly in our favor, with typical improvements of orders of magnitude, up to 5 and 6 orders of magnitude in the extreme cases. Considering that partial-order reduction and unfolding are venerable techniques into which sustained research effort was invested since decades, while star-topology decoupling was only just invented, we find this remarkable.

The major weakness evident from Table 1 is the *absence* of data for all the other competition domains. We show only those domains where a simple automatic factoring strategy succeeded – taking a few milliseconds to identify what we call an *X-shape*, a simple special case of star topologies where the interaction between the center and each leaf is one-way. X-shapes do occur in planning competition domains, but not widely.

Preempting the conclusion section a bit, one major conclusion here is the need for more powerful factoring strategies. *Every* planning task has star-topology factorings. We currently do not lose any runtime on cases we cannot handle, but the number of such cases is large. Another major conclusion is that domain-independent planning may not be the prime target application for star-topology decoupling – why go search for star topologies in arbitrary input problems when there are so many important problems that come with a star topology by definition?

2   Combination with Strong Stubborn Sets Pruning

As star-topology decoupling is complementary to all previous methods, the question arises whether it can be combined with these methods to mutual benefit. The question is especially pertinent as star-topology decoupling essentially just reformulates the state space into a component-wise fashion, and should thus leave many of the technicalities of other methods intact. In the IJCAI'16 paper [11] this extended abstract is based on, we show that this is indeed so for strong stubborn set pruning, the most well-known and wide-spread partial-order reduction method.

Given a state s during search, a stubborn set for s is a subset S of actions so that, in s, to preserve optimality it suffices to branch over those actions from S applicable in s. To ensure this, S collects actions that (1) make progress to the goal, that (2) are required for this progress and are applicable in s, and that (3) interfere with applicable actions already included into S. For (1), it is enough to pick one open goal fact from the goal conjunction; for (2), one recursively includes actions achieving open preconditions of actions already included into S; given (3), all true alternatives at this point – all conflicting decisions one may take in s – are included in S and will be branched over.

As we show in detail in the paper, (1)–(3) transfer directly, almost straight-forwardly, to decoupled search, when restricting to *fork* topologies where the leaf components depend on the center but not vice versa. In this setting, reachability within each leaf factor can only grow along a search path (along a transition path by the center), and one can view a decoupled search state s as the union $\overline{s}$ of all leaf states reachable at that point. Given this, in a nutshell, (1) remains as-is, (2) redefines "applicability" relative to $\overline{s}$, and (3) needs to consider only interference with applicable center actions as all applicable leaf actions (more precisely, their effects) are already incorporated into $\overline{s}$.

The only additional complication is that, to guarantee optimality, decoupled search has to proceed beyond decoupled goal states, as cheaper leaf-goal costs may become available on a longer center-component path. Standard strong stubborn sets are undefined for goal states, so a new concept is required here. That can be achieved by replacing (1) with a simple notion of "making progress towards cheaper leaf-goal costs".

In theory, the combination of star-topology decoupling with strong stubborn sets dominates each of its components, and is exponentially separated from each of its components. Indeed, there are cases where the combination is exponentially stronger than *both* its components, i.e., there can be synergistic effects where, thanks to the decoupling, strong stubborn sets are able to exploit a structure they are unable to exploit in the original state space. For example, this happens in simple transportation-style domains akin to the planning competition "Logistics" benchmarks, where a decoupling over packages enables partial-order reduction over trucks.

In practice, the proposed combination is almost as strong as in theory. It inherits the strengths of its components in almost all cases, and it outperforms both its components in some cases. Table 2 shows coverage data. Observe that the benefit of star-topology decoupling is much stronger for blind search, where the search space reduction does not compete with the reduction already provided by the heuristic function (the state-of-the-art admissible heuristic LM-cut [13]). The additional advantage brought by using strong stubborn sets on top of the decoupling is similar in both settings though.

Table 2. Coverage data. Best results highlighted in **boldface**. "SSS": standard search with strong stubborn sets pruning; "DS": star-topology decoupled search; "DSSS": our combination of the two. Results shown on planning competition benchmarks with a fork topology.

Domain	#	Blind heuristic				LM-cut			
		A*	SSS	DS	DSSS	A*	SSS	DS	DSSS
Driverlog	20	7	7	**11**	**11**	13	13	13	13
Logistics'00	28	10	10	22	**24**	20	20	**28**	**28**
Logistics'98	35	2	2	4	**5**	6	6	6	6
Miconic	145	50	45	35	**36**	**136**	**136**	135	135
NoMystery	20	8	7	**17**	15	14	14	**20**	19
Pathways	29	3	3	3	3	4	4	4	4
Rovers	40	6	7	7	**9**	7	9	9	**11**
Satellite	36	6	6	6	6	7	**11**	7	**11**
TPP	27	5	5	**23**	22	5	5	**18**	**18**
Woodworking'08	13	4	6	5	**7**	6	**11**	10	**11**
Woodworking'11	5	0	1	1	**2**	2	**5**	4	**5**
Zenotravel	20	8	7	**11**	**11**	13	13	13	13
Σ	418	109	106	145	**151**	233	247	267	**274**

3 Conclusion

Star-topology decoupling is a powerful new approach to state-space decomposition. The possible benefits are dramatic, the space of opportunities is wide open, the research questions are manifold.

The most obvious direct follow-up on our work here regards the extension of decoupled strong stubborn sets to general star topologies, beyond forks. We believe that this is possible and will lead to similar theoretical and practical results, but that remains to be proven. More generally, the combination with alternate search enhancements is a whole research line in its own right: symmetry reduction; heuristic functions exploiting the star topology; BDDs compactly representing leaf state spaces; adaptations to multi-core search; adaptations of bitstate hashing; etc.

Regarding domain-independent planning, the most pressing question regards more powerful factoring strategies. Much more interesting factorings than our current ones – X-shapes and forks – definitely exist. As a simple rim case, every partition into 2 subsets of state variables is a star-topology factoring, already opening an exponentially large space of factorings to choose from. The more practically pertinent factorings, though, presumably are the ones with maximum number of leaves. These correspond to maximum independent sets in the input task's causal graph, so approximations to the latter could form the starting point for factoring strategies.

A cute thought is to generalize from the idea to fix and exploit a star-topology profile: *target-profile factoring* could, perhaps, work also for different structural profiles, like chains, trees, DAGs, etc. This suggests an entirely new way of exploiting structure in planning. Instead of *relaxing* the planning task into a (structurally defined) fragment to obtain a heuristic function, try to *factorize* the task into a fragment to obtain a plan. The huge amount of effort invested into tractability analysis (e.g. [3, 5, 17]) could then be redirected to the design of fragments suited to specialized combinatorial search algorithms. In the long term, this could lead to an entire portfolio of target profiles.

Lastly and probably most importantly, the world is full of star topologies so we should go out there and apply star-topology decoupling to those. For AI, a highly suggestive thought is that of multi-agent systems interacting via a set of shared variables – so the agents are the leaves, and the shared variables are the center? Star topology also is a classical system design paradigm, which cries out for applications in model checking. A highly relevant recent direction are concurrent programs under weak memory models (e.g. [1, 16]). Processes run on separate processors (leaves), yet a consistent view of shared memory (center) needs to be guaranteed. The objective is verification, i.e., exhausting the state space, for which star-topology decoupling is especially beneficial (compare Table 1 against Table 2). Key challenges include the adaptation to model checking languages, and the extension to properties beyond reachability.

Acknowledgments. Daniel Gnad was partially supported by the German Research Foundation (DFG), as part of project grant HO 2169/6-1, "Star-Topology Decoupled State Space Search". Martin Wehrle was supported by the Swiss National Science Foundation (SNSF) as part of the project "Automated Reformulation and Pruning in Factored State Spaces (ARAP)".

References

1. Abd Alrahman, Y., Andric, M., Beggiato, A., Lafuente, A.L.: Can we efficiently check concurrent programs under relaxed memory models in maude? In: Escobar, S. (ed.) WRLA 2014. LNCS, vol. 8663, pp. 21–41. Springer, Heidelberg (2014). doi:10.1007/978-3-319-12904-4_2
2. Amir, E., Engelhardt, B.: Factored planning. In: Proceedings of the 18th International Joint Conference on Artificial Intelligence (IJCAI 2003), pp. 929–935 (2003)
3. Brafman, R., Domshlak, C.: Structure and complexity in planning with unary operators. J. Artif. Intell. Res. **18**, 315–349 (2003)
4. Brafman, R., Domshlak, C.: On the complexity of planning for agent teams and its implications for single agent planning. Artif. Intell. **198**, 52–71 (2013)
5. Chen, H., Giménez, O.: Causal graphs and structurally restricted planning. J. Comput. Syst. Sci. **76**(7), 579–592 (2010)
6. Domshlak, C., Katz, M., Shleyfman, A.: Enhanced symmetry breaking in cost-optimal planning as forward search. In: Proceedings of the 22nd International Conference on Automated Planning and Scheduling (ICAPS 2012) (2012)
7. Esparza, J., Römer, S., Vogler, W.: An improvement of mcmillan's unfolding algorithm. Formal Meth. Syst. Des. **20**(3), 285–310 (2002)

8. Fabre, E., Jezequel, L., Haslum, P., Thiébaux, S.: Cost-optimal factored planning: promises and pitfalls. In: Proceedings of the 20th International Conference on Automated Planning and Scheduling (ICAPS 2010), pp. 65–72 (2010)
9. Gnad, D., Hoffmann, J., Beating LM-cut with h^{max} (sometimes): Fork-decoupled statespace search. In: Proceedings of the 25th International Conferenceon Automated Planning and Scheduling (ICAPS 2015) (2015)
10. Gnad, D., Hoffmann, J.: Red-black planning: a new tractability analysis and heuristicfunction. In: Proceedings of the 8th Annual Symposium on Combinatorial Search (SOCS 2015) (2015)
11. Gnad, D., Wehrle, M., Hoffmann, J.: Decoupled strong stubborn sets. In: Proceedings of the 25th International Joint Conference on Artificial Intelligence (IJCAI 2016) (2016)
12. Helmert, M.: The fast downward planning system. J. Artif. Intell. Res. **26**, 191–246 (2006)
13. Helmert, M., Domshlak, C.: Landmarks, critical paths and abstractions: what's the differenceanyway? In: Proceedings of the 19th International Conference on Automated Planning and Scheduling (ICAPS 2009), pp. 162–169 (2009)
14. Hickmott, S.L., Rintanen, J., Thiébaux, S., White, L.B.: Planning via petri net unfolding. In: Proceedings of the 20th International Joint Conference on Artificial Intelligence (IJCAI 2007), pp. 1904–1911 (2007)
15. Hoffmann, J., Kissmann, P., Torralba, Á.: "Distance"? Who Cares? Tailoring merge-and-shrink heuristics to detect unsolvability. In: Proceedings of the 21st European Conference on Artificial Intelligence (ECAI 2014) (2014)
16. Jonsson, B.: State-space exploration for concurrent algorithms under weak memory orderings. SIGARCH Comput. Archit. News **36**(5), 65–71 (2008)
17. Jonsson, P., Bäckström, C.: Incremental planning. In: European Workshop on Planning (1995)
18. Khomenko, V., Koutny, M.: Towards an efficient algorithm for unfolding petri nets. In: Larsen, K.G., Nielsen, M. (eds.) CONCUR 2001. LNCS, vol. 2154, pp. 366–380. Springer, Heidelberg (2001). doi:10.1007/3-540-44685-0_25
19. Knoblock, C.: Automatically generating abstractions for planning. Artif. Intell. **68**(2), 243–302 (1994)
20. McMillan, K.L.: Using unfoldings to avoid the state explosion problem in the verification of asynchronous circuits. In: Bochmann, G., Probst, D.K. (eds.) CAV 1992. LNCS, vol. 663, pp. 164–177. Springer, Heidelberg (1993). doi:10.1007/3-540-56496-9_14
21. Rodríguez, C., Schwoon, S.: Cunf: a tool for unfolding and verifying petri nets with read arcs. In: Proceedings of the 11th International Symposium on AutomatedTechnology for Verification and Analysis (ATVA 2013), pp. 492–495 (2013)
22. Starke, P.: Reachability analysis of petri nets using symmetries. J. Math. Model. Simul. Syst. Anal. **8**(4/5), 293–304 (1991)
23. Valmari, A.: Stubborn sets for reduced state space generation. In: Rozenberg, G. (ed.) ICATPN 1989. LNCS, vol. 483, pp. 491–515. Springer, Heidelberg (1991). doi:10.1007/3-540-53863-1
24. Wehrle, M., Helmert, M.: Efficient stubborn sets: generalized algorithms and selectionstrategies. In: Proceedings of the 24th International Conference on Automated Planning andScheduling (ICAPS 2014) (2014)

State-Dependent Cost Partitionings
for Cartesian Abstractions in Classical Planning

Thomas Keller[1], Florian Pommerening[1], Jendrik Seipp[1], Florian Geißer[2],
and Robert Mattmüller[2(✉)]

[1] University of Basel, Basel, Switzerland
{tho.keller,florian.pommerening,jendrik.seipp}@unibas.ch
[2] University of Freiburg, Freiburg Im Breisgau, Germany
{geisserf,mattmuel}@informatik.uni-freiburg.de

Abstract. Abstraction heuristics are a popular method to guide optimal search algorithms in classical planning. *Cost partitionings* allow to sum heuristic estimates admissibly by partitioning action costs among the abstractions. We introduce *state-dependent* cost partitionings which take context information of actions into account, and show that an *optimal state-dependent cost partitioning* dominates its state-independent counterpart. We demonstrate the potential of state-dependent cost partitionings with a state-dependent variant of the recently proposed *saturated cost partitioning*, and show that it can sometimes improve not only over its state-independent counterpart, but even over the optimal state-independent cost partitioning.

Keywords: AI planning · Abstraction heuristics · Cost partitioning · State-dependent cost partitioning

1 Introduction

Abstraction heuristics [2, 14] are a popular method to guide optimal heuristic search algorithms in classical planning. Since a single abstraction often provides poor guidance, we would like to combine the information from *several* abstractions admissibly. This can be accomplished either by *maximizing* over a set of admissible heuristics, or even better, by *adding* admissible heuristics, provided that one can guarantee that the sum of heuristic values is still admissible. This can be guaranteed either by restricting oneself to additive abstractions [3, 11], or by *cost partitioning* [7, 8]. The latter approach counts only some fraction of the original cost of each action in each abstraction, such that the accumulated cost of each action over all abstractions does not exceed its original cost.

This extended abstract is based on an IJCAI 2016 paper by the same authors [9]. Full proofs can be found there and in an associated technical report [10].

G. Friedrich et al. (Eds.): KI 2016, LNAI 9904, pp. 285–290, 2016.
DOI: 10.1007/978-3-319-46073-4

Interesting instances of cost partitioning include *optimal cost partitioning* that leads to highest possible accumulated costs per state, *general cost partitioning* [12] that also allows negative costs, and *saturated cost partitioning* [15], where the cost partitioning is computed iteratively by "consuming" the minimum costs in each abstraction such that the costs of all shortest paths are preserved.

In this paper, we show that even more information can be extracted from a collection of abstractions if *context information* is taken into account and abstract action costs are allowed to differ from state to state. To that end, we define *state-dependent cost partitioning* and show that its optimal version dominates optimal state-independent cost partitioning. Since computing *optimal* state-dependent cost partitionings is usually infeasible, we also consider *saturated* state-dependent cost partitioning, which is cheaper to compute. Whereas saturated state-*independent* cost partitioning loses valuable information when maximizing over all transitions incurred by the same action, saturated state-*dependent* cost partitioning, where costs are consumed only in a given context, does not suffer from this loss of information.

Besides the definition of state-dependent cost partitioning, the major contribution of this paper is a complete analysis of theoretical dominance relationships between the four combinations of optimal and saturated, and state-dependent and state-independent cost partitionings.

2   Preliminaries

Planning. We consider SAS$^+$ planning tasks [1] Π with the usual components, i. e., variables $\mathcal{V}$, actions A, initial state s_I, and goal description $s_\star$. The set of states is denoted with S. Applicability of actions and action sequences to states as well as the result of their application is also defined as usual via preconditions and effects. In addition, we allow non-negative *action costs* to be specified by *cost functions* $c : A \to \mathbb{R}_0^+$. At several places in this paper, we are interested in costs that are based on modified cost functions. An important aspect of this work are *general* and *state-dependent* cost functions $c : A \times S \to \mathbb{R}$ that determine transition costs $c(a, s)$ that depend on the state s in addition to the action a that is applied. Since state-dependent cost functions are more general, we define the following concepts in terms of state-dependent instead of regular cost functions unless we want to emphasize that the cost function of the original task is used.

An action sequence $\pi = \langle a_1, \ldots, a_n \rangle$ is an s-plan if it is applicable in s and leads to a state satisfying the goal condition. It is a *plan* if it is an s_I-plan. The *cost* of s-plan π under cost function c is the sum of action costs along the induced state sequence $\langle s_0, \ldots, s_n \rangle$, i.e., $c(\pi, s) = \sum_{i=1}^{n} c(a_i, s_{i-1})$. A plan π is *optimal* under c if it minimizes $c(\pi, s)$. A *heuristic function* h estimates the cost of an optimal s-plan under cost function c with values $h(s, c) \in \mathbb{R} \cup \{-\infty, \infty\}$. Note that we allow negative heuristic values to support general cost partitioning [12]. A heuristic h is called *admissible* if it never overestimates the true optimal cost. A planning task Π and a cost function ct induce a weighted labeled transition system $\mathcal{T}$ in the usual way. Edge weights in $\mathcal{T}$ are the (possibly state-dependent) action costs of the planning task.

Abstraction Heuristics. The core idea of *abstraction heuristics* is to collapse several states into a single abstract state, which reduces the size of the transition system and allows the computation of abstract goal distances that can be used as admissible heuristic estimates in the original task. Given a planning task Π with induced transition system $\mathcal{T}$, we denote abstraction mappings from concrete to abstract states preserving initial state, goal states, and transitions, by α, and the induced abstract transition system by $\mathcal{T}^\alpha$. In defining the weight of an abstract transition in $\mathcal{T}^\alpha$ between abstract states t and u with transition label a, we follow Geißer et al. [4, 5] and define it to be the *minimal* weight of all concrete transitions labeled with action a that start in a state s with $\alpha(s) = t$. Together with the fact that every plan in the concrete transition system is a plan in the abstract transition system, this ensures that the cost of each optimal abstract plan is an admissible heuristic estimate. Abstractions where all abstract states are Cartesian products of domain subsets of the state variables are called *Cartesian abstractions.* Since we only consider Cartesian abstractions here, we simply call them *abstractions* in the following.

3 State-Dependent Cost Partitioning

Early work on additive admissible heuristics has mostly focused on techniques that allow to generate or identify heuristics that can be added up admissibly because each deals with a sub-problem of the planning task that can be regarded independently from the rest [3, 6]. An equivalent view on these techniques is to regard them as cost partitionings [8] that distribute action costs such that each operator is assigned its full cost in one heuristic and a cost of zero in all other. However, cost partitionings are more general as costs can be distributed arbitrarily between the heuristics as long as the sum over the individual costs does not exceed the original cost. Given such a cost partitioning, heuristic values are then computed on a copy of the planning task where actions cost only the fraction of the actual action cost that is assigned to the heuristic. In this paper, we continue developing more accurate cost partitioning techniques by presenting state-dependent cost partitionings, a generalization where context information of applied actions is taken into account.

Definition 1 (State-dependent cost partitioning). *Let Π be a planning task. Then a general state-dependent cost partitioning for Π is a tuple $P = \langle c_1 \ldots, c_n \rangle$, where $c_i : A \times S \to \mathbb{R}$ for $1 \leq i \leq n$ and $\sum_{i=1}^{n} c_i(a, s) \leq c(a)$ for all $s \in S$ and $a \in A$. If P is* state-independent, *i.e., if $c_i(a, s) = c_i(a, s')$ for all $s, s' \in S$, $a \in A$ and $1 \leq i \leq n$, then P is a general* state-independent *cost partitioning for Π.*

Let $h_1, \ldots, h_n$ be admissible heuristics and $P = \langle c_1 \ldots, c_n \rangle$ a cost partitioning. Then the corresponding *cost partitioning heuristic* is denoted as $h_P(s) = \sum_{i=1}^{n} h_i(s, c_i)$, where the sum is defined as ∞ if any term in the sum is ∞, even if another term is $-\infty$. We want to point out that the introduction of state-dependent cost functions does not break admissibility of h_P.

State-dependent cost partitionings differ from their state-independent counterpart in that each state-action pair can have its own cost instead of a cost that is shared among all possible applications of an action.

Definition 2 (OCP$_D$ and OCP$_I$). *Let $h_1, \ldots, h_n$ be admissible heuristics for a planning task Π, $\mathbb{P}_D$ the space of state-dependent cost partitionings and $\mathbb{P}_I \subseteq \mathbb{P}_D$ the space of state-independent cost partitionings for Π. The optimal state $-$ dependent cost partitioning (OCP$_D$) heuristic estimate for $h_1, \ldots, h_n$ in state s is $h^{ocp_D}(s) = \max_{P \in \mathbb{P}_D} h_P(s)$, and the optimal state $-$ independent cost partitioning (OCP$_I$) heuristic estimate for $h_1, \ldots, h_n$ is $h^{ocp_I}(s) = \max_{P \in \mathbb{P}_I} h_P(s)$.*

State-dependent cost partitionings allow the computation of more accurate heuristic estimates.

Theorem 1 (OCP$_D$ dominates OCP$_I$). *Let $h_1, \ldots, h_n$ be admissible heuristics for a planning task Π. Then $h^{ocp_D}(s) \geq h^{ocp_I}(s)$ for all $s \in S$. Moreover, there are planning tasks where the inequality is strict for at least one state.* $\square$

Although Theorem 1 provides an encouraging result, its practical impact appears limited. This is mostly because the computation of an optimal state-dependent cost partitioning with a method designed for state-independent cost partitionings [8, 12] would require a compilation with one action for each state-action pair, a number that is exponential in the number of state variables. Whereas there are techniques like context splitting [13] that allow to compute a more compact compilation, the worst-case exponential blowup cannot be avoided in general. We therefore turn our attention to saturated cost partitioning [15], a technique that is tractable in practice.

4   Saturated Cost Partitioning

Seipp and Helmert [15] introduced the concept of *cost saturation*. Iteratively, they compute an abstraction, reduce the action costs such that all goal distances are preserved, and use the remaining costs for subsequent abstractions. The result is a *saturated cost partitioning*. Due to the greediness of the procedure, the resulting cost partitioning usually provides poorer estimates than the optimal cost partitioning. However, we can compute the saturated cost partitioning much faster and more memory-efficiently. Following Seipp and Helmert [15] and extending their definition to potentially negative, but still state-independent action cost, we can define saturated state-independent cost partitioning as follows.

Definition 3 (SCP$_I$). *Let Π be a planning task with cost function c and $\alpha_1, \ldots, \alpha_n$ abstractions. Let $\langle c_1, \ldots, c_n \rangle$ and $P = \langle \hat{c}_1, \ldots, \hat{c}_n \rangle$ be tuples of cost functions with the following properties: $c_1 = c$; $\hat{c}_i(a) = \max_{s \in S} h_i(\alpha_i(s)) - h_i(\alpha_i(s[a]))$, where h_i is the goal distance function of T^{α_i} with cost function c_i; and $c_{i+1} = c_i - \hat{c}_i$. We call c_i the remaining cost for T^{α_i}, $\hat{c}_i$ the saturated cost of T^{α_i} and P the saturated state $-$ independent cost partitioning (SCP$_I$) for $\alpha_1, \ldots, \alpha_n$.*

We denote the associated heuristic by h^{scp_I}. Seipp and Helmert [15] show that the saturated cost function preserves the goal distances of all abstract states in all abstractions, and is minimal among all distance-preserving cost functions. The same holds for the potentially negative cost partitioning that we use.

As state-independent cost functions do not allow assigning costs to actions in the context of the current state, saturated cost functions are computed by maximizing over all weights of transitions that are labeled with the same action. State-*dependent* cost partitioning offers an opportunity to overcome this weakness by allowing to reduce the costs of state-action pairs rather than actions.

Definition 4 ($\mathbf{SCP_D}$). *Let Π be a planning task with cost function c and let $\alpha_1, \ldots, \alpha_n$ be abstractions. Let $\langle c_1, \ldots, c_n \rangle$ and $P = \langle \hat{c}_1, \ldots, \hat{c}_n \rangle$ be tuples of cost functions with the following properties: $c_1(a, s) = c(a)$ for all $a \in A$ and $s \in S$; $\hat{c}_i(a, s) = h_i(\alpha(s)) - h_i(\alpha(s[a]))$, where h_i is the goal distance function of $\mathcal{T}^{\alpha_i}$ with cost function c_i; and $c_{i+1} = c_i - \hat{c}_i$. We call c_i the* remaining cost *for $\mathcal{T}^{\alpha_i}$, $\hat{c}_i$ the* saturated cost *of $\mathcal{T}^{\alpha_i}$ and P the* saturated state − dependent cost partitioning *(SCP$_D$) for $\alpha_1, \ldots, \alpha_n$.*

We denote the associated heuristic by h^{scp_D}. In analogy to Theorem 1, we might be tempted to expect a similar theoretical dominance of SCP$_D$ over SCP$_i$. However, it turns out that this is not the case due to the inaccuracy caused by the greediness of saturated cost partitionings.

Theorem 2 ($\mathbf{SCP_D}$ and $\mathbf{SCP_I}$ are incomparable). *There are planning tasks Π and Π' with states $s \in S$ and $s' \in S'$ such that $h^{scp_D}(s) > h^{scp_i}(s)$ and $h^{scp_I}(s') > h^{scp_D}(s')$.* □

In Theorems 1 and 2, we investigated the relationship between OCP$_D$ and OCP$_I$, and between SCP$_D$ and SCP$_I$. Dominance of OCP$_D$ over SCP$_D$ and of OCP$_I$ over SCP$_I$ is clear. What is left is comparing SCP$_D$ to OCP$_I$.

Theorem 3 ($\mathbf{SCP_D}$ and $\mathbf{OCP_I}$ are incomparable). *There are a planning tasks Π and Π' with states $s \in S$ and $s' \in S'$ such that $h^{scp_D}(s) > h^{ocp_I}(s)$ and $h^{ocp_I}(s') > h^{scp_D}$.* □

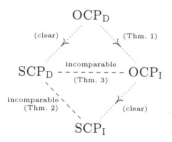

The figure to the left shows a summary of our theoretical results (where $A \succ B$ means A dominates B). Optimal state-dependent cost partitioning combines the best of both worlds, but computing it is exponential. Saturated state-dependent cost partitioning may not always result in better heuristic estimates, but it has the potential to surpass optimal state-independent cost partitioning.

5   Conclusion

We generalized cost partitionings and showed that additional information can be extracted from a set of abstractions if context information of applied actions is taken into account. We showed that an optimal state-dependent cost partitioning dominates all state-independent cost partitionings and that there are planning tasks where the dominance is strict. As it is unclear how an optimal state-dependent cost partitioning can be computed efficiently in practice, we applied the idea to the efficiently computable saturated cost partitioning. We showed that saturated state-dependent cost partitioning does not dominate its state-independent sibling, but may still surpass optimal state-independent cost partitioning. Preliminary experimental results are generally in line with what our theoretical results suggest.

Acknowledgments. This work was supported by the European Research Council as part of the project "State Space Exploration: Principles, Algorithms and Applications" and by BMBF grant 02PJ2667 as part of the KARIS PRO project.

References

1. Bäckström, C., Nebel, B.: Complexity results for SAS$^+$ planning. Comput. Intell. **11**(4), 625–655 (1995)
2. Culberson, J.C., Schaeffer, J.: Pattern databases. Comput. Intell. **14**(3), 318–334 (1998)
3. Felner, A., Korf, R., Hanan, S.: Additive pattern database heuristics. JAIR **22**, 279–318 (2004)
4. Geißer, F., Keller, T., Mattmüller, R.: Delete relaxations for planning with state-dependent action costs. In: Proceedings of the IJCAI 2015, pp. 1573–1579 (2015)
5. Geißer, F., Keller, T., Mattmüller, R.: Abstractions for planning with state-dependent action costs. In: Proceedings of the ICAPS 2016 (2016)
6. Haslum, P., Botea, A., Helmert, M., Bonet, B., Koenig, S.: Domain-independent construction of pattern database heuristics for cost-optimal planning. In: Proceedings of the AAAI 2007, pp. 1007–1012 (2007)
7. Katz, M., Domshlak, C.: Structural patterns of tractable sequentially-optimal planning. In: Proceedinngs of the ICAPS 2007, pp. 200–207 (2007)
8. Katz, M., Domshlak, C.: Optimal admissible composition of abstraction heuristics. AIJ **174**(12–13), 767–798 (2010)
9. Keller, T., Pommerening, F., Seipp, J., Geißer, F., Mattmüller, R.: State-dependent cost partitionings for cartesian abstractions in classical planning. In: Proceedings of the IJCAI 2016 (2016)
10. Keller, T., Pommerening, F., Seipp, J., Geißer, F., Mattmüller, R.: State-dependent cost partitionings for cartesian abstractions in classical planning: Full proofs. Technical report CS-2016-002, University of Basel, Switzerland (2016)
11. Korf, R.E., Felner, A.: Disjoint pattern database heuristics. AIJ **134**(1–2), 9–22 (2002)
12. Pommerening, F., Helmert, M., Röger, G., Seipp, J.: From non-negative to general operator cost partitioning. In: Proceedings of the AAAI 2015, pp. 3335–3341 (2015)
13. Röger, G., Pommerening, F., Helmert, M.: Optimal planning in the presence of conditional effects: extending LM-Cut with context splitting. In: Proceedings of the ECAI 2014, pp. 80–87 (2014)
14. Seipp, J., Helmert, M.: Counterexample-guided cartesian abstraction refinement. In: Proceedings of the ICAPS 2013, pp. 347–351 (2013)
15. Seipp, J., Helmert, M.: Diverse and additive Cartesian abstraction heuristics. In: Proceedings of the ICAPS 2014, pp. 289–297 (2014)

Group Decision Making via Probabilistic Belief Merging

Nico Potyka[1(✉)], Erman Acar[2], Matthias Thimm[3],
and Heiner Stuckenschmidt[2]

[1] University of Osnabrück, Osnabrück, Germany
nico.potyka@uni-osnabrueck.de
[2] University of Mannheim, Mannheim, Germany
[3] University of Koblenz, Mainz, Germany

Group decision making [4, 5, 8, 9, 11, 14] addresses the problem of finding a reasonable decision when multiple decision makers have different preferences. In this extended abstract, we give a high-level description of the key ideas from [20]. We explain how probabilistic belief merging can be applied to solve Group decision problems when the preferences can be derived from agents' individual utilities and beliefs. Subsequently, we discuss some guarantees that our approach can give regarding the relationship between the individual preferences and the derived group preferences.

Some group decision approaches consider dynamic aspects like communication between agents [16, 23]. Our group-decision approach is static, similar to social-choice approaches that take individual preferences for granted and apply voting rules to make a group decision from the individual preferences [3, 21]. However, instead of aggregating individual preferences directly, we aggregate their beliefs and utilities that (as we assume) constituted their preferences.

Our agent framework extends the single agent framework from [1]. Each agent is associated with an *individual knowledge base* that contains its personal beliefs, which are represented by probabilistic conditionals [12, 13]. Additionally, we consider a *public knowledge base* (again consisting of probabilistic conditionals) that contains beliefs shared by all agents. The *alternatives* from which our agents can choose are evaluated by different *criteria*, which can be expressed by relational formulas. Agents can assign different utility values to these criteria and can have diffent beliefs about which alternative satisfies which criterion. The following example illustrates these abstract terms.

Example 1. Let us consider two agents, which we will call 1 and 2 for simplicity. Our agents are about to choose a politician from a set of alternatives $\mathcal{A} = \{peter, nicole\}$. Our agents evaluate the candidates with respect to the criteria $\mathcal{C} = \{Honest(x), Intelligent(x)\}$. Agent 1 believes

---

Original paper appeared at the 25th International Joint Conference on Artificial Intelligence (IJCAI), 2016.

G. Friedrich et al. (Eds.): KI 2016, LNAI 9904, pp. 291–296, 2016.
DOI: 10.1007/978-3-319-46073-4

$$(Honest(peter))[0.2], (Honest(nicole))[0.9],$$
$$(Studied(peter, harvard))[1],$$
$$(Intelligent(x) \mid Studied(x,y) \wedge Prestigious(y))[0.9].$$

Note that a conditional $(B|A)[x]$ can be read as 'the probability of B given that A holds is x'. If A is tautological, we just write $(B)[x]$ and read this as 'the probability of B is x'. In particular, if $x = 1$, we basically have a logical rule. So, for instance, agent 1 believes that *nicole* is probably honest, while *peter* is probably not. Agent 2's knowledge base contains

$$(Honest(peter))[0.9], (Honest(nicole))[0.6],$$
$$(LooksIntelligent(nicole))[1],$$
$$(Intelligent(x) \mid LooksIntelligent(x))[0.8].$$

Our public knowledge base contains only the conditional (*Prestigious (harvard*)) [1]. We consider the utilities $u_1(Intelligent) = 70, u_2(Intelligent) = 80, u_1(Honest) = 40, u_2(Honest) = 95$. Note that agents cannot only have different beliefs about candidates, but also about the causes of different alternatives.

Given a set of agents along with their beliefs, we want to derive preferences from their expected utilities. Formally, we let *agent i's expected utility of alternative a* be

$$EU_i(a) = \sum_{C \in \mathcal{C}} \mathcal{B}_i(C(a)) \cdot u_i(C).$$

The sum ranges over all criteria and multiplies the belief $\mathcal{B}_i(C(a))$ that alternative a satisfies criterion C with agent i's utility of C. The individual beliefs $\mathcal{B}_i(C(a))$ are derived from the public beliefs and agent i's individual beliefs by means of *probabilistic entailment* [10, 13, 15]. $\mathcal{B}_i(C(a))$ is a probability interval, whose lower and upper bound corresponds to the minimum and maximum probability of $C(a)$ among all probability distributions that satisfy both the public beliefs and agent i's individual beliefs. If all agents's beliefs are consistent, we could also derive group beliefs for the agents by considering the multiset-union of all individual knowledge bases and the public knowledge base. However, in general this union can be inconsistent. That is, there exists no probability distribution that satisfies all the probabilistic conditionals in the union and so we will be unable to derive a group belief for $C(a)$. However, in order to overcome this problem, we can replace the distributions that satisfy the knowledge base with those that 'minimally violate it' [7, 17, 19]. This is the basic idea of *generalized probabilistic entailment* [19]. We can measure the violation of a knowledge base with respect to different norms, see [20] for more detailed explanations. Generalized probabilistic entailment indeed generalizes probabilistic entailment in the sense that the derived probabilities coincide whenever the knowledge base is consistent. We let $\mathcal{B}_G(C(a))$ denote the generalized probabilistic entailment result for $C(a)$ when using the multiset-union of all individual knowledge bases and the public knowledge base. The *group's expected utility interval of an alternative a* is

Table 1. Individual Beliefs $\mathcal{B}_1$, $\mathcal{B}_2$ and group belief $\mathcal{B}_G$ for Example 1 when measuring violation by the 1-norm.

	Honest		Intelligent	
	Nicole	Peter	Nicole	Peter
$\mathcal{B}_1$	$[0.9, 0.9]$	$[0.2, 0.2]$	$[0, 1]$	$[0.9, 0.9]$
$\mathcal{B}_2$	$[0.6, 0.6]$	$[0.9, 0.9]$	$[0.8, 0.8]$	$[0, 1]$
$\mathcal{B}_G$	$[0.6, 0.9]$	$[0.2, 0.9]$	$[0.8, 0.8]$	$[0.9, 0.9]$

Table 2. Expected utilities of individuals and the group for Example 1 when measuring violation by the 1-norm.

	Nicole	Peter
EU_1	$[36, 106]$	$[71, 71]$
EU_2	$[121, 121]$	$[85.5, 165.5]$
EU_G	$[100.5, 120.75]$	$[81, 128.25]$

$$EU_G(a) = \frac{1}{|N|} \sum_{i \in N} \sum_{C \in \mathcal{C}} \mathcal{B}_G(C(a)) \cdot u_i(C).$$

Intuitively, $\mathcal{B}_G(C(a))$ corresponds to the merged belief of the agents that alternative a satisfies C and $\frac{1}{|N|} \sum_{i \in N} u_i(C)$ corresponds to the agents' average utility of criterion C. Again, $\mathcal{B}_G(C(a))$ can yield a probability interval rather than a point probability. Given that the beliefs can be probability intervals in general, we get expected utility intervals rather than expected utilities. Tables 1 and 2 show the agents' beliefs and expected utilities for Example 1 to illustrate this.

Let us denote these intervals in the form $EU(a) = [\underline{EU(a)}, \overline{EU(a)}]$. We consider optimistic, pessimistic and cautious inference relations. Alternative a_1 is preferred over alternative a_2 iff

- Optimistic: $\overline{EU(a_1)} \geq \overline{EU(a_2)}$
- Pessimistic: $\underline{EU(a_1)} \geq \underline{EU(a_2)}$
- Cautious: $\underline{EU(a_1)} \geq \overline{EU(a_2)}$

At this point, our framework is completely defined. Starting from agents individual beliefs and utilities, we can derive group preferences from the group expected utilities. Of course, the question remains whether this approach can give us some meaningful guarantees. We will now discuss the intuition of several properties that group decision making by means of generalized probabilistic entailment satisfies. For a thorough formal investigation, we refer to [20] and the corresponding proof appendix.

To begin with, what can we say about the influence of the interactions between agents' beliefs on the expected utilities and the corresponding preference relations? Since it is difficult to make an objective statement about what we should expect in the presence of conflicts between agents' beliefs, we start with some intuitive properties that hold if there are no conflicts.

- *Cautious Dominance*: If the decision base is conflict-free and alternative a is cautiously preferred over b by all agents, then a will be cautiously preferred over b with respect to the group preferences.
- *Cautious Condorcet-Consistency*: If the decision base is conflict-free and alternative a is cautiously preferred over all b by all agents, then a will be cautiously preferred over all b with respect to the group preferences.
- *Consensus*: If the decision base is conflict-free, the expected utility of the group will be a refinement of the individual expected utilities in the sense that it yields a subinterval of the averaged individual belief intervals.

Dominance and Condorcet-Consistency correspond to social-choice-theoretic properties [21]. We conjecture that these properties also hold for optimistic and pessimistic preference relations, but proved this only for cautious preference. These properties actually still hold if there are only minor conflicts in the decision base as we can show formally by continuity arguments. Roughly speaking, we have the following result.

- *Continuity of Expected Utilities*: Minor changes in the agents' beliefs and utilities will result only in minor changes in the expected utilities. In particular, if there are only minor conflicts in the knowledge base, Consensus, Cautious Dominance and Cautious Condorcet-Consistency will still hold.

The computational problem of computing expected utilities can sometimes be simplified by exploiting independence structure.

- *Decomposition of Utility*: If the agents' beliefs are independent of each other, the problem of computing expected utilities can be decomposed.
- *Modularity*: If the agents' beliefs and utilities are independent of each other, then the expected utility of the decision base will be a weighted sum over the expected utilities of independent sub decision bases.

Finally, the choice of the norm that we use for generalized probabilistic entailment can control the influence of large interest groups.

- *Majority*: The influence of large interest groups on the aggregated group beliefs and preferences can be regulated by the choice of the norm.

Please consult [20] for a more thorough discussion of these properties.

In summary, we found that group decision making via generalized entailment satisfies several intuitive properties. The corresponding computational problems can be solved by convex optimization techniques [19], that is, non-global local minima are not an issue. Since we use generalized entailment for belief merging, we have to work with expected utility intervals rather than with point utilities. While this approach is unbiased in the sense that we consider all possible probability distributions that satisfy (minimally violate) agents' beliefs, it might be interesting to restrict to particular probability distribution in order to obtain stronger guarantees for the group decision. Interesting candidates are, for instance, selecting the probability distribution that maximizes entropy or minimizes some notion of distance to a prior distribution [2, 6, 18, 22]. We are planning to investigate this in more detail in future work.

References

1. Acar, E., Thorne, C., Stuckenschmidt, H.: Towards decision making via expressive probabilistic ontologies. In: Walsh, T. (ed.) ADT 2015. LNAI, vol. 9346, pp. 52–68. Springer, Heidelberg (2015). doi:10.1007/978-3-319-23114-3_4
2. Adamcik, M.: Collective reasoning under uncertainty and inconsistency, Ph.D. thesis. University of Manchester (2014)
3. Brandt, F., Conitzer, V., Endriss, U.: Computational Social Choice, pp. 213–283. MIT Press (2012)
4. Chambers, C.P., Hayashi, T.: Preference aggregation under uncertainty: savage vs. pareto. Games Econ. Behav. **54**(2), 430–440 (2006)
5. Crès, H., Gilboa, I., Vieille, N.: Aggregation of multiple prior opinions. J. Econ. Theory **146**(6), 2563–2582 (2011)
6. Daniel, L.: Paraconsistent probabilistic reasoning, Ph.D. thesis, L'École Nationale Supérieure des Mines de Paris (2009)
7. De Bona, G., Finger, M.: Measuring inconsistency in probabilistic logic: rationality postulates and dutch book interpretation. Artif. Intell. **227**, 140–164 (2015)
8. Gajdos, T., Tallon, J.M., Vergnaud, J.C.: Representation and aggregation of preferences under uncertainty. J. Econ. Theory **141**(1), 68–99 (2008)
9. Gilboa, I., Samet, D., Schmeidler, D.: Utilitarian aggregation of beliefs and tastes. J. Polit. Econ. **112**, 932–938 (2004)
10. Hansen, P., Jaumard, B.: Probabilistic satisfiability. In: Kohlas, J., Moral, S. (eds.) Handbook of Defeasible Reasoning and Uncertainty Management Systems, Handbook of Defeasible Reasoning and Uncertainty Management Systems, vol. 5, pp. 321–367. Springer, Netherlands (2000). http://dx.doi.org/10.1007/978-94-017-1737-3_8
11. Keeney, R., Raiffa, H.: Decisions with Multiple Objectives: Preferences and Value Tradeoffs. Wiley, New York (1976)
12. Kern-Isberner, G. (ed.): Conditionals in Nonmonotonic Reasoning and Belief Revision. LNCS, vol. 2087. Springer, Heidelberg (2001)
13. Lukasiewicz, T.: Probabilistic deduction with conditional constraints over basic events. J. Artif. Intell. Res. **10**, 380–391 (1999)
14. Nehring, K.: The impossibility of a paretian rational: a bayesian perspective. Econ. Lett. **96**(1), 45–50 (2007)
15. Nilsson, N.J.: Probabilistic logic. Artif. Intell. **28**, 71–88 (1986)
16. Panzarasa, P., Jennings, N.R., Norman, T.J.: Formalizing collaborative decision-making and practical reasoning in multi-agent systems. J. Log. Comput. **12**(1), 55–117 (2002)
17. Potyka, N.: Linear programs for measuring inconsistency in probabilistic logics. In: Proceedings KR 2014, pp. 568–578. AAAI Press (2014)
18. Potyka, N., Thimm, M.: Consolidation of probabilistic knowledge bases by inconsistency minimization. In: Proceedings ECAI 2014, pp. 729–734. IOS Press (2014)
19. Potyka, N., Thimm, M.: Probabilistic reasoning with inconsistent beliefs using inconsistency measures. In: International Joint Conference on Artificial Intelligence 2015 (IJCAI'15), pp. 3156–3163 (2015)

20. Potyka, N., Acar, E., Thimm, M., Stuckenschmidt, H.: Group decision making via probabilistic belief merging. In: International Joint Conference on Artificial Intelligence 2016 (IJCAI'16) (2016)
21. Shoham, Y., Leyton-Brown, K.: Multiagent Systems: Algorithmic, Game-Theoretic, and Logical Foundations. Cambridge University Press, New York (2008)
22. Wilmers, G.: A foundational approach to generalising the maximum entropy inference process to the multi-agent context. Entropy $17(2)$, 594–645 (2015)
23. Wooldridge, M., Jennings, N.R.: The cooperative problem-solving process. J. Log. Comput. $9(4)$, 563–592 (1999)

Simulating Human Inferences in the Light of New Information: A Formal Analysis

Marco Ragni[2(✉)], Christian Eichhorn[1], and Gabriele Kern-Isberner[1]

[1] Technische Universität Dortmund, Dortmund, Germany
{christian.eichhorn,gabriele.kern-isberner}@cs.tu-dortmund.de
[2] Technical Faculty, University of Freiburg, Freiburg Im Breisgau, Germany
ragni@informatik.uni-freiburg.de

1 Introduction and Overview

Being able to reason nonmonotonically is crucial both for many practical applications of artificial intelligence and for humans in their everyday lives. It has been shown that humans deviate systematically from classical logic, in particular with respect to revising previously drawn conclusions, and they are very successful in solving their everyday problems this way. Although many approaches to default and nonmonotonic reasoning in artificial intelligence have been developed in close correspondence to human commonsense reasoning, only few empirical studies have actually been carried out to support the claim that nonmonotonic and default logics are indeed suitable to formally represent human reasoning (e.g., [9, 11], and they are mostly motivated from the points of view of computer science. In this paper, we focus on a core research problem that had been raised first in psychology and was one of the first examples to make the nonmonotonicity phenomenon obvious for psychologists: The so-called *suppression task* was introduced in [1] to show that additional information may cause humans to give up conclusions which they have drawn previously via modus ponens. More precisely, three groups of participants received one of three types of problems: $\alpha\delta$ (Group 1), $\alpha\beta\delta$ (Group 2, also referred to as *β-case*), and $\alpha\gamma\delta$ (Group 3, also referred to as *γ-case*), where α, β, γ are symbols for the following sentences:

(α) *If she has an essay to write (e),*
then she will study late in the library (l) and
(β) *If she has a textbook to read (t) ,*
then she will study late in the library (l) and
(δ) *She has an essay to write. (e)*

(α) *If she has an essay to write (e),*
then she will study late in the library (l) and
(γ) *If the library stays open (o),*
she will study late in the library (l) and
(δ) *She has an essay to write. (e)*

Both for Group 1 and 2, most participants (98 %) in the study concluded: *She will study late in the library.* However, for Group 3, the γ-case, only 38 % of the

---

Original paper appeared at the 25th International Joint Conference on Artificial Intelligence (IJCAI), 2016.

G. Kern-Isberner—This work is supported by DFG-Grants KI1413/5-1 to G. Kern-Isberner and by RA1934 2/1 and a Heisenberg DFG fellowship RA1934 3/1 to M. Ragni. C. Eichhorn is supported by Grant KI1413/5-1.

G. Friedrich et al. (Eds.): KI 2016, LNAI 9904, pp. 297–302, 2016.
DOI: 10.1007/978-3-319-46073-4

participants made a modus ponens inference [1] and concluded that *She will study late in the library* while 62 % concluded that *She may or may not study late in the library.* This example shows that although the conclusion "she will study late in the library" is still correct, it is suppressed by the γ-conditional, but not by the β-conditional. This study shows not only that humans are capable of drawing *non-monotonic* inferences but that the semantical contents of the additional conditional that may hint a reasoner to exceptions of the α-conditional is crucial to suppress inference.

The aim of the paper [12] is to analyze the inferences provided by major formal approaches to nonmonotonic reasoning in the suppression task, more precisely, we investigate system P [8], logic programming under weak completion semantics [2, 18], Reiter's default logic [14] under skeptical semantics, system Z [3], and c-representations [5, 6]. In particular, we evaluate whether they can reflect human inferences observed in the empirical studies. A bit surprisingly, not many of them succeed in modeling the suppression task. We discuss formal properties of successful theories and general insights of how to improve the inferences.

This paper is an extended abstract of [12], more detailed information, in particular on formal background and technical issues, can be found in that paper.

2   Nonmonotonic Reasoning and the Suppression Task

There are at least two ways how a formalism can be evaluated: The so-called *conceptual cognitive-adequacy* (Is the formal representation of a reasoning system similar to human mental representations?) and the so-called *inferential cognitive-adequacy* (Are the inferences a reasoning system draws similar/identical to human inferences?) of a reasoning system [7, 15, 18]. With respect to the suppression task, it is crucial how we interpret the conditional statements (conceptual cognitive-adequacy) and the inference system that we apply (inferential cognitive-adequacy). There are different ways how a conditional given in natural language as, e.g., "if e then l" can be interpreted. The first possibility is to interpret it as material implication (in propositional logic) which, however, is linked to monotonic reasoning. A nonmonotonic inference $e \mathrel{|\!\sim} l$ expresses "if e is true, then *typically* l is true as well", weakening the strong deduction relation. On the syntactical level, conditionals $(B|A)$ express such weakened relationships between antecedent A and consequent B; in particular, conditionals are often used to express rules that may have exceptions, "if A then *usually* B". In logic programming approaches, this is represented by a weakening of a conditional by an abnormality predicate (ab), and with this the implementation of the γ-case is

$$\{l \leftarrow e \wedge \neg \, \mathrm{ab}_1, l \leftarrow o \wedge \neg \, \mathrm{ab}_2, \mathrm{ab}_1 \leftarrow \overline{o}, \mathrm{ab}_2 \leftarrow \overline{e}, e \leftarrow \top\}. \qquad (1)$$

We used conditional knowledge bases for system P, system Z, and c-representations, default rules for Reiter's default logic, and logic program rules from [2, 18] to model the suppression task. We translated the sentences α, β, γ

as literally as possible into the respective language. Except for logic programming under the weak completion semantics [2, 18], all nonmonotonic systems failed to reproduce the suppression task – even in the γ-case, from "she has an essay to write", the systems inferred "she will study late in the library". In the following we will exemplify our studies by briefly reporting on the conclusions c-representations draw and show how making background knowledge explicit can indeed lead to reproduce the suppression task.

2.1   A Case Study: Modeling by C-Representations

As demonstrated above the way humans understand conditionals can be modeled using logic programming with WCS with an adequate implementation of the knowledge. We can also consider to model and predict inferences based on an epistemic state in the sense of [4], for instance based on a preferential model [10] with a preference relation induced by an *Ordinal Conditional Function* (ranking function, OCF [16, 17]). An OCF is a function $\kappa : \Omega \to \mathbb{N}_0^\infty$ that assigns to each world $\omega \in \Omega$ an implausibility rank, that is, the higher $\kappa(\omega)$, the less plausible the world is, where the most plausible worlds have a rank of 0. c-representations [5, 6] assign to each conditional in the knowledge base $\mathcal{R} = \{(\psi_1|\phi_1), \ldots, (\psi_n|\phi_n)\}$ an impact $\kappa_i^- \in \mathbb{N}_0$. The rank of a world is the composed impact of all falsified conditionals, so a c-representation κ_Δ^c is an OCF defined by

$$\kappa_\Delta^c(\omega) = \sum_{\omega \models \phi_i \land \neg \psi_i} \kappa_i^-, \tag{2}$$

where the individual impacts $\kappa_i^- \in \mathbb{N}_0$ are chosen such that κ_Δ^c is admissible with respect to Δ, which is the case if the impacts satisfy the following system of inequations [5, 6]:

$$\kappa_i^- > \min_{\substack{\omega \in \Omega \\ \omega \models \phi_i \land \psi_i}} \left\{ \sum_{\substack{1 \le j \le n, j \ne i \\ \omega \models \phi_j \land \neg \psi_j}} \kappa_j^- \right\} - \min_{\substack{\omega \in \Omega \\ \omega \models \phi_i \land \neg \psi_i}} \left\{ \sum_{\substack{1 \le j \le n, j \ne i \\ \omega \models \phi_j \land \neg \psi_j}} \kappa_j^- \right\} \tag{3}$$

The (as literal as possible translated) knowledge base of the γ case is the set

$$\Delta^\gamma = \{\delta_1 = (l|e), \delta_2 = (l|t), \delta_3 = (e|\top)\}. \tag{γ-case}$$

The values $\kappa_1^- = 1$, $\kappa_2^- = 0$ and $\kappa_3^- = 1$ are a minimal solution of the system of inequations (3) applied to this knowledge base, and with (2) these values result in the OCF $\kappa_{\Delta^\gamma}^c(\omega)$ given Table 1. Here, $\kappa_{\Delta^\gamma}^c(l) = 0 < 1 = \kappa_{\Delta^\gamma}^c(\bar{l})$ and thus we can infer that "she will study late in the library", so no suppression effect occurs.

This could be the result of a different understanding of the sentence (γ), in such a way that it could be understood as "if she studies late in the library, the library is open", named the γ'-case.

$$\Delta^{\gamma'} = \{\delta_1 : (l|e), \delta_4 : (o|l), \delta_3 : (e|\top)\} \tag{γ'-case}$$

The computations for the minimal c-representations for this knowledge base can be found in [12], Table 1 gives the resulting OCF. In this modeling, we also do not find a suppression effect: we obtain $\kappa^c_{\Delta\gamma'}(l) = 0 < 1 = \kappa^c_{\Delta\gamma'}(\bar{l})$ and therefore can infer l.

2.2 Modeling the Suppression Effect by Expliciting Background Knowledge

As we have seen in the previous subsection, c-representations and system Z do not replicate the suppression effect. In the following, we show that it is possible to mimic the suppression effect using c-representations and system Z, as it was already demonstrated for logic programming with WCS. In the implementation of the γ-case in logic programming (1) [18], the weak completion steps connect the variables o and e in the head of a rule via the abnormality predicate. This connection is crucial for the retraction of the MP inference in the γ-case. We hence modeled this connection for the γ and γ' cases, but not in the β-case where the additional information (β) does not represent an additional requirement for "studying late in the library" (as (γ)), but an additional explanation for "studying late in the library"; this differentiation between the models of the different cases can also be found in the implementation of the suppression task in logic programming [18]. The different modelings as well as the results of these modelings are summarized in Table 1, the computations can be found in [12]. Since the set of maximally plausible worlds is identical both for system Z and c-representations, these results hold for both approaches. We obtain that in the modelings of the β-case, the inference l can be drawn, which is not the case both in the cases γ and γ', so we find a suppression effect for these cases, but not for the β-case, which follows the inference pattern found in the original study [1]. It can be seen that the connection of the premises (second row of the γ-case in Table 1: right) is sufficient for evoking a suppression effect, which is then preserved in the completion step (fourth row of the γ-case in Table 1: right).

Another line of thought that, in general, might cover human inferences even better would be to generate the OCF κ from the generic knowledge (in this example the default rules (α), (β), and (γ)) and revise this epistemic state with

Table 1. Left: OCFs obtained by system Z and minimal c-representations for the cases γ, γ', and γ''. **Right:** System Z and c-representations mimicking the weak completion semantics approach for the β, γ, γ'-cases. Tables taken from [12].

ω	elo	$el\bar{o}$	$e\bar{l}o$	$e\bar{l}\bar{o}$	$\bar{e}lo$	$\bar{e}l\bar{o}$	$\bar{e}\bar{l}o$	$\bar{e}\bar{l}\bar{o}$
$\kappa^c_{\Delta\gamma}(\omega)$	0	1	1	1	1	1	2	1
$\kappa^c_{\Delta\gamma'}(\omega)$	0	1	2	1	1	2	1	1

Problems	β	γ	γ'
knowledge base	$(l\|e)$ $(l\|t)$	$(l\|eo)$	$(l\|eo)$ $(o\|le)$
Belief sets	$Cn(el)$	$Cn(el \vee e\bar{l}\bar{o})$	$Cn(elo \vee e\bar{l}\bar{o})$
wcs knowledge base	$(l\|e)$ $(l\|t)$ $(e \vee t\|l)$	$(l\|eo)$ $(eo\|l)$	$(l\|eo)$ $(eo\|l)$ $(o\|le)$ $(le\|o)$
Belief sets	$Cn(el)$	$Cn(elo \vee e\bar{l}\bar{o})$	$Cn(elo \vee e\bar{l}\bar{o})$
Percentage	96%	38%	n/a

the evidential knowledge (in this example the statement (δ)). This modeling follows the view that (α), (β), (γ) represent generic knowledge that is applied to (δ) [13]. For the small examples considered here, that is, the knowledge bases of the β- and γ-case, having ($e|\top$) in the knowledge base or revising with e does not make a difference, technically, that is, using this modeling yields the same results as already given in Table 1.

3 Discussion

The differences in the results produced by the different nonmonotonic systems cannot be explained by formal properties. In this sense the suppression task can form a further benchmark for many nonmonotonic systems to evaluate their fitness to simulate human common sense reasoning. One advantage is that the formal properties of these nonmonotonic systems are known. By and large, system P has been accepted as a good formal standard of nonmonotonic inference relations, system Z and c-representations are even stronger since both satisfy rational monotony [10]. Both Reiter's default logic and logic programming under weak completion semantics fail to satisfy system P, more precisely, they do not fulfill cautious monotony [10, 12]. Analyzing the different modelings more closely, we find that the logic programming rules allow for making slight differences in the β- and γ-case that reflect background knowledge. By enriching our conditional knowledge bases so that the inference procedure can also make use of such background knowledge, we find that both system Z and c-representations can reproduce the suppression effect.

This opens a long debate in psychology that has not yet been resolved satisfactorily: How much on the reasoning process depends on a cognitively-adequate inference system (be it syntactically, semantically, heuristic or probabilistic) and how much depends on possible background information that can ease the inference process? While such a question is rather difficult to answer if we consider non-formal systems and reasoning about everyday reasoning scenarios abstract domains may help further to distinguish the influence of these two sources for reasoning [9].

References

1. Byrne, R.M.: Suppressing valid inferences with conditionals. Cognition **31**, 61–83 (1989)
2. Dietz, E., Hölldobler, S., Ragni, M.: A computational approach to the suppression task. In: Miyake, N., Peebles, D., Cooper, R. (eds.) Proceedings of the 34th annual conference of the cognitive science society, pp. 1500–1505. Cognitive Science Society, Austin (2012)
3. Goldszmidt, M., Pearl, J.: Qualitative probabilities for default reasoning, belief revision, and causal modeling. Artif. Intell. **84**(1–2), 57–112 (1996)
4. Halpern, J.Y.: Reasoning About Uncertainty. MIT Press, Cambridge (2005)
5. Kern-Isberner, G. (ed.): Conditionals in Nonmonotonic Reasoning and Belief Revision. LNCS, vol. 2087. Springer, Heidelberg (2001)

6. Kern-Isberner, G.: A thorough axiomatization of a principle of conditional preservation in belief revision. Ann. Math. Artif. Intell. **40**, 127–164 (2004)
7. Knauff, M.: The cognitive adequacy of allen's interval calculus for qualitative spatial representation and reasoning. Spat. Cogn. Comput. **1**(3), 261–290 (1999)
8. Kraus, S., Lehmann, D., Magidor, M.: Nonmonotonic reasoning, preferential models and cumulative logics. Artif. Intell. J. **44**, 167–207 (1990)
9. Kuhnmünch, G., Ragni, M.: Can formal non-monotonic systems properly describe human reasoning? In: Bello, P., Guarini, M., McShane, M., Scassellati, B. (eds.) Proceedings of the 36th Annual Conference of the Cognitive Science Society, pp. 1222–1228. Cognitive Science Society, Austin (2014)
10. Makinson, D.: General patterns in nonmonotonic reasoning. In: Gabbay, D.M., Hogger, C.J., Robinson, J.A. (eds.) Handbook of Logic in Artificial Intelligence and Logic Programming, vol. 3, pp. 35–110. Oxford University Press, New York (1994)
11. Neves, R., Bonnefon, J., Raufaste, E.: An empirical test of patterns for nonmonotonic inference. Ann. Math. Artif. Intell. **34**(1–3), 107–130 (2002)
12. Ragni, M., Eichhorn, C., Kern-Isberner, G.: Simulating human inferences in the light of new information: a formal analysis. In: Proceedings of the 25th International Joint Conference on Artificial Intelligence, IJCAI 2016 (2016, to appear)
13. Ramsey, F.P.: General propositions and causality. In: Philosophical Papers, pp. 145–163. Cambridge University Press, Cambridge (1929)
14. Reiter, R.: A logic for default reasoning. Artif. Intell. **13**(1–2), 81–132 (1980)
15. Renz, J., Rauh, R., Knauff, M.: Towards cognitive adequacy of topological spatial relations. In: Freksa, C., Habel, C., Brauer, W., Wender, K.F. (eds.) Spatial Cognition II. LNCS, vol. 1849, pp. 184–197. Springer, Heidelberg (2000)
16. Spohn, W.: Ordinal conditional functions: a dynamic theory of epistemic states. In: Proceedings of the Irvine Conference on Probability and Causation. Causation in Decision, Belief Change and Statistics. The Western Ontario Series in Philosophy of Science, vol. 42, pp. 105–134. Springer, Dordrecht (1988)
17. Spohn, W.: The Laws of Belief: Ranking Theory and Its Philosophical Applications. Oxford University Press, Oxford (2012)
18. Stenning, K., Lambalgen, M.: Human Reasoning and Cognitive Science. Bradford Books, MIT Press, Cambridge (2008)

Efficient Determination of Measurement Points for Sequential Diagnosis

Kostyantyn Shchekotykhin[1], Thomas Schmitz[2(✉)], and Dietmar Jannach[2]

[1] Alpen-Adria University Klagenfurt, Klagenfurt, Austria
kostyantyn.shchekotykhin@aau.at
[2] TU Dortmund, Dortmund, Germany
{Thomas.Schmitz,Dietmar.Jannach}@tu-dortmund.de

Abstract. Model-Based Diagnosis is a principled AI approach to determine the possible explanations why a system under observation behaves unexpectedly. For complex systems the number of such explanations can be too large to be inspected manually by a user. In these cases *sequential diagnosis* approaches can be applied. In order to find the true cause of the problem, these approaches iteratively take additional measurements to narrow down the set of possible explanations.

One computationally demanding challenge in such sequential diagnosis settings can be to determine the "best" next measurement point. This paper summarizes the key ideas of our recently proposed sequential diagnosis approach, which uses the newly introduced concept of "partial" diagnoses to significantly speed up the process of determining the next measurement point. The resulting overall reductions of the required computation times to find the true cause of the problem are quantified using different benchmark problems and were achieved without the need for any information about the structure of the system.

Keywords: Model-based diagnosis · Sequential diagnosis · Conflicts

1 Introduction

Model-Based Diagnosis (MBD) techniques are used to determine the possible causes when an observed system behaves unexpectedly. To find the possible causes, these approaches use knowledge about the system's expected behavior when all of its components work correctly. Since their development in the 1980s [1, 9, 7], MBD-based approaches were applied to many different problem settings like electronic circuits and software artifacts, e.g., java programs, knowledge bases, logic programs, ontologies, and spreadsheets.

When applying MBD for complex systems, the number of possible diagnoses can be too large to be checked individually by a user. For example, even when we

This work was supported by the Carinthian Science Fund (contract KWF-3520/26767/38701), the Austrian Science Fund (contract I 2144 N-15) and the German Research Foundation (contract JA 2095/4-1).

This paper summarizes the work from [14], presented at IJCAI'16.

© Springer International Publishing AG 2016
G. Friedrich et al. (Eds.): KI 2016, LNAI 9904, pp. 303–309, 2016.
DOI: 10.1007/978-3-319-46073-4

only search for diagnoses up to a size of five, there are already 6,944 diagnoses for the system *c432 (scenario 0)* of the DX 2011 diagnosis competition benchmark.

Different approaches to deal with the problem exist. One option is to rank the diagnoses based on weights or fault probabilities and return only the highest ranked ones. However, these methods might be incomplete in cases when existing information is not sufficient to give a high rank to the correct explanation of a fault. Another possibility is to take additional measurements to discriminate between fault causes [7], thereby ensuring completeness. A recent work of Shchekotykhin et al. compared two different strategies for taking the next measurement, applied to the problem of ontology debugging [11]. The result indicates that the computation of a query, i.e., a suggestion for a next measurement to be made by a user, can be computationally expensive. Therefore, the approach of [11] first searches for a few *leading* diagnoses and then determines the optimal query to the user. However, for some real-world cases the computation of even a few leading diagnoses remains challenging [12].

In our work we address this problem setting and aim to reduce the diagnosis computation time. Specifically, the technical contribution of our work is the new notion of "partial" diagnoses, which can be efficiently computed using only a subset of the minimal conflicts. The partial diagnoses are then used to determine the best next query, i.e., we determine the best possible partitioning of the partial diagnoses, which typically form a smaller search space than in the original problem setting. In [14] we proved that our method remains complete, i.e., it is guaranteed that the true problem cause – called *preferred* diagnosis – will be found. An experimental evaluation on different benchmarks shows significant reductions of the diagnosis time compared to previous works. Our method furthermore is not dependent on the availability of application-specific problem decomposition methods and can therefore be applied to efficiently diagnose all kinds of systems without exploiting problem-specific structural characteristics.

2   Sequential Diagnosis

Our technique is based on the approach to sequential (interactive) diagnosis developed in [7, 9]. A diagnosable system in this approach is represented by a *model*, which describes the normal behavior of a system in terms of components and relations between them. In many scenarios models are encoded using constants representing the components and first-order sentences representing the relations. A diagnosis problem arises when the observed behavior of the system – represented as a finite set of consistent first-order sentences – differs from the expected one, represented by the model. In this case, a diagnosis Δ corresponds to a set of components that, if assumed to be faulty, explains the observed misbehavior.

In our approach – as in many others – the computation of diagnoses is based on the concept of conflicts. Informally speaking a minimal conflict is an irreducible set of components that cannot all work correctly at the same time given the observations. To resolve a minimal conflict every diagnosis therefore needs to comprise at least one of its components. Given a method for computing minimal conflicts such as QUICKXPLAIN [5] or PROGRESSION [8], algorithms like HS-Tree [9] find *all diagnoses* **D** by enumerating all subset-minimal hitting sets of the set of *all minimal conflicts* **CS**.

If an MBD system returns more diagnoses than can be manually inspected, additional information is required in order to find the so-called *preferred* diagnosis Δ^*, which corresponds to the set of actually faulty components. This information is usually specified by means of measurements expressed as first-order sentences [2, 7, 9]. However, it is often unclear which measurements must be taken to uniquely determine Δ^*. In order to find Δ^*, sequential methods ask a user or some oracle a number of queries. The answers to these queries provide measurements required to rule out irrelevant diagnoses [7, 11].[1] The problem in this context is to determine "good" measurement points and correspondingly construct a set of first-order sentences Q, called *query*. Given a set of diagnoses $D \subseteq$ **D**, queries are designed such that at least one element of D can be ruled out regardless of the answer. If more than one query is possible, the best one can be selected using strategies like split-in-half, entropy, or risk-optimization [7, 10].

3   Query Computation with Partial Diagnoses

Our algorithm operates on the basis of "partial" diagnoses, which can informally be defined as follows: Given a set of minimal conflicts $C \subseteq$ **CS**, a set of components δ is a *partial diagnosis* iff it is a subset-minimal hitting set of C. Our algorithm repeatedly searches for preferred partial diagnoses and thereby incrementally identifies the preferred diagnosis Δ^*. In contrast to existing sequential approaches, we do not compute *all* conflicts required to find a set of diagnoses D in each iteration, but only determine a subset of the minimal conflicts. Finding such a subset of the existing minimal conflicts can be done, e.g., with the MERGEXPLAIN method [13]. Then, we find a set of minimal hitting sets *for this subset of the conflicts*, which correspond to partial diagnoses.

In the first step of our overall diagnosis algorithm, we compute at most k minimal conflicts C. In case there are no conflicts, i.e., the provided system description is consistent with all observations and measurements, the algorithm returns $\Delta^* = \emptyset$ as a diagnosis. Next, for the minimal conflicts C it finds a set of partial diagnoses PD. If PD comprises only one partial diagnosis, then its only element δ^* is returned as the *preferred partial diagnosis*. Otherwise, the algorithm determines a query Q to discriminate between the elements of PD and provides it to the oracle. The query computation method internally uses the underlying problem-specific reasoning engine to derive the consequences of the different answers to possible queries. This engine can for example be a Description Logic reasoner in case of ontology debugging problems [4, 11] or a constraint solver when the problem is to diagnose digital circuits [7].

Given an answer of the oracle the algorithm adds the corresponding first-order sentences to the set of measurements. This update requires the set C to be

---

[1] As in previous works we assume the oracle to answer correctly.

reviewed because some of its elements might not be minimal conflicts given the new measurements. Then, the set of partial diagnoses is updated by removing all elements of PD that are not partial diagnoses with respect to the updated set of minimal conflicts C. Finally, the algorithm recursively calls itself and continues the search until the preferred partial diagnosis is found.

Given a preferred partial diagnosis, we declare all its components as faulty and check whether the model is consistent with the observations. If this is the case, the set of all faulty components, corresponding to the preferred diagnosis, is returned. Otherwise, the algorithm starts searching for the next preferred partial diagnosis. The suggested algorithm is shown to be sound and complete given correct answers of an oracle to its queries.

Example 1. Let us consider the system 74L85, Scenario 10, from the DX Competition 2011 Synthetic Track (DXC 2011). There are three minimal conflicts: $\mathbf{CS} = \{\{o1\}, \{o2, z2, z22\}, \{o2, o3, z7, z9, z10, z11, z12, z13, z14, z17, z18, z19, z22, z27\}\}$. These conflicts are not known in advance. The number of minimal hitting sets (diagnoses) for $\mathbf{CS}$ is 14, i.e., $|\mathbf{D}| = 14$. The preferred diagnosis Δ^* as specified in the benchmark is $\{o1, z22\}$.

The interactive diagnosis process starts with the computation of a subset C of all minimal conflicts using MERGEXPLAIN, e.g., $C=\{\{o1\}, \{o2, z2, z22\}\}$. We then compute the minimal hitting sets of C and partial diagnoses $PD=\{\{o1, o2\}, \{o1, z2\}, \{o1, z22\}\}$. Next, we use PD to find the query o2 asking the user if component $\{o2\}$ is faulty. Since o2 is correct, the user answers "no". Given the answer we update the conflicts in C, i.e., $C=\{\{o1\}, \{z2, z22\}\}$ as well as PD. From the latter we remove all elements that are no partial diagnoses for the updated set of C resulting in $PD=\{\{o1, z2\}, \{o1, z22\}\}$.

In the second iteration we first search for new partial diagnoses. Since we have already found all partial diagnoses for the conflicts in C, PD remains unchanged and non-empty. Therefore, we compute a new query asking if $\{z22\}$ is faulty and the user answers "yes". This means that the preferred diagnosis must be a superset of $\{z22\}$ and we can remove all elements of PD that do not contain z22, resulting in $PD=\{\{o1, z22\}\}$. The third iteration returns $\{o1, z22\}$ as the preferred partial diagnosis δ^*, since no additional partial diagnosis can be found.

Next, the algorithm declares the components $\{o1, z22\}$ as faulty and finds that this assumption explains the observed misbehavior. Therefore, it returns $\Delta^*=\{o1, z22\}$ as the preferred diagnosis and ignores the third conflict in $\mathbf{CS}$. As a result, only two queries were required to find the true diagnosis.

4   Experimental Evaluation

We evaluated our method on two sets of benchmark problems: (a) the ontologies of the OAEI Conference benchmark as used in [12], (b) the systems of the DXC 2011. As the main performance measure we use the wall clock time to find the preferred diagnosis. The oracle's deliberation time to answer a query was assumed to be independent of the query as done in [12]. In addition, we evaluated how many queries were required to find the preferred diagnosis and how many statements were queried. We compared the following strategies:

1. INV-HS-DFS: The Inverse-HS-Tree method proposed in [12] which computes diagnoses using Inverse QuickXplain and builds a search tree in depth-first manner to find additional diagnoses.
2. INV-HS-BFS: A breadth-first variant of INV-HS-DFS, similar to [3].
3. QXP-HS-DFS: A depth-first variant of Reiter's Hitting-Set-Tree algorithm [9] using QUICKXPLAIN to find all conflicts required for complete diagnoses.
4. MXP-HS-DFS: Our proposed method which uses MERGEXPLAIN to find a set of conflicts and a depth-first variant of Reiter's Hitting-Set-Tree algorithm [9] to find partial diagnoses based on the found conflicts.

We compared our approach MXP-HS-DFS to these other three, because the performance of each of them highly depends on the problem characteristics. Overall, we expect the Inverse-HS-Tree methods to be faster than QXP-HS-DFS for most of the tested problems. For all strategies, we set the number of diagnoses n that are used to determine the optimal query to 9 as done in [12], and used the best-performing Entropy strategy for query selection. We did not set a limit on the number of conflicts to search for during a single call of MERGEXPLAIN. For the ontology benchmark, the failure probabilities used by the Entropy strategy are predefined. For the DXC problems, we used random probabilities and added a small bias for the actually faulty components to simulate partial user knowledge about the faulty components. The components were ordered according to the probabilities, which is advantageous for the conflict detection process for all tested algorithms. To simulate the oracle, we implemented a software agent that knew the preferred diagnosis in advance and answered all queries accordingly. All tests were performed on a modern laptop computer. The algorithms were implemented in Java. Choco was used as a constraint solver and HermiT as Description Logic reasoner.

For the ontologies the runtime improvements of our approach compared to the fastest of the other ones range from 28 % for one of the simplest ontologies to 93 % for the most complex one, for which the calculation time could be reduced from 6 min to 23 s. On average the improvements are as high as 80 %. Looking at the number of required interactions and queried statements, our method is also advantageous for the most complex problems. For some ontologies, however, using partial diagnoses requires the user to answer more questions.

The results for the DXC problems corroborate these observations. Except for the tiny problems, which can be solved in fractions of a second with all approaches, significant improvements in terms of the running times could be achieved with our method compared to all other approaches. For the DXC problems, INV-HS-DFS was the fastest of the other approaches. The strongest relative improvement of our approach compared with this method is at 86 %; on average, the performance improvement is at 58 %. For those systems where the computation times of INV-HS-DFS were more than one second, the average improvement is as high as 77 %. Some of the benchmark problems could not be solved by some of the other approaches at all in 24 h. QXP-HS-DFS, which was the fastest of the other methods for the ontologies, could, for example, not find the preferred diagnosis for the three most complex systems. The most complex system could not be diagnosed in 24 h by any of the other approaches, while our new approach MXP-HS-DFS finished in about 40 min.

5   Conclusion

In this work we presented a new approach to speed up the sequential diagnosis process. Our approach uses the new concept of partial diagnoses to reduce the computation time needed to determine the next best question to ask to the user. This can be particularly useful in cases when many conflicts exist.

In our future work we plan to additionally speed up the process of determining the leading diagnoses by incorporating additional information, e.g., the system's structure or prior fault probabilities of the components, and will explore if such information can help us to generate more informative queries.

References

1. Davis, R.: Diagnostic reasoning based on structure and behavior. Artif. Intell. **24**(1–3), 347–410 (1984)
2. Felfernig, A., Friedrich, G., Jannach, D., Stumptner, M.: Consistency-based diagnosis of configuration knowledge bases. Artif. Intell. **152**(2), 213–234 (2004)
3. Felfernig, A., Schubert, M., Zehentner, C.: An efficient diagnosis algorithm for inconsistent constraint sets. AI EDAM **26**(1), 53–62 (2012)
4. Horridge, M., Parsia, B., Sattler, U.: Laconic and precise justifications in OWL. In: Sheth, A., Staab, S., Dean, M., Paolucci, M., Maynard, D., Finin, T., Thirunarayan, K. (eds.) ISWC 2008. LNCS, vol. 5318, pp. 323–338. Springer, Heidelberg (2008). doi:10.1007/978-3-540-88564-1_21
5. Junker, U.: QUICKXPLAIN: preferred explanations and relaxations for over-constrained problems. In: AAAI 2004, pp. 167–172 (2004)
6. de Kleer, J.: Readings in model-based diagnosis. In: Focusing on Probable Diagnosis, pp. 131–137 (1992)
7. de Kleer, J., Williams, B.C.: Diagnosing multiple faults. Artif. Intell. **32**(1), 97–130 (1987)
8. Marques-Silva, J., Janota, M., Belov, A.: Minimal sets over monotone predicates in boolean formulae. In: Sharygina, N., Veith, H. (eds.) CAV 2013. LNCS, vol. 8044, pp. 592–607. Springer, Heidelberg (2013). doi:10.1007/978-3-642-39799-8_39
9. Reiter, R.: A theory of diagnosis from first principles. Artif. Intell. **32**(1), 57–95 (1987)
10. Rodler, P., Shchekotykhin, K., Fleiss, P., Friedrich, G.: RIO: minimizing user interaction in ontology debugging. In: Faber, W., Lembo, D. (eds.) RR 2013. LNCS, vol. 7994, pp. 153–167. Springer, Heidelberg (2013). doi:10.1007/978-3-642-39666-3_12
11. Shchekotykhin, K., Friedrich, G., Fleiss, P., Rodler, P.: Interactive ontology debugging: two query strategies for efficient fault localization. J. Web Semant. **12–13**, 88–103 (2012)
12. Shchekotykhin, K., Friedrich, G., Rodler, P., Fleiss, P.: Sequential diagnosis of high cardinality faults in knowledge-bases by direct diagnosis generation. In: ECAI 2014, pp. 813–818 (2014)

13. Shchekotykhin, K., Jannach, D., Schmitz, T.: MergeXplain: fast computation of multiple conflicts for diagnosis. IJCAI **2015**, 3221–3228 (2015)
14. Shchekotykhin, K., Schmitz, T., Jannach, D.: Efficient sequential model-based fault-Localization with partial diagnoses. In: IJCAI 2016 (2016)

Discriminatively Trained Recurrent Neural Networks for Continuous Dimensional Emotion Recognition from Audio

Felix Weninger[1][✉], Fabien Ringeval[2], Erik Marchi[2], and Björn Schuller[2,3]

[1] MISP/MMK, Technische Universität München, Munich, Germany
weninger@tum.de
[2] Chair of Complex and Intelligent Systems, University of Passau, Passau, Germany
[3] Department of Computing, Imperial College London, London, UK

Abstract. In many sequential regression problems, the goal is to maximize correlation between sequences of regression outputs and continuous-valued training targets, while minimizing the average deviation. For example, in continuous dimensional emotion recognition sequences of acoustic features have to be mapped to emotion contours. As in other domains, recurrent neural networks achieve good performance on this task. Yet, the usual squared error objective functions for neural network training do not fully take into account the above-named goal. Hence, in this paper we introduce a technique for the discriminative training of neural networks using the concordance correlation coefficient as cost function. Results on the MediaEval 2013 and RECOLA databases show that the proposed method can significantly improve the evaluation criteria compared to standard mean squared error training, both in the music and speech domains.

Keywords: Discriminative training · Recurrent neural networks · Concordance correlation coefficient · Dimensional emotion recognition · Audio

1 Introduction

Continuous dimensional emotion recognition from audio is a sequential learning problem that has recently attracted increasing attention [1, 8, 9]. There, sequences of acoustic features from, e.g., speech utterances or excerpts of music have to be mapped to emotion contours in dimensions such as arousal and valence. Defining the target labels as real-valued mappings from time instants to targets helps capturing the temporal dynamics of emotion, which cannot be assumed to be constant over time [8]. To learn such mappings, deep recurrent neural networks are a promising model [1], as they take into account temporal dependencies in inputs and outputs and can handle correlated features.

Original paper appeared at the 25th International Joint Conference on Artificial Intelligence (IJCAI), 2016.

© Springer International Publishing AG 2016
G. Friedrich et al. (Eds.): KI 2016, LNAI 9904, pp. 310–315, 2016.
DOI: 10.1007/978-3-319-46073-4

Continuous emotion recognition is typically evaluated in terms of the correlation between the learner's outputs and the target values, as well as the average deviation of outputs and targets, such as by the mean linear or mean squared error (MLE/MSE). Since neural networks are usually trained using criteria such as the (root) MSE, this only takes into account the latter while neglecting the former. However, as the correlation coefficient (CC) is insensitive to scaling and shifting, it may lead to an infinite number of local minima with different prediction behavior. To alleviate these problems, we propose to use the concordance correlation coefficient (CCC) [4] as a differentiable objective function that unites both correlation and mean squared error [12].

2   Discriminative Objectives for Emotion Regression

In this work, we consider three different objectives in training. The standard sum of squared errors (SSE) training objective for a mini-batch $\mathcal{B}$ is given by

$$\sum_{i \in \mathcal{B}, f \in \mathcal{F}} \sum_t (y^i_{f,t} - y^{i}_{f,t}{}^*)^2, \tag{1}$$

where $\mathcal{F}$ is the set of target variables and t denotes the index of a time step at which the target variable is annotated. Further, we introduce two new objectives based on CCC. These are discriminative on the sequence level, while the standard SSE objective is not. Let us define y^i_f as the regression outputs for sequence i and target variable f (in case of neural networks, the sequences of activations of unit f of the output layer), while $y^i_f{}^*$ denotes the corresponding training targets (i.e., gold-standard). The objective denoted by $\varSigma$CCC below is based on the CCC applied to each sequence, and pertains to minimizing the function $\mathcal{O}$:

$$\mathcal{O} = - \sum_{i \in \mathcal{B}, f \in \mathcal{F}} \text{CCC}^i_f. \tag{2}$$

The CCC per sequence i and target f is defined in accordance with [4] as:

$$\text{CCC}^i_f = \frac{2\text{Cov}(y^i_f, y^i_f{}^*)}{\text{Var}(y^i_f) + \text{Var}(y^i_f{}^*) + \left(\text{E}(y^i_f) - \text{E}(y^i_f{}^*)\right)^2}, \tag{3}$$

where E, Var, and Cov denote sample mean, variance, and covariance, respectively. An alternative objective (denoted simply by CCC below) is the 'total' CCC on the training set. This can be achieved by simply considering the entire training set as a single sequence i in (2). The $\varSigma$CCC objective differs from the CCC objective in that it necessarily enforces accurate prediction of the target contour within each sequence, while the CCC objective would assign a good score to over-smoothed regression outputs that simply predict the average gold standard per sequence.

In this study, optimization of the discriminative objectives is performed by stochastic gradient descent. To this end, we compute the gradients $\nabla_y \mathcal{O} =$

$(\partial \mathcal{O}/\partial y_{f,t}^i)_{i,f,t}$. The gradients w.r.t. the weights, $\partial \mathcal{O}/\partial w$ are determined by back-propagation as usual. Discriminative training is implemented on top of the open source, GPU-enabled neural network training software CURRENNT [10], which supports deep feed-forward and recurrent neural networks.

3   Experiments and Results

We present in this section the performance obtained in time-continuous dimensional emotion (arousal and valence) prediction on two different corpora from different domains (speech and music), comparing the ΣCCC, CCC, and SSE training objectives.

3.1   Emotions from Music: MediaEval

Experiments on emotion recognition from music are done on the 'Emotion in Music Database' which was used in the MediaEval 2013 evaluation campaign [9]. The data set includes excerpts of 45 s randomly extracted from 744 songs taken from the Free Music Archive[1]. It is split into a development set (619 songs) and an evaluation set (125 songs). Ratings of emotion were performed on a crowd-sourcing platform (MTurk) by a pool of 100 selected workers.

Both feature extraction and machine learning steps are based on the setup reported in [11]. The 6 373-dimensional ComParE set of generic affective features, and the Long Short-Term Memory (LSTM) [3] architecture for deep recurrent neural networks (DRNNs) are used. LSTM networks have two hidden layers with 192 or 256 hidden units. The training parameters are preserved from [11].

In accordance with the MediaEval challenge, the evaluation metrics comprise the overall Pearson's correlation coefficient (CC)[2] as well as the average Kendall's rank correlation coefficient per sequence (E$\{\tau\}$), which is related to our ΣCCC objective function but not differentiable. Furthermore, we report the average CCC (E$\{(CCC)\}$) per sequence, which directly corresponds to the ΣCCC objective.

3.2   Emotions from Speech: RECOLA

Time-continuous prediction of emotion has also been investigated on speech data by using the RECOLA database [6]; the full dataset was used for the purpose of this study, which corresponds to speech recordings from 46 French-speaking participants with five minutes for each. Ratings of emotion were obtained by six French-speaking research assistants. Traces were then interpolated at a 40 ms frame rate and averaged as a gold-standard [5]. The dataset was split equally

---

[1] http://www.freemusicarchive.org.

[2] Note that MediaEval uses the determination coefficient, which is the square of the CC, but we report CC as it is in the same order of magnitude as the CCC, which is the focus of our evaluation.

in three partitions – train (16 subjects), development (15 subjects) and test (15 subjects) – by balancing the gender, the age and the nationality of the speakers. The extended Geneva minimalistic acoustic feature set (eGeMAPS – 102 features) [2] has been applied at a rate of 40 ms using overlapping windows of 3 s length [7].

For the prediction task, we used LSTM-DRNNs with three hidden layers with 128 units each. Input noise with $\sigma = 0.1$ is added and early stopping is also used to prevent overfitting. The networks were trained with stochastic gradient descent on a batch size of five sequences with a fixed momentum of 0.9. An optimal learning rate η was chosen based on the CCC on the development set for each emotional dimension and objective function [12]. The CCC metric was computed on the gold-standard and prediction values concatenated over all recordings, in accordance with the AV$^+$EC challenge. In addition, we also report the average CCC (E{CCC}) per sequence in analogy to the experiments on music.

3.3 Results

The results on the MediaEval 2013 database are shown in Table 1. We can observe that the evaluation metrics achieved on the test set exactly reflect the choice of the objective function for training: SSE training works best for minimizing the MLE, while CCC based training yields the best CCC on the test set.

The official Challenge evaluation metric, E{τ}, is significantly (according to a z-test, $\alpha = .05$) improved by using the ΣCCC objective function for arousal (.221 → .251), but only slightly (.189 → .199) for valence. Generally, it is observed that the larger network with 256 hidden units performs worse on the test set, which can be attributed to the relatively small data set which causes over-fitting. The discrepancy between E{CCC} and CCC on this data set is astonishing; we found that for some test sequences, the variance in the annotated emotion contours is very low, which makes it hard to achieve good CC on these. One may further

Table 1. Emotion recognition performance on the MediaEval 2013 test set (music domain). The best achieved Challenge metric (E{τ}) is highlighted. Obj. denotes the objective function in network training and η the learning rate, determined in cross-validation.

| Layers | Obj. | η | Arousal | | | | | Valence | | | | |
			CC	CCC	E{CCC}	E{τ}	MLE	CC	CCC	E{CCC}	E{τ}	MLE
192-192	SSE	10^{-5}	.795	.778	.148	.221	.136	.637	.632	.118	.189	.149
256-256	SSE	10^{-5}	.732	.724	.119	.174	.152	.623	.609	.109	.151	.142
192-192	CCC	10^{-2}	.792	.790	.149	.224	.140	.653	.648	.119	**.199**	.156
256-256	CCC	10^{-2}	.764	.761	.128	.161	.149	.648	.646	.130	.191	.154
192-192	ΣCCC	10^{-4}	.723	.719	.166	**.251**	.158	.547	.546	.136	.198	.168
256-256	ΣCCC	10^{-4}	.720	.717	.153	**.211**	.158	.587	.582	.130	**.198**	.158

notice that the best performance in terms of CC on valence is obtained with the CCC objective. The improvement over the SSE objective is significant (.637 → .653). Regarding the optimization of the network, results show that each objective function requires a specific learning rate to perform best.

Table 2. Emotion recognition performance on the RECOLA development and test partitions (speech domain). The best achieved Challenge metric (CCC) is highlighted. Obj. denotes the objective function in network training and η the learning rate, determined on the development results.

Partition	Obj.	η	Arousal				η	Valence			
			RMSE	CC	CCC	E{CCC}		RMSE	CC	CCC	E{CCC}
DEV	SSE	10^{-4}	.117	.412	.397	.227	10^{-4}	.105	.210	.201	.066
TEST	SSE	10^{-4}	.128	.109	.097	.161	10^{-4}	.108	.133	.131	.052
DEV	CCC	10^{-3}	.193	.373	.373	.294	10^{-2}	.133	.179	.179	.112
TEST	CCC	10^{-3}	.193	.257	.254	.212	10^{-2}	.130	.155	.155	.080
DEV	ΣCCC	10^{-5}	.217	.412	**.412**	.313	10^{-2}	.188	.249	**.242**	.150
TEST	ΣCCC	10^{-5}	.200	.351	**.350**	.268	10^{-2}	.192	.227	**.199**	.139

Next, in Table 2 we report the metrics on the RECOLA database. Here, we observe a significant improvement in the CC, CCC and E{CCC} metrics by using the ΣCCC objective function, particularly on the test set, where SSE training does not deliver useful results in the arousal dimension: Here, CCCs of .097 and .350 are achieved with SSE training and ΣCCC training, respectively. Since this difference is less pronounced on the development set, for which the network is tuned, we have some evidence that the ΣCCC objective function leads to better generalization. In fact, when training using the SSE criterion, we observed a tendency of the network to predict the mean annotation on the training set, which leads to good RMSE but low correlation; conversely, the RMSE is significantly increased by using the CCC-based criteria. This result can also be observed on the CC evaluation metric, where a significant improvement over the SSE objective function is obtained when using ΣCCC for both arousal and valence.

4   Conclusions

In this study, we introduced neural network regression based on maximizing correlation of the output and target sequences. The CCC was chosen as a differentiable objective that can effectively replace the traditional SSE objective. We could confirm that the CCC is an elegant solution to the issue of scaling and shifting time-continuous predictions, as it is sensitive to both of these variations and thus alleviates the problem of local minima in neural network training. The choice of training objective had a significant impact on the performance in the recognition of emotion in the arousal and valence dimensions from speech and music.

Furthermore, note that the proposed approach based on CCC optimization can be applied to any sequence regression task where the correlation between the regression outputs and the ground truth should be maximized. There are no assumptions made on the underlying problem, other than that there be one or more continuous-valued target labels and that the regression model can be effectively trained by a first-order method such as stochastic gradient descent. Thus, we will verify its efficiency on other recognition tasks involving time-continuous measurements.

Acknowledgments. The research leading to these results has received funding from the European Commission's Seventh Framework Programme through the ERC Starting Grant No. 338164 (iHEARu).

References

1. Coutinho, E., Cangelosi, A.: A neural network model for the prediction of musical emotions. In: Nefti-Meziani, S., Grey, J. (eds.) Advances in Cognitive Systems, pp. 331–368. IET Publisher, London (2010)
2. Eyben, F., et al.: The Geneva minimalistic acoustic parameter set (GeMAPS) for voice research and affective computing. IEEE Trans. Affect. Comput. **7**(2), 190–202 (2015)
3. Gers, F.A., Schmidhuber, J., Cummins, F.: Learning to forget: continual prediction with LSTM. Neural Comput. **12**(10), 2451–2471 (2000)
4. Lin, L.I.: A concordance correlation coefficient to evaluate reproducibility. Biometrics **45**(1), 255–268 (1989)
5. Ringeval, F., Eyben, F., Kroupi, E., Yuce, A., Thiran, J.P., Ebrahimi, T., Lalanne, D., Schuller, B.: Prediction of asynchronous dimensional emotion ratings from audiovisual and physiological data. Pattern Recogn. Lett. **66**, 22–30 (2015)
6. Ringeval, F., et al.: Introducing the RECOLA multimodal corpus of remote collaborative and affective interactions. In: Proceedings of the of EmoSPACE (Held in Conjunction with ACM FG), p. 8, Shanghai, China, April 2013
7. Ringeval, F., et al.: AV+EC 2015 - The first affect recognition challenge bridging across audio, video, and physiological data. In: Proceedings of AVEC (Held in Conjunction with ACM MM), pp. 3–8. Brisbane, Australia, October 2015
8. Schmidt, E.M., Kim, Y.E.: Modeling musical emotion dynamics with conditional random fields. In: Proceedings of ISMIR, pp. 777–782, Miami, FL, USA (2011)
9. Soleymani, M., et al.: 1000 songs for emotional analysis of music. In: Proceedings of CrowdMM (Held in Conjunction with ACM MM). ACM, Barcelona (2013)
10. Weninger, F., Bergmann, J., Schuller, B.: Introducing CURRENNT - the Munich open-source CUDA RecurREnt neural network toolkit. J. Mach. Learn. Res. **16**, 547–551 (2015)
11. Weninger, F., Eyben, F., Schuller, B.: The TUM approach to the MediaEval music emotion task using generic affective audio features. In: Proceedings of MediaEval. CEUR, Barcelona, October 2013
12. Weninger, F., Ringeval, F., Marchi, E., Schuller, B.: Discriminatively trained recurrent neural networks for continuous dimensional emotion recognition from audio. In: Proceedings of IJCAI, p. 7. AAAI, New York City, July 2016 (to appear)

Author Index

Printed in the United States
By Bookmasters